T3G

MANAGING
BY
COMMUNICATION

MANAGING BY COMMUNICATION

AN ORGANIZATIONAL APPROACH

Michele Tolela Myers
Trinity University

Gail E. Myers
Trinity University

McGraw-Hill Book Company

New York St. Louis San Francisco Auckland Bogotá Hamburg Johannesburg
London Madrid Mexico Montreal New Delhi Panama Paris São Paulo
Singapore Sydney Tokyo Toronto

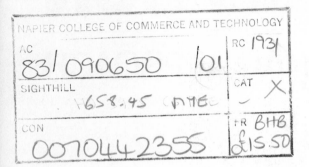
MANAGING BY COMMUNICATION
An Organizational Approach

1234567890DODO8987654321

This book was set in Hanover by Graphic Technique, Inc. The editors
were Kaye Pace and James R. Belser; the designer was Anne Canevari Green;
the production supervisor was Diane Renda. New drawings were done by
VIP Graphics.
R. R. Donnelley & Sons Company was printer and binder.

Library of Congress Cataloging in Publication Data

Myers, Michele Tolela, date
    Managing by communication.

    Bibliography: p.
    1. Communication in management.   I. Myers,
Gail E., date   II. Title.
HF5718.M93   658.4'5   81-1696
ISBN 0-07-044235-5   AACR2

To Erika and David

CONTENTS FOR TEXT

PART FOUR
THE SKILLS OF MANAGING BY COMMUNICATION

CONTENTS FOR LABORATORY MANUAL

INTRODUCTION

This is a book about communication, management, organizations, and their interface. It is a book about organizational theories, management practices, and communication applications. Above all, it is a book about people and their behaviors in organizational settings.

In many significant ways, this book is different from most business communication, organizational behavior, management, and communication theory texts.

Managing by Communication differs from organizational behavior and traditional management texts which typically treat communication as only one facet of organizational life and one among the many managerial functions. Our thesis is that communication is the central, binding force which permits coordination among people and thus allows for organized behavior. We believe that managing is ultimately a process of influencing other people, and we contend that such influence is exerted through communication. *Managing by Communication* is unique in its attempt to analyze the managerial process from a broadly defined communication base. It is an original effort designed to help you make intellectual connections between managing and communicating and to develop your interpersonal skills in organizational settings.

Managing by Communication differs from interpersonal communication texts in that it squarely and specifically focuses on business and organizational contexts for interpersonal transactions. *Managing by Communication* also differs from many of the newer texts in organizational communication by providing an in-depth study of dyadic relationships which, we believe, represent most of the day-to-day interpersonal encounters in the work environment. Yet, this book does not ignore the structural and organizational variables which affect communication behaviors in the business setting.

For the future manager and the future communication professional, this text offers a thorough introduction to the relationship between organizational and management theories and communication theory. Your work will inevitably focus on human behavior. Our intentions are to help you explore the relationship between management and communication, and view communication as the methodology of management. This, we think, is facilitated in a course with a laboratory component.

Managing by Communication provides such a component with its laboratory manual. The laboratory section will permit you to become personally involved in testing out the applications we suggest are derived from the theoretical formulations.

You do not need a cookbook of solutions to the human problems you will encounter in most organizations. It would be nice if we could provide you with a checklist of ten easy steps for solving communication problems. However, communication and management problems are not simple, nor are they amenable to cookbook answers. Rather, you need a sound theoretical base to guide you through the challenges and intricacies of human interactions. You need the flexibility that comes from good grounding in communication theory integrated with management theory. You need to be fast on your communication feet as the dynamics of managing call on special applications of communication techniques.

This book's uniqueness comes largely from the laboratory component which provides you with exercises, activities, problems, cases, simulations, role plays, small group work, and individual assignments, as well as assessment tools to learn more about yourself, your communication and management styles, your ways of relating to others in a work environment.

In the give-and-take of laboratory activities and with the guidance of your instructor, you will test your understanding of communication and management principles and your skills in the practice of communication behaviors which will enhance your future managerial performance. Whether in marketing, sales, accounting, production, research and development, administration, personnel, quality control, records, procurement, compliance, information systems, internal communication, or public relations, you will be a practicing communicator. This book will help you do your job more effectively.

Our goals were to make this book readable, interesting, provocative, and current. This is what we have done to accomplish these objectives.

Readable: Our writing style is clear and conversational, yet we neither talk down to you nor water down the concepts we explain. We use extensive examples and minimize jargon. When we do use technical terms, we define and clarify them.

Interesting: We have kept chapters short and concise. We cover a lot of territory, yet, at each stage of our analysis, we emphasize relationships between concepts and implications for actual behavior on the job.

Provocative: We challenge you to think through the implications of the theories for action. We describe opposing views and approaches and urge you to think for yourselves how they can be integrated into a coherent framework which will work for you.

Current: Although we present material typically found in organizational behavior, management, and communication theory books, we emphasize those concepts which have gained current importance in the 1970s. We describe recent developments in areas such as interpersonal transactions, communication rules, conflict management, negotiations, trust, power, and influence.

As readers of *Managing by Communication*, you are ultimately the judges of whether we have successfully reached our goals. We hope that after reading this book you will share with us our excitement for the truly challenging field of business communication.

Managing by Communication was written to meet the needs of the following students:

1. Undergraduates enrolled in organizational communication courses, usually offered in speech communication departments for their majors or as electives for business administration majors.
2. Undergraduates enrolled in business communication courses which emphasize oral and interpersonal skills. Such courses are usually taught in business schools, although a few may be offered in speech communication departments for business students.
3. Practicing managers who participate in executive development seminars and workshops.

This book is truly the product of organized efforts and effective communication among a number of people whom we wish to thank. The McGraw-Hill editorial staff under the direction of Jim Belser has done, we think, an outstanding job. Our friends Jane Stieren, Barbara Czachowski, and Eva Turner assisted expertly in the many stages of manuscript preparation. Our professional debt, however, is to our many students who have listened patiently to our ideas, who have participated in countless class activities, and whose reponses have helped us to change, refine, and sharpen so much of this material. To the Trinity University business administration and speech communication undergraduate students, to the health care administration graduate students, and to the practicing managers and executives who have worked with us in our classes and seminars, we give thanks. This book is truly theirs.

PART ONE

THE THEORIES OF MANAGING BY COMMUNICATION

In the first three chapters of this book, we are going to take you through a tour of the theoretical foundations of the field of human communication and its relationship to the fields of organizational and management theories. Like Kurt Lewin, we believe that nothing is as practical as a good theory. While this tour may simply serve as a review for many of you who study business administration and/or have a management background, it will give a solid introduction to the organizational field to those of you who are beginning your study of organizational behavior. What is new about our review, however, is our deliberate effort to tie in the findings of communication scholars to organizational analysis and the use of communication concepts to evaluate organizational and management theories. This, we believe, will provide you with a fresh look at managerial theory as well as a good introduction to the specific communication analyses to follow in Parts Two and Three.

Chapter 1 presents an introduction to communication as it pervades organizational life. It presents our view that communication is the necessary foundation for organizing activities—the mortar that holds the organizational edifice together. Chapter 2 presents a survey of the major organizational theories and their communication implications, and Chapter 3 introduces you to communication theory and how it can be used to deepen your understanding of organizational life and processes.

CHAPTER 1

COMMUNICATING AND ORGANIZING

"Like all living systems, organizations establish and maintain themselves through communication with their environments and amongst their parts." Lee Thayer

**YOU AND
ORGANIZATIONS**

Take a minute and jot down some of the organizations you are a part of. Even without a scholarly definition of what an organization "is," it is relatively easy to come up with a list looking something like:

> Member of a family (spouse, parent, child)
> Student in a college
> Major in a department
> Member of PTA
> Voter in a city election
> Patient in a local hospital
> Rider in a car pool
> Salesclerk in a department store
> Member of a student/faculty/administration committee
> Chairperson of fund-raising committee for a local philanthropic group
> Basketball coach at the YMCA
> Member of a church congregation

Much of your life unfolds within a complex web of organizations where you take care of your economic, social and recreational, educational, spiritual, and political needs. You work, play, learn, and worship in a more or less structured social context. The organizations in which you participate may vary in size, structure, complexity, purposes, and longevity, but they all represent the dynamic elements of society as you know it.

While the neighborhood car pool may consist of five people riding together for a few months, General Motors may own assets in the billions of dollars, employ over half a million people, and have been in existence for several generations. Both the car pool and GM are the product of organized efforts, and thus they share some common characteristics.

**WHY
ORGANIZATIONS**

An organization comprises essentially two kinds of resources: technical (raw materials, equipment, capital) and human (work, ideas, skills). Basically, an organization exists because by pooling resources individuals can accomplish potentially more together than they can singly. Two persons, working together, can lift an object which is too heavy for either one of them to lift alone. However, in order to lift the object the two persons must work together and their efforts need to be coordinated: If one lifted while the other rested, the object would not be moved and the goal not accomplished.[1]

[1]James D. Mooney, *The Principles of Organization*, Harper and Brothers, New York, 1974, p. 5.

Although Americans admire and boast about individual achievement, most human accomplishments today are made possible by people working together in concerted and organized efforts. Neil Armstrong's first and giant step on the moon was an awesome testimony to the power of human and technical organization at its best.

Organizations exist primarily because certain goals can be achieved only through the joint efforts and actions of groups of people. GM and the car pool of our earlier example both pursue objectives that can be more effectively met by the collective efforts of a group of people.

When we talk about organizing, we mean that people routinely go beyond their individual limitations and engage in concerted and coordinated action with others.

A few basic elements are shared by all organizations:

Size (two or more people): You can't organize all by yourself.
Interdependent actions: Members work together to achieve goals.
Bounding in space and duration: Organizations involve people, places, and time.
Input of resources from the environment: Organizations involve some of the people and things around them.
Communication: Members get it all together by coordinating their activities to process and transform resources.
Output: Goods or services are returned to the environment as a result of the activities of the organization.

Size

The basic organizational unit is the two-person group, or dyad. By definition, interdependence cannot be achieved with one isolated individual. The dyad is thus the most basic unit of organizational studies. As size increases, the organization becomes more complex, coordination becomes more difficult, and communication becomes both more necessary and more difficult.

Interdependence

The concept of interdependence is crucial in understanding organizational dynamics. Interdependence refers to the notion that people mutually and reciprocally influence each other. The behavior of one person affects the behavior of another.

Interdependence reflects the difference between a collection of isolated individuals and an organized group of people. A collection of individuals will not necessarily act together to achieve common goals. Individuals need use only their individual talents and resources; they don't need to relate to anyone else to achieve their goals. But when isolated individuals develop common goals, act cooperatively, and join efforts and resources to achieve a common goal, then interdependence develops and organizing takes place.

Bounding in Space and Time

Organizations do not exist in a vacuum any more than individuals do. Organizations exist in a context, an environment they must respond to, and it is their boundaries which set them apart from that environment. What's good for General Motors may or may not be good for the country; the fact is, General Motors is not the country. GM exists within the context of the American economy and the American social and political system.

Organizations continually interact and enter into relationships with other individuals and organizations in the larger environment. Clients, suppliers, stockholders, unions, and governmental bodies all make claims on organizations and have expectations about their performance. These constituencies make demands on organizations—often conflicting demands which must be understood and managed.

The interdependent activities of the organization members form a repeated and relatively enduring pattern. Doing the same things over and over, or the stability of activity, can be looked at in relation to the input of resources, the processing of resources, and the resulting output. For example, in a factory, the cycle of input, processing, and output has the goal of an increase of financial resources which then permits acquisition of new resources to be processed and put on the market. If the cycle is incomplete—for example, the product does not sell—new financial resources will not be available, new inputs ultimately will not be possible, and production will have to stop, thus ending the life of the organization.

Input

In a manufacturing organization, inputs may consist of raw materials, energy, and revenues. In a social organization, inputs may be human resources such as talents, skills, or ideas.

Coordinated Activities

Materials and energy enter the organization and are acted upon by people working together to produce desired results. Ongoing activities which take place every day may include the work people do: their thinking, talking, reading, writing, listening, operating machinery, etc. Activities of people are coordinated because the tasks to be done are subdivided into individual assignments which are often departmentalized. The familiar principles of division of labor, departmentalization, span of control, and delegation of authority are traditional ways of talking about coordinated activities. *Coordinated activities are made possible through communication.* People can work together only because they can communicate. This important point will be developed in a later section.

Output

Outcome of the cycle of coordinated activities is usually put into the environment. GM sells automobiles. By doing so it can buy new energy and new raw materials, and thus the cycle of input, coordinated activities, output can continue.

Throughout our discussion, we have used the two terms "organizations" and "organizing." We want to call your attention to the difference, which is based on Weick's[2] discussion of the organizing process. The term "organization" is used in a static sense to describe stable patterns of coordination. In that sense, GM is an organization. "Organizing" refers to the ongoing process by which coordinated activities and actions are accomplished. An organization is the result of organizing at any given time. The college or university you attend is a different organization now from what it was twenty years ago. Organizing processes over the years changed the shape of the organization in a number of ways, some trivial (the color of the cheerleaders' uniforms), some more fundamental (the addition of a new major in ecology).

Communication is what permits people to organize. It permits people to coordinate their activities to accomplish common objectives, but there is more to communication than a mere transmission of information or transfer of meaning.

WHAT PERMITS PEOPLE TO ORGANIZE

Our view of communication, which we will develop more fully below and in Chapter 3, comes from general system theory and implies a transactional process where people *construct meaning* and *develop expectations* about what is happening around them and with one another *through the exchange of symbols*. Three parts of this definition are crucial: (1) constructing meaning, (2) developing expectations, and (3) exchanging symbols.

In much of the management and organizational behavior literature, communication is viewed as one of the processes taking place in organizations. Many authors admit communication is important and central to organizational life, but also view it simply as *one of a number* of processes which go on in organizations. Many writers define communication as the transmission of information through a hierarchical structure. Katz and Kahn,[3] for example, contend that "communication—the exchange of information and the transmission of meaning—is the very essence of a social system or an organization." Davis[4] defines communication as the "process of passing information

[2]K. Weick, *The Social Psychology of Organizing*, Addison-Wesley, Reading, Mass., 1969.

[3]Daniel Katz and Robert Kahn, *The Social Psychology of Organizations*, John Wiley and Sons, New York, 1978, p. 428.

[4]Keith Davis, *Human Relations and Organizational Behavior*, 4th ed., McGraw-Hill Book Company, 1972, pp. 379–380.

and understanding from one person to another" and adds that "the only way that management can be achieved in an organization is through the process of communication." Some writers, however, have regarded communication as a much more pervasive activity in organizational life. Chester Barnard,[5] one of the early scholars of organizational behavior, emphasized that "in any exhaustive theory of organization, communication would occupy a central place, because the structure, extensiveness, and scope of organizations are almost entirely determined by communication techniques." Simon[6] stated that case even more directly when he wrote that "the question to be asked of any administrative process is: How does it influence the decisions of the individual? Without communication the answer must always be: It does not influence them at all."

The view of communication coming from these writers is that communication is a dominant force in organizational life. Communication is the essence of the organization. It is the binding element that keeps the various interdependent parts of the organizational system together. Without communication there is no organized activity. Communication allows organizational structures to develop by giving separate individuals the means to coordinate their activities and thus achieve common goals.

Communication is necessary for two people to decide that their combined efforts will permit them to lift a heavy object which neither could lift alone. It takes communication for their efforts to be coordinated so that their combined energies are channeled into the actual lifting. "Let's lift it together on a count of three. One . . . two. . . ."

Constructing Meanings

What permits you to organize is the fact that (1) you can use symbols to describe your experience with your environment and (2) you can develop a common symbol system (language) for sharing your experience with others. The process of making your symbols fit your experience is a highly personal, individual, or idiosyncratic one. It is in that sense that each of you constructs meaning in your head—that is, develops a specific relationship between a symbol and a personal experience. When you want to share your meanings with others you need to go back to symbols and hope that, upon receiving these symbols, others will construct in their heads a meaning similar to yours. You hope the symbols will call up in the other person's head an experience similar to the one you intended to share.

[5]*The Function of the Executive,* Harvard University Press, Cambridge, Mass., 1938, p. 8.
[6]Herbert Simon, *Models of Man,* Wiley, New York, 1956, p. 109.

In some instances this translating cannot be done. As many a tourist in a foreign land knows, you simply cannot engage in sharing meaning when your symbols are not like the other person's symbols. However, sharing the same symbol system does not guarantee that meanings will be shared. For meanings to be constructed in similar ways by two people, the two need to share common experiences.

If I construct my own meaning and you construct yours, how is it possible ever to understand each other and thus coordinate our activities? Even though meanings are always highly personal, they are not developed in a total social vacuum. Communication is transactional in the sense that you learn *with others* to use symbols and construct meanings. You learn many meanings by watching and listening to others—parents or peers. As a result you develop a pool of common information, knowledge, intelligence[7]—what you know about your world. The more frequently and regularly you communicate with another person, the more you come to share meanings. The more you work with and communicate with those around you, the more likely you are to develop a consensus on how you view certain facets of your world.

Developing Expectations

Learning symbols and learning to associate symbols with experiences come about by paying attention to people and by observing what they do when they use symbols. As a result of these observations you not only learn to construct meanings that are fairly similar to those of the people around you, but you also develop expectations or make predictions about what people will do and think. By exchanging symbols you create expectations. For example, Mrs. Jones asks her secretary to make ten copies of a report and to distribute them among the members of her department. Mrs. Jones expects from previous experience with the secretary that this person will (1) understand the instructions, (2) be willing to carry them out, (3) perform the task with reasonable accuracy and speed. Mrs. Jones' behavior is based on her expectations about the secretary's behavior. When Mrs. Jones holds a staff meeting, she will expect her staff to be familiar with the content of that report since she will assume it has been distributed and read. It is only when expectations are shared that coordination is possible and organizing takes place.

When meanings and expectations are not shared, individuals simply function in their own private worlds, doing their own things, uninvolved with others, unpredictable to others.

[7]Bonnie McDaniel Johnson provides an excellent discussion of organizational intelligence in her book *Communicating: The Process of Organizing,* Allyn and Bacon, Boston, 1977, pp. 4–6.

Exchanging Symbols

Exchanging symbols with others provides you with the impetus for creating meaning and developing expectations. Let's look at symbolic behavior in organizations in terms of its form and its context.

Form

The symbols people exchange with one another can take several forms. They can be *verbal* when you use words to speak or write to others. Much of the communication within organizations is of that kind. Giving instructions to a subordinate, interviewing a candidate for a job, giving information, receiving information, are all examples of verbal-oral communication. Letters, memos, and written reports, regulations, and procedures are examples of verbal-written communication. Symbols, however, can also be *nonverbal*. Gestures, facial expressions, postures all can mean something. Office furnishings and equipment, clothes, and jewelry are also powerful nonverbal symbols in the context of an organization. Other nonverbal symbols, such as intonation, pitch, and intensity of the voice, also contribute to creation of meaning and expectations, as the following dialogue illustrates:

Harry: I saw you go into Mrs. Brown's office. Did you have a chance to tell her our idea about that sales meeting?

Sally: Well, no. She sounded rather abrupt, and I got the feeling she did not want me to take up much of her time.

Context

Exchange of symbols can take place within a variety of contexts in an organization. Much of the communication in organizations occurs in a dyadic context, between two people. A job interview typically includes the applicant and one interviewer; instructions and procedures are frequently given and explained on a one-to-one, face-to-face basis. The boss-secretary dyad is a common pair. The boss-subordinate pair found at all levels of the organization structure is the context in which much communication takes place.

Small groups constitute another context for communication: peers or managers and staff getting together in meetings to share information, make decisions, solve problems; informal groups at coffee or chatting in a hallway; team workers in a small production unit.

Large groups are another context for communication. Such groups can include large departments in an organization or the entire organization.

Still another context for communication is represented by the external environment in which the organization functions. Clients, customers, groups, and government agencies are the targets of much

ORGANIZATIONAL CONTEXTS AND COMMUNICATION ACTIVITIES   **TABLE 1-1**

CONTEXTS

	Dyad	Small Group	Large Group	Mass (Environment)

Who	Manager/subordinate
	Peers
		Manager/subordinates
		Peers
		  Managers
		  Staff
			Departments
			Total organization
				Customers
				Civic groups
				Governmental
				agencies
				Public

What	Interviews
	  Hiring
	  Appraisal
	  Information
	Discussion about
	  Problems
	  Policies and
	  Procedures
	Instructions
	Informal
	conversations
	  Lunch
	  Breaks
	  On-the-job
		Executive meetings
		Board meetings
		Regular department meetings
		  Information
		  Decision-
		  making
		  Problem
		  solving
		Brainstorming
		Specialized meetings
		  Budget
		  Sales
		  Production
		Training meetings
		Production team
		Informal meetings
		Etc.
			Sales meetings
			Union meetings
			Chief executive
			and all employees
			Stockholder
			meetings
			Social functions
			  Picnics
			  Holiday parties
			Interdepartmental
			meetings
			Board meetings
			Etc.
				Advertising
				Public relations
				Customer relations
				Fund raising
				Etc.

How	Oral
	  Face-to-face
	  Telephone
	Written
	  Letters, memos
	  Reports
		Oral
		  Face-to-face
		Written
		  Letters, memos
			Oral
			  Public communications
			Written
			  Policy manuals
			  Operating procedures
			  Contracts
			  Internal organs
			  Newsletters
			  Bulletins
			  Memos
			  Reports
				Oral
				  Public communications
				Media
				  (TV, Radio)
				Written
				  Proposals
				  Media
				  (Newspapers)
				  Letters

Communication Activities

communication from the organization by way of advertising, public relations efforts, lobbying.

Table 1-1 presents a summary of organizational contexts in terms of (1) who communicates, (2) what communication activities take place, and (3) how the communication activities are carried out.

COMMUNICATION IN ORGANIZA-TIONS—WHAT IT IS LIKE

So far we have used the term "communication" without actually defining it. We have presented our view that communication is the basis for the organizing processes which take place in organizations. We wrote in an earlier section that constructing meaning and developing expectations were the result of exchanging symbols and that shared meanings and expectations were the basis for coordination which permitted organizing to take place. In this section, we will (1) describe how communication is different from information and (2) discuss what communication does in organizations.

Information and Communication

What is information?

The environment in which you live is a constant source of sensory stimulations for you. You hear sounds, see objects, events, and people, and generally are bombarded by energy inputs. The human nervous system, just like organizational systems, gets input from its environment, processes the inputs, and comes up with an output in the form of thoughts, feelings, and behaviors. This sequence of input, processing, and output which occurs within the individual is a communication process. It is the basic mechanism by which you make sense of your environment. You are thus able to behave in ways which are adaptive within that environment. A more thorough discussion of communication will be presented in Chapter 3. At this point, however, it is important to mention the process to help you distinguish between information and communication.

Here is an example. As we are writing these lines, we are bombarded by a variety of sounds. This energy input from our present environment is constituted by sound waves of different frequencies and intensity. Before we started writing this paragraph, these sound waves were undifferentiated, unpatterned "background noises." As we focus attention on them, we begin to distinguish among traffic noises, the hum of the typewriter, the rustling of leaves in the breeze, the cats chasing each other, the baby softly cooing to himself, the mail carrier dropping mail in the mailbox. In other words, we are beginning to discern *patterns* in the energy inputs, the raw sensory data, that reach us, and begin to differentiate sounds. The undifferentiated "background noises" were just unpatterned or random sound energy. *Patterning* is the basic process by which you transform energy input into information. By repeated exposure to certain sounds you develop the capacity to pattern them and set them apart from other sounds. A baby crying and a Siamese cat meowing may sound alike to many people unfamiliar with both babies and Siamese cats. They are distinctive sounds, however, to parents of small babies who own Siamese cats. Patterning is the basis for information.

Another example will illustrate what we mean by patterning. Hearing a foreign language spoken for the first time is an example of unpatterned sound energy. You can get no information from that exposure. However, should you hear the language repeated over a period of time, patterns will emerge which will permit you to tell when words begin and end. The foreign sentences will finally appear to be made up of individual words rather than of sounds, rapidly and endlessly strung together. This first step in patterning is crucial and is the beginning of more and more refined patterning sequences.

When you perceive no pattern, no information is possible. The lost feeling you get in a totally new place or situation (your first few days as a freshman on campus, or your first day on a new job) result from a bombardment of stimuli which form no pattern yet. Little by little you get a feel for where things are and who people are. "CGC 213" and "R&D Labs" become known rooms in known buildings rather than a mumbo jumbo of letters and numbers without information value.

When you recognize patterns you have information. The implications of this statement are far-reaching. Pattern perception is something a person does, it is something *learned* by individuals. For this reason, the patterns one individual recognizes can be different from the patterns another person will pay attention to. The information value of any one stimulus is likely to vary from individual to individual, a crucial point to which we will return in Chapter 3. Although some patterns are set by law or common practice and can be called the product of cultural consensus (red and green traffic lights, for example, or the playing of the "Star-Spangled Banner" at the start of a sports event), *most patterns are the product of individual learning experiences.*

Patterning is only one facet of information. Another important concept that must be discussed in relation to patterning and information is *uncertainty.*

Uncertainty refers to how predictable something is for you. It involves the degree of structure things and events have for you and if there are recognizable patterns. The more structured a situation is, that is, the more predictable some patterns are, the less uncertainty is present.

A totally new situation is potentially very high in uncertainty, You have no way to predict what patterns you will recognize, and at first, the patterns will seem random. Randomness, in the information theory sense, means that the probability of occurrence of one pattern is the same as the probability of occurrence of any other pattern. In other words, out of all the things which could happen, there is no particular thing that is more likely to happen than anything else. In random situations you really don't know what might happen next.

The greater the number of potential patterns, the greater the uncertainty. If one pattern is no more likely to occur than another, there is more uncertainty and therefore more information value derived from that pattern when it occurs.

If you have one penny and toss it in the air, the number of potential patterns is limited to heads, tails, and the very slim chance of standing on edge. Now, if you take a handful of mixed coins and toss them in the air you have those same three potential patterns multiplied by all those pennies, nickels, dimes, and quarters you tossed in the air. Think of all the things you might say about what happened! For example, maybe most of the dimes fell heads, while the quarters were almost all tails, and the nickels and pennies were evenly divided. The information value was much greater in this situation because so many more things could happen.

Here's a real-life example: You start a new job as a bank teller. You have never been a bank teller before. You know nothing about what the job entails. You have no way to predict which patterns are likely to occur. As you begin work, you notice that certain things and events recur frequently. For example, your supervisor is always grumpy before her first cup of coffee. You take a coffee break with two other tellers. There are longer lines of customers at the noon hour than at 8:30 in the morning. As these patterns occur, they give you information about something previously unknown. As you recognize these patterns and are able to predict their recurrence, you have gained information and thus reduced the uncertainty of the situation. You have learned to depend on certain things to happen. From a random situation, where you had no way to guess the probability of occurrence of anything, you have moved to a more structured one. Now, when the pattern occurs, it no longer gives you information, as you are able to predict its occurrence. Imagine you now quit this job and go to work as a teller in a competing bank. Although the new situation is unstructured in many ways, your uncertainty will not be as high as for your very first job. At least you now have a way to predict the likelihood of occurrence of some patterns related to the job of bank teller which you presumably learned in the first job. You may not be able to predict the behavior of your new supervisor in the morning, but you are likely to accurately figure out the rush hours at the bank. Information you gained in your first job helps you reduce some uncertainty in your new job.

Information, then, refers to (1) recognizing patterns and (2) determining the predictability of their occurrence. The function of information is to reduce uncertainty.

While all communication contains information, not all information has communicative value. Information is like an enormous umbrella, a broad concept which covers communication as one particular type of information. Information is a global concept referring to any pattern of energy input you are exposed to. "Communication" refers to a special kind of patterning: patterning which is expressed in *symbolic form*. For communication to take place between or among people, two requirements must be met: (1) a symbolic system must be shared by the people involved (we need to speak the same language or jargon or dialects) and (2) the associations between the symbols and their referents must be shared (words or symbols should mean very nearly the same to both of us). Let us examine these two requirements.

Communication

A symbolic system must be shared. Information which cannot be translated into a symbolic form has no communicative value. A pattern may have information value for one person, but unless it can be translated into a shared symbolic code, it has no communication value. An American and a French person may not be able to communicate unless they use a symbol system they both understand. It may be English or French, or it may be a third language they have in common. Use of technical jargon by chemists, philosophers, lawyers, or doctors sounds like a foreign language to many people.

Associations between symbols and their referents must be shared. Referents are the actual things, events, people, or feelings that symbols stand for. If people make similar associations between symbols and referents, they are potentially successful in their communication with each other. To the extent those associations differ, communication loses its effectiveness. Sharing the same language does not ensure communication. You and I may both speak English, yet my associations between the word "mother" and my experiences may be quite different from your associations between the same word and *your* experiences. For that reason we say that people have meanings inside themselves; words don't. Communication, as we pointed out earlier in this chapter, involves the exchange of shared symbols which call up similar associations between symbols and referents (or meanings) in the people involved in the process and who can then make predictions (have expectations) about their environment and each other. Communication is information because it allows us to reduce uncertainty and to develop expectations. It is more specific than information because while information broadly deals with the recognition of patterns, communication only deals with patterns which can be put into symbols or words.

Functions of Communication in Organizations

The function of communication, that is, what communication does or brings about, can be studied at different levels. As we said above, communication in a very global sense permits patterning. At the level of the total organization, communication can be analyzed in terms of three broad functions: (1) production and regulation, (2) innovation, and (3) socialization or maintenance.

At a more specific level, communication functions can be examined within specific contexts: (1) manager/subordinate or downward communication, (2) peer or horizontal communication, and (3) subordinate/manager or upward communication. Box 1-1 and Box 1-2 present summaries of communication functions. In this section we analyze the functions of communication at the organizational level.

Production and regulation

Communication which deals mainly with getting work done and which helps meet the organization output objectives (products, services, etc.) is regulatory or production-oriented. Examples of production communication include sales information, quality control messages, budgets, and policy and regulatory messages which instruct organization members on how to perform their tasks. This function of communication includes messages which permit managers and organization members to[8]:

1. Determine goals and objectives
2. Define problem areas
3. Assess performance
4. Coordinate functionally interdependent tasks
5. Determine standards of performance output
6. Command, tell people what to do, give orders
7. Instruct, tell people how to carry out an order, develop procedures, get policies
8. Lead and influence

The *production* function involves any communication activities directly related to doing the main work of the organization. In a manufacturing organization we include communication about production or whatever must be communicated in order to turn out the widgets or cars or bottles of beer. In an educational institution it is the actual teaching and training of students. All communications related

[8]Lee Thayer, *Communication and Communication Systems*, Richard D. Irwin, Inc., Homewood, Ill., 1968.

FUNCTIONS OF COMMUNICATION IN ORGANIZATIONS　　　　　　**BOX 1-1**

1. Production and Regulation
   A. Determine goals and objectives.
   B. Define problem areas.
   C. Assess performance.
   D. Coordinate functionally interdependent tasks.
   E. Determine standards of performance output.
   F. Command, tell people what to do, give orders.
   G. Instruct, tell people how to carry out an order, develop procedures and policies.
   H. Lead and influence.

2. Innovation

3. Social or Maintenance
   A. Whatever affects members' self-esteem.
   B. Interpersonal relationships in the organization.
   C. Motivation to integrate individual goals and organizational objectives.

---

to purchasing, packaging, hiring or firing personnel, generating capital, sales, finding jobs for graduates are examples of the production function of communication.

Communication messages which govern work are not the only messages within organizational settings. An organization does not exist apart from its environment, and constant pressures from that environment force the organization to adapt to changes. External changes ultimately result in internal changes if the organization is to

---

COMMUNICATION FUNCTIONS IN RELATIONAL CONTEXTS　　　**BOX 1-2**

1. Manager/Subordinate—Down the Line
   A. Specific task directives: *job instructions.*
   B. Information designed to produce understanding of the task in relation to other organizational tasks: *job rationale.*
   C. Information about organizational *procedures and practices.*
   D. *Feedback* to the subordinate about performance.
   E. Information of an ideological character to inculcate a sense of mission: *Indoctrination of goals.*

2. Peer or Horizontal Communication
   A. Provide socioemotional support among peers.
   B. Coordinate between peers and work process.
   C. Diffuse locus of control in the organization.

3. Subordinate/Manager—Up the Line
   A. Communication about self, performance, and problems.
   B. Communication about others and their problems.
   C. Organizational practices and policies.
   D. What needs to be done and how to do it.

stay in business or grow. For example, companies that made and sold car seat covers in the fifties, had to completely change product lines and diversify to stay alive after car manufacturers produced cars with more durable and more aesthetically pleasing seat covers. The innovation function of communication includes all messages about new ideas and changing procedures in the organization. The innovation function of communication includes communication activities such as organizationwide suggestion systems, research and development work, market research and analysis, brainstorming sessions, and "think tank" committees. This function of communication is especially vital in organizations which find themselves in a fluid and changing environment.

Socialization or maintenance

This third function of communication includes communications which affect (1) organization members' self-esteem, (2) their interpersonal relationships in the organizations, and (3) their motivation to integrate their individual goals with the organization's objectives.

Social communication activities are directed not at the material being worked on but at the means of getting the work done, in most cases, people themselves. Social communication is concerned with rewarding and motivating personnel, morale, etc. For people to remain in an organization and to perform adequately, their experiences in the organization must be rewarding. Rewards may include money, prestige, status, interesting work, identification with the organization products, and satisfaction from such factors as involvement in decision making. Social communication includes information which confirms a person's relationship with the physical and human environment. For example, information which confirms your view of yourself as a competent and worthwhile individual is integrative and affects your self-esteem. The social function of communication helps build shared expectations by organizational members—expectations about each other, the work to be done, how to do the work, and the organizational context and environment in which the organization itself exists. Routines, rituals, and procedures are ways organization members develop common expectations which link them together as part of the organization. It is because of the social function of communication that members of an organization can identify and relate to each other as members of that organization. Only with social or maintenance communication can people become personally involved in the goals of any organization.

Specific relational contexts

Let's look at communication from the vantage point of specific relational contexts.

Manager/subordinate or downward communication. Communication from manager to subordinates has five basic functions:

1. Specific task directives: *job instructions.*
2. Information designed to produce understanding of the task in its relation to other organizational tasks: *job rationale.*
3. Information about organizational *procedures* and *practices.*
4. *Feedback* to the subordinate about performance.
5. Information of an ideological nature to develop a sense of mission: *indoctrination of goals.*[9]

Job instructions may include direct orders, job description, procedure manuals, and training programs. They are designed to tell organization members what they are supposed to do and how to do it.

Job rationale involves communication to provide organization members with a larger understanding of their jobs and especially how their jobs are related to other activities in the organization. This kind of information tells you how you fit into the company or department.

Information about organizational *procedures* acquaints organization members with organizational practices, regulations, benefits, and privileges. Employee handbooks and personnel manuals are examples.

Feedback allows organization members to know how well or how poorly they are doing their jobs. In complex jobs, such feedback is difficult to give and few guidelines are usually available to the managers of evaluating their subordinates' performances. Periodic job evaluations and appraisals and self-evaluation programs are examples of such communication. Feedback lets you know how you're doing.

Ideology.   The mission of the organization must be communicated to members if they are to identify with the organizational goals. An extension of job rationale, ideological information permits organization members to understand the "big picture" and carry out their jobs more effectively. They may develop a sense of belonging to the organization.

Peer or horizontal communication.   Communication between people at the same levels of the hierarchy has three basic purposes: first, to provide socioemotional support among peers, or to help everybody get along better; second, to permit coordination between peers in the work process so they can do a more efficient job; third, to diffuse the locus of control in the organization, or to spread the authority and responsibility. When horizontal communication is restricted, the locus of control (power) rests primarily on the higher levels of the hierarchy. Vertical communication with no horizontal flow is a common way to keep control in many organizational systems. The more authoritarian

[9]Katz and Kahn, op. cit., p. 440.

the structure, the more restricted the horizontal flow. For example, the academic vice-president in a university may know about all the deans and their respective schools while each one of the deans may only know what pertains to his or her own school. Allocation of resources in other schools may remain an unknown factor for any one dean. The vice-president has the information regarding all schools and is thus in a powerful position to manipulate the deans and the resources. If horizontal flow is not restricted, however, the deans of our example will get together, formally or informally, and share with one another information about the resources each was allocated. Pressure can thus be placed on the vice-president if any of the deans is dissatisfied about the allocation process.

Subordinate/manager or upward communication.   Upward communication has to do with what the organization members say:

1. About themselves, their performance, and their problems
2. About others and their problems
3. About organizational practices and policies
4. About what needs to be done and how to do it[10]

You can see from these topics that it takes a special kind of manager to listen effectively to those messages. It also takes a special kind of relationship of trust and objective openness to have good lines of communication in this direction. For example, a subordinate who wants to report to a boss is restricted by many norms or common practices: (1) Talking about one's own achievements is difficult because our culture frowns on braggarts. (2) Telling the boss how other workers are doing is difficult because our culture frowns on the squealer or stoolie. (3) Telling superiors about better systems or procedures is difficult because our mythology says you just do your job and don't try to give the boss advice. "That's the way we do it around here . . ." has turned off many sincere attempts to improve the business. Whether looked at from the total organization level or from the more specific relational contexts, functions of communication are complex and all-pervasive in organizational life.

BUSINESS COMMUNICATION: A POINT OF VIEW

Every book written reflects the point of view, biases, philosophy, and values of its author or authors. In the preface, we traced our intellectual origins, and explicitly stated our philosophy about the kind of communication course we believe is helpful, useful, and

---

[10]Ibid., pp. 446–448.

practical both for business administration students and for speech-communication students who study organizational communication. Such a course is also relevant for sociology, political science, and psychology. Students in these disciplines each bring to the study of organizations a framework different from ours, but their studies can be enriched by the perspective we believe communication provides.

In this section we want to spell out the major points of our perspective in the study of communication in organizations.

We pointed out earlier in this chapter that a car pool and General Motors are both organizations from an organizing process standpoint. The statement, we believe, is accurate. The two examples were chosen to represent extremes in a continuum ranging from the small, loosely knit, informal, almost spontaneous organization up to the large, complex, formal organization.

Communication in Formal Work Organizations

In this book we choose to concentrate on formal work organization. Although much of what we write could apply to informal organizations, our discussions and examples will primarily center on organizations like businesses, government and social agencies, health care systems, educational institutions, and other organizations which employ human and physical resources to produce goods and/or services.

The most useful theoretical foundation for the study of organizations is represented by open system theory, which says that any organization depends upon its outside environment. In social organizations, people are the carriers of energy input, and this theory provides useful analytical tools for the study of human behavior.

Organizations as Open Systems

The way people think about communication profoundly affects how they communicate. We wrote earlier in this chapter that we view communication as a transactional process where people construct meaning, develop expectations, and exchange symbols. Communication involves a complex interrelationship of many variables over time and within situations. Communication between people never occurs in a vacuum. It happens in a certain place at a certain time. The people involved are not cardboard figures. They are the result of their lifetime of experiences, perceptions, and previous communications. How you construct meaning and develop expectations in the present is based on the ways you constructed meaning and developed expectations in your past. As you and I speak to each other we are both simultaneously sender and receiver of symbols. We simultaneously construct and possibly share meanings and develop expectations of each other, the situation, and the environment. As our communication continues, our

Communication as a Transactional Process

meanings and expectations may change, either drastically or slightly, and thus provide a basis for a new understanding of what is going on between us.

How you view yourself and your world is related to your communication with yourself and with others. How you see yourself depends on how you see others' responses to you. Your perception of other people's responses is itself built on prior perceptions and prior responses, the history of your communication. How you see yourself will affect how you communicate with others, which in turn affects how others will respond to you, which in turn affects how you see yourself. Do you get the feeling of an unending spiraling process? If you follow our argument that there is truly no beginning and no end to communication, you understand what we mean when we write that communication is a transactional process in which you are both cause and effect of whatever is happening.

Behavioral Approach

This book has a very clear focus: We are interested in the *behaviors* of people in organizational settings. Although we devote some attention to the reciprocal relationship between organizational structure and communication, our emphasis will remain on communicative behaviors. That includes how people can experience them, describe them, interpret them, predict them, control them, and change them.

We will be concerned with what managers and other organization members *do* in relation to one another and with how communicative behaviors are at the core of organizational activities. This approach differentiates our book from other organizational behavior and management texts which treat communication as only one of the processes of organizational life. We contend that managing is a process of influencing others, and that influence occurs through communication. This makes communicative behaviors and activities the central influence in the organization.

Laboratory Approach

We believe very strongly that knowledge which is not applied does little good. If what you learn is not translated into behavior, then you gain little from your knowledge. It is our objective to describe communicative behaviors in organizations in such a way that you will be able to see the practical applications of what we talk about. We do not intend for this book to have a cookbook approach with simple oven-tested recipes on how to manage communication. Not enough is known and understood yet about organizations and communication to present a complete theory from which adequate and tested principles can be derived to cover all occasions. However, we will continually urge you to think how you can use what you have learned about communication in practical situations you encounter and in organizations in which you participate.

The laboratory manual will provide you with situations to analyze and discuss with your classmates and your instructor. The situations we chose are realistic representations of people engaging in communication in organizations. As we repeatedly stress relationships between concepts discussed in the book and their applications to "real" situations and as we provide you with analytical tools, you will be able to use your knowledge in the cases, simulations, and various exercises. We intend for you to develop a feel for what communication is like in organizations, a curiosity about why certain events happen, a sensitivity to the complexity of human communication, and the skill to transfer what you learn in the classroom to situations you will encounter as a member or a manager of an organization.

SUMMARY

People organize to get more done than they can accomplish working alone. Our basic definition of the organization or the organizational unit is two or more persons functioning in space and time, giving each other resources, and coordinating their activities to accomplish some output. Without communication, efforts cannot be combined, inputs expressed, or outputs articulated.

Communication is not the same as information, which consists mainly of patterns. Because the way we pattern information is special to each of us, it is necessary also to communicate about the system we are using. We need to tell each other the information and also how we are putting the information together.

In organizations there are three main functions for communication. When you are mainly concerned with production or getting work done, your communication helps meet the organization's objectives of regulation and output. When you are concerned with relating to the outside environment, you are using communication to adapt to change or innovation. When you are concerned with how members of the organization feel about themselves and their work and their motivation, then you are using communication to help the social or maintenance functions of people to get the purposes realized.

There are also relational elements in communication such as the difference between a manager addressing a subordinate, peers talking, or communication upward, or from subordinates to superiors.

Our view, as authors of this text, is that communication study should look at the organization as an open system, using a transactional model as a way of thinking and theorizing about it from a behavioral approach. Learning in this area can be, in our opinion, greatly helped by the laboratory approach to studying organizational communication which gives you practice in looking at communication in action, analyzing it, and practicing it.

CHAPTER 2

ORGANIZATIONAL THEORIES AND THEIR COMMUNICATION IMPLICATIONS

"The authoritarian organizational hierarchy contains key factors which are counterproductive to the quality of life within and outside the organization." Chris Argyris

INTRODUCTION

Each of you is a student of human behavior. Ever since you were born you have learned that certain things you do are likely to bring certain responses from people. As an infant, if you cried, you were fed, picked up, or in some way paid attention to. As you grew older, you learned more sophisticated ways to explain, control, and predict other people's behaviors, and in a sense, you learned to make relationships between events you observed.

When you develop generalizations to explain and predict what people do and will do, you become a theorist. You already know a great number of generalizations about people and organizations. Some may be accurate, some may not. Think, for example, of the following statements:

1. People are basically lazy.
2. People are only motivated by money.
3. Everyone wants a challenging job.
4. Happy workers are productive workers.
5. A camel is a horse produced by a committee.

How many of these statements are true? It may surprise you to learn that none is totally accurate. We will discuss generalizations later in the book. What matters here is not so much the validity of these generalizations, but rather the fact that you do really hold many generalizations about human behavior. While some of these may be based on your personal experience, many are hand-me-down clichés you have always heard and perhaps never challenged.

In this chapter we are going to take you on a tour of the major theories which have attempted to give us generalizations about the way people behave in organizations. For some of you, this may be new material. For the many students of organizational behavior and management, we suspect this chapter may serve as a review. However, one important factor sets this review apart from most: its emphasis on *communication*. Because our focus in this book is on communicative behaviors, we have deliberately chosen to classify the major theories in terms of their stated or implicit assumptions about the role of communication in the organization. As you will see later in this chapter, concern for communication by these theorists ranges from almost none to very much. Figure 2-1 summarizes the various schools, their major theorists, and their basic concepts.

THE CLASSICAL SCHOOL

The classical school, by and large, ignored communication as a key variable in the study of human behavior in organizations. Such oversight appears incredibly naive, yet you must remember that the

---

MAJOR SCHOOLS OF ORGANIZATIONAL THEORY **FIGURE 2-1**

CLASSICAL	**BEHAVIORAL**
Contributing disciplines:	*Contributing disciplines:*
Industrial engineering	Psychology
Economics	Sociology
Experience	Social psychology
	Anthropology

Scientific Management	**Human Relations**
Taylor	Mayo
	Roethlisberger

Bureaucracy	**Human Resources**
Weber	McGregor
	Likert

Administrative Management	**Systems**
Fayol	Open systems:
Barnard	Katz and Kahn
	Contingency:
	Woodward
	Lawrence and Lorsch

MAJOR CONCEPTS

Division of labor	Motivation
Pay as motivator	Group norms
Narrow span of control	Flat organization designs
Unity of command	Contingency leadership
Authority-responsibility	Job enrichment
Line-staff	

---

theorists of that school were mostly engineers who were instrumental in the development of mass production. Machines were their new gods. Efficiency and scientific rigor were the key words. People were little more than extensions of the all-powerful machinery. Emphasis was clearly on structure, order, formal organization, and objective rationality.

In this section we will review Taylor and scientific management; Weber and bureaucracy; and Fayol, Barnard, and administrative theory. We will close the section with a summary of the major implications for communication of the concepts set forth by the classical school.

Taylor and Scientific Management[1]

In the early 1900s, a group of engineers spearheaded by Frederick W. Taylor became interested in the techniques of work. Taylor was a mechanical engineer who held a top executive position in the steel and

[1]*Scientific Management*, Harper and Brothers, New York, 1947.

metal industry. These engineers felt that work and managing work were processes which could be analyzed in a scientific manner. They believed that an objective analysis of facts collected through scientific experimentation would reveal the best way to organize work in organizations. They focused essentially on blue-collar work (shoveling and metal cutting) and felt it was management's responsibility to organize the tasks of the workers. Time-and-motion studies were the trademark of Taylorism. Box 2-1 describes the major points of scientific management.

Communication implications

Scientific management theorists had a faith in machines which typified scientific thinking at its best. Workers were considered simply extensions of machines and were to be treated as inter-

---

BOX 2-1*   **SCIENTIFIC MANAGEMENT: FREDERICK W. TAYLOR**

Assumptions

Labor-management conflict stems from inefficient use of scarce resources.
The supply of economic goods can be increased through more efficient use of human resources.
Managing work efficiently is the main objective.
Man is basically motivated by economic needs.
Man behaves rationally to improve monetary income.

Characteristics

1. Science, not rule of thumb, is stressed.
2. Harmony, not discord, is the goal.
3. Cooperation, not individualism, is required.
4. Maximum output, not restricted output, is to be achieved.
5. Development of each worker to his greatest efficiency and prosperity is considered desirable.

Principles of management

1. Develop a science for each element of a man's work to replace the old rule-of-thumb method.
2. Scientifically select, then train, teach, and develop the workman.
3. Management should cooperate with workers to ensure work is done in accordance with principles of the science which has been developed.
4. There is almost equal division of work and responsibility between management and workers.

*Frederick W. Taylor, *Scientific Management*, Harper and Brothers, New York, 1947, pp. 36–37, 140.

changeable parts. Coordination and organization were thought to be design problems, and organizational theory was a branch of engineering.

Taylor had little to say about communication and its function in the organizing process. For the engineers of the scientific management school, downward communication from supervisors to workers was the best way to instruct workers to perform their tasks. The assumptions were that workers would (1) understand what they were told and (2) agree to do it. These assumptions were never questioned. Rather, Taylor assumed that since it was to their best economic advantage to produce satisfactorily, workers would logically and rationally heed instructions. Absolutely no attention was paid to the fact that workers talked to one another on the job, that work groups interpreted instructions in ways often unintended by supervisors, and that independent decisions to maintain low production standards were frequently made by these groups.

In short the role of informal communication activities was simply ignored.

BOX 2-2

Characteristics of Bureaucracy*

1. Division of labor and specialization.
2. Hierarchy.
3. Rules and procedures.
4. Professional qualifications.
5. Impersonal relationships.

Functions of Bureaucracy†

1. Specialization permits productivity.
2. Structure gives form to organization.
3. Predictability and stability are worked for.
4. Rationality is admired.

Dysfunctional Consequences

1. Problem with specialization: communication and lack of overall view.
2. Problem with rules and regulations: red tape.
3. Problem with impersonality: no room for enthusiasm.
4. Problem with stability: in fast-changing environment—lack of flexibility.

*Max Weber, *The Theory of Social and Economic Organization*, translated by A.M. Henderson and Talcott Parsons, Oxford Univ. Press, New York, 1947.
†Herbert G. Hicks and C. Roy Gullett, *Organization: Theory and Behavior*, McGraw-Hill Book Company, N.Y., 1975, pp. 134–38.

**Weber and
Bureaucracy**

Max Weber, a German sociologist, is generally recognized as the father of bureaucracy, which he claimed was superior to any other form of organization "in precision, in stability, in the stringency of its discipline and its reliability."[2]

Warren Bennis[3] strongly indicted bureaucracy. Some of his criticisms are summarized in Box 2-3.

**Communication
implications**

Bureaucracy portrays a model of organization structure in which communication is highly formalized and flexibility minimal. The emphasis on rules and procedures demands that communication be initiated at the top of the hierarchy or chain of command. Communication among peers is almost nonexistent, one of Bennis's criticisms. The production function of communication is strongly emphasized at the expense of its innovation and social functions. At best, bureaucracy represents a limited view of what functions communication performs in the organization. It ignores the complexity of human motivation and the richness of human resources. Many of Bennis's criticisms

[2]*The Theory of Social and Economic Organization,* Trans., A.M., Henderson and Talcott Parsons, Oxford University Press, New York, 1947, p. 334.

[3]"Beyond Bureaucracy," *Trans-Action,* July–August 1965, p. 31.

BOX 2-3   **BENNIS'S CRITICISMS OF BUREAUCRACY***

1. Bureaucracy does not adequately allow for personal growth and the development of mature personalities.
2. It develops conformity and "groupthink."
3. It does not take into account the "informal organization" and the emergent and unanticipated problems.
4. Its system of control and authority are hopelessly outdated.
5. It has no juridical process.
6. It does not possess adequate means for resolving differences and conflicts between ranks, and most particularly among functional groups.
7. Communication (and innovative ideas) are thwarted or distorted due to hierarchical division.
8. The full range of human resources is not utilized because of mistrust, fear of reprisal, etc. Play-it-safe behaviors are reinforced.
9. It cannot assimilate the influx of new technology or scientists entering the organization.
10. It modifies personality structure so that people become and reflect the dull, gray, conditioned "organization man."

*Warren Bennis, "Beyond Bureaucracy," *Trans-Action,* p. 31, July–August 1965.

HENRI FAYOL*   BOX 2-4

Structural Principles

1. Division of work
2. Unity of direction
3. Centralization
4. Authority and responsibility
5. The scalar chain

Process Principles

1. Equity
2. Discipline
3. Remuneration
4. Unity of command
5. Subordination to the general interest

End-Result Principles

1. Order
2. Stability
3. Initiative
4. Esprit de corps

Functions of Management

1. Planning
2. Organizing
3. Commanding
4. Coordinating
5. Controlling

   *The division of Fayol's fourteen principles into structural, process, and end-result principles is based on the analysis in James L. Gibson, John M. Ivancevitch, and James H. Donelly, *Organizations: Behavior, Structure, Process*, Business Publications, Inc., Dallas, Tex., 1976, pp. 267–270.

---

center on the fact that the bureaucratic model simply misunderstands or ignores communication factors.

Fayol, Barnard, and Administrative Theory

Administrative theory and bureaucracy are very much related. Both emphasize specialization, hierarchy, and professionalism. Both potentially generate rigidity, impersonality, and goal displacement. However, there are differences between the two models, which may stem from their origins. Bureaucracy was the product of sociologists who intended to prescribe efficient organizational structures. Administrative theory was the child of practicing managers who were interested in prescribing *principles to manage* formal organizations.

BOX 2-5   **CHESTER BARNARD'S THEORY OF ACCEPTANCE***

Chester Barnard was president of New Jersey Bell Telephone Company. Barnard is often credited with a great deal of influence on the break from classical thinking which he felt was too superficial. Barnard's emphasis on communication as the means for developing cooperation was unique at the time. Barnard believed that the communication system of an organization was the means to induce cooperation. He was dissatisfied with the classical view that authority came from the top down. Rather, he maintained that authority came from the bottom up.

In his *theory of acceptance*, Barnard contended that it is subordinates who decide whether an order is legitimate and whether to accept it or reject it. Before a person decides to accept a communication as authoritative, four conditions must be met:

1. The receiver can and does understand the communication.
2. At the time of decision the receiver believes that it is not inconsistent with the purpose of the organization.
3. At the time of decision the receiver believes it to be compatible with his or her personal interest as a whole.
4. The receiver is able mentally and physically to comply with it.

*Chester I. Barnard, *The Function of the Executive*, Harvard University Press, Cambridge, Mass., 1938, p. 165.

Henri Fayol, the Frenchman, and Chester Barnard, the American, are two outstanding representatives of the action-oriented administrative theorists.

Fayol's[4] fourteen principles and five functions of management are listed in Box 2-4. Barnard's[5] theory of acceptance is summarized in Box 2-5.

Communication implications

Although Fayol gave some attention to communication processes, his notion of the role of communication in the organization remained fairly similar to that of the bureaucratic model. Communication was essentially the process of moving information up and down the formal chain of command. Information and orders, both production concerns, were basically the focus of managerial activities. Although Fayol does mention the need for two-way communication and oral communication between managers and subordinates, the flow of communication is essentially from top to bottom. Fayol, however, was aware of the slowness of the process in large organizations and of the time element

[4]*General and Industrial Management*, Trans., Constance Storrs, Pitman and Sons, Ltd., London, 1949.
[5]Chester I. Barnard, *The Function of the Executive*, Harvard University Press, Cambridge, Mass., 1938, p. 165.

involved in passing information up and down the line. His "gangplank" principle is designed to permit the bypassing of formal channels when two managers at the same level need to communicate to accomplish a common activity. This horizontal or peer communication, however, must be authorized by the immediate superiors of the two managers and must be clearly limited to the business at hand or joint activity. Figure 2-2 diagrams the "gangplank" concept. Here again, the concern is clearly production, and the role of communication is never discussed from a perspective of innovation and social functions. Informal communication among managers or between managers and subordinates is not mentioned. The coordinating function of the managerial process, the one function which is essentially based on communication, is not particularly highlighted. It is very interesting that Fayol, who writes much about the personality of the manager as a kind and fair person knowing his or her employees well, did not write more about informal communication and the social function of communication. However, remember that he wrote in France in 1915, a time when workers were still generally considered little more than extensions of machines or cogs in a wheel. Only later was there reluctant recognition that human factors—not just pure logic and reason—were at work in organizations.

It was Barnard who first asserted that the existence of a formal chain of command and a formal structure did not guarantee compliance with orders communicated from above. These were the assertions that paved the way for recognition of the importance of human factors in organizations. Barnard was the first writer who formally challenged the assumption that simply because an order or a communication was sent through the proper channels it was necessarily (1) understood, and (2) complied with. For the first time, organization members were viewed as people rather than as machines, and it was recognized that their personal needs, perceptions, and interests played a part in the way they functioned in the organization. Barnard was truly the forerunner of the human relations movement and the human resources school.

FIGURE 2-2

Fayol's scalar chain of organization and the gangplank idea.

The Concept of Structure and its Communication Implications

The structure of an organization refers to the way people and work and activities are grouped together. The classical school reflects a great concern for the concept of structure and has dealt with it in a number of ways. On one hand the classical school deals with *vertical* structure and the notions of centralization, delegation of authority, span of control, and hierarchy. On the other hand, it deals with *horizontal* structure and notions of departmentalization—a direct by-product of specialization, and line/staff division.

Centralization versus decentralization

There are several types of centralized structures. The term "centralized" can refer to *geographical* centralization when an organization has its activities grouped in one place, such as a city or region. Geographical decentralization means the higher degree of dispersion of an organization's operations throughout the country.

The term "centralized" can also refer to *functional* centralization when, for example, the accounting functions for all departments are accomplished in one department. Decentralized in that case means that each department performs its own accounting operations.

In a third sense, "centralization" can refer to the delegation or retention of decision-making and command authority. It is concerned with how many different people and at what levels hold power positions in an organization.

The bureaucratic school advocates centralization, a tall structure over a narrow span of control. Such a structure gives managers tight and close control over subordinates, and calls for strict discipline. The nature of flat structures, on the other hand, rules out close control over subordinates since the wide span of control makes it hard for a manager to keep in touch with so many subordinates. Some of the work has to be delegated, which may promote decentralization of authority.

In a tall structure, communication flows mostly along vertical lines. There may be more opportunities for close contact between superiors and subordinates since the span of control is usually narrow. Although it is often assumed that such contact remains impersonal and is of a disciplinary nature, it need not be. However, the number of levels involved in tall structures increases the risk of distortion in the communication process and fosters the red tape so often associated with large bureaucracies. Flat structure permits a simplification of vertical communication since fewer levels of the hierarchy are involved. Fewer distortions are present. However, the equality which exists between a large number of managers in a flat structure may itself create some communication problems. Horizontal communication may not work well if it is not carefully facilitated. As mentioned earlier, horizontal communication in bureaucracies—that is, communication among managers at the same level of the hierarchy— is not encouraged except in special cases where Fayol's "gangplank" provides a shortcut for otherwise cumbersome communication channels.

Departmentalization is one of the major components of any organizational structure. Traditionally, the bureaucratic structure recognizes several bases for departmentalization: In *functional* departmentalization—sales, production, accounting, and personnel are examples— people who do the same things are grouped together. *Geographical area* and *product lines* are other bases for departmentalization.

    Functional departmentalization is by far the most common in large organizations. Its greatest single advantage is that it incorporates the strengths of specialization, allowing for the most efficient use of employees' skills. It also risks the disadvantages of specialization if it encourages excessive interdepartmental competition rather than cooperation, or reduces communication among competing departments, or fosters empire building.

Departmentalization

The concept of staff persons to advise managers who have primary command authority—line managers—is not a new one. Its origins are credited to the military. In the early 1900s, the European version of the military staff concept was adapted in the United States armed forces. In the thirties, the line-staff was widely used in American business and industry.[6]

    Staff members provide information, expert advice, and counsel to line managers. Line managers have authority over those members of the organization who directly accomplish its objectives. The staff concept permits an expansion of management abilities through specialization. Executive assistants, special assistants, or assistants-to are usually people with special qualifications to whom a line office can delegate work. Other staff positions, such as personnel, accounting, and research and development, perform broad supportive functions of the organization. These functions support the main goal of the organization. It is not uncommon for line and staff personnel to be in conflict with one another. Staff people often feel like second-class citizens. Tensions between line and staff are often stereotypically described as the conflict between the old-line supervisor who has been in the company for thirty years and has no formal education but a wealth of experience on the job, and the young college graduate full of bright and innovative ideas on how to run the business. In a classic

Line/staff division

[6]Fred Luthans, *Organizational Behavior*, 2d ed., McGraw-Hill Book Company, New York, 1977, p. 142.

study of line-staff conflicts, Dalton[7] found that by and large, staff personnel were younger and better-educated than line supervisors. Line managers often feel threatened by and suspicious of staff advice.

THE BEHAVIORAL SCHOOL

From the 1930s on, a new school of thought developed which challenged the basic economic-man assumption of the classical school. The behavioral school, with its origins in psychology, sociology, social psychology, and anthropology, began to shed a different light on organizational behavior. It emphasized the crucial role played by individuals—or human behavior—in the effectiveness of an organization.

The Human Relations Movement

Between the 1930s and the 1950s, a group of researchers under the direction of Elton Mayo studied the behavior of individuals and work groups and focused on the relationships between the two. They were interested in the *social* environment surrounding the job rather than the *physical* environment which the classical school had emphasized. While the classical school stressed structure, order, formal organization, and objective rationality, the human relations movement focused on social factors, informal organization, and individual motivation.

Mayo, a professor of industrial research at the Harvard Graduate School of Business Administration, began a series of studies with his associates in the Hawthorne plant of the Western Electric Company. These studies[8] produced results which had considerable influence on the current thinking about human behavior and motivation in organizations. The Hawthorne studies, as they are generally known, are described in Box 2-6.

Although they grew out of the mechanistic thinking of the time-and-motion studies, the Hawthorne studies eventually challenged the classical view. Researchers happened on some interesting, confusing, and revolutionary results in their attempt to get the workers to cooperate with the experimenters. They had consulted the workers about every change to be made in the work conditions. They had listened to workers about their reactions to the experimental conditions. They had allowed workers to talk as they worked in contrast to regular plant policy. They had held meetings with workers in supervisors' offices where they had asked the workers about their

[7]Melville Dalton, "Conflicts between Staff and Line Managerial Officers," *American Sociological Review*, June 1950, pp. 342–350.

[8]Fritz J. Roethlisberger and William J. Dickson, *Management and the Worker*, Harvard University Press, Cambridge, Mass., 1939.

THE HAWTHORNE STUDIES

BOX 2-6

1. *The illumination experiment and the "Hawthorne effect."*
   In the mid-1920s, the National Research Council's Illuminating Engineering Society conducted a series of studies on industrial lighting at the Hawthorne (Illinois) plant of the Western Electric Company. The Council intended for the researchers to determine the relationship between lighting conditions and workers' productivity.

   Results of these experiments were startling. As illumination went up in the room of the experimental group, productivity also went up, as expected. However, surprisingly, productivity went up also in the control group where lighting had remained constant. When the experimenters *decreased* the intensity of the lighting in the experimental room, expecting productivity to go down, productivity still went up. As lighting further decreased, productivity continued to go up.

   Something peculiar was obviously at work, and it did not seem to have much to do with lighting conditions. It seemed that the workers' productivity was related to their perception of the special attention they were getting. As "research participants," workers felt motivated to produce more. This effect, the "Hawthorne effect" as it came to be known, refers to the tendency of people to behave in unusual ways when they know they are singled out, observed, and generally given special attention. Clearly, the Hawthorne effect could not be accounted for in the terms of classical theory.

2. *The relay assembly test room experiment.*
   In the relay assembly test room, a group of six women were assigned to assemble telephone relays. A variety of changes were introduced in the conditions of the job: a group payment incentive, breaks, shorter working hours, refreshments. After each of these treatments was introduced, productivity went up. Then the relay assembly test room went back to its original 48-hour, six-day week, with no incentives, no breaks, and no refreshments, and productivity went . . . *up*. And it went up to the highest level yet recorded.

   At that point it became clear to the researchers that *human elements* such as workers' motivation and attitudes, social relations, and supervisory attitudes and *not* the purely physical and technical conditions of the job had an effect on workers' productivity.

3. *The bank wiring assembly observation room experiment.*
   The last phase of the Hawthorne studies, the bank wiring observation room experiment, was set up to test some of the premises formulated at the conclusion of earlier interviews. A group of nine male workers who assembled terminal banks for telephone exchanges were involved in that phase of the study. They were a highly integrated group with their own norms and code of conduct. The researchers wanted to test the effects of a group piecework incentive pay plan. They assumed that the workers would seek their own economic interest and increase their production by having faster workers pressure the slower ones to improve their output. Yet group pressure did not quite work the way the researchers had anticipated. Once the worker group had defined what constituted the acceptable output for a day's work, and once they knew they could reach it, the workers slacked off, particularly the faster ones. Violating the group norm by being a "rate buster" and overproducing or by being a "chiseler" and underproducing was definitely unacceptable by the group's own standards. The researchers concluded that wage incentives were less effective in determining an individual worker's productivity than the sense of security and acceptance offered by the work group, which not only set its own standard of production, but exerted strong group pressure to achieve, maintain, and not exceed that standard.

opinions, goals, and worries. Researchers were totally unaware at the time that changes in *how the workers were dealt with* would be more significant than the actual changes in working conditions.

Communication implications

The Hawthorne studies were a landmark in organizational thinking and questioned the basic assumptions of the classical school about human behavior in organizations. The human relations theorists saw the worker as a social being responding to interpersonal pressures of informal work groups. What became clear, particularly after the bank wiring observation room experiment, was that workers did not follow a rate of production set by their supervisors or by other experts, but one that *they themselves set as a group.* Clearly the *informal communication* which existed in work groups was at the root of workers' motivation in these groups. Formal outside efforts to pressure individual workers toward greater production appeared futile in the context of the work group. The belief that workers' motivations rather than organizational design and structure are central elements in productivity became evident with the Hawthorne studies. Mayo felt that people are not necessarily guided by logic and rationality but respond mainly to their relationships with other people. Too much attention had been placed on standardization and specialization of work which contributed to the exclusion of workers from social participation. It prevented workers from understanding the value of their individual work and their contribution to the organization and to society.

For the human relations movement, organizing related to motivating. For the classical theorists, motivating was simply a process of informing workers of more efficient ways to do their work. Workers would thus become better at their jobs and receive more money as a reward. When workers did not use the "better" methods of doing their work, something was wrong with them because they did not respond to the monetary incentive. That the "incentive" may not have been a real incentive was never questioned.

Human relations theorists felt that motivation was a much more complex phenomenon. Simple dollar inducements were not enough. They felt that human relationships were much more of a crucial factor in motivating workers. Satisfied workers, that is, workers happy with their relationships at work, would produce more than workers placed in a social vacuum and treated like machines. Workers produced more when they were treated like people and made to feel important, and when supervisory attitudes permitted them or encouraged them to participate in decisions which affected them. Motivation depended on the leadership and communication skills of supervisors. The social function of communication was emphasized. To the extent that a supervisor could meet workers' social needs and acceptance needs, workers would respond positively to management.

Informal communication in the peer group and with immediate supervisors was the central idea of the human relations movement. The interview phase of the Hawthorne studies made it very clear that "just talking" to an understanding person was beneficial to the workers. Communication was no longer thought of solely as a way to give information and issue orders about getting the job done. Communication was now seen as a way to get at the internal world of the workers and to make it clear to them that they were all individuals, different from all others, with feelings and opinions that mattered.

Workers were recognized as individuals, not machines. The work group was a fundamental entity in the organization, shaping the workers' perceptions, attitudes, values, and needs. These new ideas were also coupled with the notion that involving workers in decisions that affected them was a powerful tool for developing workers' satisfaction.

Researchers stumbled upon the notion of participative management when they explored the workers' feelings in a series of interviews. That the workers had been consulted at each phase of the experiment, that they had been listened to, and that their suggestions had sometimes been implemented gave them a sense of participation which undoubtedly was related to their high productivity. A new style of supervision—with a new emphasis on communication—was to emerge from these studies and pave the way for the human resources school.

The Human Resources School

As Mayo represented the human relations movement, Douglas McGregor and Rensis Likert are the men whose thinking shaped the content of the human resources school.

Douglas McGregor: theory X and theory Y

In his book *The Human Side of Enterprise*, McGregor[9] contrasted the classical view of man as rational and economic with a conception of man as growth-oriented and responsible. McGregor labeled *theory X* and *theory Y* the two sets of assumptions described in Box 2-7.

The human relations movement earlier had challenged theory X assumptions and had demonstrated that simplistic statements about human behavior were just not adequate to guide managerial strategy. These assumptions nevertheless persisted for a long time. They are

[9]McGraw-Hill Book Company, New York, 1960, pp. 33–34.

consistent with the often-expressed belief that people are motivated only by money, security, and the threat of punishment. On the other hand, much of what we can see going on among people does not agree with this negative, pessimistic, and in many ways childlike view of man.

Theory X assumptions imply that the blame for ineffective organizational performance rests on human nature and the limitations of the human resources ("That's the way people are . . .") with which management has to work. Theory Y assumptions challenge the view that human resources are so basically limited. It puts the responsibility squarely on management itself to discover ways to realize the vastly untapped potential of available human resources to the organization.

Communication implications.   According to theory X, communication is primarily a process of passing information and commands from the top of the hierarchy to the bottom with little encouragement to subordinates to initiate communication with their supervisors. Although lip service is paid to the innovation function of communication, an impersonal, organizationwide suggestion box system is often all that is implemented to find out what employees down the line think and feel. Communication with or among employees is not encouraged

---

BOX 2-7   **HUMAN RESOURCES SCHOOL**
DOUGLAS McGREGOR
THEORY X AND THEORY Y: BASIC ASSUMPTIONS

Theory X

1. The average human being dislikes work and will avoid it.
2. Most people must be coerced, controlled, directed, threatened with punishment to get them to put forth adequate effort toward achievement of organizational objectives.
3. The average person prefers to be directed, wishes to avoid responsibility, has little ambition, and seeks security above all.

Theory Y

1. Expenditure of physical and mental effort is as natural as play and rest.
2. External control and threat of punishment are not the only means to bring about effort toward organizational objectives. People will exercise self-control and self-direction in the service of objectives toward which they are committed.
3. Commitment to objectives is a function of the rewards associated with their achievement.
4. The average person learns under proper conditions to seek rather than avoid responsibility.
5. The capacity to exercise a relatively high degree of imagination and creativity in the solution of organizational problems is widely distributed among the population.
6. Under the conditions of modern industrial life, the intellectual potential of the average human being is only partially utilized.

and, as a result, little stock is placed on the information which circulates informally in the organization through the grapevine. Decisions remain in the hands of top-level managers who often have to make decisions on the basis of partial and sometimes distorted information. McGregor claimed that such styles would not promote job satisfaction and good job performance because closely supervised people tend to resist constraints and do only the minimum required of them. People in the theory X system tend to lose initiative and creativity and end up acting in accord with the assumptions which generated the style in the first place—a nice example of a self-fulfilling prophecy. McGregor suggested that management practices should reflect theory Y assumptions, more in tune with the newer developments in the behavioral sciences, particularly in the area of human motivation.

The central idea in McGregor's framework is *integration* of individual needs and goals with organizational objectives. It is up to management to create conditions that will allow organization members to achieve their own goals by fulfilling the organization's objectives.

In this new framework, management of human resources cannot rest on direction and control through the exercise of authority. The unexpressed needs of the individual can no longer be automatically second to organizational objectives. The notion of integration and self-control means that the organization will achieve its objectives better if it makes significant adjustments to the needs of its members.

Supervisory styles more in line with theory Y assumptions include less control and structure, less direct supervision of the work environment. Supervisors and managers who believe in these newer assumptions must develop management and communication practices which permit their subordinates to assume more control over their work. In that way workers can satisfy their social, esteem, and self-actualization needs. By being more openly communicative, managers demonstrate they trust their subordinates to enjoy their work, to show initiative and creativity, and basically to fulfill the organization's goals if those are compatible with their own.

From a communication viewpoint, theory Y managers focus less on formal regulations and more on informal oral communication. The innovative function of communication gets some attention as organization members' suggestions and ideas are sought and encouraged. Decision making is not limited to higher management but is encouraged at all levels of the organization. Frequent communication among all organization members is a must, and its flow is allowed in all directions: up, down, and laterally. Organization members thus feel informed, are part of what is going on, know what they need to know in order to make decisions—and hence are likely to make better decisions. More trust will exist among members of the organization as a result of these communication practices.

Rensis Likert: the linking pin model and the four systems of management

Likert was one of the first theorists to develop ways to measure human variables within the organization. He has been the leading force behind large-scale research on management and leadership styles in industry. With his colleagues at the Institute for Social Research at the University of Michigan, Likert conducted many empirical studies and summarized his findings in two widely read books, *New Patterns of Management* and *The Human Organization*.[10] Likert dealt explicitly with communication concerns. His analysis of leadership and management style relies heavily on the communication aspects of organizational behavior.

The linking pin model.   Instead of the traditional model of individuals relating to individuals within the traditional hierarchy and chain of command, Likert sees the organizational structure as one where groups relate to groups and where individual managers perform the role of "linking pins." Each group is composed of managers and those who report to them. In Likert's description or model, managers are members of at least two groups: one which links them to a group led by their superior and one in which they participate with their subordinates. By belonging to both groups, managers represent their level of the organization both to the next higher level and to the next lower level of the hierarchy. By being the linking pin between these groups, managers represent the overlapping structure which lets the organization develop upward communication. In such a design, shared leadership and decision making are possible since there are no sharp distinctions between the roles of superior and subordinate. Figure 2-3 shows the linking pin model which Likert described. Although it may appear to be no more than a hierarchy of triangles, the main advantage of the group structure from a communication viewpoint is that it fosters loyalty to several groups and thus permits free exchange of information in these groups. Likert also stressed that more real influence can be exerted upward, which affects not just morale and satisfaction but ultimately productivity and performance.[11]

---

[10]McGraw-Hill Book Company, New York, 1961; 1967.

[11]Ludwig von Bertalanffy, "General System Theory," *General Systems*, 1956, pp. 1–10; "General Systems Theory: A Critical Review," *General Systems*, 1962, pp. 1–20; *General Systems Theory*, Braziller, New York, 1968, p. 37.

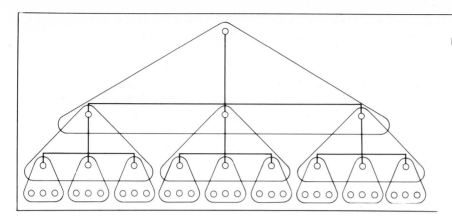

FIGURE 2-3
Likert's linking pin model.
Source: Rensis Likert,
New Patterns of Management, McGraw-Hill
Book Company, New
York, 1961, p. 105.

The four systems of management.   Likert was interested in differentiating between effective and ineffective organizations. His research led him to believe that the difference could be found along a number of structural dimensions and organizational processes: (1) leadership, (2) motivation, (3) communication, (4) interaction, (5) decision making, (6) goal setting, (7) control, and (8) performance. Likert developed a fifty-one-item questionnaire designed to tap managers' perceptions of the nature of these eight characteristics for their organization. When the averages for each characteristic are plotted along a continuum, an organizational profile emerges which can fall into one of four systems of management:

System 1:   Exploitative-authoritarian
System 2:   Benevolent-authoritarian
System 3:   Consultative
System 4:   Participative

Figure 2-4 provides a fictional example of an organizational profile based on Likert's questionnaire. System 1 closely resembles McGregor's Theory X and Taylor's scientific management. System 4 parallels McGregor's Theory Y. The other two systems fall somewhere between the two. A description of the four systems and their characteristics appears in Box 2-8.

Communication implications.   Likert clearly points out the valuable and central role that communication plays in these systems. Communication is much more than simply one of the characteristics he describes. Communication is truly the basis for practically all the dimensions which are part of an organizational profile.

LIKERT'S FOUR SYSTEMS OF MANAGEMENT　　　　BOX 2-8

	System 1	System 2	System 3	System 4
Leadership	No trust. No supportive behavior. No freedom to discuss.	Condescending trust. Condescending support. Little freedom to discuss.	Substantial confidence. Good support. Rather free discussions.	Complete confidence. Complete support. Free discussion.
Motivation	Appeal to physical, economic, and status needs. Hostility toward organizational goals. Top management only feels responsible for goal accomplishment.	Appeal to economic, status, achievement needs. Some hostility to organizational goal. Management responsible for goal accomplishments.	Economic needs and desire for new experiences. Favorable attitude toward organizational goals. Subordinates feel responsible for goal accomplishment.	All needs. Participation and involvement in goal setting. All feel responsible for goal accomplishment.
Communication	Little. Downward. No upward. Viewed with suspicion. No responsibility for accuracy is felt by subordinates. Great distortions.	Little. Downward. Some upward. Viewed with caution. Some distortions. Suggestion box system.	Quite a bit. Upward and downward. Reasonably accurate. Lateral is fair to good.	A great deal. All directions. Accurate and trusted. Accurate interpersonal perceptions. Closeness.
Interaction and Influence	Little interaction. Distrust. No cooperation. Subordinates have no influence except through unions. Superiors have influence if they can use punishments.	Little interaction. Cautiousness. Little teamwork. Subordinates have little influence except through unions. Influence exerted vertically.	Moderate interaction. Fair confidence. Moderate influence from subordinates. Fairly good structure enabling mutual influence of parts of the organization.	Extensive interaction. Friendly. Trust. Good teamwork. Extensive influence of subordinates. Highly effective structure enabling mutual influence.
Decision Making	Only at top. Information inadequate. Adverse motivation to implement decisions. Teamwork discouraged. Technical skills of top only are used.	At the top. Some made lower but checked with top before action. Information inadequate. Little motivation to implement decisions. Teamwork discouraged. Technical skills of top and middle.	Policy at top. Specific decisions lower. Reasonably accurate information. Motivation to implement since most involved. Partial teamwork. Technical skills of all levels.	Widely done. Complete and accurate information. Powerful motivation to implement. Teamwork encouraged. Technical skills of all levels.
Goal Setting	High performance goals ordered by top; resisted by subordinates.	High performance goals sought by top; overtly accepted by subordinates but moderately resisted.	Goals set after discussion with subordinates; occasional resistance by subordinates.	Goals set through group participation; fully accepted.

BOX 2-8 (CONTINUED)

	System 1	System 2	System 3	System 4
Control	Top only. Great distortions. Informal system opposes formal system goals. Control data used for punitive purposes.	Mainly at top, some at middle. Strong forces to distort. Informal system partially resists formal system goals. Control data for policing and guidance.	Mostly top and middle. Some distortions. Moderate delegation of review and control process. Informal system sometimes supports, sometimes resists formal system goals. Control data used for policing but emphasis on reward, guidance, and self-guidance.	Throughout. Accurate information. Reviews at all levels. Informal and formal systems are in accord. Control data are used for self-guidance and coordination.
Performance Goals	Average level. Resources fairly good.	High levels. Good resources.	Very high levels. Very good resources.	Extremely high levels. Excellent resources.

For example, the leadership characteristic centers around the issue of trust. The degree of trust and confidence superiors and subordinates have for one another is very much related to how freely subordinates can talk to their superiors about their jobs. This in turn affects the amount and accuracy of the information superiors get when they need to make decisions or to delegate decision making. In considering motivation, group involvement and participation based on group communication can be used as a most powerful motivator for performance and satisfaction.

Communication is the basis for teamwork, interaction, and influence throughout the organization. Communication drives development of a structure which permits part of the organization to influence other parts. Communication directly affects decision making in terms of (1) making decisions on the basis of accurate information, (2) placing the locus of decision making where the needed information is, or (3) moving the necessary information to the decision-making point in the organization. Communication is vital in goal setting as it tells people down the line what the goals are or involves them through group discussion in setting their own departmental or personal goals. Communication plays a vital role in control processes; if measurements and information are not accurate or complete, the control function cannot be realistically performed.

Likert was truly the first theorist to list and study the multitude of communication functions behind all organizational activities. In system 4, which he clearly advocates, communication is the least

FIGURE 2-4
Organizational profile for two manufacturing firms* based on Likert's questionnaire.

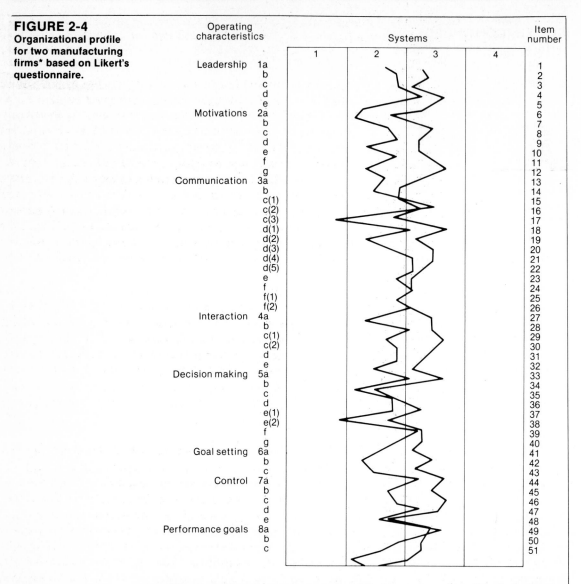

*These two profiles are based upon responses to the fifty-one-item version of Likert's questionnaire. Copies can be obtained from the Foundation for Research on Human Behavior, Ann Arbor, Michigan. A facsimile is included in J. H. Donnelly et al., *Fundamentals of Management*, Business Publications, Dallas, Tex., 1971, pp. 258–272.

restricted. Communication is the force which thus encourages the greatest utilization of human resources with a resulting effect on performance and organizational effectiveness. Likert's model stresses the importance of communication functions in the organization. Although there is emphasis on the production function of communication (communication which helps reach organizational goals), the social and innovative functions are not ignored. In fact, the linking pin model provides a mechanism for coordination of activities and encourages social and innovative messages to flow through the organization.

The Systems School

Origins of the systems school are traced to the theoretical work of a biologist, Ludwig Von Bertalanffy. He defined his *general systems theory*[12] as the "science of wholeness" which deals with wholes made up of interdependent parts, the relationships between the parts, and the relationships between the wholes and their environments.

The central idea of general systems theory is the *synergistic effect*, a complex term which refers to the rather simple notion that the whole is more than the sum of its parts. General systems theory with its emphasis on structure, interdependence, and relationships is concerned only with the parts of a system as they relate to the whole. This particular perspective considers communication an essential process which permits interdependence among the parts of any system.

The open system theory of Katz and Kahn

The greatest impetus for applying general systems theory to the study of social organizations came from Daniel Katz and Robert Kahn,[13] two social psychologists from the University of Michigan Survey Research Center. Major concepts of open system theory are briefly described in this section.

Boundaries.   The concept of boundaries says that an organization is differentiated from and dependent on the environment in which it exists. In open systems, energy comes into the organization from the environment, is transformed within the organization, and is returned to the environment. Interestingly, boundaries are not physical entities but rather are defined in terms of communication flows. As Rogers

[12]Ibid.

[13]*The Social Psychology of Organizations*, John Wiley and Sons, Inc., New York, 1978, 2d ed.

and Rogers point out,[14] "the units in a system have a greater degree of communication with each other than—across the boundary, with units in the external environment." This means, for example, managers of a corporation spend more time communicating with one another than with people from outside the company. Or, at a lower level of a subsystem, people in a given department spend more time and energy communicating with one another than with people from other departments in the company.

Entropy. Open systems are different from closed systems because they continuously exchange energy with the environment while closed systems do not. Open systems depend on interaction with the environment to continue to exist. Closed systems are subject to entropy, which means they eventually move toward disorganization and death. They run down. Entropy is a measure of the degree of disorganization in closed systems. To survive, an open system must counteract the entropic process by constantly getting new energy from the environment, by maximizing the energy it gets, and by minimizing the energy it spends. As long as there is a balance, the system maintains itself. In simple terms, if a company spends more money producing products than it gets from selling its products, it will soon go out of business. The fact that open systems can potentially maintain themselves indefinitely does not mean that they always will.

Information input and negative feedback. The kind of input a system receives is not limited to raw materials which are subsequently transformed. Information is also a basic input for any system by providing signals to the system about its environment and about its own functioning in relation to that environment. For example, information about an antipollution piece of legislation on emission standards of noxious gases represents information input for the automobile industry. It will give the automobile industry the signal to change the way cars are manufactured if those cars are to be put on the market. The most basic kind of information a system can receive is *negative feedback* which tells the system about its deviations from its planned course. The thermostat controlling the temperature of a room is the typical example of a regulatory device operating on the basis of negative feedback. Without negative feedback, the system cannot correct itself and get back on course after a deviation. As a result, it could end up spending more energy than it receives and thus eventually run down. The control function in organizations is vital

[14]Everett M. Rogers and Rekha Argawala-Rogers, *Communication in Organizations*, The Free Press, New York, 1976, p. 50.

since it produces the information which permits managers to determine whether they are on course in relation to their objectives.

The steady state and dynamic homeostasis.   A balance between energy input and energy output characterizes open systems which survive and are not subject to entropy. This balance or *steady state* permits the system to be in equilibrium or balance. It is not complete homeostasis or static balance but a state in which deviations on one side of the balance are compensated by deviations of approximately similar magnitudes on the other side. Any disruption in the equilibrium of a system is countered by forces trying to return the system as closely as possible to its previous steady state. For example, when a manager retires or resigns from a company, the replacement is likely to perform the function somewhat differently; the function will be, in effect, "under new management." But company functions will continue to be performed in a recognizable pattern.

Steady state is perhaps easiest to see in the processes in the human body which maintain body temperature constant in spite of changes in the environment. When these regulatory processes break down, the system loses its balance and a fever or chills signal that something "wrong" is happening.

Differentiation.   Open systems grow in the direction of greater differentiation and specialization. The management function, which, fifty years ago, could well be performed by one person who knew everything about the company and could do most of the work single-handedly, has become increasingly complex and differentiated. Even in modest-sized companies the same manager would not be expected to run accounting, personnel, sales, and production. These functions now require specialists with specific knowledge and skills. Attorneys, who used to be able to perform almost any service for a client, are now increasingly becoming specialized as the law increases in complexity. A tax attorney seldom handles litigation, and a divorce lawyer rarely represents utilities companies.

Equifinality.   The principle of *equifinality* states that, in an open system, the same final state can be reached from different initial conditions and in different ways.

One implication of the equifinality principle is the rather simple notion that there are many ways to reach a given objective: there is no one single method which will be the best under all conditions.[15]

---

[15]Long before the invention of the term "equifinality," people exchanged much the same sentiment in the inelegant expression, "There's more than one way to skin a cat."

Managing, for example, is a complex process which can be done effectively in a number of different ways. Effective leadership styles are many. Their effectiveness depends on, among other things, the conditions of the system in which they are applied.

For Taylor, Weber, and to some extent the human relations and human resources theorists, there was *one best way* and only one to manage and to organize. For the open system theorists, objectives can be reached through a number of different paths, each having some effectiveness in relation to the conditions of the system. Open systems theory forces managers to ask different questions about an organization. The old questions were: "What is the best way to manage?" "What is the best style of leadership?" and "What is the best way to motivate workers?" The new questions are: "What are the forces, external and internal, affecting the system now?" and "Which particular management and leadership styles best fit these internal and external conditions and can best bring about the desired objectives?"

This approach, the *contingency* approach, will be discussed at length in the next section. The questions are designed to determine the contingencies of a given situation, or what is going on now. Then various methods are matched appropriately to various situations, and through feedback processes, vital information is gathered about environmental forces and how these forces affect the organization.

Communication implications.   This dynamic, process view of the nature of organizations is in harmony with the authors' ideas of what communication is about. It parallels our belief that the production function of communication is second in importance only to the social function of communication. A manager who looks at communication as only a process of transmitting information and giving orders, designed to get workers to perform a job and to reach certain objectives, remains attached to the old physical model and fails to realize that social organizations cannot be understood in mechanistic terms.

The unit of analysis in organizations is not a thing, a person, an event in isolation, but a *relationship*—between people, and between people and environments. Social communication is crucial in organizations because what holds social structures together is essentially a system of attitudes, perceptions, beliefs, expectations, motivations, and meanings shared by the people who are a part of the system. Production inputs which come from the environment are only one way in which social systems are open. Openness also exists in relation to social inputs because people bring to their work the lifetime of learnings, past experiences, expectations, and motivations which makes them what they are and influences how they behave with each other.

There are limited or finite ways to repair, maintain, and run a machine, and its functioning is predictable under controlled conditions. Not so with the human elements in the social system. Social communication cannot be described in a repair manual or a list of standard operating procedures; there is almost never a cause-and-effect relationship between what people do and the effects of that behavior on the social system. There are no simple recipes for dealing with the human problems encountered in organizations, and so we will not in this book try to provide simple answers or easy steps for solving communication problems. In fact, our answer to most questions is "It all depends."

The classical model and the human relations and human resources schools developed universal prescriptions ("This is the only way to do it") for organizational design and management practices. Then open system theory introduced a significant shift in thinking about organizations. The essence of the systems school is that different situations require different organizing styles in order to get the most out of the organization. Contingency theory strengthened this notion by focusing on the basic question of which organizational design and management practice best suits a particular situation. Contingency theory starts where Katz and Kahn left off and builds on the premise that situational and environmental factors must be included in any organizational analysis. Contingency theorists, as we will see in this section, have simply begun to study situational factors and to relate them to organizational design.

Contingency theory

Two classical significant research studies investigated key situational factors. The first looked at situational factors from the standpoint of *technology*, the second from the standpoint of the *environment*.

Technology and the Woodward study. Joan Woodward's research[16] on the organizational structure of 100 manufacturing companies in South Essex, England, is generally recognized as the starting point for contingency theory. Woodward and her colleagues discovered vast differences in structure among the companies they studied. They determined that these differences are related to the type of technology used in the manufacturing process. They found out that, as the technology becomes more advanced, the number of managerial levels increases, the chain of command lengthens, and the span of control of the chief executive widens. Although technology may not be the only

[16]*Industrial Organization: Theory and Practice*, Oxford University Press, London, 1965.

important variable in determining how an organization is structured, there are clearly prescribed and predictable relationships between structure and technical demands. It takes a more complex management system to produce goods in a very complicated factory.

The environment: Lawrence and Lorsch contingency study.   Paul Lawrence and Jay Lorsch[17] of the Harvard Business School studied the relationship between internal organization and environmental factors. Definitions of three concepts are needed to understand their research.

Differentiation.   Specialization means that an organization will be subdivided into units and subunits. Each of these generally develops special qualities or attributes which are related to the requirements imposed by that unit's own environment. Differentiation refers to *differences in behavioral attributes found among the managers of an organization.* Three attributes are particularly important: (1) the degree to which managers are production-oriented or people-oriented, (2) whether they think in terms of long- or short-term spans, and (3) whether they are more concerned with organizational goals or departmental goals.

Integration.   Integration refers to the *process of coordinating* among *the various units and the degree of collaboration necessary to accomplish organizational goals.* For the classical theorists, integration was achieved by creating rules and procedures which told people what to do. For open systems theorists, integration is based on communication through open channels throughout the organization.

Environment.   The environment of an organization can be *stable* or *unstable.* A company in a relatively stable environment faces little change in the kinds of products it sells. Banks and insurance companies are examples of companies which function in stable environments. At the other end of the continuum, rapidly changing environments are characterized by quickly changing technology and by frequent changes in products to meet the pressure of the competition and consumers demands. The electronics and space industries are two that function in unstable environments.

Because of differentiation, each major subunit in a company deals with a different facet of the total environment. For example, the sales department is mostly involved with the market environment, the production department with the technical and economic environ-

[17]*Organization and Environment: Managing Differentiation and Integration,* Harvard University Press, Cambridge, Mass., 1967.

ments, the research and development department with the scientific environment.

Each subenvironment also varies in its degree of stability, and the variations occur along three dimensions: (1) how fast conditions change over time, (2) how certain the information about these conditions is at any time, and (3) how long it takes managers to get feedback about their decisions.

Results of Lawrence and Losch's studies basically support the notion that parts of the organization must deal with different aspects of the environment and therefore must be organized internally in a way which best fits the demands of that particular related subenvironment. In essence, the more different the subenvironments are, the more differentiation must exist in the organization. As a result the need for integration is greater and also more difficult. Following this argument, effective organizations are those which achieve optimum differentiation yet are able to integrate the various subunits to deal with the total environment.

An example is the plastics industry, in which research departments deal with the most unstable environment and are constantly faced with demands for new products and ideas. In contrast, production units deal with a rather stable environment, and production department managers have rather short-term concerns of quality control and meeting customers' needs on time. Sales departments are somewhere in between. Successful companies in the plastics industry are those which permit a great amount of differentiation among their subunits. Research departments have a loose structure and a wide span of management with few levels. Decision making is decentralized. Production units, in contrast, are more highly structured, have narrower spans of control, and have many more levels of hierarchy as well as centralized decision making. Production and sales departments have short-term concerns; research departments have a long-term perspective. Production and research have production-oriented managers; sales departments have people-oriented managers. In summary, units dealing with stable environments function rather well under the bureaucratic structure, while units facing unstable environments are more effective when they rely on the integrative techniques proposed by Likert in his system 4 type of management.

When the organization as a whole faces a stable environment and when its departments are rather homogeneous, there is little need for differentiation. Because internal structure and attitudes are similar among subunits, integration can be achieved quite easily by relying on the bureaucratic structure, narrow spans of management, many hierarchical levels, and emphasis on standardization. When the organization faces an unstable environment or when its units face different types of subenvironments, differentiation must be high and the task of integration is much more complex. Each unit must develop a system which is best for the type of subenvironment it faces. While production departments operate effectively on a bureaucratic system, sales and research may operate better in a more decentralized fashion. Integration among these departments is difficult. Overall operation of the organization and integration of highly differentiated units may be best achieved with an overall flexible, decentralized system of management with heavy emphasis on open communication at all levels and across levels in the spirit of system 4.

Communication implications.   The major point made by Lawrence and Lorsch is that *there is no one best way to organize.* Each organization has to adapt to the demands of its environments, and furthermore each organization contains units which themselves must deal with separate subenvironments with specific demands. Many different management systems can coexist within the same organization quite successfully, provided the integration tasks required by the internal diversity are attended to. These integrative tasks can also be done successfully in different ways ranging from the classical model of integrating through the hierarchy to the open system model of mutual adjustments through communication.

Lawrence and Lorsch found that the least effective organizations were those which operated under the same system of management in all units in spite of the fact that the units were highly differentiated. The most effective organizations were those which were highly differentiated and had high integration. To be effective, different units must be different from one another. This naturally makes it difficult for the members of those units to understand members of other units. As a result, the sense of "working for the same company" often disappears, unless—and this is the key—integration takes place. To get useful information from its many environments, the organization must be differentiated. When that happens, it becomes more difficult to integrate. The dilemma of differentiation and integration cannot be resolved by attending to one process to the exclusion of the other. Both are necessary when the environment is not homogeneous. For integration to take place in a highly differentiated organization, managers must develop open attitudes and skills which permit them to communicate with people different from themselves, people who have differing views on organizational objectives and different attitudes about people. A production supervisor concerned with immediate production to meet immediate demands may often resent the fact that organizational resources are diverted for the benefit of the research engineer who works on a new product to be developed over the next ten years. If the production supervisor treats the research engineer as a person whose head is in the clouds, and if the research engineer resents the production supervisor's shortsightedness, the two will have a hard time communicating and pooling their energies on common tasks. The fact is, both short- and long-term attitudes are needed in the organization. If they are not somehow integrated, the organization will lose its effectiveness by wasting energy on needless interpersonal conflicts. To integrate successfully, people need to learn to mediate conflict successfully. For Lawrence and Lorsch, organizational communication is conflict resolution achieved both through organizational design (formal structure) and through effective face-to-face interaction.

Lawrence and Lorsch contend that the unit with the most information on the most important issue in the industry needs to have the most influence on decision making. For example, the most important issue in the plastic and food industries is innovation, and thus the most effective companies are those which give their research and development department the most influence in organizationwide decision making.

Contingency theory is truly predicated on communication variables.

SUMMARY

Major theories about organizations and how people work together were reviewed from the communication viewpoint. The classical school avoided identifying communication as the significant force we believe it to be. Frederick Taylor represented scientific management theories which had great faith in machines and considered workers merely extensions of the machines. Communication in this science-oriented theory was used only to give workers their orders and to direct machine operations; no attention was given to informal communication. Max Weber and bureaucracy proposed very highly structured communication, rigorously controlled to take care of production needs only, and offered little chance for personal involvement of organization members. The administrative theory of Henri Fayol and Chester Barnard was much like the bureaucracy theory except it was designed by practicing managers rather than sociological theorists. Communication was primarily a means of moving information up and down a formal chain of command. Although the personality of the manager was considered, the human element in workers was almost ignored.

Structure was very important to the classical school. Whether an organization is centralized or decentralized, how it is departmentalized, and the workings of line/staff divisions are all parts of structure.

Any structure is subject to the limitations, styles, and basic attitudes and assumptions of the people working in them—at all levels.

The behavioral school developed in the 1930s and represented human relations theories of Elton Mayo and others. They contended that communication of an informal nature was of great importance to the organization, and that communicating related to motivating. The human resources group (Douglas McGregor's theory X and theory Y) also relied on oral communication to motivate and to get the job done but made a specific study of the managerial attitudes which seemed to affect the outcome of organizations. Rensis Likert developed the linking pin model to describe an informational and communication function in managers' roles. His four systems of management trace the authoritarian styles on system 1 through a developing involvement of organization members into the participative styles in system 4. In system 4, much leadership centers on trust and confidence as motivators, and communication is an imperative to that understanding. The systems school of Ludwig von Bertalanffy states that the whole is greater than the sum of the parts, and communication is related to the essential role of moving the parts together in a task. Daniel Katz and Robert Kahn suggest an open system theory which makes extensive use of boundaries to relate to an environment and to maintain its momentum, again with communication taking a central role. The "contingency approach" to meeting internal and external conditions for managing seems to us best suited to studying relationships in organizations—not the static or rigidly mechanistic elements of production. This theory states that there is no one best way to organize. Each organization must find its own best way based on (1) the internal and external factors and (2) the abilities of the managers and their styles as (3) they relate to subunits which also may have different organizational demands. Joan Woodward, Paul Lawrence, and Jay Lorsch, among others, are associated with the contingency theory.

CHAPTER 3

COMMUNICATION THEORY AND ORGANIZATIONAL IMPLICATIONS

"Accurate and adequate communication between groups and peoples will not in itself bring about the millenium, but it is a necessary condition for almost

all forms of social progress. . . . Physical barriers to communication are rapidly disappearing but the psychological obstacles remain. These psychological difficulties are in part a function of the very nature of language; in part they are due to the emotional character and mental limitations of human beings."   Daniel Katz

This is a book about human communication in organizational and business settings. The one specific behavior which sets humans apart from other species is the use of symbols for the purpose of communicating. *Communication is at the core of your humanness.* It is the essential process through which you develop your individuality and your relationships with others. These two major human concerns provide a convenient way to approach the study of communication processes and to understand the complex, often perplexing behaviors of people in organizations.

In this chapter, we want to guide you through a tour of the communication field, which has grown rapidly over the past thirty years and which has earned both academic respectability and conceptual strength.

As we span the major theoretical contributions to the field of human communication, we will emphasize the relationships to be made with organizational behavior and managerial practices. We will spell out some of the axioms of interpersonal communication which have grown out of the theories. Finally, we will introduce you to what we think is the most promising model of the human communication process, one which describes communication as a transactional process.

THE ROOTS

As you study communication and its implications for understanding human behavior, you will discover that for the past thirty years, communication has been discussed from various perspectives. No fewer than twenty-four approaches to the study of human communication have been identified, ranging from anthropology, art, biology, speech, and zoology to encounter groups, general semantics, information theory, neuphysiology, psychology, and sociology.[1]

Naturally, as each discipline studies communication, it chooses to focus on one or two central concepts. For example, information theory isolated the *bit* of information, a mathematical construct. Cybernetics gave us *feedback*. Psychology and sociology concerned themselves with the *self* and *roles*. What do all these approaches have in common? Why such eclectic and diverse contributions to the field of communication?

The answer is relatively simple. The basic characteristic which distinguishes humanity from other species is the ability to create and manipulate symbols, and as a result to create and share meaning. This, in short, is what human communication is about. To understand human behavior in its totality, you need to understand the symbolic processes of creating and sharing meaning—communication.

Let us take you through a brief tour of those fields which contributed the major concepts of communication theory.

Although the symbolic interactionism school is most frequently associated with sociologists like George Herbert Mead and Charles Horton Cooley, the philosopher John Dewey and the psychiatrist Harry Stack Sullivan also made major contributions to this approach. Herbert Blumer[3] credits himself with having coined the label "symbolic interactionism" in an article he contributed to a book published in 1937.

The core of symbolic interactionism rests on three major premises:

People act toward things in terms of the meanings these things have for them. Things include physical objects as well as people, categories of people, organizations, and ideas. Simple enough. Yet much previous theorizing in the social sciences ignored this view. Sociologists often analyze human behavior in terms of social roles, status, attitudes, motives, etc., rather than in terms of the meanings things have for people. But to bypass meaning for other factors which are supposed to explain human behavior is a grave oversight for the symbolic interactionist who believes that meaning is central in the formation of behavior.

Symbolic Interactionism[2] and the Concept of Meaning

Meaning and people

[1]Richard W. Budd and Brent D. Ruben (eds.), *Approaches to Human Communication*, Hayden Book Company, Rochelle Park, N.J., 1972.

[2]This discussion of symbolic interactionism is largely based on the work of Herbert Blumer, *Symbolic Interactionism: Perspective and Method*, Prentice-Hall, Englewood Cliffs, N.J., 1969.

[3]Ibid., p. 1.

Meaning and social interaction

The meanings people have for things are derived from social interaction with others.   How do you come to have a meaning for a thing? Where does the meaning come from? Is it in the thing itself, a natural attribute of the thing? Or is it rather an expression of your psychological makeup, of you as a person? Symbolic interactionists say: neither. Meaning, in their view, has a different source altogether. It is neither an intrinsic quality of things, nor does it come from your insides. *Your meaning for a thing grows out of the ways in which other people act toward you when you are dealing with the thing.* For example, a baby learns the meaning of "hot stove" as "danger" when someone consistently pulls her away from the stove as she gets close to it. Meanings are social products, and they are formed as people interact with one another.

Meaning and interpretation

Meanings are mediated through your interpretations of situations and things.   Interpretation is a two-step process. You must first select the things that you will act toward and then use, revise, and apply meanings to guide your actions.

In addition to the three premises just described, some other ideas are important for the symbolic interactionist.

1. Your actions are mostly a response to the actions of others. What you do is not just the product of internal forces, but is your way of fitting your activities to those of others.

   For George Herbert Mead, symbolic interaction consists of presenting a message and responding to the meaning of that message. The message has meaning for both the person who sends it and the person who receives it. When the message has the same meaning for both, sender and receiver understand each other.

   Basically, the message tells the person to whom it is directed what to do, and indicates what the person sending it plans to do. It is through such messages that people are able to fit their actions to those of others, and organized activities become possible.

2. The world in which human beings exist is made up of "objects," a loose term to describe anything that can be referred to (a physical object, a person, an idea). The nature of any object consists of the meaning it has for a person. A car is a different object to a salesperson, a mechanic, a police officer, a junk dealer, an environmentalist, a stockholder in Chrysler Corporation. This notion has vast implications. First, the environment for any person consists only of those objects the person recognizes and knows. What the environment is like is determined by the meaning these objects have for the person. This means that my world may be quite different from your world because (1) what I recognize and know

may be different from what you recognize and know, and (2) even if we recognize and know the same objects, my meanings for these objects may be quite different from yours.

People have to deal with and act toward their own worlds. To understand people's behavior, you need to find out what their worlds are like and "where they are coming from."

Meanings of objects are social creations. Meanings are formed, learned, and transmitted through social interaction. Objects have no fixed meanings in themselves. Some things or ideas have enduring meaning because people continue to define them in the same manner over long periods of time, but all objects can change in meaning as people themselves change.

3. The *self* is also an object. People can act toward themselves and can guide their actions toward others on the basis of what they are to themselves. A person may recognize and know herself as a young woman, a student, an accounting major, and a divorced person. What each of these characteristics means to her determines how she acts toward herself and toward others. The self emerges out of a process of social interaction. You learn the meaning of your self as you learn the meaning of any other object: by interpreting the actions of others toward you as you relate to that object. You see yourself as how others define you.

The fact that you can take your self into account means you can communicate with yourself. Being conscious and aware means that you make observations to yourself about what is happening around you and use these observations to direct your actions. What you do, then, is not the product of internal or external forces which play upon you, but rather the outcome of a process of interpretation of what you note and define. You act on the basis of the things you take into account and their meanings. You live in a world you must interpret in order to act. You construct your actions, for better or for worse, on the basis of how you interpret what you take into account. If you want to understand the behavior of any person, you must come to understand the defining process of that person.

4. *Joint action.* Group life—that is, organized life—consists of the fitting of any individual's actions with others. Organizing means acting jointly. Some joint actions are fairly repetitive and stable simply because people know in advance how they and others will act. This is possible because they share common and preestablished meanings about expected actions and guide their behavior according to these meanings. Values, norms, policies or rules prescribe what you are to do in different situations. They permit you, by the strength of the preestablished shared meanings they imply, not only to shortcut the interpretative process but also to develop fairly secure expectations about your role and the roles of others.

Organizational implications

Symbolic interactionism is a powerful theoretical approach to the study of human behavior. It has direct implications for (1) communication and (2) human organizing processes. Symbolic interactionists put communication or social interaction clearly in the center of their formulations when they discuss meaning. Meanings grow out of social interaction and in turn guide, form, and shape social interaction. There can be no organizing without common meanings which permit integrated actions of several individuals. It is only when there is some common agreement among different people's meanings that these people can develop stable expectations of one another's behavior and thus engage in reasonable coordinated and integrated action. *Organized life grows out of communication processes.*

Different people often hold different meanings for things and events. You can see that the chances for communication messages to be interpreted totally as they were intended are relatively slim. For example, a question of whether to modify an existing product or to keep it unchanged for this season while developing a totally new product will be perceived quite differently by people in marketing, production, and research and development. Each department will pit the potential decision against selected data from its own environment and will interpret it accordingly. Labor and management groups typically interpret events differently because each comes from a different perspective and evaluates the information at hand from that perspective.

Information Theory: The Concept of Uncertainty

Development of information theory is usually traced to Claude E. Shannon and Warren Weaver.[4] In contrast with symbolic interactionism, which sought to explain human behavior in its broad social context, information theory had a much narrower scope and was specifically concerned with the technical problem of transmitting signals from one point to another. Shannon, an engineer at the Bell Laboratories, saw communication as a mechanistic system composed of five basic elements: (1) an *information source* which uses (2) a *transmitter* to convert a message into a transmittable signal and which sends the signal through (3) a *channel*; (4) a *receiver* reconstructs the message from the signal so that it can reach (5) its *destination*, the person (or machine) for whom it is intended. In addition to these five elements, Shannon introduced four other components to the system: the *message* itself, the *transmitted signal*, the *received signal*, and a *noise source* which could be anything that

[4]*The Mathematical Theory of Communication*, University of Illinois Press, Urbana, Ill., 1949.

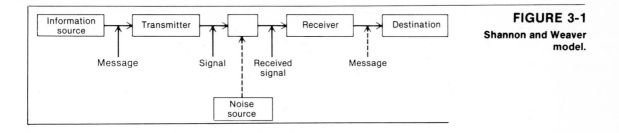

FIGURE 3-1
Shannon and Weaver model.

affects the signal as it travels through the channel and which prevents the received signal from being identical to the transmitted signal. Figure 3-1 gives a diagram of the Shannon and Weaver model.

The important question in information theory is, How can an information source get a message to a destination with a minimum of distortions and errors in spite of the noise source and in spite of the fact that the source may be different from the destination? The concepts of *redundancy* and *coding efficiency* will be used in this section to answer this question.

Shannon's key idea is that the message transmitted represents a choice made by the source from among many other possible messages potentially transmittable. In other words, what you choose to say or write at any time is only one of many possible messages you could transmit. The receiver's problem is to figure out what it does not already know—namely, what your choice is. The more possible alternative messages that are available to you to transmit, the more uncertainty the receiver has in reconstructing the message that you send.

Information theory will not be thoroughly discussed here; what we are presenting is a vastly oversimplified description. Our reason for going quickly past information theory is that it is not concerned with interpretation of messages, the meaning of messages, or information in the most common sense of the term. As a mathematical theory, it has revolutionized some of the information-processing systems of humankind. The formulation of what the theorists called the "bit" (a contraction of "binary digit") is associated with spectacular developments of information machines and the sophisticated hardware of computer technology.

An adaptation of the principle of "redundancy" from information theory is of special interest to the organization communicators. Remember the idea of "noise"? Noise was described as any disruption in the communication system which made the received messages different from the transmitted ones. To help prevent this from happening, in channels or exchanges which are likely not to be free of noise, we build in "redundancy" or repetition. Most spoken languages have developed some sort of compromise between efficiency (saying it briefly) and redundancy (saying it enough ways to avoid error). It has been estimated that only about half of what we say to each other is really needed to reconstruct a message, and the other half is a sort of "noise insurance." We need a backup against the forces of confusion. Redundancy does not cut out noise, but it does reduce the harmful effects of noise at a price of speed and, perhaps, efficiency.

When brevity is important—as when you are charged for your messages on the basis of number of words (telegram or newspaper ad) or time (long distance phone calls, computer time, radio or TV commercials)—you try to reduce redundancy. However, the risks incurred if noise is present can be great. If the consequences of an error may be serious, redundancy as noise insurance becomes crucial and must be used. Air traffic controllers, for example, routinely require repetition and confirmation of messages before they authorize any aircraft maneuver. You intuitively know to repeat an important point to a listener. You spell out key words in a message by identifying each letter with a common name ("c as in cat," for example) or by using whole words for each letter (Alpha, Bravo, Charley, Delta, Easy, Fox . . .).

Organizational implications

Information theory played a vital role in solving the technical problem of signal transmission through noisy channels. However, those principles cannot be literally applied to human communication. For one thing, human beings are generally interested in more than the mere occurrence of a message.

A possible exception is small talk and ritualistic communication. In these instances, what matters is the exchange of words or gestures rather than the literal meanings of the words or gestures. There is very little difference between "Hi" and "Nice day, isn't it?" since primarily what matters in the casual encounter is that something be said rather than the content of what is said.

Generally, however, what you say does matter. When that is the case, information theory provides no insight into meaning, one of the central concepts in communication. For one thing, there is a huge number of possibilities for what one person may choose to say to another. Uncertainty is generally very high in human communication, and what you do *not* say, the choices that are *not* made, may have great communication value.

Ideas of information theorists are useful for understanding human communication if you do not expect to duplicate the rigor which mathematics brought to the study of technical communication. For example, you can use the concepts of information theory to understand why clichés and ritualistic small talk convey practically no information about the meanings a person attaches to a situation or an idea. Clichés are interchangeable, and so are the phrases used in cocktail party chatter. Such conversation is highly predictable; and as information theorists explain, what is highly predictable carries little information value. A very personal disclosure about yourself, however, carries a great deal of information. In human communication, generalities, small talk, and clichés are some of the ways you may reveal nothing or little about yourself. The very predictability of such conversations is what makes them so uninteresting and gives small talk or "party chatter" a bad name.

The concepts of noise and redundancy, however, have important organizational implications. In human systems, noise is not simply physical but refers to internal distractions experienced by people. Noise in a social sense is whatever interferes with accurate transmission of messages. Headaches, worries, lack of confidence, defensiveness, lack of motivation, and inadequate training are all examples of noise in human communication. Noise is always present and must always be counteracted by some measure of planned redundancy.

In terms of practical behavior, this means that when you send a message, oral or written, you must build in redundancy. Important key words should be highlighted and repeated. Drawings, charts, or other visual aids should help reinforce your communication. Telephone messages often need to be backed with written reminders of the conversation contents. Oral interviews must generally be documented in writing. When you give instructions to people, you cannot assume that because you said it once, the message is automatically received and understood.

Cybernetics: The Concept of Feedback

Norbert Wiener, while a professor of mathematics at the Massachusetts Institute of Technology, adapted the word "cybernetics" from the Greek word *kubernētēs*—meaning "steersman"—the same Greek word which also gave us "governor."

You live in a world which you perceive through your sense organs. Information you receive through your senses is coordinated through your brain and your nervous system. It is finally translated into action through your muscles, and this, in turn, permits you to act on the outside world. The process of receiving and using information is a process of adjusting to various forces in your environment. "To live effectively is to live with adequate information. Thus communication and control belong to the essence of man's inner life, even as they belong to his life in society."[5]

[5]Norbert Wiener, *The Human Use of Human Beings*, 2d ed., Doubleday Anchor Books, Doubleday and Company, Inc., Garden City, N.Y., 1954, p. 18.

Wiener's emphasis is on *control* and *communication*. When you communicate with another person, you send a message and the receiver of that message sends back a message. Each message contains information that the sender alone has access to. When you control the actions of another person, the process is essentially the same. You send a message (a command, an order), and if your control is to be effective, you must receive messages from that person which tell you that he or she has understood the order and has followed through with it.

You exert control over your environment by sending commands, that is, information, to that environment. Like any other messages, these commands have a tendency to get garbled as they travel through channels which are not noisefree. Because of noise, they usually come out less clear than they were sent. In communication and control, as Wiener points out, you "are always fighting nature's tendency to degrade the organized and to destroy the meaningful; the tendency . . . for entropy to increase."[6] To act effectively, you must receive information concerning the results of your own actions. That information is needed for you to continue to act. It is crucial that the information be about the *actual* results of your actions and not just the *expected* results. Control of a machine is based on its actual performance rather than its expected performance and is called *feedback*. In machines, this control is made possible by building in elements which give information on performance monitors. These monitors control and reverse the mechanical tendency toward disorganization or entropy.

Very much the same thing happens with human behavior. Human beings and the newest communication machines function alike because both attempt to control entropy or disorganization through feedback. In human beings and machines, a special sensory apparatus collects information from the external world and makes that information available for the operations of the human being or the machine. In both, the performed action and not solely the intended action is reported back to a regulatory center. Feedback allows the human being and the machine to adjust future behavior on the basis of past performance. "The (human) nervous system and the automatic machine are fundamentally alike in that they are devices which make decisions on the basis of decisions they have made in the past."[7]

Feedback permits you to monitor your communication on the basis of information you receive about the discrepancy between what you intended to communicate and what you actually communicated.

[6]Ibid., p. 17.
[7]Ibid., p. 33.

Feedback systems are used with self-propelled missiles which seek their targets, antiaircraft fire control systems, and other servo-mechanisms. Many biological phenomena operate under the principle of feedback. For example, maintaining health or homeostasis in the living organism is based on the existence of feedback. Breathing harder to bring more oxygen into the system during energy-demanding exertions is one example; others are maintaining viable body temperature and sleeping when tired.

The concept of feedback is crucial for your understanding of the human communication system at work in organizations. Feedback is what permits managers to monitor performance, their own as well as their subordinates'. In fact, as most of you know, the control function of management is essentially one of developing systems to collect information on performance and to compare it with what was expected. Management by objectives (MBO) is also based on the feedback process when performance is checked against objectives. Without feedback, you cannot know whether you are on course, whether you are headed in the planned direction, whether you are communicating adequately.

Organizational implications

There is much discussion in business circles about the respective merits and costs of two-way versus one-way communication. Two-way communication involves sending a message and receiving feedback about what was sent. A subordinate questioning a supervisor about instructions just given is making use of two-way communication. The supervisor then gets a chance to repeat, clarify, and add information to what was already said to ensure better understanding of the message. One-way communication goes from the sender to the receiver and stops there. No response from the receiver is encouraged to flow back to the sender who then has no way to check whether the message was correctly understood. Each system naturally has advantages and disadvantages, and those are listed in Figure 3-2.

In general, feedback allows you to determine whether the message has been sent and received as intended. The fewer the intermediaries between sender and receiver, the more immediate the feedback, and therefore, the more useful it is in modifying subsequent communication and behavior. However, we must point out that in large and formal organizations, subordinates may feel reluctant to make use of feedback mechanisms for fear they might appear incompetent. For some people, asking questions and checking communication may be perceived as a sign of weakness or ignorance. Also, some supervisors are hard to talk to and do not really encourage two-way communication.

FIGURE 3-2

**One-way versus two-way
communication.**

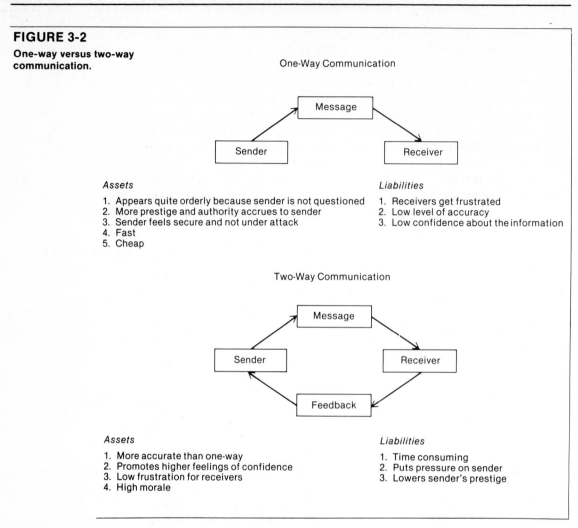

One-Way Communication

Sender → Message → Receiver

Assets
1. Appears quite orderly because sender is not questioned
2. More prestige and authority accrues to sender
3. Sender feels secure and not under attack
4. Fast
5. Cheap

Liabilities
1. Receivers get frustrated
2. Low level of accuracy
3. Low confidence about the information

Two-Way Communication

Sender → Message → Receiver → Feedback → Sender

Assets
1. More accurate than one-way
2. Promotes higher feelings of confidence
3. Low frustration for receivers
4. High morale

Liabilities
1. Time consuming
2. Puts pressure on sender
3. Lowers sender's prestige

**General Systems
Theory: The
Concept of
Transaction**

In Chapter 2, we described the major points of general systems theory. Basically, general systems theorists look at *relationships* rather than at isolated elements.

**The study of
relationships**

The recognition that the whole is greater than the sum of its parts led to the idea that transactions are important in analyzing communication events. To study an individual, a message, a receiver's feedback, a method of transmission is simply not enough when you want to understand what goes on when people communicate and transact business. What is important is the relationship each of these elements has with the others and how they mutually influence one another.

A system—and any organization is a system—is made up of parts that are interrelated. What happens to one part affects other parts and, subsequently, the whole system. Compare a family of four or five with a group of four or five people picked at random in a social situation, say a movie theater. The five people picked at random at the theater are not connected to one another in any way except that they are attending the same movie. If one leaves the theater, for example, it is unlikely that the other four will be affected by the move of a person they may not even be aware of. The family, on the other hand, is a different matter. What one member of the family does will definitely affect other members of the family. What happens to one member affects every other member of the family. The family is a system.

An additional insight offered by general systems theory is the concept of mutual causality. In a mechanistic universe, causality is a one-way phenomenon. One element acts on another and causes a reaction. In open systems, you cannot ignore the interplay of elements among one another and with the environment in which the system is embedded. Everything affects everything else. An individual and the world he or she experiences are in mutual and reciprocal interaction, or transaction, as each one determines the other. The way you think influences what you perceive. Conversely, what you perceive influences what you think, in an endless spiraling process. As you will see later in this section, the concept of hen-and-egg beginnings and endings is crucial in understanding human communication processes. This concept is a direct outcome of the notion of mutual causality.

Mutual causality

Each element of a system can be broken down into its own components and looked at as a subsystem within the system. In that case, the system becomes the environment within which the subsystem exists, separated from it by its own boundary. The system itself can be looked at as one element of a still larger system, a suprasystem.

Levels of analysis

Joske's of Texas, a San Antonio department store, is a system. It is composed of a variety of selling departments, including men's, women's, and children's clothes; sporting goods; notions; bookstore; cosmetics; housewares; furniture; and linens. It also has accounting, advertising, credit, personnel, and other managerial departments. Joske's operates within a professional environment, the local retail industry, itself a system which functions within a geographic environment, the city of San Antonio. If you switch your level of analysis to look at the San Antonio retail industry as a system, then Joske's becomes one of the subsystems within the retail industry system along with other department stores and other retail stores. If you continue to switch levels of analysis to look at the city of San Antonio as a system, then the retail industry itself, a system in which Joske's is a subsystem, becomes a subsystem along with other subsystems such as the financial industry, the manufacturing industry, the transit industry, the city government, and the educational institutions. San Antonio, naturally, is also a subsystem—one city among others, in the state of Texas, which is in itself a subsystem within the United States. At the other end of the scale, you can look at one of Joske's departments, such as the personnel department, and study it as a system composed of the various elements normally present in a personnel department, including a manager, an assistant manager, and some secretaries.

You can conceive of all these levels as a "hierarchy of encompassing systems,"[8] or a ladder of abstraction, as general semanticists describe it.[9] What you view as a whole system from the perspective of one level of analysis may be viewed as only a small part within the perspective of another level of analysis.

Choice of level of analysis depends upon your purpose. If you were interested in the economic impact of the retail industry in San Antonio, a look at the personnel department of Joske's would give you irrelevant information. The notion of levels of analysis has significant implications for your study of human communication. The level you select to look at depends very much on your purpose and perspective. College students' perspectives and purposes are different from those of the professors, the deans, the president, the trustees, the alumni, and the potential donors. People at each of these levels have conceptions of what the college system is like based on their own purposes and how they are related to that system. The company as it is known to its president is indeed different from the company the workers see.

Applications to human communication

Widespread application of general systems theory to the study of human communication is relatively recent. In the middle sixties, a team of mental health researchers at the Palo Alto Mental Research Institute started paying attention to the behavioral effects of human communication. Although they were concerned primarily with disturbed and pathological patterns of communicative behavior, they nevertheless produced the first general theoretical treatment of human communication as a transactional system.[10]

[8] Kenneth Boulding, "General Systems Theory—The Skeleton of Science," *Management Science,* 1956, vol. 2, p. 60.

[9] S. I. Hayakawa, *Language in Thought and Action,* Harcourt, Brace and World, New York, 1964.

[10] Paul Watzlawick, Janet H. Beavin, and Don D. Jackson, *Pragmatics of Human Communication,* W. W. Norton & Company, Inc., New York, 1967.

The focus on behavior is extremely significant. Because communication is analyzed from a system perspective, at least three hierarchical levels are necessary to understand what goes on in a communication transaction. The first level is the subsystem, one individual. The second level is the system, the relationships of one individual with one or several other individuals. The third level is the suprasystem, the social environment in which the system functions. For example, a boss and her employee represent a system. The boss herself is a subsystem. The department in which they both operate is a suprasystem. The only way individuals can affect a system is through their behaviors. In a social situation, people can affect other people only by providing them with something directly observable through their senses. You do not affect each other through feelings, thoughts, or beliefs, unless these are translated into observable behaviors. Behaviors are the only commodities of your communication systems, the only "observable manifestations of relationships."[11]

There are several communication rules or axioms which we briefly present in this section. We will discuss them more fully in Chapter 4 as we describe their implications for interpersonal communication.

THE RULES

Communication truly does not have an opposite. There is no way for human beings not to behave, and all behaviors have communication value. Whether you speak or are silent, whether you act or choose not to act, you will affect others in some way. Others, in turn, cannot *not* respond to your behaviors and, thus, are communicating also. If you intently read your book as you sit next to someone in the library, you are in effect communicating that you do not wish to speak or be spoken to, and usually your neighbor "gets the message" and leaves you alone. You are no doubt familiar with the experience of waiting at some counter while the clerk on the other side of the window occupies himself with paperwork and thus communicates to you that he is busy and you'll just have to wait. As you wait in silence for a while, you indicate that, although no words were spoken, you understood the message.

Communication does not take place only when it is planned, conscious, or successful. You communicate many things you may not intend to communicate. You are not always aware of what indeed you communicate, and you may not always be understood. Yet, communicate you do, and in many behavioral modes. You use spoken

Rule 1: You Cannot *Not* Communicate

[11]Ibid., p. 21.

words and written words. You use the inflection of your voice and the stresses you put on certain words or parts of words. You use the intensity of your voice, as when you whisper or yell. Your facial muscles form a smile, frown, or express a host of different feelings. You use your body postures and you gesture. You use the many contexts of your communication—space, time, objects, etc. All these communicative behaviors are used simultaneously, and each qualifies in some way the meaning of the other. A moderately loud "Hi," a smile, and a wave of the hand at ten o'clock in the morning in the company coffee shop are all communicative behaviors which fit together, reinforce one another, and communicate one kind of message. A "Hi" whispered in a raspy voice over the telephone at four o'clock in the morning communicates something else. A simple "No" may mean "Yes" or "Maybe," depending on how it is said and on the context of the communication, which includes not only the present space and time dimensions, but probably past history. All these elements of communicative behaviors can be organized in highly complex ways and can be *congruent* with one another, as when a friendly comment is spoken in a friendly tone of voice and accompanied by friendly gestures; or they can be *incongruent*, as when verbal and nonverbal messages say opposite things. We will return to the notions of congruency and incongruency in Chapter 4.

Rule 2: Communication Occurs at Two Levels

Information conveyed through communication is the *content* level of communication and refers to *what* is said. In addition, however, communication of any kind always implies a definition of the relationship between communicators. It always contains instructions about *how* to interpret the content of that communication. Statements such as "I was only joking," "I mean it," and "This is an order" are verbal expressions of the relationship level of communication. The relationship level need not be expressed in words, and in fact, more often than not it is expressed nonverbally. When I speak to you, I give you information, the content of my communication; and simultaneously, I give you information *about* that information. I tell you in some way whether this is a serious conversation or a friendly one, a stern lecture, a put-down, a tease, a joke. Nonverbal and contextual clues will often help you determine which it is and thus will tell you how to behave toward me.

A clerk in a store does not need to preface her "May I help you?" with an elaborate description of her relationship with the customer. She does not need to state that she is a salesperson here and that her job is to help customers find and buy things. Nonverbal and contextual clues such as a nametag, possibly a uniform, her demeanor, all contribute to your understanding that she will help you buy what you need.

The distinction between content and relationship levels is not a theoretical one dreamed up to satisfy the intellectual needs of fuzzy-headed academicians. The distinction has enormous implications for an understanding of communication as behavior. In Chapter 5, we will discuss at length the practical implications of this distinction.

Communication is seldom seen as the dynamic, flowing, uninterrupted sequence it really is. Our thinking habits have trained us to look for stopping and starting, cause and effect, stimulus and response, action and reaction, sender and receiver, beginning and ending. Although the concept of feedback adds the notion of circularity to an otherwise linear thought process, feedback is often conceived as little more than a reaction to an action. Communication events are grouped and sequenced to become meaningful units. How this sequencing is done depends very much on who does it. What you might see as the cause of a communication event may well be the effect of some preceding event. So, what you may choose to focus on as the beginning of a communication series may not be at all what I may choose as the beginning of the series. These starts and stops are similar to punctuation in writing, and the term "punctuation" has indeed been used by some writers to describe what we are calling the hen-and-egg dilemma.

Rule 3: Communication Is Like the Hen-and-Egg Dilemma

Take the example of a department chief who likes to ride herd on her employees. She may tell you that she feels she has to supervise the employees' work closely *because* they take no pride in their work, are careless, and therefore make errors, unless she is on their backs all the time. The department chief sequences the events by asserting that employees' carelessness is the cause of her strict supervision. If you ask the employees how they see the situation, you may get a different picture. Although the events themselves may be seen the same—everyone may well agree that the employees are indeed careless in their work and that the department chief is a martinet—the sequence of communicative events will be described differently. The employees may tell you that it makes them nervous to have the chief stand over their shoulders all day long; that she actually expects them to make mistakes; that they are left with no opportunity for initiative and thus do not feel inclined to take pride in their work. They see the chief's behavior as a cause for theirs. In essence, the chief is strict because the employees are careless, and they are careless because she is strict. A classic hen-and-egg dilemma. If you see your behavior only as a response to that of the other person, you may forget that your actions may also be a stimulus and a reinforcement to the other person. When you forget, you may well find yourself involved in useless circular arguments which may go on and on about who is the cause of what and who started what. Blaming is usually based on who started the problem, or which came first, the hen or the egg.

Rule 4: Communication Transactions Are Either Between Equals or Between Nonequals

For Watzlawick and his associates, relationships are based on equality or difference. Communicative behaviors can be between equals or nonequals. The most typical example of a nonequal relationship is that of the mother-infant pair. The mother clearly takes care of the baby, and the baby is clearly taken care of. The two cannot exist without each other, and this is not just a biological truism. There can be no *taking care of* if there is no one to be *taken care of*. Relationships among nonequals include two different positions. One communicator is in the superior, one-up, or primary position, while the other occupies the secondary, one-down, or inferior position. The words "one-up" and "one-down" should not be equated with "good," "bad," "strong," or "weak." Such nonequal relationships are often set by social or cultural contexts as in the case of doctor-patient, student-teacher, and parent-child relationships. In these nonequal relationships, the one-up person is usually the one who defines the nature of the relationship, while the one-down position refers to the person who accepts and goes along with this decision.

In relationships among equals, the communicators are on a par. In a positive sense, this allows for mutual respect and trust. It is a relationship in which people see each other as equals.

A TRANSACTIONAL MODEL OF HUMAN COMMUNICATION

Many influences have shaped the field of human communication. Early rhetorical tradition gave way to the mechanistic perspective offered by the mathematics model of information theory. The social-psychological contributions of symbolic interactionism matured into the newer cybernetics and general systems theory. Human communication has continued to pique the curiosity of scholars and laymen. Indeed, no other field touches you so deeply, for you are a communicating being. Communication is not only at the heart of your humanity, but is also the vehicle of your intentions toward others. Only through communication can you realize your potential. Without communication, you would be an evolutionary misfit.

Let us now review briefly the major threads that run through the various approaches to the study of human communication.

The Action View: The Bull's-eye Theory of Communication

The rhetorical tradition and information theory share the view that communication consists of a one-way act like shooting an arrow into a target. You fire, and you hit the bull's-eye, get close, or miss. The whole activity of communication is centered on the one-way action of doing something to someone. How good you are depends mostly on how well you shoot the arrow, or on how well you make your point. Emphasis is on the sender and the encoding skills. This means that how you construct a message, organize it, and deliver it is just as crucial as sharpening your arrow, testing its feathers, flexing your bow, and shooting straight would be in target practice. The key questions in this view center on what a *speaker* must *do* in order to persuade, sell, help, or in some other way change someone else's behavior. This view is also based on the idea that words have meanings and that if the sender knows the correct meanings and uses the words properly, no misunderstanding should arise. Note the "should" in there. The fact is that misunderstandings do occur. But when that happens, when communication is not perfect, information theory says it is because you did not perform adequately. Somewhere along the line, you used the "wrong" words, did not organize your message clearly enough, did not possess enough credibility (as though credibility were a quality a speaker owned); in essence, you did not shoot straight at your target and therefore you missed. This view is still popular and shows up in statements like, "I don't know why she does not understand this; I explained it fifty times," or "I don't understand why they don't know about this; I told them."

Another favorite way to look at communication is to compare it with taking turns at a table tennis match. You say something; I answer. You say more; I reply. I serve; you respond. We take turns at being sender and receiver. This view accounts for more of the complexities of human communication than does the bull's-eye theory. It includes the receiver by adding the concept of linear feedback which permits the sender to exert more control over the communication. The communication process is still oversimplified, however, by being treated as linear cause and effect: I speak, you answer; one way at a time.

The Interaction View: The Ping-Pong Theory of Communication

The weakness in the interaction view is that communication is really not divided into ping and pong, stimulus and response, shot and return, action and reaction. Senders and receivers do not simply alternate in sending and receiving, and the simple linear model of cause and effect does not explain enough of the dynamic complexities of our communication.

What general systems theory emphasized was the transactional nature of human communication. "Transactional" means more than a simple interaction between senders and receivers. A transaction implies *interdependency* and *mutual, reciprocal causality* among the parts of a system. Human communication is best understood as a system in which senders are simultaneously receivers and receivers

The Transaction View: The Spiral Theory of Communication

are senders. Communication is not static like still photography. Communication is more like the continuous flow of motion pictures, persistently jumping to the next frame as we try to make sense out of the last one.

Communication in its process view is characterized less by the actions of a sender and the subsequent reactions of a receiver than by the *simultaneity of their reciprocal responses*, or more simply, by things going on at the same time which affect each other. Who starts the process is an irrelevant question since processes have no specific beginnings nor ends. Human communication comes from somewhere and is going somewhere. Any communicative behavior which you may want to isolate for the purposes of analysis has a history and a future. It has been born in the mind of the speaker and relates to the mind of the receiver, and these minds do not simply come into existence as the words are spoken. They have lived in many places; they have said many things before, possibly to each other. In a transactional view of communication you are both cause and effect, stimulus and response, sender and receiver. You are not only the product of your previous communicative behaviors, but, very important, what you see yourself to be shapes your communicative behavior. What you see yourself to be is strongly affected by how you see others behave toward you, or how you perceive others' communication. Your perception of other people's responses is itself the product of your lifetime of previous communication. To isolate a communicative act is to punctuate falsely, to set an arbitrary beginning and an arbitrary end to an unending process. Starting and stopping communication in order to understand the process is very common, but communicative acts are best understood within the transactional framework.

The study of communication as a transaction comes closer to encompassing the complexities of the process than any of the other theories or ideas. Communication as transaction is the direct outcome of general systems theory, and we will discuss the far-reaching implications of that view in the next chapters.

SUMMARY

The use of symbols is what distinguishes humanity from other forms of life. Symbolic interactionism, one theoretical approach to studying communication, contends that (1) people act toward things in terms of the meanings these things have for them, (2) meanings are derived from interaction with others, and (3) meanings are modified by people's interpretation of situations, objects, and events. Symbolic interactionists also say that people's actions are mainly a response to actions of others, that the world as it is known to people consists of objects, that the self is also an object, and that we organize into group life when we fit our needs with others.

Information theory was developed as a mathematical model for transmission of information by mechanical means, but has proved very useful as an analogy to human communication of many kinds. Cybernetics and feedback principles are also of scientific and mathematical origins but have significant relations to human organizational communication.

General systems theory as a study of relationships has many applications to organizational communication and has been most recently applied in behavioral studies by the Palo Alto Mental Research Institute. Study of relationships gives rise to a transactional focus for understanding organizations.

There is no opposite to communicating; you cannot *not* communicate. Communication occurs on two levels, the level of what is said (content) and the level of how it is said (relationship). It is difficult sometimes to figure out the punctuation of a communication transaction, when it started or ended, what was the cause and what was the effect. Communication occurs either between people on the same level (equals) or between people who see each other as above or below one another (nonequals).

You cannot take yourself out of communication, and therefore in order to study communication, you must study yourself in the middle of a dynamic series of events.

PART TWO

THE PROCESS OF MANAGING BY COMMUNICATION

Part One took you through a tour of the theoretical foundations of human communication and its relationship to organizational and management theories. In the three chapters of Part Two we will concentrate on the processes of communication. What happens between people when communication takes place. Chapter 4 will present an overview of communication transactions. Communicative behaviors between two people are stressed because we believe them to be at the core of business communication. Chapter 5 will describe information flow in organizations, and Chapter 6 will focus on human motivation and the influence process.

PART TWO

THE PROCESS OF HUMAN
COMMUNICATION

CHAPTER 4

COMMUNICATION TRANSACTIONS

*"There is only
one corner of
the universe you can
be certain of improving;
that's your own self."* Aldous Huxley

When you exchange messages with other people, the symbols you trade back and forth do not in themselves constitute communication. Meaning must be created, and the process of creating meaning is called *communication*. Meanings are highly personal and are based on reactions to life experiences. However, in some way you learn to construct meanings in social contexts and this means that you tend to construct meanings like those of the people you live with, work around, and interact with.

Because you collaborate with others in learning to construct meanings, you can engage in coordinated activities with other people. Because you are able to take other people into account, you can develop expectations of what others will do or what they expect of you. Sharing meanings and sharing expectations, as Bonnie Johnson explains it,[1] are the prerequisites for organized action.

THE STRUCTURE OF TRANSACTIONS

The transactional nature of communication makes it possible for you to learn to construct meanings with others and to learn to develop mutual expectations. A transaction, the basic unit of study in communication, can be quite simply described as involving *two or more people who mutually and simultaneously (1) take one another into account, (2) differentiate their role relationship, and (3) conduct their interaction by a set of rules.*

We will now explore further the three components of a transaction.

Taking One Another into Account

A transaction takes place when two or more people pay attention to each other at the same time, or are "mutually and simultaneously taking one another into account." As an outsider observing other people, you may not always be able to tell whether other people are taking each other into account. When you are a participant, however, you are quite aware of the process. Say, for example, while stopped at a red light you casually look at the man driving the car stopped next to you. For a moment, perhaps the other driver is not aware that you are looking in his direction. All of a sudden, however, he turns around and *sees you seeing him*. If you are still looking, you *will see him seeing you seeing him*. This is now a communication transaction.

It frequently happens that you are aware of someone else's presence and that person may not be aware of you at all. The child who waits until her mother has turned her back to stick her tongue out is well aware of the mother's presence and acts on the basis of the

[1]Bonnie McDaniel Johnson, *Communication, the Process of Organizing,* Allyn and Bacon, Inc., Boston, 1977, pp. 5–8.

mother's momentary unawareness of the child's behavior. This is communication, since the child constructs meaning out of the situation and behaves on the basis of that meaning. But it is not a transaction.

A communication transaction takes *mutual* awareness, and is the prerequisite for organized behavior. Only when mutual awareness exists is mutual influence possible. The actions of one person may affect the actions of the other, and vice versa. A transaction only occurs when you perceive yourself being perceived by another person, when you see yourself being seen.

Transactions do not require physical interdependence. For one thing, communication transactions can occur on the telephone. For another, what matters is the perception of the other person's perception. Standing in a room full of strangers at a party, your eyes may meet someone else's. You may acknowledge the mutual look by a smile or a nod of the head. Contact is established. You perceive the other person and are aware of his or her perception of you. The process is mutual. A transaction takes place, and meaning is constructed which potentially can lead to organized activity.

The concept of transaction as mutual perceptions is rich in implications. Your behavior is fair game for the other person, who constructs meaning out of it and then behaves accordingly. As you observe the other person's behavior, you too construct meaning which subsequently shapes your behavior. Because constructing meaning and making mutual perceptions occur practically simultaneously, it is very difficult to untangle the process. To figure out another person's behavior, you must always figure out the part you may have played in shaping that behavior. What you perceive in another person may depend in part on what the other person perceives in you.

To take the party example again, perhaps the stranger looked at you, perceived you as a friendly type and, because you were smiling, smiled. Simultaneously, you looked at the stranger, perceived him or her as a friendly sort because he or she was smiling, so you smiled too. Who smiled first? As far as you are concerned, you smiled because the other person smiled. But your smile may have been the trigger for his or her smile. As far as the other person is concerned, he or she smiled because of your smile. The important thing here is that in transactions, meanings are constructed out of reciprocal and often interdependent behavior. What you perceive in others may well depend partly on what they perceive in you. We will return to the implications of this concept when we discuss the notion of "punctuation" or hen-and-egg sequencing.[2]

[2]William W. Wilmot, *Dyadic Communication, a Transactional Perspective*, Addison-Wesley, Reading, Mass., 1975, p. 81.

**Mutual Role
Definitions**

Transactions are characterized by the fact that people assume roles in relation to one another. Roles play a significant part in shaping people's behaviors. Roles limit the range of behaviors you can expect from an interpersonal encounter, and they also permit you to develop expectations about other people's behaviors. Roles serve as guides to interpret behaviors and construct meaning.

Roles are patterns of behaviors felt to be appropriate for specific situations. They are expected behaviors of people in certain positions. For example, when you are in the role of a student, you are expected to go to classes, listen to your professors, take examinations, read books, write papers, and so forth. Your role as a student is defined in relation to the roles of other people such as professors, school administrators, and fellow students. Your behavior as a student is different from your behavior as a mother, or as a supervisor. Certain behaviors are expected of mothers, students, and supervisors; these behaviors are not defined in isolation, but in relationship to other complementary sets of behaviors—other roles. You are not a mother without a child to mother; you are not a student without a teacher to learn from; and you are not a supervisor without someone to supervise.

Behaviors expected in a given role relationship are usually the product of the value system of a society, a group, or an individual. You learn to enact these behaviors as you grow up in your society and begin imitating people around you. Role relationships reflect consensual meanings in a given society.

In any transaction, you are faced with a decision about what role you need to take in relation to the role you think the other person will take and the role you think the other person expects you to take. All transactions reflect *negotiated role relationships*. In your communication transaction with others, you must always face the issue of role relationship negotiations. Because everyone can be cast in many different roles, you need to determine which role is appropriate for you, considering your evaluations of: (1) the situation, (2) the other person, and (3) yourself.

The situation

The context in which an interpersonal situation occurs is a powerful guide in determining which role is appropriate. You would not behave the same way at a funeral and in a bar, at home and at the office. You are expected to behave differently in different situations: in study and at play, at a football game and at a symphony performance, at a formal dinner party and at a picnic. The professor who always "lectures," whether in class, at the coffee shop, at home, or at parties, exhibits role rigidity and does not understand that professorial behavior is inappropriate outside the classroom.

Because you can assume a large number of possible roles with others, the situation or the context of the transaction is crucial in determining your role at a given time. The example of Greg is not uncommon. Greg is a graduate student at State University where he teaches an introductory management course. He also works three afternoons a week in a local retail store. The store assistant manager, Bob, is a few years older than Greg, and they are very good friends. They go out frequently together. Bob is also taking a few courses at the university and happens to be in the class Greg teaches this semester. Possible role relationships between the two men are numerous. They can relate as supervisor-employee in the store, friends and peers when they go out, and teacher-student when they are at the university. It is important that both define each situation in the same way. Both must agree that these three situations call for different behaviors. Trouble may arise if they don't agree. If Greg defines the store situation as a friendship situation and talks to Bob in a very informal fashion there, while Bob feels that at the store he is boss and should be treated with some deference, their relationship is likely to experience stress.

The other person

Whenever you communicate with another person, you have some idea of how that person is going to behave based on (1) the role you expect that person to play, (2) the person's age, and (3) the person's sex. How you know what roles other people play is based partly on your previous personal experiences with them, partly on what you know about how people in that role generally behave. Different salesclerks may act differently, but you can at least expect them to wait on you and help you when you want to buy something. You do not expect them to invite you for coffee or lecture on nuclear energy.

Professional roles.   Role expectations are often tied to professional labels and you expect certain behaviors from a physician, a minister, a police officer, a social worker, etc. Once you know what role you may expect a person to play, it becomes easier to construct meaning about his or her behavior. If you see an adult jerk a child by the arm and push the child forcefully into a parked car, you may construct a different meaning about the situation if you know that the adult is the father of the child or if you think the adult is not related to the child. In one case you may observe a frustrated father dealing with a recalcitrant child, while in the other you may witness a kidnapping.

Age roles.   Aside from professional expectations, you may have ideas about how people of a certain age are supposed to behave. A tantrum by a 3-year-old does not "mean" the same thing as a tantrum by a 50-year-old. The same behavior is to be interpreted differently, depending on the age of the person.

Sex roles.   Another important source of role expectations comes from sex differences. Although sex role stereotyping is now being challenged seriously, you may still have learned to expect that boys don't cry, girls play with dolls, boys become engineers or doctors, and girls become housewives or secretaries. The same behavior in a man or a woman may be interpreted quite differently simply because of the sex difference. For some, a man who cries is weak, while a woman who cries is just emotional. The same behavior which in a man can be seen as appropriately assertive, ambitious, and go-getting, may be seen in a woman as pushy and aggressive. Figure 4-1 satirically implies different sex role expectations for business persons of the two sexes.

FIGURE 4-1
How to tell a businessman from a businesswoman.

A businessman is aggressive; a businesswoman is pushy.
A businessman is good on details; she's picky.
He loses temper because he's so involved in his job; she's bitchy.
When he's depressed (or hungover), everyone tiptoes past his office; she's moody, so it must be her time of the month.
He follows through; she doesn't know when to quit.
He's confident; she's conceited.
He stands firm; she's hard.
His judgments are her prejudices.
He is a man of the world; she's been around.
He drinks because of the excessive job pressure; she's a lush.
He isn't afraid to say what he thinks; she's mouthy.
He exercises authority diligently; she's power mad.
He's close-mouthed; she's secretive.
He climbed the ladder of success; she slept her way to the top.
He's a stern taskmaster; she's hard to work for.

Claire Levesque,
Michigan State University

Yourself

We have discussed in Chapter 4 the role which self-concept plays in your perception of the world around you. How you see yourself affects also not only the roles you choose to play but also, and very importantly, how you will play them. You may decide to become a physician, and the professional role of a physician is in part set for you by the generations of doctors who have preceded you and what society demands from its healers. But you can choose to be a distant, impersonal, disease-oriented doctor or a warm, compassionate, people-oriented physician. You may decide to be a professor; and here again, there are many ways for you to enact that role, from the high-minded and scholarly researcher who lectures occasionally to hundreds of students, to the teacher who just "loves to teach freshmen."

Role definitions are important because once you figure out what role you need to take and what role the other person is likely to take, you have a great deal of information about what behavior is expected of you and what you can expect of the other person.

Roles spell out how you will dress (you do not wear a swimsuit at the office), how you will speak or be spoken to (whether swearing is permissible or not), what kinds of duties and privileges and rights you may be entitled to (whether you get the key to the executive washroom). Roles determine whom you communicate with. If you are a salesclerk, you have to wait on the customers. If you are a student, you talk to other students most of the time; to a professor fairly often; to a dean seldom; to a president rarely, if ever; and to a trustee probably never. As a new employee you will communicate with your fellow workers, supervisors, perhaps your supervisor's supervisor, and rarely directly with the top-level executives of the organization, unless you meet them at a company function.

Roles also influence the content of your communication. As a student, you may need to talk with the professor about the course. Should you meet the same professor on a bus or at the supermarket, you will likely talk about school-related topics. Roles limit conversational topics, and the professor is not obligated to talk about anything else. Some professors never feel quite comfortable stepping out of the professor-student relationship and prefer to maintain the distance they feel the role requires. Supervisors often believe rigid role boundaries are necessary to maintain their authority over their employees. Although they may act pleasant and friendly with their employees at work, they maintain a professional distance outside the organization when they see their employees in other settings. "Not mixing business with pleasure" is a way to avoid complicated role relationships and the potential problems they may create.

When you first encounter someone, you experience a lot of ambiguity. This is because the role assignment process has to be negotiated from scratch. As we mentioned earlier, you determine what role to take on the basis of (1) how you define the situation and how you think the other person defines the situation, (2) how you define your role for that situation and how you think the other person defines your role, and (3) how you define the other person's role and how you think that person defines his or her role. When you meet someone new, it is extremely difficult to figure out how that person will think, so you rely on obvious behavioral cues such as physical appearance, dress, age, and sex to make some assumptions about "who the person is." You may engage in small talk and, through a cautious process of exchanging banalities, find out more about each other. This is how you jointly build and define roles for that future

Consequences of role definition

moment which will bring some element of predictability and comfort to the relationship.

When you get your first job, you need to learn not only what tasks are expected of you, but also how to negotiate role relationships with others. Many people will help you learn how to do the work, but the guidelines for getting along in a new role are fuzzy and you will receive only a little coaching.

For example, how will you find out whether you are in a position to expect the office secretary to type your work? With whom should you go to lunch? Can you go to the boss's office unannounced, or should you make an appointment through a secretary? If you get promoted to supervisor, how are you to relate to your former peers? Will they still expect you to join them for coffee breaks? Should you? Will they perceive you as a "buddy," and will you lose their respect and jeopardize your authority? What would happen if you did not join them? Will they perceive you as "stuck-up," and will that jeopardize their support?

These are the types of questions which directly relate to role negotiations in business settings.

Rules

As we mentioned in the preceding paragraphs, your communication transactions are characterized by a mutual negotiation of the relationship with the other person(s) involved. You define not only the situation but also the nature of the relationship by determining the roles that need to be enacted in the particular circumstance. Similarly, the other person is involved in the same process and offers a definition of the situation and of the nature of the relationship, thus confirming, rejecting, or modifying yours.[3]

Role negotiation is particularly clear in new relationships where much energy is spent mutually figuring out what roles are appropriate and comfortable, and where some time is devoted to establishing the structure of the relationship. New dating couples, for example, spend much effort figuring out how their relationship is to be defined. How much intimacy, how much sexual involvement, how soon, initiated by whom, are questions which are not always explored directly and out loud. They are often worked out through a subtle trial-and-error procedure during which both partners decipher small verbal and nonverbal clues.

Although the process of negotiating a new relationship appears to be intuitive and solely based on the idiosyncrasies of the particular

[3]Paul Watzlawick, Janet H. Beavin, and Don D. Jackson, *Pragmatics of Human Communication*, W. W. Norton & Company, New York, 1967, p. 133.

situation, there are certain rules that govern the establishment of role relationships. Sometimes the rules are very explicit, as in the case of professional dyads·like doctor/patient or doctor/nurse in a hospital, foreman/worker on an assembly line, etc. In organizational settings, job descriptions usually define what a person is expected to do and give some indication of how to relate to others. Status, authority, and lines of communication are spelled out to codify the interpersonal relationships necessary to accomplish the work.

In social situations, books of etiquette and manners, commonly accepted social guides, and traditions define how people should communicate with others, what they should say, how they should say it, when they should say it, and what they are expected to do.

Most of the time the rules for establishing social transactions are implicit, that is, not formally established in written form. Many of the rules that govern nonverbal communications fall into that category. For example, one of our cultural rules says that *when you talk to others you must look at them and they must look at you*, preferably in the eyes or in the face. You will usually feel somewhat uncomfortable if your listeners look everywhere in the room but at you when you are talking to them. Students who look out the window, at the ceiling, or toward something happening in the back of the room irritate teachers because they violate the rule. Teachers who lecture without ever looking up from their notes annoy students because they, too, violate the rule. You tend to distrust and not like people who will not look at you when you talk to them. Shifty eyes mean insincerity.

Another rule about looking has to do with how long you look at someone while speaking. If you maintain eye contact for a very long period without averting your eyes, you communicate more than just passing interest. In a totally new relationship, sustained eye contact usually communicates an intensity and a level of intimacy which are not usually expected of passing or brief encounters. If someone you do not know well maintains long eye contact with you, you have the choice of either deciding that the person is violating the implicit social norm that governs length of eye contact, or you may redefine the situation, for example, as a potential sexual advance.

Another implicit rule is that *if you do not talk to someone, you should not look at them*. It is considered impolite to stare at someone you are not actively communicating with. When you are not talking to someone, you usually avoid looking at him or her. If you do look and then get caught at it by the person you were looking at, you will usually feel embarrassed and will quickly shift your eyes away, or start talking. Observe what happens in schools, public hallways, streets, and offices. Two people are walking toward each other. Most of the time they have noticed each other from a distance, but need not acknowledge each other yet (it is safe to look at another from far enough away). However, as they get closer, they must do one of two things if they are to follow the rules that govern interpersonal nonverbal communication. (1) They can act as if they do not see each other and thus not have to say anything to each other: If you don't look at someone, you don't have to talk. In this case, they may look at their feet, at the ceiling or walls, or straight ahead in order to avoid the other person's eyes. (2) They can look at each other. If they choose this course of action, they must acknowledge each other by a few words or at least a nod of the head: If you look, you must talk. It is difficult to look and be looked at and not to talk. Elevators are interesting places to study the looking and talking behavior of people. Close physical proximity makes it impossible to pretend not to see other people; yet you can stare intently at the floor numbers as the elevator moves, and keep silent, or you can make profound statements about the speed or slowness of the elevator.

Other rules are also implicit. Appropriate times for you to disclose something personal to a friend, for example, cannot be looked up in Emily Post's *Book of Etiquette* or Ann Landers' column. It ultimately depends on you and your friend, how you have defined the relationship, what kinds of interpersonal risks you are willing to take, and a host of other idiosyncratic factors.

In ongoing relationships, the rules that govern communication transactions come partly from the explicit cultural and social norms which broadly define the type of relationship you are involved in, but also from jointly developed rules that are implicitly agreed upon by the parties involved. Married couples, for example, over the years evolve a system for dealing with each other and with events that come up in their lives. What topics of conversation are taboo, who does the dishes, who picks up kids at school, who initiates sex, who invites people over for dinner, who handles money matters, who makes decisions, etc.—all these and many other aspects of the relationship follow a pattern which, for better or for worse, gives the relationship some degree of stability, predictability, and meaning.

Families develop their own rules for their transactions; and children as well as spouses know that if these rules are broken, heated arguments, misunderstandings, hurt feelings, anger, and confusion may follow.

As a newcomer in an organization, you have to learn not only the formal rules or policies which regulate your work, but also the implicit rules which regulate people's interpersonal communication and which give the organization its personality. You may learn that there is no use speaking to your supervisor until she's had her first cup of coffee, that shop talk is a no-no during breaks, that if you want to get something done Mike's secretary is the one to talk to, etc.

Communication transactions are not simple phenomena. To understand them fully, you must first realize that they operate at two distinct, but simultaneous, levels.

As we mentioned in Chapter 3, the *content* level of communicative transactions deals with what a message refers to. This level has to do with what you normally consider the information of the message. A statement like "Get out of here" gives information about a possible course of action, a movement someone must make from here to somewhere else. The words of the sentence help you call up the denotative meaning implied. However, should you read this sentence out of context, not knowing who said it to whom, with what tone of voice, facial expressions, and gestures, you would have difficulty interpreting what was really meant. Was the person angry or joking? Was the person in a proper authority position to make such an order? These questions uncover the fact that some information is missing, and there is more to the statement than the simple denotative or content level. What is missing in this example is the *relationship*, or *metacommunicative*, level, which performs two basic functions: the first of these functions is *interpretive*, the second is *relational*.

Communication transactions (unless they are purposefully taken out of context or stripped of all inflections) contain information which tells you how to interpret the content or informational level of the transaction. Interpretive metacommunication consists of (1) nonverbal cues generated along with the verbal messages, which qualify the message, or (2) verbal cues which specifically give information about the interpretation to be made. "Get out of here" takes on different meanings when said with a smile or a shout or a frown. If the nonverbal cues are insufficient to help the other person figure out what was meant, the addition of "I am only joking" or "I mean it, damn it!" can provide additional verbal data for the interpretation of the message. Your every gesture and expression, how you handle physical distance and time, how you dress, how you choose to organize the words of your messages, how you stress specific words, all convey information which is crucial in helping others understand your intentions.

The Interpretive Function of Meta-communication

Although interpretive metacommunication is not exclusively nonverbal, much of the information you need to decipher messages comes from this dimension of your communication. The following treatment of nonverbal communication relies heavily on our discussion of this topic in *The Dynamics of Human Communication*.[4]

[4]Gail E. Myers and Michele T. Myers, *The Dynamics of Human Communication: A Laboratory Approach*, McGraw-Hill Book Company, New York, 1980, pp. 203–222.

Paralanguage The spoken word is never neutral. It is always affected by tone of voice, emphasis or inflections given, breaks in the sentence, speed of delivery, degree of loudness or softness, and pitch of the voice. These nonverbal factors are called *paralanguage*. As you know, a simple "yes" can express a lot of different feelings such as anger, frustration, resignation, disinterest, agreement, or challenge. A short sentence such as "I'll do it" may "mean" any of the following:

"I'll be really happy to do it."
"I'll do it, but it's the last time."
"You always make me do what you want."
"All right, you win."
"Don't worry, I'll take care of it."
"You're so dumb I better take care of it myself."

Which "meaning" is implied can usually be determined by the tone or inflection of the voice or by the stress placed on each separate word. The meaning of the sentence does not lie in the words alone, but also in the vocal expressions, or paralanguage, which are always associated with the words.

Some years ago a record came out in which two renowned actors carried on a seven-minute dialogue using only two words, "John" and "Marsha." The two talented artists managed to express so many different feelings and emotions that the story they were telling came through loud and clear. Meaning was exclusively carried through the paralanguage.

In everyday life, you naturally rely on the words themselves *plus* their paralanguage features to develop your meanings about what people are telling you. There are times, however, when you get distracted and miss the words themselves. If you have to respond and do not wish to admit you have not been paying close attention, you will rely on the paralanguage features alone to interpret what was said. This happens often at cocktail parties where people involved in small talk do not pay full attention to what is said and respond almost automatically. It may be pouring rain, but if someone says in a convincing tone, "It is really nice out, isn't it?" chances are the response will be an equally convincing "It sure is."

You often get upset not so much at *what* people say, but at *how* they say it. "He sounds so sure of himself, I always feel like contradicting him." You tend to respond to people in relation to these paralanguage features without quite realizing what exactly you react to. If you can learn to pay attention to how you respond to people's tone of voice or intonations, you will understand better why you may be attracted to some people and turned off by others.

Gestures were probably one of the first means of communicating human beings developed, long before oral language appeared. All cultures have a system of meaningful gestures which either accompany spoken language or stand alone in conveying a particular message. You nod your head to say "yes" (in some cultures, nodding means "no") and shake your head sideways to say "no." The hitchhiker's hand gesture is recognizable in most automobile-using cultures. You extend your hand to shake someone else's as a greeting and not as a hostile gesture. The language of the deaf is one of the most sophisticated systems of sign language.

You usually accompany your speech with a considerable number of hand gestures. If you've ever tried to give directions to someone over the telephone, you probably have caught yourself uselessly waving a hand in the air. Some cultures are known to be more expressive with the hands than others. The French, Spanish, and Italian, for instance—generally Mediterranean cultures—are quite effusive with their hand gestures. Sometimes certain gestures become automatic. Students are quick to recognize the familiar gestures of their professors. Impersonators of famous people rely on pose and gestures, in addition to their voice imitations, to create their characters. Gestures are often used to give emphasis to words. Sometimes, if a person's timing is bad and the emphasis occurs on the wrong word, you get the impression that he or she may not be sincere.

You are seldom immobile or expressionless. Your face moves and your body moves, and these movements communicate a great deal about your feelings, emotions, reactions, etc. Some of the time these movements are conscious and intentional, as when you deliberately smile at a friend, frown to express dissatisfaction, or raise an eyebrow to show surprise. Much of the time, however, these movements are so much a part of you they appear unintentional and unconscious. When you attempt to hide a feeling, you often give yourself away without realizing it: the way you move toward or away from a person, the way you sit—tense, relaxed, on the edge of the chair, slouched, etc. You tend to lean forward when you feel involved and interested, and to lean back when you are not. The way you walk often indicates to others whether you feel good, happy, and cheerful or sad, gloomy, tired, and dejected. You indicate your perception of status by your postures. You tend to relax around people of equal or lower status and tense up around people whom you perceive as having higher status. You sometimes feel that someone is disrespectful simply because he or she talks in a more relaxed manner than you think is appropriate.

How you look at a person communicates a great deal. A teacher sensitive to nonverbal movements and expressions can identify a resistive, belligerent, challenging student before that student ever says a word. There is no magic or, as we often call it for lack of a better word, "intuition" involved. It is a simple interpretation of subtle, yet visible, cues which are sent or given away by the student's posture and the way he or she looks at the teacher. We discussed earlier the rules that regulate how long you can look at another person. Whether you look too long or too briefly will communicate something.

Object language   Object language refers to the meanings you attribute to objects with which you surround yourself. The clothes and jewelry you wear, your hairstyle, and the decorative objects in your house are all object language. They say something about you because they represent deliberate choices you make. Clothing and jewelry are particularly revealing. You usually dress differently for different occasions; and if you don't, you are still communicating something about yourself, your attitudes toward others, your sense of appropriateness, your up-bringing, your values. Clothing is symbolic. Some young people choose attire rich in colorful symbols. Some people are so concerned about what they communicate with their clothes that they will only buy them in certain stores which guarantee them the particular kind of status they seek, whether they be secondhand stores, army surplus stores, or fashionable boutiques. A wedding band or an engagement ring communicates something quite specific about a person.

How you dress on the job is an important aspect of what impression you will make on other people. Business uniforms vary according to positions and status in the organization. Although for some professions the uniform is a clearly prescribed one (the military, the police, physicians' white coats, construction workers' hard hats), rules that govern what you should wear on the job may be just as compelling. The executive look (three-piece suit, tie, briefcase for men; skirted suit, blouse, high heels, briefcase for women) is different from the professorial look, the secretarial look, the blue-collar look. Recent popular books give very specific advice on how men and women can dress for success.[5] While the "right" outfit may not automatically get you that raise, it may be important in creating a feeling about you and your perceived competence.

All material objects help you make inferences about the person who displays them. You cannot ignore these objects and decide they do not count, just as you cannot decide that a person's words do not count.

[5] John T. Molloy, *Dress for Success Book*, Warner Books, New York, 1980; John T. Molloy, *The Woman's Dress for Success Book*, Warner Books, New York, 1978.

Too often, unfortunately, the inferences you make may be wrong, or the objects' meaning misinterpreted. Verbal breakdowns in communication also happen. You must be cautious in interpreting the nonverbal messages communicated through dress and other material objects, just as you must be careful in interpreting a person's words; but you must remember that the choice of what to wear and what to say is still yours. You have to take the responsibility for, and sometimes the consequences of, any misunderstandings your choices might generate. If you truly wish to communicate effectively with others, you cannot operate on the assumption that it's totally their responsibility to understand you. You have some responsibility to help them understand you. Just as you do not speak Chinese to a Frenchman and expect him to understand, you perhaps should not be surprised that certain clothes or hairstyles may be misunderstood in some situations. If you think that you should not be judged for what you wear, remember that—whether you like it or not—clothes are a part of communication, and therefore they say something about you.

Tactile communication

Touch is one of the first modes of communication of the human being. Infants learn much about their environment by touching, feeling, cuddling, and tasting. Linus's security blanket in Charles Schultz's cartoons is a symbol of all the objects children become attached to, which they particularly like to touch, feel, or keep. You communicate a great deal by touching. A pat on the back, shaking hands, or holding hands can express more than a lengthy speech. Lovers know this. Mothers do too.

In the American culture, except in a few well-defined situations, touching is linked with intimate interpersonal relationships, and is thus taboo for most other types of relationships. Many people refrain from touching others in casual encounters for fear their behavior might be misconstrued or simply because they are afraid of or do not like physical contacts. When they must stand in line, Americans will usually form an orderly single line in which everyone waits patiently for a turn. In Arab countries, on the other hand, lines are almost unheard of; considerable pushing, shoving, and touching are involved in most gatherings, and such behavior is not considered distasteful. American children learn relatively young to kiss their relatives hello and goodbye sparingly. Spanish children frequently kiss not only their relatives, but adult friends and acquaintances as well when they encounter them and depart from them.

Touching is a powerful communicative tool and serves to express a tremendous range of feelings such as fear, love, anxiety, warmth, and coldness.

Time

The anthropologist Edward T. Hall in his fascinating book, *The Silent Language*,[6] was one of the first scholars to probe into the time dimension of interpersonal communication. Time is a form of interpersonal communication. In our culture, time is almost treated as a thing; you gain time, waste it, give it, and take it. Time is precious, a rare commodity in rushed lives. Time speaks.

In the American urban white culture, punctuality is valued and tardiness is considered insulting. Being late for an appointment or in turning in an assignment may lead to unpleasant consequences. However, what is considered "late" varies not only with each individual and his or her personal sense of time, but also with the situation, the other people involved, and the geographic area. For example, you may have a very important appointment with a person of higher status than yours—perhaps a job interview. Usually, you will try to be "on time," and this may mean from about five minutes before the appointed time to five minutes after. If you arrive fifteen minutes after the appointed time, you will probably apologize and offer some explanation for your delay. The kind and extent of your apologies and explanations will vary according to how late you are and how important the situation is to you. If you are only five minutes late, you may not have to say anything; if you are ten minutes late, you may feel you have to briefly apologize but not give any reason for the delay; if you are half an hour late, you will probably apologize profusely and explain thoroughly what kept you; if you are an hour late, you may not expect the other person to be still waiting for you. If the other person is still there (as when you are to pick up your date at her house and show up an hour late), you expect her to be very upset.

With a close friend, the extent of tardiness may be increased without drastic consequences; but here, too, a scale will be established in terms of whether or not you owe an apology and, if so, the extent of that apology. An apology does become appropriate at some point, because extreme tardiness may be taken either as an insult or as a sign of irresponsibility.

In some cultures, tardiness may not be perceived as insulting, and one can go to a meeting hours after the appointed time without upsetting anyone. In Mexico, for example, it is not uncommon to arrive an hour and a half after the appointed time and still be considered on time. In America this would, of course, be considered very late and very rude. An American meeting a Mexican would feel insulted to have to wait so long and would probably expect a good story to account for such a delay. The American would be quite upset hearing no story, for the Mexican would, in his or her eyes, be on time

[6]Fawcett Publications, Inc., Greenwich, Conn. 1959.

and thus would not feel any need to explain anything. Unless you know and understand the other culture's sense of time, you may get very frustrated, and this naturally will affect the way you communicate with members of that culture.

Arriving early for an appointment communicates as much as arriving late. In circles where it is fashionable to be late to parties, the early arrival of a guest may throw the hosts into a panic, and they may be quite upset that their guest was not polite enough to arrive later.

Time communicates in other ways. A phone call at 3 A.M. communicates urgency and importance. People don't usually call you at that time of the night just to ask you how you are and to say, "Gee, it's been a while since we saw each other."

If you are two hours late coming home during the day, your family or friends may be quite worried and upset; but their fears will be less intense than if you were two hours late after midnight.

Space

The space in which your interpersonal communication takes place affects you in many subtle ways that you are not always aware of. Each of you has a "personal space," a sort of invisible bubble around you, which you feel is yours and which you do not like to see intruded upon without express permission. Although each of you sets your own personal boundaries, there are recognizable cultural patterns which regulate the handling of personal space and interpersonal distance.

Edward T. Hall[7] has identified three major interpersonal distances he calls "intimate," "social," and "public," which govern most of your interpersonal relationships. The "intimate" distance ranges from very close (3 to 6 inches—for soft whispers, secret or intimate communication) to close (8 to 12 inches—for giving confidential information) to near (12 to 20 inches—for speaking in a soft voice). The "social" distance ranges from 20 inches to 5 feet, and the "public" distance from 6 feet to about 100 feet.

When people violate the unspoken rules of interpersonal distance (get too close when they should be at a social distance or stand too far away when they are expected to be more intimate), you feel uncomfortable. When someone comes too close to you uninvited, you tend to move away. Your territory is marked, and you may let others approach but not come too close unless you specifically decide to allow them. The uncomfortable feeling one gets in a crowded room often comes from the fact that too many people are too close to one another. If someone crowds you at the library or at the cafeteria by sitting too close to you, you unconsciously try to avoid the intrusion by moving your books, tray, or chair away from the intruder. If for

[7]Ibid., pp. 163–164.

some reason the intruder moves closer, you try other avoidance behaviors. However, you rarely ask people in words to move away from you. If they do not respond appropriately by understanding your nonverbal avoidance moves, you usually change places in the library or leave the cafeteria as soon as you can, feeling your lunch was spoiled.

Appropriate interpersonal distances vary from culture to culture. As Hall points out, the comfortable distance for most Americans to stand for social conversation is about 2 to 3 feet. In France, Mexico, Brazil, and Arab countries, however, the comfortable distance is somewhat shorter than 2 feet. Should an American engage in conversation with an Arab, a subtle ballet is likely to occur: The Arab moves close to the American and looks intently into his or her eyes. The American, uncomfortable because the other is too close, tries to reestablish a less disturbing distance by moving back. The Arab, feeling the American is too far away for social conversation, moves in closer, and the American moves back. Each feels somewhat upset about the behavior they perceive as "pushy" (the Arab moving in too close) or "unfriendly" (the American moving away).

Interpersonal distance is one of the ways you have to express feelings. You tend to move close to people you like and away from people you do not like, if you have a choice. People sometimes take great precautions to avoid walking near others they do not like.

Special elements other than interpersonal distances also affect you. The arrangement of a room, the shape of a meeting table, or the size of a classroom in relation to the number of students occupying it all influence the development of interpersonal communication. Researchers have found, for example, that communication is distributed more evenly among people sitting at a *round* table than among people at a *rectangular* table. At a rectangular table, people sitting at the ends are more likely to be talked to and to talk than the other group members.

The Relational Function of Meta-communication

This second function of metacommunication serves to tell others how you see yourself, how you see them, and how you see the relationship. A statement such as "Please, Jill, have this letter typed and make three copies" conveys the expectation that Jill will carry out the order and indicates that the relationship between the two people is such that one can legitimately make the request and expect it to be fulfilled. If the answer to the request is "Yes, right away, Mrs. Jones," Jill confirms that she, too, sees the relationship as one where Mrs. Jones can expect to request things done. Compliance with the request is, in itself, a confirmation of the definition of the relationship; and the use of first and last names shows that both agree to define the relationship as a superior-subordinate one, where Mrs. Jones has some degree of authority over Jill. In some cases, the definition of the relationship may be challenged, directly or indirectly. The challenge is direct and clear when the other person tells in some way that he or she does not intend to comply. There are many ways to refuse compliance, and each way will communicate something about the nature of the relationship. If Jill says, for example, "I am sorry, but I just don't have time right now; ask Susan," she implies that Mrs. Jones probably had a right to ask, but not authority to enforce her request. Relationship in this case is redefined as one of superior and subordinate who treat each other almost on an equal basis. If the answer is "I don't work for you," the statement is a clear rejection of Mrs. Jones' attempted authority, and Jill indicates that she clearly rejects Mrs. Jones' right to make requests of her. Sometimes the noncompliance and the redefinition of the relationship are quite indirect and more subtle. For example, Jill might not overtly challenge the authority implied in Mrs. Jones' request, but might simply not do what was asked, or she might do it sloppily or do it late.

Nonverbal cues such as voice inflections, tone of voice, facial expressions, and gestures are particularly rich in their potential for yielding information about the relational level of metacommunication. Distance, how far away from or how close to people you stand, also indicates much about the nature of your relationship with them. In watching other people interact, you need not hear the words exchanged to interpret what kind of relationship they have.

The relational level of metacommunication gives information about three essential dimensions in a given relationship. Watzlawick and his associates have called two of these dimensions *complementary* and *symmetrical* communication.[8] (See also the discussion of Axiom 4, Chapter 3.) The third dimension has to do with the degree of *intimacy* present in a relationship.

Complementary communication

Complementary communication is based on differences among the people in a relationship, and these differences are usually expressed in terms of a dominance-submission or authority dimension. Teacher-student, mother-child, doctor-patient, and boss-subordinate are complementary relationships which imply that communication will take place along dominant-submissive lines and that some degree of agreement exists about who's in charge or the locus of authority and control in the relationship. One person is up, dominant, and has authority; the other person is down, submissive, and has less or no authority.

[8]Watzlawick, et al., op. cit., pp. 67–70.

As Watzlawick points out, a complementary relationship may be implied by social and cultural contexts as in the case of mother-child, doctor-patient, teacher-student, or boss-subordinate. But it may also develop in any relationship where tacit agreement exists about who has authority and who is dominant. Husbands and wives often behave in such a way which "presupposes, while at the same time providing reasons for, the behavior of the other: their definitions fit."[9] Usually, the more dominant one of the partners acts, the more submissive the other becomes; and more submissive behavior invariably brings on more dominant behavior. Both partners collude or tacitly agree to maintain the relationship on clearly, if implicitly, defined authority lines. The characteristic of complementary communication is that such communication provokes its complement. Submission elicits authority; directing provokes obedience.

Symmetrical communication

Symmetrical communication is based on similarities between people involved in a relationship who tend to mirror each other's behaviors. People in symmetrical communication perceive each other as equals. Friends tend to operate their transactions on a symmetrical level and so do professional colleagues. If you recall our earlier example of Greg and Bob—who were not only friends, but boss and employee, and student and teacher—you can see that the same two people will engage in symmetrical communication sometimes and complementary communication at other times. The ability to switch back and forth is a sign that little role rigidity exists and that people are sensitive to the communication styles associated with different role definitions. Symmetrical communication provokes similar behavior; generally love provokes love, hostility provokes hostility.

Intimacy

Relational metacommunication provides information about the degree of intimacy present in a given relationship. "Jill, please type this letter" and "Jill, honey, type this letter" and "Miss Smith, type this letter" are three statements that imply three different degrees of closeness and informality. Here again, information about the level of closeness and intimacy between people is revealed through the non-verbal cues people constantly give each other. Touching people, standing close to them, looking at their eyes as you talk to them, and smiling in certain ways all powerfully communicate that you define the situation as one which permits a certain amount of closeness and intimacy. You all know some people who clearly communicate by

[9]Watzlawick, et al., op. cit., pp. 69.

their demeanor, tone of voice, and attitudes that the relationship is formal and demands distance and no intimacy.

Because of the nature of transactions, and because they evolve as people negotiate roles and meanings simultaneously and mutually with one another, numerous potential problems may seriously affect communication and jeopardize your ability to organize activities and get things done. In this section, we will review some possible problems that you may encounter in your transactions with other people. There are basically four types of issues which can affect the effectiveness of your communication: (1) role conflict and ambiguity, (2) incongruent punctuation and sequencing, (3) relational disconfirmation, and (4) double binds.

TRANSACTIONAL INCONGRUENCIES AND COMMUNICATION PROBLEMS

One of the difficulties with roles is that you fill many of them, and often several at the same time. The woman who gets promoted to a supervisory position and now must be boss to those who were formerly her peers may experience confusion about which role she is to be in when she deals with her employees. Is she still a friend, or is she a superior? In addition, while she is a supervisor to her subordinates, she is also subordinate to her own boss.

Role Conflict and Role Ambiguity[10]

In filling any role, there are difficulties which stem from the fact that the various expectations you have about how to fill the role may not be consistent with one another. This is called *role conflict*.

You experience role conflict when one set of expectations about how you should perform the role disagrees with another set of expectations. The conflicts may have several sources.

Role conflict

Intrasender conflict arises when you receive inconsistent directives from the same person on how to perform your work. For example, you may be told by your boss that you must increase the production of your department but keep costs down. If the hourly productivity of your employees cannot be increased, you need to either increase your work force (a cost increase) or have your present work force do overtime (also a cost increase). There seems to be no way to meet both of your boss's expectations.

[10]This section is based on a discussion about organizational roles by Frederic E. Finch, Halsey R. Jones, and Joseph Litterer, *Managing for Organizational Effectiveness: an Experimental Approach*, McGraw-Hill Book Company, New York, 1976, pp. 49–57.

Intersender conflict occurs when different people send you expectations which conflict with one another. For example, a nurse may be told by a supervisor not to perform certain routine tasks which must be done by physicians, yet the nurse may be expected by a rushed physician to perform these same tasks. Secretaries who work in a typing pool and report to a pool supervisor often find themselves in this kind of role conflict when they are asked by an executive to perform certain duties which may not be part of the job description given to them by their supervisor. For example, a secretary may be asked by an executive for whom she does a lot of typing to run an errand which results in her getting back to the typing pool late, and thus earns her a reprimand from her immediate and direct supervisor.

Role overload is present when the expectations others have of you far exceed the amount of energy, time, and skills you have to fill them. Your boss may expect you to work overtime on a special project to meet a crucial deadline; your husband may expect you home early to go with him to a dinner party to which both of you just got invited; your daughter may insist that you keep your promise to attend her last baseball game of the season and cheer her as yet undefeated team; your neighbor may be depending on you to keep her children while she attends a very special event; your instructor may have assigned several articles to be read and reported on at the next class meeting in a night course you are taking. The sheer quantity of what is expected of you in the various roles you perform generates a conflict.

Person-role conflict occurs when you are expected to do things which are quite out of character for you. You may at times be expected to do things which do not fit your self-concept. If you see yourself as a compassionate person, it will be difficult for you to fire someone, particularly when the person to be fired may have great difficulty in finding another job, five children to feed, no spouse, etc. Yet your supervisory position may require that you let that person go. Some teachers find it difficult to give an F to a student they have come to like and whom they consider a friend.

Role ambiguity

Role ambiguity arises from lack of clarity in communicating expectations. You may have had the experience of starting a new job and being told very little about what exactly you are accountable for. For example, you may not have been told whether starting and quitting times are rigidly enforced, when you should take breaks, whom you specifically report to, etc. Sometimes expectations about what you are to do are expressed in very general terms such as "50 percent of your grade in this course will depend on your participation in class." What exactly is meant by "participation in class" often remains unclear throughout the semester.

Bateson and Jackson facetiously wrote,[11] "The rat who said, 'I have got my experimenter trained. Each time I press the lever he gives me food,' was declining to accept the punctuation of the sequence which the experimenter was seeking to impose." As you recall, a characteristic of transactions is that one person's behavior may be both cause and effect of another person's behavior. Punctuation is a way to organize a sequence of communicative interactions and decide that one behavior is the cause of another. Disagreements about how to punctuate a sequence of events account for many communication difficulties among people.

Punctuation and Sequencing: The Hen or the Egg

It is not uncommon to find a supervisor-subordinate pair facing a communication problem which goes like this. The supervisor constantly rides herd on the subordinate, checks and double-checks everything, leaves no room for initiative or responsibility, and generally feels the subordinate is, if not totally incompetent, at least in need of constant guidance. The supervisor explains her behavior toward the subordinate by stating that the reason for her close supervision is the inability of the subordinate to think for himself and take initiative. If the subordinate did not make so many mistakes, she, the supervisor, would not have to check and double-check everything. In other words, the supervisor is punctuating the sequence of events by labeling her behavior a response to the subordinate's behavior. "I have to decide everything because he can't take any initiative."

The subordinate, however, perceives and punctuates the situation quite differently. For him, there is no way he can take any initiative since the supervisor won't ever let him. He feels that there is absolutely no room for making even small decisions, so he's given up trying. He also feels that, because the supervisor constantly breathes down his neck and makes him nervous, it is easy to make mistakes. Also, there is no need to be that accurate, because the supervisor will check and recheck everything; and no matter how well you did, she will always find something to correct. In other words, the subordinate labels his behavior a response to the supervisor's behavior. "I don't take initiative because she makes all the decisions."

The issue is not whether one punctuates more accurately than the other. The fact is each behavior is *both* cause and effect of the other. In a sense, both supervisor and subordinate are right in their perception of the events. Yet, because they punctuate the same events differently, each gets caught in a spiral of mutually reinforcing behaviors which will lead inevitably to more and more aggressive

---

[11] G. Bateson and Don Jackson, "Some Varieties of Pathogenic Organizations," in David McK. Rioch, ed., *Disorders of Communication*, vol. 42, Research Publications, Association for Research in Nervous and Mental Disease, 1964, p. 274.

controlling on the part of the supervisor and less and less initiative on the part of the subordinate. Each feels absolutely justified in his or her own response. Each finds justification for his or her behavior in the behavior of the other. What is typical about punctuation problems is that the individuals involved see themselves only as reacting to, not as provoking, others' attitudes and behaviors. Self-fulfilling prophecies stem from discrepancies in punctuation. As Watzlawick writes,[12] "It is behavior that brings about in others the reaction to which the behavior would be an appropriate reaction."

For example, you may believe that people in general do not like you. You will tend to act defensively, in a distrustful manner, and sometimes aggressively. This kind of behavior is likely to generate unsympathetic reactions from other people, thus confirming your original assumption that people do not like you—a typical case of self-fulfilling prophecy. Sometimes discrepancies in punctuation occur because people involved in communicative transactions do not all have the same amount of information about a given situation, *but do not know this.* For example, if you make a friendly gesture toward someone you know, but for some reason the other person does not notice it and does not respond to you, and *you do not realize that he or she has not noticed,* you may be puzzled by the lack of friendly response to your overture and wonder why you are getting the cold treatment. While you would not get disturbed if you knew that the person was preoccupied and did not see you—a different meaning given to the lack of response—you do get annoyed when you interpret the situation as a deliberate brush-off. Let's pursue this further. If you interpret the situation as a brush-off from your friend and get angry, you may behave coolly toward that friend the next time you meet. Your friend does not know that you feel you got a brush-off on the initial encounter, is therefore confused about *your* cold treatment, and wonders why in the world you are not speaking. Such a situation can, and often does, spiral in the worst way. Each friend continues to react more and more coldly toward the other. The only way to break the vicious cycle is to confront the other person and ask what is going on. Only then may you have a chance to untangle the cumulative erroneous interpretations each of you made throughout the situation.

**Relational
Disconfirmation**   Frequent problems in communication can be traced to the lack of agreement, tacit or explicit, about the role definition people bring to a transaction. To return to the example of Greg and Bob, it is possible for Greg to relate to Bob at the store not as employee to boss, an

[12]Watzlawick et al., op. cit., p. 99.

example of complementary communication but as friend to friend, an example of symmetrical communication. If Bob also defines the role relationship as friend to friend, no problem arises. However, if Bob wants to define the store situation as one where he is the boss and Greg the employee, communication between the two will quickly become strained, frustrating, and may even stop altogether.

You may have experienced the frustration of discovering that someone who was relating to you with the casualness and friendliness you associate with social situations turns out to be a high-powered salesperson making a pitch. In this case, of course, the manipulation of the role definition is deliberate on the part of the salesperson, and your frustration comes from your being taken in, if only momentarily.

When one person insists on labeling a situation or a role in a particular way while the other refuses to label it the same way, you get annoyed at each other. You may define a situation as purely social while the other party keeps talking business. You may wish to define a relationship as a platonic friendship while the other person keeps trying to make it a sexual affair.

What may start as a complementary relationship, when indeed one of the people is in a legitimate dominant position (the parent with a very young child, for example), often needs to evolve into more of a symmetrical relationship. As the submissive person gains more information, he or she is progressively more able to make decisions. Typical communication problems occur between parents and their children when parents do not realize that normal dependency needs in children are gradually replaced by needs to be on their own. Adolescents try hard to redefine the relationship with their parents as symmetrical, while parents often cling to the old complementary one. Changing role definitions is indeed difficult, as such changes require not only a redefinition of the other person but also a redefinition of the self in the relationship.

Double Binds, Double Messages, and Other Incongruencies

Incongruencies arise in many ways in interpersonal transactions. A rather common type of incongruency occurs when the content level of your communication does not fit the relationship level. Your words "say" one thing, and your tone of voice, for example, "says" another. An aggressively yelled "I am not angry" is really a *double message*. Your words claim one thing (you *are not* angry), but your voice indicates another (you *are* angry). Which is to be believed? Which is to be reacted to?

A supervisor who says that his employees are welcome to come to the office whenever they have a problem but who consistently keeps busy in meetings outside the office or looks rushed when employees do catch him is sending a double message. The words say one thing, the behavior another. Soon, employees catch on and few will make any attempt to talk about their problems to the supervisor.

Double binds are specific cases of incongruencies and were first described in a paper on schizophrenia by Bateson, Jackson, Haley, and Weakland.[13] A double-bind situation exists when (1) two people are involved in a significant relationship from which they cannot withdraw and (2) one person sends a message which is paradoxical in the sense that the other person must engage in *simultaneously mutually exclusive behaviors.*

For example, if the message is an order, it must be disobeyed to be obeyed. Because this is impossible, double binds eventually put a person in the "damned if you do, damned if you don't" type of predicament. One humorous example is "Ignore this sign."

Sometimes a double bind can be experienced when two different people who are important to you make mutually exclusive demands on you. For example, Mrs. Jones, one of your two supervisors, may tell you: (1) "Always comply with Mr. Black's requests." (2) "Don't overuse the copying machine; make carbon copies." Mr. Black may tell you: (1) "Always comply with Mrs. Jones' requests." (2) "Stop making those illegible carbon copies; use the copying machine instead." Result: You are in a double bind. You cannot obey either supervisor without disobeying the other. You cannot obey her without disobeying him. The next time you must type something, you will be hard-pressed to figure out what to do. No matter what you decide, you will be disobeying someone you were specifically asked to obey. If you are stuck in a department where you have to report to both Mr. Black and Mrs. Jones, there is nothing you can do that will be right.

Sometimes one person places you in a double bind. An instruction such as "Be spontaneous" is itself a paradox. It cannot be obeyed without being disobeyed, for how can you respond spontaneously if you are ordered to do so? If you behave spontaneously, you are obeying the command and are thus not being spontaneous. A command such as "Don't be obedient" is another paradox, for if you are not obedient any more, you are in effect still obeying the command.

TRANSACTIONAL PERSPECTIVES

Newcomb's Co-orientation Model[14]

Newcomb's work on coorientation provided an early impetus to analyze communication in transactional terms. In his system, two individuals, A and B, have some relationship with (1) an object (call it X) and (2) each other. Each individual is *cooriented*; that is, has an

---

[13] Gregory Bateson, Don Jackson, Jay Haley, and John Weakland, "Toward a Theory of Schizophrenia," *Behavioral Science*, vol. 1, pp. 251–264, 1956.

[14] Theodore M. Newcomb, "An Approach to the Study of Communicative Arts," *Psychological Review*, vol. 60, 1953, pp. 393–404.

orientation toward both the object and the other person. The crux of Newcomb's model is that how A and B orient toward X is determined not only by the nature of X, but by the relationship each person perceives the other has with X.

Newcomb suggested what he called a "strain toward symmetry." If an object is important to you and if you are attracted to another person, how that other person feels about the object will influence your own feelings about it. If you like someone, you expect him or her to like what you like. There is a strain in the relationship if you perceive some discrepancy between your orientation toward an object and how you perceive the other person to feel toward that object. Somehow, you will feel compelled to reduce the dissonance created by the unbalanced system and take some action. The alternatives may be to (1) diminish the importance of the object—decide it really isn't that important to you, (2) decrease your attraction to the other person—decide that the friend isn't that important to you, or (3) attempt to make the other person change his or her mind about the object.

You do not function in a vacuum; and your actions are dependent, not just on your own orientations toward things and events, but also on how you see other people responding to things and events.

Other scholars[15] have refined Newcomb's coorientation model and

[15]Steven H. Chaffee and Jack M. McLeod, "Sensitization in Panel Design: a Co-orientation Experiment." *Journalism Quarterly*, vol. 45, no. 4, 1968, pp. 661–669; William W. Wilmot, *Dyadic Communication*, Addison-Wesley, Reading, Mass., 1975, p. 170; Renato Tagiuri, Jerome S. Bruner, and Robert R. Blake, "On the Relation between Feelings and Perception of Feelings among Members of Small Groups," in *Readings in Social Psychology*, Eleanor Maccoby, Theodore M. Newcomb, and Eugene L. Hartley (eds.), Holt, Rinehart and Winston, New York, 3d ed., 1958, pp. 110–116.

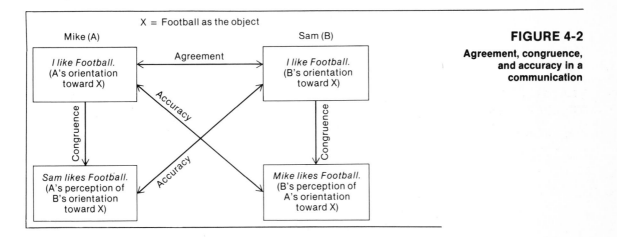

FIGURE 4-2

Agreement, congruence, and accuracy in a communication

provided still more dimensions to analyze transactional communication. *Agreement* occurs when two people have the same orientation toward an object. If you like football and your friend Sam also likes football, there is agreement. *Congruence* refers to the relationship between A's orientation toward the object and A's perception of B's orientation toward the object. If you like football and think your friend Sam also likes football, there is congruence. *Accuracy* refers to the relationship between A's perception of B's orientation toward the object and B's actual orientation. If you think Sam likes football and he actually does, there is accuracy. Figure 4-2 summarizes the relationships described in this discussion.

**Laing's
Interperception
Method**

Laing, Phillipson, and Lee[16] have expanded the coorientation model and have written that behavior of people toward one another is mediated by how much they experience the other. That clearly makes it transactional. The interperception method offers a technique for analyzing transaction from a variety of perspectives: (1) the first-level perspective, (2) the second-level perspective, and (3) the third-level perspective.

Let's use the example of two executives to illustrate the various perspectives and how the interperception method works.

Let's assume that Pete and Sue are colleagues who must decide whether the company should buy or lease a fleet of cars. Sue's preferences (leasing) represent her first-level perspectives. Pete's preferences (buying) represent his first-level perspective. Figure 4-3 illustrates the first level of perspective. This is the level of how each views the object—in this case, the type of fleet the company should have.

Sue's view of Pete's preferences is her second-level perspective (Pete wants the company to buy the cars), and Pete's view of Sue's preference is his second-level perspective (Sue wants the company to lease the cars). This is the level of how each views how the other views the object. (See Figure 4-3.)

Sue's view of what Pete thinks is her preference, or her own third-level perspective (Pete thinks I want the company to lease the cars). Pete's view of what Sue thinks he wants is his third-level perspective (Sue thinks I want the company to buy the cars). This is the level of how each thinks how the other thinks about the object. (See Figure 4-3.)

Relationships between people are always characterized by these

---

[16]R. D. Laing, H. Phillipson, A. R. Lee, *Interpersonal Perception: A Theory and Method of Research*, Springer Publishing Co., New York, 1966.

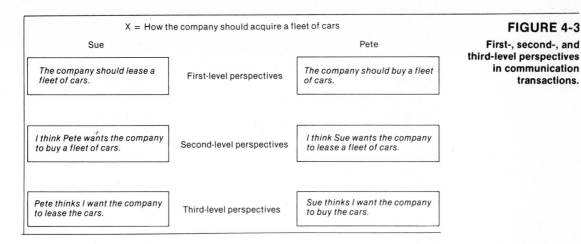

X = How the company should acquire a fleet of cars

Sue	First-level perspectives	Pete
The company should lease a fleet of cars.		The company should buy a fleet of cars.
I think Pete wants the company to buy a fleet of cars.	Second-level perspectives	I think Sue wants the company to lease a fleet of cars.
Pete thinks I want the company to lease the cars.	Third-level perspectives	Sue thinks I want the company to buy the cars.

FIGURE 4-3

First-, second-, and third-level perspectives in communication transactions.

three perspective levels. In the example diagrammed in Figure 4-3 and discussed above, the only existing discrepancy is between Pete and Sue's first perspective levels: they do not agree on what they think the company should do about cars.

Laing, Phillipson, and Lee propose that there are four possible comparisons between these perspective levels which shed light on interpersonal communication. These comparisons are described in Figure 4-4.

1. The first comparison is between the two first perspective levels and yields *agreement or disagreement*. In our example, there is disagreement. Pete wants to buy cars; Sue prefers leasing them.
2. The second comparison is between one person's second perspective level and the other person's first perspective level and yields *understanding or misunderstanding*. In our example, both Sue and Pete understand each other's preferences. Sue understands that Pete wants the company to buy cars. Pete understands accurately that Sue prefers leasing.
3. The third comparison is between the third perspective level of one person and the second perspective level of the other and yields *awareness of understanding or unawareness of understanding*. This comparison indicates whether a person is aware that the other person understands or misunderstands her or him. In our example, Sue is aware that Pete understands her. At this level, she is guessing about Pete's guesses about her preference. In this case she is accurate. And so is he.
4. The fourth comparison is between the third perspective level of a person and the first perspective level of that person and yields *a*

FIGURE 4-4

Comparisons between first-, second-, and third-level perspectives in transactional communication as related to interpersonal agreement, understanding, and the realization of understanding and agreement. Accurate understanding of each other's position is shown. Disagreement is on the first level only.

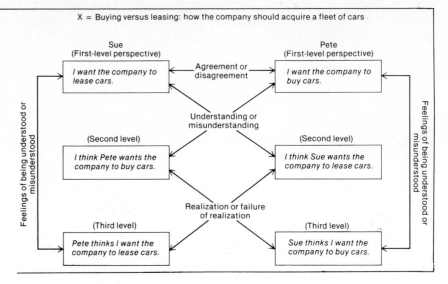

feeling of being understood or misunderstood. In this example, Sue feels that Pete understands her since she wants to lease the cars and she thinks Pete knows it. Pete also feels understood, since he wants to buy the cars and believes Sue knows where he stands.

Although the two disagree on the issue at hand—their opinions about what the company should do do not match—they each know what the other wants. They both feel understood. They are both accurate in feeling understood.

You can see from the previous discussion that transactional communication is anything but simple. All the levels described intermingle. Communication takes place and affects the participants of a relationship at all these levels. It appears that the most functional pattern of relationship among all the perspectives happens when there is agreement, understanding, a feeling of being understood, and realization for both the partners. However, this is not always achieved and many other possibilities are available. In the example we describe, Pete and Sue do not agree on the issue of leasing versus buying. Yet they are both accurate in their estimates of what the other likes, they both feel understood, and they are both accurate in feeling understood.

When the time comes to make a decision about what to do, the potential conflict, being at the first level, is relatively simple and straightforward and may be resolved in a number of ways. They can agree to recommend leasing and please Sue. They can agree to recommend buying and please Pete. They can agree to use one system for a time, then switch to the other. They can decide to study the cost data further, or they can follow any other alternative their imaginations will let them come up with.

Imagine, however, that the second-level perspectives do not match. Figure 4-5 describes a case where not only do Sue and Pete disagree on their preferences, but one person (Pete) estimates inaccurately the preferences of the other. In this new example, you can see that Sue understands Pete (she knows he wants to buy) and Pete is aware of that, which leads him to feel understood. Pete misunderstands Sue (he guesses wrong about her choice), and Sue is aware of that fact, which leads her to feel misunderstood. When time comes to actually make the decision, the problem is no longer one of simply deciding leasing versus buying. Faulty assumptions will cloud the issue. It is easy to see that, from Pete's point of view, there is really no problem. He wants to buy, thinks Sue wants to buy, and believes she knows he wants to buy. As far as he is concerned, all he has to do is get bids from the local dealers. Sue's point of view, however, is quite different. She knows Pete wants to buy, inaccurately believes that Pete knows she prefers leasing, and expects that the two of them will sit down and discuss the issue of what to do. Because she feels understood but is in error, she will attribute meaning to Pete's preparations to call the local dealers as "proof" of his total insensitivity or bossiness. What she tells herself may go something like this: "He's got some nerve. He knows I don't like the buying option, but does not even consult me about what to do. He does not care what I want and will only do what he wants." She may get quite angry at her

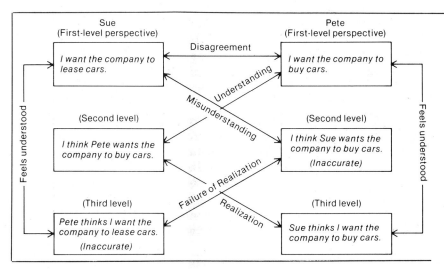

FIGURE 4-5

Comparisons between unmatching perspectives when Pete's second-level perspective is in error. A new set of relationships develops when people do not accurately evaluate the wishes of others. Disagreement on the first level is more simple to settle than that involving the other levels.

perception of what she calls Pete's "insensitivity" and may get back at him in a number of ways. Pete may be in for a surprise when, instead of getting interested in their mutual assignment, Sue appears sullen and resentful and he may wonder what is the matter with her, or decide that women are hard to work with, furthering a stereotype. Unless they are both willing to talk about their perceptions and discuss their perspectives with each other, the issue may easily go beyond the simple decision of what to do about cars. The issue can escalate from the content level to the relationships or metacommunication level. The relational dimension of Pete and Sue's communication becomes the significant issue and takes the forms of: (1) Who makes decisions in this department? (2) Who is insensitive? (3) What are women like? These deeper issues are more difficult to resolve.

It is important to note here that, although two people may agree on a content issue, they may inaccurately perceive each other's positions on the issue, and their second-level perspectives may not match. They may both feel misunderstood and resentful, even though they agree but do not know it. Conversely, two people may disagree on a content issue, but not experience any stress in their communication if their second-level perspectives are congruent. They may agree to disagree.

How you assess another person's perspectives is itself a process of transactional communication. Some people give clear messages about what they feel and think. Some do not. Sue reads Pete accurately, perhaps because he is forthright about his opinions regarding the advantages of buying cars and consistent about the messages he sends about cars. In the example of Figure 4-5, Pete's error about Sue's preference may stem from (1) her sending unclear messages about what she likes, (2) her sending inconsistent messages about it (sometimes she thinks buying cars is best, sometimes she is high on leasing), and (3) his own insensitivity and failure to pay much attention to the messages she sends. Perhaps he cannot imagine that someone will just not agree with him. Perhaps he sees what he wishes to see.

What is important here is to realize how much effort it takes to keep the perspectives clear. Both partners in a communicative relationship must strive to send clear messages. Both must pay attention to messages that are being sent verbally and nonverbally. Finally, if you are in doubt, check whenever possible.

Communication permits you to talk about your communication; that is, to metacommunicate. You can always talk about how you see a situation and check with the other person to determine whether he or she sees it the same way. It is through this mutual process of checking interpersonal perceptions that you can increase the effectiveness of your communication transactions with others.

Communication transactions depend on your taking others into account, knowing what your relationships are, and being able to communicate according to special rules.

SUMMARY

You need to take into account the complex nature of communication, to recognize that it goes on at two identifiable and distinct levels at the same time. There is communication at the *content* level where messages carry information. There is simultaneously the *relational* level where your communication carries information about the messages and how you should interpret them. In the "meta" systems your communication involves paralanguage, gestures, facial expressions, object language, touch, and certain cultural patterns of time and distance from each other. These meta processes carry information if you can "read" their messages.

In addition, there are relational aspects to the "meta" system. These include consideration of whether you are in a dominant position with another or are equals. Levels of personal intimacy affect how your messages are taken.

Your communication transactions may be unsuccessful if you do not perform well in the roles demanded of you and if you do not understand who you are in relation to others. A second difficulty arises when you have problems figuring out when a communication transaction starts. A third consideration concerns how you see yourself in relation to others and how they act toward the situation and you. A fourth set of difficulties includes classic communication incongruencies such as "double bind" and double or mixed messages.

You communicate in relation to other people and objects in your world, expressed by Newcomb's theory of "coorientation." Agreement, congruence, and accuracy are components of this theory which says you act toward other people and toward things in the way that makes your world most comfortable to you.

Another way of looking at relationships is in terms of levels of communication. At the first level you may agree with another person on an issue, but at the second level, you may not understand accurately how the other person feels. A third level involves whether you are aware of your understanding and that of the other person. The quality of your communication relates to how well you figure out the three levels and how well you help the other person understand them.

CHAPTER 5

INFORMATION AND FLOW

"Within every organization there is a straining toward completeness in the overall communication system." Anthony Downs

INTRODUCTION

In the first two chapters of this book, we discussed concepts such as linking-pin, gangplank, and upward and downward communication. In this chapter, we are going to take a closer look at information needs in organizations and at the process of information transmission.

The structure of the organization itself places certain inevitable restrictions, barriers, and requirements on the content, amount, and flow of information. What superiors want to know, for example, is not always what subordinates want to tell. What subordinates feel they should know may not always match what their superiors think is necessary to tell. Because of such discrepancies and because of the pervasive desire by most people to know what is going on, informal channels of communication always develop in organizations. The grapevine supplements formal networks, and members of an organization almost always will turn to associates to discuss informally what they know about what's going on.

In this section we will discuss three basic rules or axioms of organizational communication: First, human interaction creates information. Second, information creates the need and market for more information. Third, information flow in the human organization can be both studied (analyzed) and changed (improved).

Human Interaction Creates Information

In the discussion of information theory (in Chapter 3), we used the mathematical definition of "information," one which has developed much currency with the influence of computer technology. Although necessary for quantified analysis of communication, this definition is too specialized for purposes of the present chapter. While our use of the term may implicitly include measurable units, like the Shannon and Weaver "bit," we are here painting organizational interaction with a broader brush.

We use the term "information" in at least two ways. One is a data-interpretative concept: Data becomes information when processed by the human recipient or when run through a person's nervous system. Another is the loose, common definition of information as a sort of commodity which people get from one another as they ask and answer questions, talk, make reports, read instructions, remember past events, and share secrets. Korzybski's[1] principle of "time binding" which says human beings can store, retrieve, and exchange data about their lives and their world is consistent with our definition of information. Korzybski wrote that animals, with their "space-binding" ability, are more free than the plants. The "chemical-binding" propen-

---

[1] A. Korzybski, *Science and Sanity*, 4th ed., The International Non-Aristotelian Library Publishing Co., Lakeville, Conn., 1958.

sity of plant life, although remarkable and wonderful as a scientific fact, nevertheless resulted in a plant's limited ability to cope with an environment. Plants are generally stuck with the conditions they find in the immediate surround of where the seed grows. Adaptation of plants is limited, therefore, to a response to conditions of that one environment. Animals, moving from place to place, can change some features of their environment such as food supply, temperature, flooding, and oxygen level, and they also have adaptation abilities within their systems as do plants. Human beings, asserts Korzybski, as symbol-using animals, have achieved the further and most significant adaptability of being able to carry commodities from place to place (space binding as with the animals), and they can also bind time in libraries, written history, and records of inventions and advancements. Human beings can carry information.

For our purposes, information is the material of interaction in organizations and is uniquely human. It includes socioemotional qualities in interactions as well as task functions, or the work of conducting business with each other.

Stated another way, when people have to work together they monitor or watch carefully their behaviors with each other: (1) to see what needs doing, (2) to tell each other about it, and (3) to maintain control of each other's behavior through communication. Monitoring and control require a constant flow of information among members of an organization, whether it is as loosely organized as a family or as tightly structured as a military unit. Thus, human transactions are by definition messages with information.

Information Creates the Need and Market for More Information

Once the organization is set up, its processes go on in relation to its own inner workings and, except in a most unusual situation, by communicating with its environment. Actions in the organization create further need to monitor and control additional actions. Information about these actions and controls multiplies as people do more and as they need to know more about how others are doing in relation to them. Adjusting and adapting to the flow of messages in an organization and to the interdependence with the environment develops a whole new set of communication needs. Such needs are met by adapting the frequency of communication, the volume of information per contact, and the efficiency of both the information-moving systems and the messages themselves. The discussion of load and message fidelity will cover these adaptations more fully.

Information Flow Can Be Studied and Changed

An organization has a responsibility to design its communication structure and functions so it can control the time and effort with which this part of an organizational resource is expended. Network design is one response to the problem of finding the most effective way to cover the necessary activities: how much information must go to whom under what conditions. Much study has gone into analyses of organizational networks and the flow of information. Researchers have pointed the way to better understanding of how communication relates to the size, purposes, needs, and individual and group resources of organizations. It is hard to draw general conclusions from much of the existing research. However, there have been excellent analyses of communication in organizations which lead to both philosophical understanding and action recommendations.

So much of communication effectiveness depends on the persons in the jobs which are studied, that we urge you to use the chapters discussing human communication transactions as your basic starting point for looking at message flow. Anyone who forgets or denies the impact of the individual communicator on the outcomes of information flow makes a serious error.

INFORMATION

Some of the ideas about information we will discuss in this section have been mentioned earlier. The content of messages is crucial as it relates to the information itself, what may happen to the information, and possible deterioration or loss of meaning. How much fidelity does the message preserve from the sender to the receiver? Besides the chapter on transactions (Chapter 4), we discussed the relations between messages and the structure of networks in Chapter 2. In the following review of content, we propose a four-part category system for looking at messages and information. Next comes a discussion of how content may be distorted and how distortion may be minimized. Load, including concerns of overload and underload, and information cost are also covered.

Types of Information

The pie of communication experience can be sliced many ways. The types of messages and their information value are sometimes classified by arbitrary systems, or by systems that may be of value to one student but of no value whatsoever to another. Here we are not concerned with the mathematical efficiency of encoding, transmission, decoding—a system which was developed by Shannon and Weaver and has been refined by many writers and researchers since. Here we shall study the effects of different types of information as implied by the categories "preemptive," "informative," "evaluative," and "imperative." This typology is more closely related to the "what" of the information than to the "to whom" or "what effect" or "how much." This system enables the student to categorize information exchanges by what seems to be going on in the exchange.

Preemptive messages occur during contacts in which people are not directly engaging in getting or giving either information or orders. Rather, preemptive communication takes the place of normal task exchanges or business talk. It is designed to set up future communication rather than to accomplish an information job by itself. Malinowski called it "phatic communion," and it is called by many other names such as "small talk," "water-cooler conversation," and "cocktail chatter." It all tends to be preliminary to other actions.

Preemptive messages

As a meeting begins, one member says to another, "Sure hot out today . . . ," which is not designed to give any information not already known by the person who just walked in from the heat. The message preempts silence. Asking about the other person's family is not necessarily useful in conducting company business except on a personal level of contact, separate from the information value of the messages. Even some messages which sound like orders may be considered preemptive in that they supply neither orders to be immediately obeyed nor significant information on which to base decisions. An example is, "Please come to the Board Room at 5:00 for a meeting with the chairman." While this is a distinct order, the recipients don't have to do anything right then to reply. Most preemptive messages, however, are of the getting-ready-to-communicate kind in which one person seeks socioemotional information about the mood and the interests of others, or attempts to establish contact or build toward transactions of a more lasting or complex nature. Such messages do not directly affect the organization's business.

Preemptive messages occur frequently among peers as they exchange information about bowling scores, kids in the Little League, food in the cafeteria, or the weather. Subordinates are permitted to ask superiors about their families and general matters, but are not supposed to be told too much or to become detailed in their questions. On the other hand, a leader or manager who asks a subordinate about the same topics may be told in much detail about the lousy lunch the employee bought or the braces on the kids' teeth.

Informative messages contain the data on which the conduct of business is based. A report on the stock market. A syllabus for a class. A manual for assembling a wheelbarrow. Textbooks. Signs which tell you where things are, which way to the exits (but signs which demand you do something are in another category). The Chapter 3 discussion of "uncertainty reduction" is important for this category. For example, when you ask a question, you are giving information to the other person that you are uncertain; there is something ambiguous or confusing about your environment or your relations with it as you understand things at the moment.

Informative messages

Preemptive answers to questions give so little information that uncertainty is not reduced. Example: You ask, "When can we expect to get delivery on those items?" and you receive the answer, "Well, you know how the postal service is. . . ." Nothing in this nonanswer cliché says when the items will arrive. Hidden in this exchange is one of the dangers of informative messages—believing that vague statements or answers actually provide information or actually answer the question asked. In the give-and-take of conversation, you can be fooled into thinking that an information exchange has taken place when, more likely, the messages were preemptive or nonsubstantive and will add to, rather than reduce, uncertainty or confusion. Reasons for these distortions will be discussed later. For now, let's just say that people who talk to each other do not always realize that conversations may have a net result of *increased* rather than *decreased* uncertainty if the total options are greater at the end of the talk than they were at the beginning. Too much information may immobilize a decision maker unless the person has a well-defined system for sorting out the most useful or valuable data.

In relation to the up, down, and sideways communication directions, the flow of information messages covers them all. Downward from a superior comes information about how to do the job and expectations of performance level, as well as completion criteria, general outlines of organizational activities, timetables, audit reports, budget speed printouts, results of administrative decisions, and all kinds of data backing up what the organization does for a living. Upward-directed messages include responses to requests for data, reports of progress, ideas for expansions or innovations, budget requests, accounts, grade reports, committee minutes, and all the ways a subordinate keeps the superior informed on what is happening in that echelon. Sharing information sideways in most organizations is more likely to occur in informal channels than in formal ones, but is just as much relied on.

Information messages from the *environment* are very important. Not only must an organization have a system for exchanging information within its own structure, but it is called on frequently to give data to outside agencies and to collect data from outside. The quality of messages from outside will have a serious effect on operation of the organization. The reverse is just as true. An organization must supply accurate, timely, complete messages about itself to its environment if the continuing relations are to be adequate. Government agencies announcing guidelines for application for grants, reports of high school enrollments being sent the college admissions office, and demographic data about voting habits of Americans collected by a political organization are all examples of information coming into an organization from its environment. The company annual report goes from the organization to its environment (including stockholders and the general public), as do the results of a football game sent to the press, or an announcement of a job opening published in a newspaper or journal.

Evaluative messages are the "shoulds." They contain a value judgment or a moral or ethical admonition. They provide neither neutral nor decision-producing information, as information messages do. Nor do they demand an action, as imperative messages do. They suggest there might be a more honest or a preferred course to be taken because of a conscience, spiritual, or ethical need. Goals of a company are usually expressed in this way. The philosophy of a college or university is couched in value-oriented language, "To develop in our young people a sense of religious, moral, and ethical. . . ." A cartoon legend under a picture of a corporate board meeting reads, "If honesty is the best policy, what's the SECOND best policy?" Evaluative messages are those in which people confront each other with *what ought to be done*, rather than possible, logically derived options or rigidly controlled compliance. The company which sponsors a television series on the environment supplies the message that the public good is of great importance to the conduct of that company's business. The company's annual report includes data about the public service items of its operation not just as information but in the hope that the company will be perceived cordially by its publics. Affirmative action statements on job opening announcements are a compliance device at one level, but at another level they tell employees and prospective employees that the company recognizes its social responsibilities as well as its economic ones.

Evaluative messages

Evaluative messages seldom flow upward. Subordinates seldom speak to superiors about their superiors' responsibilities. It is also not generally well accepted for peers to tell one another how to run their affairs, especially when value judgments are involved. Peers may talk about the questionable ethics of others (such as the boss) behind their backs, but are not as likely to discuss each other's ethics. On the other hand, outsiders from the environment seem to take pleasure in asserting moral and ethical value judgments on organizations: newspaper editorials about the President of the United States, the letter to the editor about gas prices, an Action Line complaint about mistreatment by a large corporation or political entity. An organization may be formed for the purpose of impressing values about the environment: clean air, nonsmoking, truth in lending, voter indignation, and religious orders. Individual forces in the environment send strong evaluative messages to existing organizations whose practices come under public control or view.

Imperative messages

A course of action is demanded. A result is asked for. A move is directed. "Report on the effects of the new accounting procedure by noon tomorrow." "All candidates for the football team report at 3:00 in the gym." "Close cover before striking." So much of what is carried on in organizations is order giving and order-response that we can assume great familiarity with this type of message. Probably most parents raise their children by imperatives. In our later discussions of leaders, the use of power relates to this item.

One caution: Even when hidden in the language of inquiry or conciliation, the imperative is still there. "How would you like to pick up this junk around the machines?" A literal-minded person might mistake this question for a valid inquiry. Actually, it is a disguised imperative: "Pick up the junk."

A classic, but doubtless apocryphal, dunning letter from a collection agency is another example. After being behind in his payments for several months, the purchaser of a new car received this letter from the collection agency: "Dear Mr. Jones: What would your neighbors think if we came and repossessed your automobile for nonpayment of your obligations?" Jones replied, "Dear Company: I've asked the neighbors, and they think it would be a lousy trick." A parent says to a child, "You don't want to put that dirt in your mouth, do you?" The kid really did want to eat the dirt, but the imperative message is, "Don't put dirt in your mouth."

Imperative messages are much more likely to flow from the top down. Very few subordinates make demands on their superiors except in angry confrontations or violent negotiations. Government demands that organizations comply with all directives, but citizens have less chance to make similar demands. See the section on power in Chapter 7 for a discussion of the power gradient which makes possible relationships that set up imperative messages. Nowhere in information exchange are authority relationships more clearly established than in imperative messages. For orders to be effective, of course, all participants must see the authority relationship the same way. Without agreement on who can send imperative messages, they won't have the intended effect. Unless the order receivers see the order givers as legitimate, nothing happens. The relationship level of the transaction is disconfirmed.

Fidelity and Distortion of Messages

This book concentrates on effects achieved by communication. If "effect" means to have a message (1) heard and understood, (2) believed in, and (3) acted on, then care must be taken that the content of messages is reliably transacted. In previous chapters we wrote about difficulties in achieving faithful reproduction of communication from source to receiver. Even when people attempt to communicate effectively, there are factors of noise, meaning, and ambiguity which get in the way. What forces are at work to distort messages (at the expense of message fidelity) and to prevent distortion (when distortion-free messages are required)?

It makes sense that the more filter points a message has to go through, the more chance there is for distortion. Message fidelity, therefore, is partly a function of whether or not the structure of the organization is tall or low, with a wider span of communication. Fayol's "gangplank" or bridge in a tall system was described as an attempt to modify the message structure to get more direct and, hence, more faithful communication content.

Besides the number of places or levels a message has to pass through, time limitations are involved. At each level the content of messages can become distorted because of lack of understanding, shoddy handling, or other quality problems. Also, the abbreviation of messages has a strong effect on their fidelity. Abbreviating usually occurs because the participants don't want to spend much time sharing information.

Factors of "load" also affect fidelity. Underloading or overloading a message channel or transmitter will have a serious effect on the way the entire organization responds—a point that will be further developed below.

Deliberate distortions in organizations are usually based on the needs and ambitions of certain organization members in relation to others in the chain of command. For example, messages sent to a manager may combine the basic information with what the subordinate thinks the manager wants to hear. This preconceived idea will have an effect on message fidelity and may be multiplied as it passes through the successive judgments of several members in a chain of communication. Each makes guesses on what parts of a message the next receiver would like to have. Slanting, interpreting, and condensing are possible ways to distort messages. Fidelity of messages may be affected both in quantity (the proportion of the original information that is sent along based on time available and on "need-to-know" condensing) and in quality (interpretations and adjustments of information to suit preconceived ideas of the system's or other people's needs).

Can zero defects be reached in messages? Can distortion-proof systems be developed and maintained? When distortion-free systems are needed, the following characteristics may be found:

1. Accuracy is of great importance to the perceived welfare of the

persons involved in the network. A surgeon does not guess about the blood pressure of an open-heart patient during the operation. When aircraft landing traffic is heavy, instructions to pilots about headings, altitudes, approach speed, and clearances cannot be approximate.

2. There is usually a high organizational structure with direct authority relationships and small power span, rather than a loosely organized, wide-span system with minimum accountability.

3. Rapid transmission from low levels to high levels of decision points is available.

4. The message content is capable of a high degree of mathematical or quantification coding. Precise terms and highly denotative rather than connotative nomenclature are used.

5. The grammar, procedures, or regimen used is highly simplified or rigorously imposed, with no provision for ambiguous meanings and no tolerance for discrepancies in prescribed methods of handling the information.

Aircraft landing and takeoff procedures are highly prescribed, and military orders follow a specific form to minimize distortion of message content. The grammar of military marching orders consists of a preparatory command which describes in only a few words what maneuver is to take place, followed by an even shorter execution command to tell the soldiers when to do it. Operating room procedures have a special grammar as well as language of precise words used by all medical personnel. Information travels from anaesthesiologist to surgeon to scrub nurse, and there is a carefully established hierarchy or authority order within a small team immediately available for message contact.

In practice, only a small amount of message transmission can be considered distortion-free. If everybody who reports to the manager tried to tell everything, the manager couldn't handle it all. What is left out, as well as what gets mixed up with something else, is part of message distortion.

Message Load   Many analogies are suggested to message load. The volume of traffic on a highway system is one visible comparison. The flow of blood carrying essential particles in a human system is another. Several characteristics of load will be discussed because of the essential nature of load/network/flow relationships. Then we will define overload and suggest some causes, before discussing how organizations respond to overload and some probable costs of high message volume in an organization.

Installers of electrical circuits design the system to take care of a normal process of distributing electricity to various parts of the structure as it is needed. Planners of highways and streets attempt to make the carrier resources available for the predicted traffic; that is, widths of streets, control signals, posted directions, and speed limits are all designed to make the traffic load move smoothly. The design of a grocery store should follow certain guidelines for where customers will arrive and exit, and the flow from section to section. An organization has specified types of contacts between and among members which are designed to handle the flow of information so the work can get accomplished. Communication rules are related to the structure involved and the way the members are supposed to interact. Message flow is formally prescribed to maintain the life of the organization.

Frequent testing of the rules of information flow can help any organization to make sure that messages go where they are needed, at the appropriate time, and with the appropriate amount of information needed to get the job done. Too much information (overload), and people get jammed up with message handling to the detriment of other activities. Too little (underload), and people have to guess about what is needed because uncertainty is not reduced by the message system. It is nearly impossible to prescribe how much load is enough. Personal factors must be considered. How much information each individual can handle varies considerably in the organization. Channel factors are important: How much information can each channel carry from one participant to another, and how much can be responded to? Time factors are important. Routine messages are handled on a different priority than messages concerning a crisis for which an immediate solution is needed. Organizational norms, situations, and types of events or activities are factors to be considered in deciding on the "right" load for a communication system. A quiet family dinner is not the same message environment as a business lunch in a noisy restaurant. A battlefield conference between the commanders of support units is not the same message environment as the long-range planning committee of a college curriculum council. There is no easy answer to the question, "What is a normal load?" It is much easier to analyze load aberrations and abuses than it is to say what the message load should be.

If an organization or person does not receive enough information to do the job, there are several possible outcomes. All are dysfunctional. Errors may result from the lack of sufficient direction or instruction—errors which will use up additional management time not only for correcting what had been done wrong, but for assessing blame (another time-consuming and message-loading event) and for developing safeguards or preventions of recurrence. The system responds to error in much the same way a human body responds to infection; the company, in effect, runs a fever, manufactures antibodies, adjusts food and drink ingestion, and develops an abnormal level of activity.

Another outcome of underload is the boredom induced by lack of data or responsibility. The Hawthorne studies demonstrated how involvement could encourage production. Management literature is preoccupied now with making work interesting to assembly-line workers (whether blue-collar workers in a factory or white-collar workers in a large organization) whose disinterest has a harmful effect on the organization. If there is any truth in the old saying "Satan finds work for idle hands," the same may apply to idle message channels and receptors. Channels between people may dry up. Unused channels will tend to atrophy if not used by other information systems. Gossip will become the main content of underused channels. Underloaded message channels signal a lack of activity which, in turn, may imply cessation of function in that part of the system. "Out to lunch" shuts off message flow, and a part of an organization which persists in isolating itself can hurt the entire operation.

A symptom of a very ill or dying organization is the message underload measured from one part of the chain of command to another. Underload may occur for various reasons: (1) The office staff may be simply tired of answering dumb questions from visitors and refuse to give information. (2) The personalities involved may cause difficulty, as when subordinates do not feel free to direct messages to a superior. (3) Contacts between people may be made so difficult by physical changes or time arrangements that participants have no opportunity to exchange messages. (4) One person in the organization may be so ambitious and energetic and may process a "normal" message load so quickly and effectively as to be constantly in a state of underload. (5) The channels may be so badly understood or ineffectively designed that parts of the organization persistently receive less than they need to get their job done.

Overload

Too much is as bad as too little. Overload may be defined as the amount of message load which exceeds the handling ability of the person or subsystem. It may be a function of the amount of data arriving to be processed; or it may be related to the complexity of the data assignment. Either quality or quantity can cause overload. Quality may be the cause when messages are so complex that the person or system cannot adequately solve problems, make decisions, collate or organize reports, or otherwise deal with the message content. Quantity may be the cause when the absolute volume of messages coming to one place during any given span of time is too great for handling.

Overload should be measured in terms of effects. Does the receiver of messages handle their processing (1) in a reasonable time and (2) with reasonable accuracy or anticipated outcome? Most research on overload has been done using the Shannon and Weaver mathematical paradigm. One problem with that design is that information *complexity* is very difficult to quantify. Also, people's individual responses are subject to many personality variables which increase the number of items to be covered and reduce the predictability of human behaviors.

One cause of overload is the increased complexity of organizational life. Early in the development of industry, government, and institutions, a manager was able to span all the activities needed to run the organization. Handling the accounts as well as production was not too great a challenge to the early-day manager. Possibly three or four people brought significant problems to that manager's desk in the course of a day. The manager initiated additional communication with ten or twelve others who supplied raw materials, transported them, or functioned as outlets for the finished product. The schoolteacher who had charge of a one-room school taught twelve different grades and also took care of heating and lighting, purchase of textbooks, enrollment, and graduation. A modern-day school system such as a college now has several persons supporting each teaching position. Imagine the messages necessary to coordinate the activities of those individuals all doing their jobs. The manager today who has charge of an industrial plant or a retail store may have so many messages coming in that attending to all of them would be impossible. Legal services send in an opinion of a new contract form; accounting recommends another computer system; research and development requests additional facilities; personnel issues new compliance directives and asks for a series of meetings to discuss affirmative action with all submanagers.

Membership in subsystems ensures that a manager will at least run the risk of occasional overload. There is no way of so perfectly controlling flow that each subsystem comes in with messages just when the manager needs the information, with just the right amount, and during a time when the manager is not assailed by an increased volume from another part of the system. Gatekeeping and liaison become significant factors in adjusting load in a system.

How much information should a message contain? Perhaps the only kind of answer to a question like that is the one attributed to

Abraham Lincoln. Someone was teasing him about his long legs and asked him just how long a man's legs should be. Lincoln replied, "Long enough to reach from his body to the ground." Messages should have enough content to produce the desired outcome. Messages should give you the salient information but should not be contaminated with other information which you cannot understand or use.

A youngster in third grade asked her teacher if penguins could fly. The teacher suggested that, since the child's father was a well-known ornithologist, an expert on penguins as well as other birds, maybe the child should ask her father. The little girl replied: "Yes, but if I ask him, I'll find out more about penguins than I want to know."

Overload may be more than an absolute amount of data, and more than the recipient can handle; it also may be more than the recipient is interested in using, especially at that moment for that decision. When the boss asked for a report on an accounting discrepancy and the reply included a long discussion of how the computer system was established and debugged, the boss found out more about penguins than he wanted to know. At some other time the issue of computer software may be exactly the answer, but in this case it was overload. Checking on your own inclinations, do you try to give everything you know about a subject when asked for only specific details? Do you give the questioner "all there is to know about penguins"?

Some causes of high message volume

"We've got too much communicating around here, and it's all the wrong kind . . ." is a complaint we heard recently. In organizations or systems which generate a very high volume of messages, there is a real danger of overload. At any moment the delicate balance of handling messages can be disturbed by (1) changes in the internal patterns or alignments, (2) changes in rules for handling data, or (3) outside influences. Like an electrical circuit in a house, the normal operations give current to the appropriate parts of the system without surges or failures. Plugging in an appliance with too much amperage demand overloads the circuit, and a fuse blows or a circuit breaker trips. If the flow of current into the house from outside is altered (as by a stroke of lightning or a transformer malfunction), then the lights and appliances inside are shut off. Fuses or circuit breakers or business safety valves are "gatekeepers" which adjust flow and respond to overloads with a reaction which neither destroys the system nor permanently damages the organization.

Such safety valves are employed by many organizations to control message volume without stopping the system. The secretarial pool is a response to word-handling fluctuations during the work week. The "hold" button on a telephone is a simple way to manage flow. Sorting mail into priority stacks is a frequent device used by busy offices.

Priority labels on teletype messages have long been an adjusting influence on order of transmission and order of response.

Because we consider messages as part of the exchange of energy and production of most organizations, it is important to consider what factors cause high message volume. If there is a slight upward swing in the volume, overload results. At any moment, any part of a system can develop a crisis which demands that the channels and the response systems of managers and subordinates handle an additional load. Much of our time in communication consulting is devoted to studying systems to absorb any sudden rise in message volume which threatens to immobilize an organization's production, at least momentarily. Some organizations, of course, are particularly subject to the ebb and flow of message volume, and some are flexible in dealing with fluctuations. Recognizing factors which contribute to high message volume may help you think of ways in which organizations you belong to typically respond to their communication needs. Their message volume may be higher than it needs to be. It is desirable to minimize the numbers of messages required to conduct company business. Reducing quantity may even have a good effect on the quality of messages which are exchanged.

The following factors affect the high volume of messages:

1. The structure of the communication network. High structures tend to produce higher volume of messages as they flow through the essential hierarchy with each level adding, summarizing, passing along, or otherwise tampering with the volume—usually by addition rather than subtraction.

2. The span of the organization in relation to the number of subsystems linked to the major system. Each subsystem generates data and thus is responsible for the flow of those data to another system or subsystem. The number of these interacting agencies will determine the amount of message load. A discussion of Tullock's model[2] of hierarchical transmission of messages is included later in this chapter.

3. Organization rules about who communicates with whom. If an administrative office operates on the "no-surprises" system, it requires information on all the activities of agencies below it. This will generate more messages than a rule giving autonomy in the subsystems. This factor is only partially related to the flat structure style, because company rules about how much information must flow and in what directions may be more important than the formal structure. People observe rules for communicating; and if those

[2]G. Tullock, *The Politics of Bureaucracy*, The Public Affairs Press, Washington, D.C., 1965.

rules develop elaborate communication networks, then the volume of messages is high.

4. The incidence of ambiguous orders or questions. Orders given, questions asked, or ideas solicited from an organization by the managing levels must be clear if they are to get brief and clear answers. Subordinates tend to play it safe in the amount of information to give, and give lots of it. Therefore, the Myers' Maxim of Message Response is that *the volume of the reply will be inversely proportional to the clarity of the question, and directly proportional to the perceived status differential between the questioner and the replier.* When in doubt, people give an overload of data just to be sure they have answered the question, especially when asked by someone more important than they are. Clear questions, briefly stated, together with a suggestion of the limits placed on a reply, can help lower message volume. Asking a class for a term paper, the professor is usually confronted with the question, "How long should it be?" Because length is often equated with depth or insight, the question persists long after a professor has given up the idea that students need to be told to write briefly, clearly, succinctly, but accurately. A subordinate in an organization, asked for a report on the point-of-purchase advertising, will likely play "guess-around" about what the question implies. Does the asker intend to use the data to plan advertising, to check on customer flow, to develop a policy about location of displays, or for some other possible use? Unless additional data are given to the subordinate, the possibilities of information acquisition and message generation are endless.

5. The degree of expertness in those attempting to develop messages. If you don't have much to say, or if you are not proud and ego-involved in knowing what you know, your answers may not be as long as your friend's answers who wants to tell you all about penguins. The idiot-savant who knows all the batting averages of major league players from the turn of the century is just waiting for someone to call for the information. Our own experience is that if you ask for the batting average of Willie Mays compared to Babe Ruth, it is possible you will get a long discourse on batting averages for many others and additional data about how batting averages have been computed over the past three-quarters of a century. A subsystem of an organization can develop vast amounts of data and be ready to share it. When asked questions or solicited for reports on items closely related to the data base, this subsystem will generate reports of such length they become almost unusable.

In one university, it was the habit at the end of each semester to provide department chairpersons with a printout of all the grades given by all the faculty for all the courses in the institution.

Although the purpose was to review the grading system of the university in the face of grade inflation, the result was an overworked computer center and some after-the-fact finger pointing at the high graders. No essential analysis was made of each instructor's performance in relation to the variables of class size, class level, nature of the course (required or elective), graduate versus undergraduate, etc. Vital information was missing for comparisons, but the volume of absolute data was very high and unused.

6. Rapidity of change within the organization. In a working system, the channels are established and message dependency is high; in other words, we expect certain things to be reported. At the end of a fiscal year, a company generates audits, annual reports, stockholder letters, etc. Weekly message exchanges involving new products or new procedures make up message volume. Committees meet periodically and publish their minutes and results of their recommendations. If things were simply going along as they were last year, the amount of message generation would remain relatively constant by simply continuing the same practices of sharing information. However, each change in the system needs explanation: breaking-in message energy must be expended to get the change assimilated. New persons in the operation must be informed. New divisions generate new message potentials. Even doing away with sections will require an increase in message flow to relocate the lost efforts and to lay the old, dead activity to rest. If changes come slowly, the normal message flow may adjust itself. Within a fast-changing internal environment, the uncertainty and confusion developed by change will, in turn, develop a great need for messages.

7. Rapidity of change and organizational sensitivity to change by the outside environment. In the past few years, government bureaus' influence on university campus activities has been highly visible: loan funds, student lawsuits going all the way to the Supreme Court, affirmative action, integration plans, safety compliance, and a great influx of federal funding to colleges and universities. Some business leaders complain about the amount of energy, time, and money spent in living up to the restrictions, policies, guidelines, and regulations from governmental agencies and from quasi-governmental systems such as volunteer consumer groups. Diversification of activity has characterized much of American industry and corporate structuring in the past score of years. To respond quickly to these changes requires high message volume from all those affected. Like changes inside the organization, changes outside the organization generate a high volume of messages both within and across systems.

8. The availability of hardware and software to store and process information. If we can do so much more message sending, receiving, and storing, then we will be tempted to take advantage of the technology offered. The fact that a lot of nonsense can be stored is less important to some enterprises than the fact or fun of storing. Citizen's band radio has been a great savior to stranded motorists, victims of flood or disaster, and lonely drivers who need help in staying awake and alert; but it has also jammed the permissible airwaves with an enormous amount of jargon and low information messages which may not represent a great leap forward in radio communication. Everyone can relate or has heard horror stories about the way in which computer responses have sent three hundred letters to the same person, written checks with the decimal point misplaced so a clerk received a paycheck for millions of dollars, or consistently mishandled billing to the dismay of angry customers. However valuable the data processing instruments and systems, they are only useful if controlled by people whose message aspirations can be curbed. In our own early experience with computers, the central processing unit had a delightful response to message overload: When asked to produce too much data too fast, it would print out "PUNT" and stop.

Responses to overload

Earlier we wrote that organizations move toward completeness in their communication. If message overload consistently occurs, there is grave danger that the organization may have to add many more systems just to handle message load. It may have to change personnel to replace those incapable of high message rates or those who have had severe psychological episodes as a result of trying to cope with overload. It may have to somehow adjust the internal responses, the external activities, or both. Or it may "punt."

Responses to overload can be categorized in several ways. Many of the same responses develop insidiously as message volume grows inside an organization without people even being aware that the adaptation is occurring. In other words, the responses listed below may not occur suddenly or dramatically as a reaction to a significant break in the message flow. They may more likely be an attrition or a slow wearing down of message effectiveness which grew most gradually.

A set of responses categorized by Miller[3] gives an idea of some ways in which an organization responds to overload:

[3] J. G. Miller, "Information Input Overload and Psychopathology," *American Journal of Psychiatry*, vol. 8, p. 116, 1960.

1. Omission of some of the messages which are considered inconsequential or of less importance. You cut out ones you think you don't need.

2. Committing errors of transmission when too much is attempted; incorrectly processed messages occur during stress times for the individual or the system, and one of the most frequent causes of stress is overload.

3. Approximation is the response of giving partial answers to questions; giving stock replies to questions or inquiries for information. Even when a form letter may not be entirely applicable, the sender must not take time to tailor it for each inquiry.

4. Escaping is a physical or psychological response depending on the situation. If there is not time to respond, don't bother. The easiest way not to bother is to not be there when called: to let a phone ring, to let people wait at your window, to change appointments or miss them completely, to tune out the other person while signing letters or shuffling through your in-box.

5. "Queuing" means delaying processing of messages during the peak periods, hoping to get to them during the slack periods. In some situations lines are formed, while in others, seekers of message handling must "take a number" and wait.

6. Multiple channels may be formed to handle messages if the overload is only occurring in part of the system. Redundancy of circuits has other functions besides taking over if an accident or malfunction of the usual type occurs. Message overload is a malfunction in the information processing system, and peaks can be helped by redundant circuits.

7. Filtering is the process of determining what should pass through immediately under some system of priority. It is different from omission in that the material is slipped through eventually in a relatively complete form, but only after a decision is made on when and to whom, under what constrictions.

Farace, Monge, and Russell[4] have expanded the discussion of coping with load to include three categories of effort. *Minimum effort strategies* usually result in dysfunctional effects, including ignoring the problem, following rules regardless, building up a backlog, setting priorities and selecting only the highest to transmit, having clients serve their own message needs, and accepting lower performance standards. *Moderate effort strategies* in their categorizations include matching up the standards with the resources, chunking or aggregating

[4]R. V. Farace, P. R. Monge, and H. M. Russell, *Communicating and Organizing*, Addison-Wesley Publishing Company, Reading, Mass., 1977.

messages systematically, turning work over to a subcontractor or a new middleman, creating branches or other improved processing capabilities or capacity, and establishing pooled or standby resources to handle peak loads. *Major effort strategies* are: creating lateral relations in a tall network structure, creating informational task forces with the purpose of message handling, implementing management information systems, and reorganizing or restructuring the organization—a very dramatic recommendation.

In an analysis of the responses of "the topmost level of communication intermediaries" to system message overload, the report by Downs[5] of a RAND Corporation study includes these predicted reactions in bureaus:

1. Slowdown of message handling without changing the network structure or rules of transmission. This, writes Downs, is the most common response to overloads because (a) until it is known whether or not the situation is temporary or permanent, the best response is to do as little as possible; (b) overloads often occur because of peaks or crises, so it is best to respond by delaying reactions; and (c) economy in the bureau may be more important than fast processing of messages, so no changes in message handling are called for.
2. Change rules so the lower echelons screen out more information, or have different "thresholds" of message importance. This may reduce the quality of the bureau's output because each successive level will have to make decisions on fewer data.
3. Add more levels and channels to the existing networks. This encourages development of "taller" networks with the accompanying disadvantage of more filter points and more information loss—and also more expense to staff than the flatter networks.
4. Group the message-exchanging subsystems so they create a balanced rate of message exchange. Subsystems which normally conduct their business together can be placed together and avoid the additional channels up the chain.
5. Improving the message-handling capabilities of participants. Capacity for handling messages varies with individuals, but one precise limit is the message-handling ability of the top officials. No amount of changes in the structure can alter that fact. Some changes in communication methods may help these managers to receive and process data more effectively in a given amount of time: (a) simplified or clearer presentation of the same data, (b) improved

[5]A. Downs, *Inside Bureaucracy*, Little, Brown and Company, Boston, 1967.

reliability of the data, (c) providing additional data or parallel data to help reduce uncertainty.

Messages do not sit around waiting to be discovered. Neither do they randomly float off to be picked up only by some lucky accident. Here we are concerned with the flow of messages as they move from sender to receiver; up or down or sideways; reciprocally, through formal or informal systems, in small and large organizations. We have already introduced you to the advantages and disadvantages of the "tall" networks as compared with the "flat" ones for handling of information. In this section we will concentrate on a few items of review and a few concepts about networking which may lead you to study further that very current and exciting research thrust.

FLOW

Networks provide the basis on which flow directions may be measured. People will respond to directions of flow in the way they can best meet their own needs. There are really only two directions, horizontal and vertical, although we usually consider vertical flow to be in two parts: upward and downward. Horizontal flow, assuming communication between peers, needs no such distinction.

Direction of Flow

According to Katz and Kahn,[6] messages sent from superior to subordinate have five basic purposes:

Downward communication

1. To provide specific task directives or instructions on *how to do the job*
2. To provide information which produces an understanding of the task and its relationship to other organizational tasks and, therefore, gives a *rationale* or reasons for the job
3. To provide information about organizational *policies*, procedures, and practices
4. To provide *feedback* on performance to the subordinate
5. To provide philosophical information regarding the organization's *mission* or orientation toward goals of the organization

   Written communication is common in downward directions, especially when the complex rationale for job orientation and company goals are involved. It has the advantage of being subject to rereading

[6]Daniel Katz and Robert Kahn, *The Social Psychology of Organization*, John Wiley and Sons, New York, 2d ed., 1978.

and filing for future reference, but the disadvantage of not easily providing feedback. Self-correction is necessary for message handling, and without some provision for a cybernetic attitude and implementation, the organization cannot catch errors or diagnose weaknesses in the system. We recommend that managers develop a two-way communication system of feedback as part of the downward flow to encourage correction of flaws in the communication operations. We have discussed earlier the greater likelihood of having very rigid channels of downward communication in the very tall networks, with the flat networks being more autonomous and subject to less message load from above.

Upward communication

Not only is an organization interested in how much of a message is received and acted on, but frequently the superiors want information about activities normally engaged in by subordinates. A manager, for example, may ask for a completion report on a project, but at the same time be interested in knowing how effectively each member of the organization performed. Upward communication, then, has many uses: feedback on progress of assignments, new information about company or project proposals, and checking up on individual performances. Earlier we discussed the value of upward communication as feedback and the advantages of "flat" networks in giving access to the top level by the subordinates.

Lateral communication

In the tall networks described by Fayol, there was mention of the "gangplank" or bridge, allowing peers to communicate directly instead of up and down the organization. This approach has been described as an "informal" system to be used when the formal system did not provide the information needed. Another way to describe it is to say that when similar subsystems need to compare their activities, the organization, however "tall," encourages lateral, or horizontal, communication. Much has been made of the advantage of not having to send messages all the way to the top and then down another long channel, but there is some question in our minds about whether message flow is thus minimized. In some tightly hierarchical systems (the military, for example), it is difficult to operate across the bridge without giving some notice up the line. When two subsystems choose to communicate horizontally, then, it is altogether possible that they will create a whole set of new messages up both "legs" of the "high crotch" system just to tell their bosses what they communicate about. Caretaking by superiors of the subsystem coalitions, we believe, may in some instances add measurably to the message load in the total system. This should be studied and evaluated against preliminary investigations on the balance of peer and vertical communication network uses.

Structures of communication networks serve as facilitators or as limiters to message handling and processing. Rules and procedures are designed to move messages, just as a conveyor is designed to move produce. Much of the message load in any organization consists of keeping the communication policies ever clear and emphasized. New members in any organization take time to learn the habits, norms, and policies which govern with whom they have information transactions, just as they take time to learn the locations of the parking lot, their desk, and the washroom, and who answers the phones.

Structure and Function

The formal system can be closely identified with the organization chart. Structure is, however, more than simply the physical relations of desk and officers, more than just the propinquities of persons or boxes on a chart. Structure determines how rules are made and applied in organizations that the flow of information will have the required results. Our view of structure represents the rules themselves and how they are formed and applied or overlooked, deliberately or by accident.

Formal and informal structures

Formal rules and systems of communication exist in an organization for at least these reasons:

1. To control and measure outputs and to articulate the rules themselves
2. To coordinate complex activities in the system and relate the subsystems to each other and to the organization
3. To regulate responses to other systems outside, to the environment, and to competing systems so a high level of predictable behavior may be maintained and consistency encouraged
4. To coordinate resource allocation of people, money, and things
5. To create a climate within which the organization can adjust its outputs as it receives and processes feedback

In our discussion of "programmed" and "nonprogrammed" decisions in Chapter 8, we set forth some types of rules followed by leaders in making decisions. In that regard, there are more rules in some organizations than others because of (1) the assumptions of the leaders, (2) the needs and attitudes of the followers, and (3) the exigencies of the situations. The number of formal rules for communicating in any organization will vary inversely with the routine nature and importance of the content of messages, and directly with the lifetime of the organization. In other words, the longer a group or system is in operation, the more elaborate its communication rules and message handling procedures are likely to be. Also, if the activities of the group are repetitive and highly predictable, there will be many rules, but if the group has unpredictable and variable activities, then the formal rules will not be so abundant or rigid. In addition, an organization which has a high degree of interdependence from one group or individual or subsystem to another will have many formal rules of how communication will take place. More simply, if you do a lot of business with others, you need lots of rules to do it.

Another observation on numbers of rules: If types of decisions are too trivial to cover with rules, the messages involved will not be subject to a set of formal rules. There is, however, a midrange of decisions which should be covered by rules (*programmed* decisions; see Chapter 8) and will depend on policy manuals, published procedures, and codified regulations for their imposition. A third level consists of decisions which are too important to make without involving superiors or other members of a hierarchy (nonprogrammed decisions; see Chapter 8). The incidence of any of these levels will indicate how much formal structure the rule system will have in an organization. Organizations which make only trivial decisions have few rules, as do those which make very significant or sweeping decisions.

If the members of the organization find the interactions prescribed by the rules are not useful, they will establish their own communicating system—the informal system. You may immediately think of the "grapevine" as this substitute for the formal channels. The term is misleading, however, if you think of it as a meandering, uncertain, unreliable channel. It is, in practice, none of these. Field research and laboratory experiments indicate that grapevine communication is very fast; predictable in its course, directions, and membership; and also far more accurate than a casual observer might imagine. Grapevine communication is less heavily loaded with task information—how to do the job—than with information about people, attitudes, relationships, interpretations, predictions, values, norms, and needs. The dysfunctional nature of the grapevine is in fostering rumors and spreading them. Because rumor, by definition, lacks substantive evidence or fact, it may be damaging when circulated and acted on. Usually full of prejudice, emotion, bias, self-serving issues, and partial truths, rumors arise in situations where (1) there is great ambiguity or uncertainty and (2) issues of high interest to group members arise suddenly. Rumor passers either support the rumor content, add to it, or suggest a counterrumor. By keeping an open ear to rumor, a manager can determine more about the mood of the organization than about the actual information on any given issue.

In its benign or friendly form, the grapevine serves as a morale-uniting force when there are high interest in new policies, innovations in procedures or personnel, and sufficient data about the organization without heavy value judgment. A grapevine also is likely to occur in organizations where people work closely together, or where they interface with other sources of information about the organization from outside.

The function of serving as a filter point for messages has been suggested by such early writers as James Harvey Robinson[7] and Walter Lippmann.[8] Likert refined the ideas in the linking-pin theory discussed earlier in this text. The liaison person manages to cross organizational lines or to cross from one subsystem to another, and helps interpret one group's rules or messages for the other group.

Liaison or "gatekeeping"

Related to this function is the message-linking function of the gatekeeper. Determining what messages should flow and who should receive them are two responsibilities of the gatekeeper. Variously referred to as the "two-step flow" of information and "opinion leading" (as in Lippmann), this function is vital to the communication networks in organizations. Not all data should be sent to all places. When rules do not specifically apply, or in systems where rules are minimal or badly understood, then the gatekeeper maintains a flow of messages either consistent with the organizational rules or parallel to them. Gatekeepers operate in both the formal and informal systems; in fact, as liaison persons, they may hold the two systems together. They support the integrity of the formal system while functioning in the informal system as "influencers" in the message flow control.

Communication makes possible—and necessary—more communication. The direction and amount of information you send and receive can be measured and analyzed, and it can also be changed by you and others.

SUMMARY

You hope that the information in your messages arrives at its receiver the way you want it to. Different kinds of messages and information have different purposes. You can engage in communicative contacts in which you are simply setting up future communication.

[7]*The Mind in the Making*, Harper and Brothers, New York, 1950.
[8]*Public Opinion*, New York, The Free Press, 1965 (paperback edition).

You may want something done or someone to know something. You may deliver "should" messages as value statements. You may give direct orders and expect some kind of action to happen as a result.

If you hope to have your message heard, understood, believed, and acted on, then you want to overcome the forces of confusion and distortion. These forces include not only the listening habits of others, but the "encoding" or delivery habits of you the speaker or writer. A large part of the problem about fidelity of messages involves "load," or how much message content people or an organization can stand. Overload and underload are potential difficulties which can be anticipated and adjusted for.

When your communication flows upward, laterally, or downward, different things happen to it. Structures of communication (or organization) networks may help move messages or may hinder them. Formal and informal structures in organizations have an effect on communication outcomes. Gatekeeping, or acting as a valve, for information flow is both an important and a generally present activity in organizations where people must influence the outcome of transactions.

CHAPTER 6

MOTIVATION AND INFLUENCE

*"I contend
that the increasing
momentum toward demotivation
in contemporary American culture
is a product of the carrot-and-stick philosophy
and the hierarchical organization structure, both of
which imprison people psychologically and assume
that they are jackasses to be manipulated."*   Harry Levinson

INTRODUCTION

One of the significant functions managers perform is the utilization of human resources. That means moving people in order to get things done and achieve organizational, departmental, and personal goals. Managers' performance is inextricably tied to other people's performance in the organization, particularly those people who work with and for them. It is little wonder, then, that managers are vitally concerned over what their employees do, how they do it, and why they do it. Performance, in most organizations, is the usual means for determining how people are compensated, how raises are determined, how promotions are decided, and how people feel about themselves and their work. However, when you take a look at how people perform in organizations, you notice quickly that there are tremendous qualitative and quantitative differences. Some people work faster and better than others. Some produce much more than others. Some perform their jobs more easily than others.

Why do some people perform better and more than others? After all, there is always a reason for the way people act, and work behavior is certainly no different from any other type of human behavior. It, too, is governed by the idea widely accepted among behavior scientists that human behavior is not random, but purposive. It meets goals and fills needs.

Performance and motivation are somehow related. Because managers constantly face questions of how to maintain high performance and how to improve marginal performance, they are concerned with employees' motivation.

Practicing managers also know that the answers to these two questions are far from simple. In fact, they are so complex that none of the abundant theoretical speculations and observations on organizational life provide perfect guidelines to assess the whys of human behavior. Frequently, seasoned managers attend special courses and seminars to learn more about motivation as it relates to organizational performance. They try to discover better ways to motivate—and thus enhance—their people's performance. Yet, understanding human motivation provides only partial answers to the practical issues of motivating specific employees. As we will discuss in this chapter, motivational factors are numerous; and many of these are not under the control or influence of the manager.

Figure 6-1 describes a model of the relationship between performance and motivation and how the two are mediated by potential managerial influence. As we discuss the various approaches to the study of motivation, you will note that four basic types of factors account for human behavior.

Psychosociobiological factors: Genetic makeup, as well as early

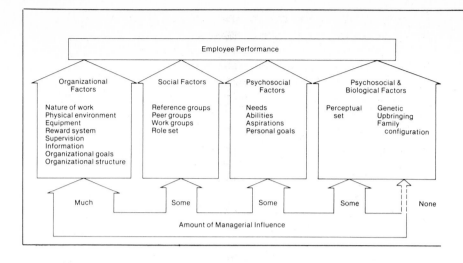

FIGURE 6-1

Motivation and performance as mediated by managerial influence. *Source:* **Adapted from Joseph L. Massie and John Douglas,** *Managing,* **Prentice-Hall, Inc., Englewood Cliffs, N.J., 1977, p. 56.**

environmental and learning influences, determine much of how you learn to interpret the world and create meaning.

Psychosocial factors: Your needs and aspirations, abilities, and personal goals have an effect on what you do.

Social factors: Your role set, peer groups, work groups, and reference groups all influence, to some degree, what you choose to do.

Organizational factors: The nature of your work, the physical environment in which you work, the equipment you use, the reward system, the type of supervision you receive, the amount, accuracy, and timeliness of the information you get, and the organizational structure and goals all affect your behavior.

When you look at these different factors, it becomes evident that a manager does not have exactly the same potential influence on all of them. There is absolutely nothing a manager can do about the genetic background of the employees. A manager has no influence on employees' upbringing and family configuration—whether a person has brothers and sisters, and whether he or she is firstborn, last, or in the middle. There is little a manager can do about the perceptual set of the people who work in the organization, although there is always the possibility a manager may help other people change their self-concept and, through communication, develop new ways to look at the world.

There is little a manager can do to influence employees' psychosocial sources of motivation. Yet it is possible, through training, to modify a person's abilities and skills; it is possible by understanding and meeting a person's needs to encourage him or her to seek fulfillment of other needs. It is possible, through communication, to help a person change his or her aspiration levels and reevaluate personal goals.

At the social level, the influence a manager can have on his or her employees can be felt more directly. Although a manager may not have much control over whom people socialize with, at times some degree of control may be exerted on who will work with whom.

Finally, at the organizational level, a manager exerts a great deal more control and influence. A manager can determine to some extent the nature of the work to be done, the quality of the physical environment, the nature of the reward system, and some other organizational factors.

The main thesis of this chapter is that it is basically through communication activities and processes that the influence a manager exerts on employees' motivation can be felt. Before examining how managers can influence their employees' motivation through communication, let us take a closer look at the major factors which motivate people in general. As we describe, first, *what* motivates people, then *how* people get motivated, you must remember that it is always the internal perception of the person which determines whether or how much a particular factor will affect that person's behavior.

WHAT MOTIVATES PEOPLE

While most behavioral scientists agree that people are motivated by the desire to satisfy many needs, not all agree about what these needs are and how each affects an individual's belief in their relative importance.

Maslow's hierarchy of needs, McClelland's achievement motive, Hertzberg's two-factor theory, and Maccoby's study of personality types and their motivational implications are discussed in this section.

Maslow and the Hierarchy of Needs[1]

Maslow's theory is based on two fundamental assumptions:

1. People all have basic needs which are arranged in a hierarchy of importance. Only when the first basic level of needs is satisfied can people devote energy to seeking satisfaction of the next needs level.
2. Only unsatisfied needs can motivate behavior. Once a need is satisfied, it no longer acts as a motivator.

Maslow identified five need levels:

[1]Abraham Maslow, *Motivation and Personality*, Harper & Row, New York, 1954.

These needs include the most basic necessities which sustain life— air, water, food, sleep, elimination, sex. They are the most basic of all needs and, if frustrated, take precedence over other needs. If you have not eaten for several days, your behavior will very likely be solely motivated by your desire to get food. It is difficult to lift a person's spirit if his or her stomach is empty. If you have not slept for a long time, that need will take precedence over any other higher need.

Physiological needs

The next level in Maslow's hierarchy is the need for safety, or for protection from danger, threat, and deprivation. From an organizational standpoint, safety needs are manifested in a desire for job security and for steady or increasing monetary income.

Safety needs

Only when physiological and safety needs are relatively well satisfied do social needs motivate behavior. Social needs are related to the desire for companionship, belonging, acceptance, friendship, and love. Some people will go to great lengths to belong to certain groups they value. The need to belong, formally as well as informally, to a variety of human groups is indeed a powerful motivator for those who derive their sense of identity from membership in social or professional groups.

Social needs

These needs do not act as motivators until the previous levels of needs have been reasonably well satisfied. Esteem needs consist of (1) the need for *self-esteem* which is characterized by a desire for self-confidence, self-respect, feelings of competence, achievement, and independence; and (2) the need for *esteem from others* which includes a desire for recognition, status, appreciation, and prestige. In most typical large organizations, there are relatively few opportunities through formal channels for the satisfaction of esteem needs at the lower levels of the organization. However, one of the functions of the informal system which exists in all organizations is to provide a means for the satisfaction of the esteem needs at all levels of the organizational structure. Respect from co-workers often means more to a person than recognition from the boss, as the Hawthorne studies clearly pointed out.

Esteem needs

These needs include the realization of one's potential, self-fulfillment, and creative expression. It is not unusual to find people who are highly respected in their field, whose lower needs are satisfied in a large measure, and yet who feel restless and discontented. The highly

Self-actualization needs

successful executive who suddenly turns artist and the eminent scholar who starts a business venture are not uncommon examples of people motivated by the need for self-actualization who shift gears in midcareer.

By and large, most organizations in this country have been successful in providing relative satisfaction of the lower needs of their members. Salary levels permit a fair amount of satisfaction of the physiological and safety needs for a majority of people. Organizations also permit the relative satisfaction of social and belonging needs by providing opportunities for association, interaction, and communication on the job. If this is true, and if Maslow's theory is accurate, these needs are no longer motivators. The implications for the management of organizations are tremendous. More money, more employee benefits, and more opportunities for socializing will do relatively little to encourage people to produce more or better. If a satisfied need is no longer a motivator, it is clear that managers must make some attempts at satisfying higher-level needs of their organization members.

This is, of course, easier said than done. For one thing, a need is a motivator only if it is felt as a frustrated need by the person himself or herself. Only *you* know whether you are hungry, need friends, or would like a pat on the back. Furthermore, only *you* know the relative importance of a given need for you at a given time. Sometimes you may forgo the satisfaction of a need—even a basic one—for the fulfillment of another, higher-level need. You may choose to deprive yourself of sleep and social activities for long periods of time in order to achieve professional goals which require a great deal of work. The student who works long hours, has little social life, and is thoroughly dedicated to getting through school is motivated essentially by esteem needs at the expense of having social, and even physiological, needs met. Not all students will make this choice, of course; and ultimately, motivation is a very personal affair. Knowing that *generally* all people have five basic needs, and that *usually* a satisfied need is not a motivator, is helpful, but it does not provide a specific answer to the question of "What should I do to motivate Susie or Jim to work harder?"

Again, you find yourself into the communication arena. Through transactional communication, employees can let you know what is important *to them*. Through your own sensitivity and attention to the messages you get from your employees, you may be able to determine (1) what their needs are, (2) what needs are particularly important to them at a given time, and (3) whether or not they perceive accurately your attempts at satisfying their needs. As a manager, you may be doing all the "right" things, but there is always the possibility your employees do not perceive what you do in the spirit in which you intended it. They may not interpret your actions in a productive manner.

McClelland and his Harvard associates identified several motives which relate closely to organizational behavior. They isolated three basic motives: (1) the need for achievement (n Ach), which is a need for success evaluated against some internal measure of excellence; (2) the need for affiliation (n Aff), which is a need for close interpersonal relationships; and (3) the need for power (n Pow), which is the need to control and influence others, directly or indirectly.

McClelland and the Achievement Motive[2]

McClelland found that people with a high need for *achievement* shared the following characteristics:

1. They prefer and seek tasks in which they can have a great degree of personal responsibility for the outcome.
2. They set realistic goals for themselves and take calculated risks.
3. They develop careful plans to help them achieve their goals.
4. They want precise feedback about their successes and failures.
5. They value competence over friendship and would much rather work with someone they feel is competent, even if they don't like the person very much, than with an incompetent but likable person.

You may fit the description or know students who do. Perhaps you prefer to do individual assignments rather than having to work on a group project. Perhaps you like to know exactly what you will be evaluated on and to get frequent feedback on your performance. You may select courses in which you feel you are likely to do well, even if your friends don't. If this is the case, you are likely to be achievement-motivated.

People with a high need for *affiliation* seek, above all, to develop pleasant relationships with others, and they value friendship. They are much less concerned with getting ahead and prefer work which provides much interaction with other people. They are the type of students who just love group projects and who are anxious to get into a group with people they know and like, even if they are not the best students in the class and if, as a result, the performance of the group may suffer.

People with a high need for *power* are primarily concerned with controlling and influencing others. They seek positions which carry

[2]David C. McClelland, *The Achieving Society*, Van Nostrand Reinhold, New York, 1964.

with them status and authority, and thus provide a built-in way to fulfill their need.

Hertzberg's Two-Factor Theory[3]

Hertzberg's two-factor theory of motivation builds on Maslow's work, but extends the analysis of motivation to the specifics of work motivation. In the fifties, Hertzberg conducted a research study using the critical incident method on 200 accountants and engineers employed in firms around Pittsburgh. He asked these people to describe to the interviewers times when they felt particularly good or particularly bad about their jobs. When the responses were all tabulated, there emerged two fairly consistent findings. Good feelings were associated with job *content*, and bad feelings were associated with job *context*. Hertzberg labeled the satisfiers *motivators* and the dissatisfiers *hygiene factors*; hence, the two-factor theory of motivation.

Hygiene factors include such things as company and administration; technical supervision; interpersonal relations with supervisor, with peers, with subordinates; salary; job security; personal life; work conditions; and status. Motivators consist of elements such as achievement, recognition, advancement, the work itself, the possibility of personal growth, and responsibility.

What is interesting in Hertzberg's theory is the relationship he discovered among satisfaction, dissatisfaction, and motivation. Hygiene factors, which are environmental and roughly equivalent to Maslow's lower levels of needs, prevent dissatisfaction but do not bring about satisfaction; hence, they do not motivate. They are necessary, but not sufficient. For employees to be motivated, more has to happen. Content elements of the job, on the other hand, are motivators and are similar to the higher levels of needs described in Maslow's hierarchy. Figure 6-2 compares the Hertzberg and Maslow systems. According to Hertzberg, a person needs to have a job with a challenging content to be truly motivated, although the absence of motivators does not necessarily lead to dissatisfaction.

Typically, managers tend to concentrate on hygiene factors. If there is a performance or morale problem, they will offer more pay, more fringe benefits, better working conditions in the hope of motivating employees. Many managers are puzzled and do not understand why well-paid employees with great fringe benefits and good working conditions are still not motivated. In terms of Hertzberg's theory, the explanation for the apparent dilemma is simple:

[3]Frederick Hertzberg, Bernard Mausner, and Barbara Block Snyderman, *The Motivation to Work*, 2d ed., John Wiley & Sons, New York, 1959.

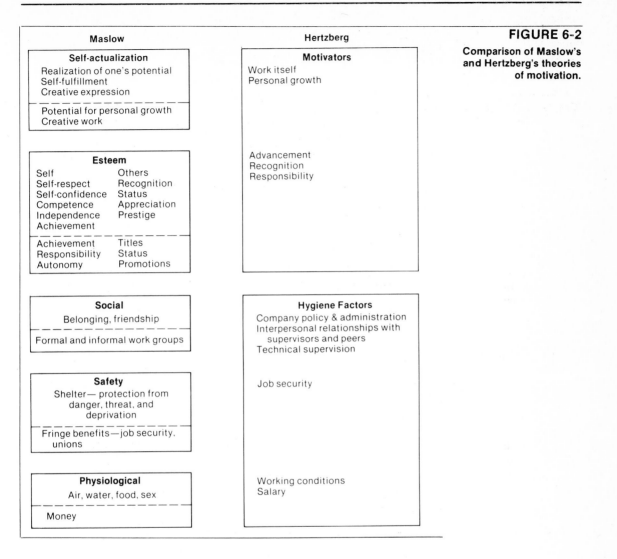

Hygienic factors are simply not motivators. If salaries were bad and working conditions poor, employees would likely be dissatisfied and motivation would drop. But to raise the motivation level above a hypothetical zero line, managers must introduce elements related to the content of the job itself, the true motivators. Employees with challenging jobs which allow them responsibility, autonomy, and a degree of creative expression, and which bring them recognition and potential advancement are motivated employees.

Hertzberg's theory gave rise to controversy and academic debate.[4] Several researchers maintain that the two-factor theory is an over-simplification of motivational processes. One factor can give rise to job satisfaction in one person while creating job dissatisfaction in another. In spite of the legitimate criticisms of the two-factor theory, Hertzberg's analysis of work motivation is a substantial contribution to the understanding of factors that relate to employee satisfaction and dissatisfaction. Hertzberg stresses the importance of the content elements of work, which have been sorely neglected and often overlooked in the past. As we will see in the application section of this chapter, his technique of job enrichment is indeed a practical method for improving work motivation.

Maccoby's Managerial Types[5]

Maccoby's study of corporate leaders sheds light on a truly fascinating dimension of motivational processes. Maccoby, a psychoanalyst and director of the Harvard Project on Technology, Work, and Character, interviewed 250 managers from twelve major companies in different parts of the country. He believed that strategies for social change must take into account the character of those people who influence the quality of work and life of others. The character and emotional attitudes of corporate leaders provide useful insights into the relationship between motivation and action. Although Maccoby's typology does not grow out of theoretical formulations, it does exemplify characteristics described by Maslow, Hertzberg, and McClelland.

The study's philosophical underpinnings come from Erich Fromm's psychoanalytic theory of character. Fromm describes character in terms of how people satisfy their basic needs (physiological and safety needs, in Maslow's terms) and their needs for relatedness, effectiveness, stimulation, and meaning. According to Fromm, people satisfy these needs in characteristic ways which can either lead to creative development or pathology.

---

[4]R. J. House and L. A. Wigdor, "Hertzberg's Dual-Factor Theory of Job Satisfaction and Motivation: A Review of the Evidence and a Criticism," *Personnel Psychology*, vol. 20, pp. 369–389, 1967; Nathan A. King, "A Classification and Evaluation of the Two-factor Theory of Job Satisfaction," *Psychological Bulletin*, p. 18, July 1970; C. A. Lindsay, E. Marks, and L. Gorlow, "The Hertzberg Theory: A Critique and Reformulation," *Journal of Applied Psychology*, pp. 330–339, August 1967; Victor H. Vroom, *Work and Motivation*, John Wiley & Sons, Inc., New York, 1964, p. 128.

[5]Michael Maccoby, *The Gamesman*, Simon and Schuster, New York, 1976.

Maccoby insists that an understanding of social character is absolutely necessary if you want to enlist the support of people for progressive social change. If your plans conflict with others' emotional attitudes rather than being supported by them, you won't get much from the people ultimately affected by the change. "Social character types are an approximation of the human reality that must be considered together with the economic, technical, and social factors that determine work organizations."[6] As one of the managers Maccoby interviewed stated, "Understanding character is ninety percent of my work."

A new type of man is taking over leadership of the most technically advanced companies in America. In contrast to the jungle fighter industrialists of the past, he is driven not to build or preside over empires, but to organize winning teams. Unlike the security seeking organization man, he is excited by the chance to cut deals and to gamble. Although more cooperative and less hardened than the autocratic empire builder and less dependent than the organizational man, he is more detached and emotionally inaccessible than either. And he is troubled by it: the new industrial leader can recognize that his work develops his head but not his heart.[7]

Thus begins Maccoby's first chapter on "Managers," with this description of the gamesman.

What are the types that emerged from Maccoby's study?

The craftsman

The craftsman is a traditional person who upholds the work ethic, is thrifty, and values respect for people and concern for quality. The craftsman enjoys the *process* of making something and loves to build and tinker. Craftsmen view other people in terms of how they can help them do a craftsmanlike job. Craftsmen are usually quiet, modest, practical perfectionists who tend to do their own thing. They may go along with goals they do not share. Above all, they will seek every opportunity to do interesting work.

The jungle fighter

Jungle fighters' primary goal is power. Life and work are a jungle where the winners destroy the losers. They see peers as potential accomplices or enemies, and subordinates as things to be used and discarded when they can be of no further use. As lions, they build empires. As foxes, they move ahead by politicking.

[6]Ibid., p. 44.
[7]Ibid., p. 34.

The company man

Company men are functionaries who derive a sense of self-identity from belonging to a powerful and protective organization. Their strong points are their concern for people and their commitment to maintain the organization's integrity. When they are weak, they are concerned with security and may be fearful and submissive. When they are strong, they develop a sense of cooperation and mutuality with other people in their group.

The gamesman

The gamesman is a new type. Gamesmen's interest is challenge, and they thrive in competitive activities where they can be winners. They are impatient with other people's cautiousness; they like to take risks and are intent on motivating others to push themselves beyond their limits. Life is a game, and gamesmen are full of enthusiasm which they communicate to others. They have a tremendous amount of energy, enjoy new ideas and new approaches. Their main goal is to win. But, not unlike company men, they are team players and feel responsible for the working of the organization. Their goals are truly merged with the company's goals, and they see people in terms of their use for the organization rather than for their own personal ambitions.

Summary

The motivations of these different types of people are quite different. The craftsman wants to do well and make money, but above all is motivated by the problem to be solved, by the work itself and its intrinsic challenges. Satisfaction comes from producing something of quality. He or she prefers working alone or in small groups on projects that are well structured and with which he or she can stay from beginning to end. Craftsmen obviously are ill-suited for the assembly line. If they have to work there or in similar types of impersonal work, they may develop all kinds of somatic symptoms as a resistance to the unpalatable.

Jungle fighters like to be feared. Suspicious and somewhat sadistic, they are totally unable to work and cooperate in interdependent teams of peers. Jungle fighters may succeed in crisis situations or in roles where trust and interdependency are not crucial. Yet, in the long run, they are divisive and generate a great deal of hostility, undermining the climate of the organization.

Company men equate their personal interests with the organization's development and success. They are motivated by hope of success, but are also driven by worry and fear. Without the organization, they feel lost and insignificant. Company men seldom rise to the top, for they lack the risk-taking ability, the toughness, the self-control, and the energy required to reach the top. They make, however, good middle managers. Because they are dependent on the organization, they are highly sensitive to the nuances of interpersonal relationships within the organization and find themselves often called to negotiate between conflicting claims.

Gamesmen are concerned about winning, and they evaluate co-workers in terms of what they can contribute to the team. They are not hostile or vindictive, but feel that generosity may not have a place in work. Their strengths are those of youth, they have energy for play and for work, and they are open for new ideas. They strive for independence, but are often unaware of the extent to which they depend on the organization and on others. They thrive on high-pressured competition. They desperately need a sense of autonomy and fear being controlled. As a result, they often create their own organization within the organization.

HOW DOES MOTIVATION WORK?

In the previous section, we looked at factors of the motivation process as they have been isolated by several theorists. Although Maslow and Hertzberg claimed they had developed a basic theory of human motivation, their critics contend that the motivational process is far more complex than either the simple need hierarchy or the two-factor approach. In this section, we will look beyond the content or *what* motivates people. We will look at the *process* of motivation; that is, the kinds of variables which go into the people's choices of actions. Theories associated with the process of motivation were developed by Victor Vroom, Lyman Porter, and Edward Lawler, and are referred to as the expectancy model of motivation.

Victor Vroom's Expectancy Model[8]

In academic circles, Vroom's model of motivation has been widely accepted and has served as the basis for a tremendous amount of research. The model may be less amenable to direct applications to industry as techniques for motivating personnel. Yet it provides a useful framework for understanding the behavior of people in organizations and how people make choices. It is also a model grounded in communication theory, since it deals less with specific determinants of motivation than with the idea that motivation is a process of cognitive variables which reflect *individual differences*. Vroom's three major concepts are summarized in Figure 6-3.

Vroom's model is based on the idea that motivation has to do with the choices people make in order to achieve personal goals. What one person will seek to achieve may be quite different from what another

[8]Op. cit.

FIGURE 6-3

Vroom's expectancy theory. This diagram represents the example from the text in which the student is motivated to work hard in the business communication class to get a B so as to be admitted to the major in business administration.

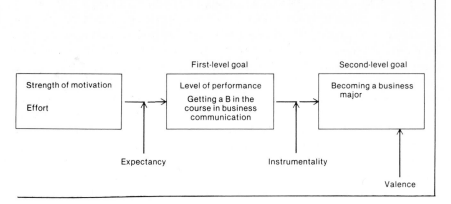

The strength of your motivation depends on
1. Expectancy—your estimate of the probability that your behavior will obtain what you want (usually a first-level goal)
2. Instrumentality—your estimate of the probability that what you want will help you reach a goal (a second-level goal)
3. Valence—the value for you of the goal in comparison with other goals

person may want. Your goals may include a career in business, with a higher salary every year and promotion within the next two years, while a friend's goals may be a year off after college to travel around. The particular needs which give rise to these different goals have no place in Vroom's model. A person usually has many goals he or she seeks to achieve, and not all have the same importance. Vroom talks about the notion of *valence* to explain the strength of a person's preference for a particular goal. Perhaps a salary hike is lower in your scale of values than a quick promotion. The valence of a salary increase is weaker than the valence of a promotion. The promotion is more important to you. Goals, however, are not always directly achievable. In order to obtain a promotion, for example, you may have to perform in a superior manner. Superior performance thus becomes your first-level goal, which needs to be achieved in order to achieve the second-level goal, the promotion. How much you perceive the first-level goal to be *instrumental* in permitting you to achieve the second-level goal is an important factor in helping you decide whether the first-level goal is worth achieving. In technical terms, the valence of the first-level goal is determined by the degree of instrumentality you perceive between first- and second-level goals. If, for example, you feel that performance is unrelated to promotion, you may simply not be motivated to perform that well.

For example, you want very much to major in business administration. In order to achieve this goal, you must at least get a B in a business communication course. Getting a B in business communication is a first-level goal, which must be met in order to achieve the second-level goal of being accepted into the department as a major. If the professor of business communication has a reputation of being tough, you know the only way you can get a B is to work hard and perform well on the tests. If majoring in business is very important to you (has a high valence), if getting a B in business communication is necessary to major in business (getting a B is instrumental in allowing you to achieve your second-level goal), and if working hard is the only way to get a B, then it is likely that you will decide to work hard in the course.

Say, however, that the professor has a reputation for being unfair. Her tests are notoriously difficult and require much more knowledge than can legitimately be expected of a beginning student in business communication. Besides, she is known to play favorites; and unless you politic your way through the course, you are not likely to get much better than a C. In this case, you would not perceive good performance and hard work to be useful in helping you achieve your goal of getting the B necessary to reach the goal of majoring in business. Your motivation to work hard and perform well would not likely be high. In this example, another variable is introduced which Vroom calls *expectancy*. Expectancy refers to whether or not you think one type of behavior will lead to the achievement of a first-level goal. If you expect that working hard won't get you a B, then you will likely not expend much effort on the course.

In summary, the strength of your motivation to behave in a particular way is the result of a combination of factors: (1) expectancy that the behavior will indeed lead to the accomplishment of a first-level goal which (2) you perceive as instrumental in helping you reach a second-level goal which (3) has a positive valence for you; that is, a high degree of importance. You will work hard if (1) you expect working hard to be related to getting a B in the course (expectancy), (2) you perceive that getting a B is necessary for being accepted as a major in the department of business administration (instrumentality), and (3) you place a high importance (valence) on becoming a business major.

The important notion here is that *you* perceive the relationship among expectancy, instrumentality, and valence. It is your perception of the relationship between working hard and getting a B that counts. If you perceive that working hard is unrelated to getting a B or that no matter how much effort you exert, the tests are impossible and unfair, you may not expend what to you would be wasted energy. It is quite possible, of course, that the reputation of the professor as unfair and amenable to political manipulation is based on totally inaccurate rumors. Nevertheless, if you believe the rumors to be true, this is what will count in your mental processes for deciding how to behave in the course.

Although Vroom's model is not directly helpful in determining specific techniques for motivating people, it clearly shows that what management may believe to be employees' goals and what employees may think are management's expectations are not necessarily accurate. Instead, the behavior of both will be a reflection of their respective mutual perceptions—how they see each other. Here again we see the close relationship between understanding motivational processes and understanding transactional communication.

Porter and Lawler's Satisfaction and Performance Model[9]

Vroom's model points out that a person must want to perform; that is, must expect that something desirable will come out of performing at a certain level. However, just wanting to perform may not be enough. In addition to motivation, there are other factors such as a person's *abilities* and *role expectations*. All these factors are important in determining how much and how well that person will perform on the job. You may want very much to become a concert pianist, but may simply not have the ability to perform at Carnegie Hall. You may want to be a successful stockbroker, but not have the financial know-how to really make a go of it.

Porter and Lawler, like Vroom, emphasize the notion of expectancy or a suspected payoff. What a person does is based on the anticipated results of the behavior. This is a tremendous departure from the content theories of motivation. Maslow's need theory and Hertzberg's two-factor theory deal with a *push* view of human behavior: Something, a need, pushes you to act a certain way. Vroom's and Porter and Lawler's approaches deal with a *pull* view of human action: The anticipated consequence of an action pulls you to act a certain way. You will do something when you think that the outcome of the action will bring positive rewards. The perceived effort/performance/ reward relationship is a major force in determining what you will do.

The actual process of decision making is not always totally conscious for most people. You do not usually sit down with pencil and paper and mathematically evaluate valences, expectancies, and instrumentality. Motivation is very interesting to study, because the consequences of actions can be described and perceptions of what constitutes a reward can be discussed and communicated. It is much

[9]Lyman W. Porter and Edward E. Lawler III, *Managerial Attitudes and Performance*, Richard D. Irwin, Homewood, Ill., 1968.

more difficult to describe needs in concrete terms. While Hertzberg's model implied that satisfaction led to higher performance, the expectancy models show that performance can lead to satisfaction—a complete turnabout in the analysis of the performance/satisfaction/ motivation relationship.

Porter and Lawler's model indicates that a person's performance is linked to the rewards that may come about as a result of the performance. There are two types of rewards, intrinsic and extrinsic. Intrinsic rewards come from the feelings you have about yourself as a result of performance. Sometimes you may feel really good about something you did and get a tremendous feeling of accomplishment, an intrinsic reward. Extrinsic rewards come from the organization and are usually associated with the satisfaction of lower-level needs in Maslow's terminology. Extrinsic rewards may include pay, status, job security, and promotions. Extrinsic rewards are only related to performance if they are perceived by the individual as being rewards. For the worker who is terrified at the prospect of performing a supervisory job, a promotion may not be a reward at all, but a cause for worry and anxiety.

Rewards by themselves are not enough, however. They must be linked to what Porter and Lawler call *perceived equitable rewards.* If you get a pay increase which brings your salary from $10,000 to $11,000, but feel that you should be getting $12,000, the pay increase may not be perceived as a reward. Instead of being pleased for getting an extra $1,000, you may feel bad that you did not get an extra $2,000, which in your eyes would be more equitable. You are satisfied only if your actual rewards are equal or superior to what you perceive are equitable rewards.

Applications: The Path-Goal Theory of Leadership[10]

One direct application of the expectancy models of motivation has been to study managers as they influence their employees' perceptions of work goals, personal goals, and ways or paths that lead to goal achievement.

Although the concept of the manager as a leader will be discussed more extensively in Chapter 7, we will deal with the path-goal theory of leadership in this section because it is directly based on our previous discussion of motivation, and it incorporates clearly some communication aspects of the managerial role.

[10]Martin G. Evans, "The Effects of Supervisory Behavior on the Path-Goal Relationship," *Organizational Behavior and Human Performance,* pp. 277–298, May 1970; Robert J. House, "A Path-Goal Theory of Leadership Effectiveness," *Administrative Science Quarterly,* pp. 321–339, September 1971.

Managers can influence their employees to meet organizational goals by rewarding employees when they achieve specific goals related to larger organizational goals. One important part of the manager's role is to clarify for the employees what behavior is most likely to result in the accomplishment of stated goals. Managers must communicate clearly what is expected of employees for goal accomplishment. Managers must also communicate path clarification, or specify behaviors which will lead to goal accomplishment.

The theory became subsequently refined as it isolated four specific kinds of managerial communication:

1. *Directive style:* The manager lets the employees know specifically what is expected of them. No participation from the employees is expected, and the manager gives directions.
2. *Supportive style:* The manager is friendly and shows genuine concern for employees. The manager may treat employees as equals.
3. *Participative style:* The manager elicits and uses suggestions from employees, although the manager retains final decision-making authority.
4. *Achievement-oriented style:* The manager sets challenging goals for employees and expects performance at high levels of excellence. The manager always seeks ways to improve performance.

A manager can use any or all of these styles, depending on two major situational factors. They are (1) the personal characteristics of the employees and (2) the pressures and demands from the environment facing employees.

The two important propositions derived from the path-goal theory of leadership are stated in communication terms. The first proposition is that employees will accept a manager's influence if they perceive the manager's behavior as (1) bringing them immediate satisfaction—that is, permitting them to achieve an immediate goal—or (2) instrumental in bringing them future satisfaction—that is, permitting them to eventually achieve a goal.[11] The key here is the employees' perception of the manager's behavior. Managers must send clear and consistent messages about how employees can use the manager to achieve their goals.

The second proposition is that a manager will motivate employees effectively when (1) satisfaction of the employees' needs depends on effective performance and (2) the manager provides guidance, support, and rewards which help employees reach their goals, particularly

---

[11]Robert J. House and Terrence R. Mitchell, "Path-Goal Theory of Leadership," *Journal of Contemporary Business*, pp. 81–97, Autumn 1974.

when such support and guidance may be lacking in the employees or in their environment.[12] For example, if you think you are particularly good at a certain job, you may not appreciate close supervision in which you get told very specifically what to do and how to do it. In this case, a manager using directive style may be counterproductive; and you may quickly lose incentive to produce if you feel that your abilities are not trusted. On the other hand, if you are new at a specific job and need to be coached, you may resent a manager who seems to expect you to learn the job totally on your own. You do expect some guidance and feel frustrated if none is offered.

The path-goal theory of leadership is interesting from a communication point of view because it is based essentially on the notion that the managers' main task is to reduce the uncertainties of the job for their subordinates. A manager who can clearly communicate what employees are expected to do, how their tasks are related to the achievement of personal goals, and how personal goals are related to larger organizational goals will be an effective motivator.

The questions, then, become: How can the manager clearly communicate to employees what is needed? How can the manager's description of what must be done to reap the promised rewards be made believable? The answers rest not in managerial techniques nor in procedural directives, but in human qualities related to basic communication attitudes and skills.

The manager ultimately must be trusted (1) to know what actions lead to the achievement of what goal, (2) to assess accurately the strengths and limitations of the employees, (3) to assign jobs that can be done, and (4) to deliver the promised rewards.

The need for trust has many implications. Not every manager inspires in subordinates the kind of trust just described. And yet, repeatedly we find that in organizations or departments where managers are so trusted, performance is high.

Of the communication factors which make a difference in the relationship between managers and subordinates, four stand out as basic: (1) the art of trusting, (2) the reduction of defensiveness, (3) the skill of listening, and (4) the appropriate communication style.

The Art of Trusting

What does it mean to trust? How does trust relate to interpersonal communication? Whom and when do you trust? How do you demonstrate that you can be trusted? These important questions do not have simple answers. In this section we present an analysis of the concept

[12]Ibid., p. 84.

of trust, based on a provocative and sensitive analysis by Rossiter and Pearce.[13]

The situational context of trust

According to Rossiter and Pearce, you can only experience trust when your relationship with another person is characterized by *contingency*, *predictability*, and *alternative options*.

"Contingency" refers to a situation in which the outcomes of another person's action significantly affect you. If the other person's actions do not affect you, there is no need for you to trust that person.

"Predictability" refers to the degree of confidence you have in your expectations about the other person's behavior or intentions. In situations where you have low predictability—where you cannot have confidence that the other person will behave in a certain way—you may hope but not trust.

Finally, "alternative options" implies that you are free to do something else besides trusting. Trust is present only by choice.

If any one of these three characteristics is missing, we cannot speak of trust. When the three characteristics are present, trust *may* develop. The word "may" is deliberately emphasized here because, as we will discuss, trust is an option, a choice, and is never automatic. If what happens to you is contingent upon another person's behavior, if you have some basis for predicting how the other person will behave, and if you have a choice about your own behavior, then you are in a situation in which trust may occur. This is usually the case in manager-subordinate relationships. The conditions are usually met for trust to occur: A manager's behavior may affect you in significant ways; you have some basis for determining whether your predictions about the manager's behavior are accurate; and at least some of the time, you have options about what to do.

The cognitive context of trust

When you trust another person, you become vulnerable or at least you increase your vulnerability to that other person. In essence, trusting means that you will let the other person's behavior affect you; and to do so, you must believe that the other person is both willing and able to behave in such a way that you will not experience serious negative consequences. In other words, you trust another person when you believe he or she won't hurt you. Intentions are not enough. Abilities are crucial. Is the other person able or competent to perform the action you predict will take place? After all, a friend may be very well

[13]Charles M. Rossiter, Jr., and W. Barnett Pearce, *Communicating Personally*, The Bobbs-Merrill Company, Inc., Indianapolis, 1975, pp. 119–145.

intentioned and may never wish to hurt you; yet you may not "trust" her to perform surgery on you unless she is a qualified surgeon. The reverse is equally true. Although you may perceive someone as quite competent, if you also perceive that person's intentions to be devious or self-serving, you may withhold trust.

Gaining others' trust does not happen to you by magic, nor can you mechanically follow a tech manual which specifies the steps to be taken to "make others trust you." In fact, there is no sure way to make other people trust you. Trusting other people sometimes encourages them to trust you. Distrusting them, however, almost always will make them distrust you.

How you develop trusting relationships

You cannot force someone to trust you. If someone is bent on misunderstanding you and refuses to perceive you as either well intentioned or competent, there is very little you can do to change that interpretation of what you are like. Anything you do can always be misinterpreted, and everything you say can always be held against you, as further "proof" of that person's original conception of you.

Trust between two people is built by taking risks. For example, you take the first risk and make yourself vulnerable to another person. You do that by accepting the fact that his or her actions may affect you adversely. If the other person accepts your initial move by not exploiting the situation, by not hurting you, that makes the other a little vulnerable to you. The process of mutual trust building has begun. You may then say or do something that makes you a little more vulnerable. The other person may respond in kind. The process goes on, mutually reinforcing itself.

Rossiter and Pearce contend that for a trusting relationship to be established, three factors must be present: (1) You must engage in trusting behavior even though you may not be completely sure that the other will reciprocate. You must take a risk. (2) You and the other person must both be able to trust; that is, you must each not follow impulses to exploit the other, and you must each interpret the other's behavior as trustworthy rather than foolish. (3) You must both be willing to negotiate the process through incremental steps, a little trust at a time.

You cannot force trust on other people. If they are intent on distrusting you, they will always find something to support their belief that you are not trustworthy. Ultimately all you can do is trust in the hope that the other can and will respond in kind. Of course, there is no guarantee that this will happen; and as you take risks in making yourself vulnerable, there is always the possibility that the other person will see you as a fool and will take advantage of you. So you always decide whether the risks are worth taking and whether you can afford to take such risks. In a sense, this implies that to have others trust you, you must actively take some initiative and not simply wait for others to make the first move. If you want to be trusted, you have to make the first gesture, and the opening gambit always involves some risk.

Developing trust in others is not simple. It is a factor of both your behavior and the ability of the other person to trust and to take risks. You have little control over another person's ability to take risks. However, you do have some control sometimes over the degree of risk involved for the other person should he or she trust you.

You can be congruent in the messages you send: Most of the time you do what you say. Your actions can match your rhetoric. Your nonverbal messages fit your verbal ones. If you behave that way, you permit the others to develop greater predictability about your actions. You thus minimize other people's "subjective probability" of guessing wrong about what you will do.

You can sometimes have some degree of control over the outcomes of risk-taking behavior. How you respond to people who take a risk and make a mistake may affect to a large extent their decision to take risks again. You may tell an employee, for example, to go ahead with a project on his or her own, and that you will support the results. If you then criticize the employee when the finished product is not exactly as you would have wished, you make it unlikely for that person to believe that you meant what you said.

If you encourage people to tell you the truth about some matter, and then punish them in some way for the behavior they confessed, they likely will learn to withhold the truth or tell lies. The risks for being truthful with you are simply too great.

How you decide to trust

There are times when you know that you had better not trust another person. Get-rich-fast-without-doing-anything deals smack of deceit. If someone appears trusting toward you, there is no sure way to know whether the person is truly wishing to build a trusting relationship with you or is only feeding you the opening lines of a con game. You must decide whether to risk trusting when you should not or not trusting when you should. If you prefer to err in the direction of trusting when you should not, you may be seen by some people as warm, compassionate, and nice and by others as guillible and stupid. If you choose to err in the direction of not trusting when you should, you may be seen by some people as hard-nosed and shrewd, but by others as distant, cynical, and not trustworthy.

As a manager, you have to come to terms with this issue. Do you buy the sob story some employee gives you to get out of work, and therefore risk being perceived a patsy? Or do you act as the hard-nosed supervisor who is not easily conned? In either case, your behavior will affect employees' behavior.

The kind of cooperation you may get from the people who work with you and for you ultimately depends on whether or not trust exists in the relationship. Your secretary's response to a request to stay overtime and finish an important report may be quite different depending on whether the relationship between the two of you is based on trust or not. Your employees will not send you accurate and open messages if they do not trust you. They must believe that you will not use the information against them. They must expect promises to be kept. They must think that you will not get even with them if they express their feelings honestly. They essentially must see you "on their side" and believe they can depend on you. Only when this happens can you rely on the quality and honesty of their communication with you. You have little control over the total organization's climate which may or may not be favorable to interpersonal trust. You cannot change the inclination of others to trust. But you can regulate your own inclination to trust others. You can choose to be fair, to hold to commitments, to be considerate of others, and not to take advantage of others' trust for your personal gain.

Much of your interpersonal communication depends on how you define your situation. You appraise how threatening or nonthreatening your interaction with others is in terms of your self-esteem. Your communication with others involves some kind of risk, since communication means presenting to others a statement of your self, your role, the situation, and the others that they may conceivably reject. The communication climate and how you can change it is an important part of your guessing how much risk is involved for you in a given situation. You behave on the basis of how safe you think you are. If you do not feel safe, you will likely use defensive strategies. Perhaps you have been in a classroom situation in which the teacher keeps insisting that students participate by discussing issues openly, and then the teacher shoots down their comments or ridicules them when they do. It does not take you long to figure out that publicly being cut down by sarcasm is not comfortable. You learn quickly that the climate is not safe. Your communication takes on defensive strategies designed to protect yourself.

The professor-student relationship is not all that different from any other dyadic relationship. People always figure out whether they are safe or not. Their communication and behavior will rest on that

Reduction of Defensive Climates

assessment. Defensive communication strategies are an indication that a person does not feel secure in some way, at some level.

Defensive strategies   As a manager, it is important for you to understand some of the defensive maneuvers which people engage in. As you learn to recognize these patterns, it may become easier for you to understand the reasons for people's actions. You may also take steps to permit people to feel safer whenever possible.

As coaches tell us, the best defense is often a good offense. People frequently follow this advice when they verbally attack others who may be threatening to them. If direct attack is too dangerous (telling your boss to go jump in the lake may cost you your job), people may resort to sarcasm and ridicule. They may question motives or competence, or put others down. They may exclude others literally or in conversation by using jargon words, the latest slang, private jokes, or topics known to be of great discomfort to the other person. Other, more indirect, aggressive techniques include passive resistance to requests which are made, or late compliance with requests, or marginal performance, doing a job just well enough to avoid blame but not really well enough to be completely acceptable.

Sometimes people will simply avoid putting themselves in a situation where they might be threatened. One way to avoid threats is to simply get out of or not enter a situation likely to produce threat. If a situation is ambiguous—you do not know whether or not it will be threatening to you—you may simply decide to avoid it. If you are not sure what mood your supervisor is in, you may avoid contact. If you are not sure whether a college course is really tough and whether you will be able to perform well, you may simply decide not to take it. If you are afraid to be turned down, you may not ask a girl out for a date or ask a favor from a friend.

The problem with defensive strategies is that they encourage a ritualistic approach to communication and discourage spontaneous interaction.[14] If you value open, free, honest, direct, and trusting communication, what can you do to help build a climate that will increase communication transactions? Again, let us emphasize that having a feeling of safety ultimately depends on the person's perception of the situation. Although you cannot control people's perceptions, you can sometimes control to some extent the stimulus for their perceptions. You may present yourself in a nonthreatening way. It is up to them to perceive you as nonthreatening.

[14]Warren Bennis, *Interpersonal Dynamics: Essays and Readings in Human Interaction*, rev. ed., The Dorsay Press, Homewood, Ill., 1969, pp. 211–212.

Jack Gibb[15] has isolated several categories of behaviors which are likely to provoke defensiveness and other categories of behaviors which are likely to help reduce defensiveness.

Communication which appears evaluative, judgmental, or blaming tends to increase defensiveness. If you feel that people are judging you, criticizing you, or even evaluating you positively, you are likely to feel threatened. Farson, for example, has openly questioned use of praise, or positive evaluations, as supportive or helping communication.[16] In his article, "Praise Reappraised," Farson contends that if you watch the way people respond to compliments or praise, you will note that they invariably seem to react with discomfort, uneasiness, and defensiveness. Their response is often a vague denial of the compliment or even a self-derogation:

Provoking and Reducing Defensiveness

Evaluation or description

> "I really can't take credit for it. . . ."
> "Well, it's nothing, really. . . ."
> "You look nice, too. . . ."
> "Oh, you're just saying that. . . ."
> "Uh, that's OK. . . ."

These statements are all defensive statements, indicating that the situation was perceived as a difficult one. Often people get so flustered when they receive compliments that their discomfort is apparent through their nonverbal behavior. They squirm, they look away, they become flushed, they make denial gestures. Part of the reason for the discomfort is that evaluation, positive or negative, is still evaluation. In Farson's words, "If we are weighed, we might be found wanting." Unless you have built a relationship you trust with the person giving the compliment, you may suspect that person's motives. "What does he want from me?" is often the nonexpressed thought of the person receiving the compliment. It is also possible to predict that a negative item will follow a positive one. When you hear a compliment, you may wait for the other shoe to fall because you are used to the "sandwich technique." Briefly, this technique consists of praising someone about something, then following up with a criticism, then back to something nice. It goes something like this:

[15]"Defensive Communication," *Journal of Communication*, vol. 11, No. 3, pp. 141–148, 1961.

[16]Richard E. Farson, "Praise Reappraised," *Harvard Business Review*, vol. 41, pp. 61–66, September–October 1963.

"Honey, this is a beautiful picture (praise), but you are so messy. You shouldn't smear paint all over the place (criticism). Well, go ahead, honey, and show your pretty picture to Daddy (praise)."

No wonder the child doesn't know what hit him or her. So you get schooled to wait for a reprimand when you hear a compliment.

To avoid as much as possible either making or reacting to evaluations, describe rather than evaluate, make unvalued statements rather than critical ones, ask questions which are relevant and information-seeking rather than rhetorically evaluative. Sometimes questions sound like information seeking when, in fact, they are evaluative or accusative. You hear it between parents and children, teachers and students, husbands and wives when, "Why did you do that?" is asked with a tone of voice which clearly reveals an accusatory reaction.

Control or approaching problems

Communication used to control others is bound to be resisted. The degree of defensiveness aroused depends on the degree of suspicion you have about the controller's motives. If you suspect ulterior motives, you get defensive. You have grown suspicious in a culture where control is often sugarcoated. "You don't want to stay up late and get all tired, do you, honey?" is a devious way of saying, "I want you to go to bed now." "What do doctors recommend?" is a question which sets up an answer that you should buy a product recommended by doctors but sold by that advertiser. Whether the message is personal, political, or mass media, it attempts implicitly to control someone who needs to be changed and is inadequate—and that makes it a threatening message. A preventative against control strategy is to address our communication to problems rather than to people, to issues rather than personalities. Repeatedly telling people what to do is a form of control. While this may be sometimes necessary when the other person needs information and direction, it need not become your habitual pattern when you deal with others. Your relationships with others are likely to be more satisfactory when you encourage them to be responsible for dealing with their own problems. By doing things for people or by telling them what to do, you may imply a subtle lack of trust in their ability. Negative reactions may follow. As a supervisor, give people fewer answers for their problems and ask them more questions. Depersonalize the problem and its possible solution. Talk about a problem/solution as if it could be anyone's. Rather than saying "your problem" or "What you should do," ask, "How does this cause us a problem?" Don't say, "I know how this works. Why don't you . . . ?", but rather, "What do you think is the problem? How could it be fixed?" In fact, "Why don't you . . ."

questions often result in "Yes, but . . ." answers—a typical defensive game.

When you would like your motive not to be known, you employ stratagems, or devious measures, tricks, devices, or games with each other. When you suspect a stratagem is being used on you, you resent it and become defensive. Most people have an aversion to deceit in any form. You do not like to be manipulated. You especially resent the idea that others might think you are foolish enough to fall for their tricks. By developing spontaneity in your relations with others and by not developing certain devices (use a firm handclasp and look someone in the eye and they're sold) for all occasions, but staying flexible in your interactions, you can avoid triggering defensive behaviors induced by obvious or obscure stratagems. The boss who mechanically memorizes employees' names or who automatically pats them on the back does not fool them. Rote rituals seldom substitute for genuine concern and care.

Stratagems or spontaneity

Any behavior which openly conveys lack of feeling, caring, or warmth says to others that you are not concerned. A detached and aloof attitude often gives the impression of rejection. Even by appearing neutral, you can make another person feel unwanted. Defensiveness based on rejection or even possibility of rejection is common. Overcoming this tendency can be described as becoming involved with others, showing empathy, and finding a level of concern for the ideas, the issues, the constraints, the abilities, the behaviors of another person. As we will describe in a later section of this chapter, an attitude of caring and involvement can be communicated by actively listening to others.

Lack of concern or involvement

When a person conveys a feeling of superiority over you, it brings out your defenses. Arrogance, distance, aloofness, haughtiness, or condescension toward you all send you a signal that the other person is not willing or ready to develop a shared or equal relationship. You have difficulty communicating in that situation. Equality is sharing of similarities and differences without having to rank each other on every item or idea, without having to compete for "first place" in every exchange of ideas or messages. In organizations, status and rank are a fact of life, and pretending to be "one of the girls" or "one of the boys" may not work. A supervisor can maintain her distance without

Superior attitude or sharing

haughtiness or any implication that she is better or superior *as a person* than her lower-rank employees.

Dogmatic attitudes or flexibility

People who come on as all-knowing, who appear to need to be right and to win arguments rather than to solve problems, and who tend to impose their views as the only right ones are classic generators of defensiveness in others. For one thing, it is hard to communicate with them unless you happen to agree exactly with their ideas. So dogmatic is this person that you must agree entirely or you will be put down and judged negatively for holding the "wrong" ideas. A person who has a provisional idea of what is going on, who acts as if there were some other ideas to be heard, and who believes that truth does not necessarily always reside in his or her own insides can reduce defensiveness in communication. Having a good idea does not mean that every other idea is wrong and must be stomped on; there is room for some error even in the best answers.

Summary

It is crucial to recognize that behaviors which provoke defensiveness are serious obstacles to effective interpersonal communication. People who communicate judgmentally and dogmatically, who need to control and manipulate others, and who appear unwilling to develop a shared relationship based on mutual trust make interpersonal communication particularly difficult. Once defensiveness is aroused, people tend to resort to shallow rituals and protective behavior. Ritualistic behavior, in turn, is likely to strengthen the motivation of the initial communicator for behaving the way he or she started. Both sender and receiver are caught in the web of self-fulfilling prophecies. Their behaviors feed each other, each person's behavior arousing additional defensiveness in the other. There is no way out of a contest of attack-defend-protect. It is unlikely that the encounter will prove satisfying for either person, because behaviors which provoke defensiveness in the first place are likely to be attacks on the self-esteem of others.

The Skill of Listening

Ask people to state one major problem in communication, and they will likely come up with lack of listening. Supervisors complain their subordinates don't listen. Subordinates complain their bosses don't listen. Parents complain about children and children about parents; teachers about students and students about teachers. Somehow, everyone is not listening.

It is obvious that unless someone listens, any effort to communicate will be lost. After all, communication is a transactional process. It involves the negotiation of mutual meanings; and how can that be accomplished if interaction is one-sided?

Listening is crucial. It is essential not only in order to comprehend the content of a message—which is called *deliberative listening* by Charles M. Kelly[17]—but also in order to understand the feeling context in which the communication is taking place. Listening for the feeling context is called *empathic listening*, or *active listening*, by Carl Rogers.[18]

There are many reasons why people's listening ability is not as effective as others might like it to be.

Some people, for example, may be so egocentric or self-centered that they prefer monologing constantly rather than sharing conversation with anyone. They want to be heard and do not care much about hearing others. At a party, they monopolize the floor and may only relinquish it when the limits of courteous behavior have been so taxed that they can no longer disregard others. While you may be able to avoid such people in social gatherings, it may not be possible to avoid your supervisor who acts that way, since the implicit rules of communication between supervisor and subordinate say that the subordinate is expected to defer to the supervisor. However, strong feelings of resentment may be harbored by the subordinate who is never allowed to say anything.

Other people may be very selective in what they listen to. They pick out only what interests them and reject everything else. A key word gets them started talking, and here again you may lose a chance to be heard.

Still others may only listen to what they want to hear. A supervisor who does not like hearing about a problem may appear to listen and may even give you some kind of an answer, but mostly in order to dispense with the subject quickly. Some people may listen defensively and take everything you say as a personal attack. Others may set you up by listening to what you have to say, only to get ammunition they can use against you in the future.

The common feeling shared by those who are not listened to is frustration, anger, hurt, and often resentment. If you want to encourage people to talk to you and to talk to you meaningfully, then you must be prepared to listen. You must let others know that you will listen. Here

---

[17]"Empathic Listening," in R. Cathcart and L. Samovar (eds.), *Small Group Communication: a Reader*, Wm. C. Brown Co., Dubuque, Iowa, 1974, pp. 340–348.
[18]"Communication: Its Blocking and Facilitating," *Northwestern University Information*, vol. 20, pp. 9–15, 1952.

again the key is congruency between what you say verbally, what you communicate nonverbally, and what you do. You may announce all over the place that you have an open-door policy to your office, but if it is not true, no one in the organization will be fooled. People will know they had better not act on your statement. Perhaps you are never there, or perhaps you make the meetings short by sending cues that you are in a hurry and that the person coming to see you with a problem is really imposing on you and disturbing you. Your half-hearted attempts at listening or at helping the person with a problem are simply not believable and you truly kid no one, except perhaps a newcomer to the organization who has not yet learned the informal rules.

As a facilitator of communication, your role as a manager requires that you facilitate communication and this means you must listen well. You must make it possible for people to talk to you about their jobs, their problems, their feelings, their suggestions. If you really want to help your employees with their job-related problems, you must hear them out in a way which will encourage them to tell you more rather than less, to tell you accurately rather than in a filtered way, to tell you what is fact rather than what you want to hear.

There is really no easy technique that can teach you how to listen. However, the work of Carl Rogers points out that listening reflects, first of all, a basic attitude about people rather than just a set of skills. Naturally, listening is a skill and, for that reason, can be taught and improved. But unless a helping attitude is present, little success can be predicted from simple mastery of a set of how-to-do-its.

As Rogers states,[19] listening reflects a whole orientation to life and people. This orientation implies that *to listen is to have the creative power to imagine how it would make sense to say what the other person is saying.* It implies that the other person is fundamentally important and worth listening to, worth giving some of your attention, energy, and time.

In a sense, you cannot fake active listening. You must *feel* deep inside that people are important in their own right, and you must feel that by listening to them you are sharing with them your feelings of respect. Active listening, Rogers points out, must be firmly based on the basic attitudes of the listener. You cannot use it as a technique if your fundamental attitudes about people are in conflict with its basic concepts. If you try, your behavior will be empty, and everyone will recognize it. Unless you have a spirit which genuinely respects the potential worth of an individual and trusts that person's capacity for self-direction, you cannot begin to be an effective listener.

[19]Ibid.

What does active listening consist of? Very simply, to listen to a person *without passing judgment on what is being said, and to mirror back what has been said to indicate that you understood what feelings the speaker was putting across.* It seems simple enough. However, the implications of this procedure are tremendous. By withholding judgment and by showing that you understand the feelings of another person, you tell that other person to be free to say more. You tell that other person there is no risk of being judged and found stupid or silly. You remove the threat that another person always presents to the personal defenses. Effective communication is free to happen once that threat has been removed. By mirroring what another person says, you help build a climate in which you can be accepting, noncritical, and nonmoralizing. People then feel safer.

All of you want to be listened to and understood. When you are not, you feel you are not worth much since people won't even think enough of you to take the time to listen to you. What do you hear most people complain about? Not being listened to. "I can't talk to my parents, they never listen." Or, "I can't talk to my son, he just won't listen." Or, "I am quitting this job. My boss never listens to anything I say. It's as if I did not exist."

To listen actively to another human being may be the greatest gift you can give a person. The power to listen is a remarkably sensitive skill, perhaps the greatest talent of the human race. It is certainly the skill that makes interpersonal communication truly effective and rewarding for all concerned.

Communication Styles

No two people behave in exactly the same manner. The same person does not act the same way all the time. However, there are regularities in human communication. Although most people are quite capable of communicating in a variety of ways, they often choose to fall back on old patterns of handling their communication transactions with others. Such characteristic ways to deal with interpersonal situations are called *styles.* People develop their own individual styles for communicating. While it is possible to use many different styles, people tend to fall back on a given and preferred style in certain situations.

Before we go on identifying some common styles of communication, let us emphasize three important points.

1. A range of styles is available to all of you. There are many different ways to respond to interpersonal situations, and you use them all at one time or another. Each way has it specific consequences.
2. Every style is effective in some specific situations.

3. The habitual use of one style indiscriminately for all situations creates interpersonal problems and may be counterproductive.

The description of communication styles is based on Virginia Satir's discussion of patterns of communication.[20] The five basic communication patterns or styles she describes include (1) the blaming or aggressive style, (2) the placating or nonassertive style, (3) the computing or intellectual style, (4) the distracting or manipulative style, and (5) the leveling or assertive style.

The blaming or aggressive style

The person using the blaming stance or the aggressive style tends to act in a demanding fashion with others. Blamers are faultfinders and come on rather critically with others. Blamers often act in a superior fashion and are often described as very bossy people. When the behavior is carried to extremes, blamers become tyrannical and loud and get their way at the expense of other people's rights and feelings. Blamers send messages which imply that everybody is stupid for not believing as they do. Other people's wants and feelings simply don't count. The major goal for blamers in interpersonal relationships is to win and dominate, forcing the other person to lose. Winning is often ensured by humiliating, degrading, and overpowering other people so they are too weak to express and defend their rights. The immediate consequences of blaming and aggressive behavior, unfortunately, are that it often works in the sense of providing emotional release and a sense of power for blamers. They get what they want without experiencing direct negative reactions from others. A blaming boss, particularly one who holds power over you, may be feared and may scare you into doing what he or she wants. If you are overpowered, chances are you will not take on the boss directly. However, in the long run, the consequences of such a style can be quite negative. Blamers usually fail to establish close relationships and feel they have to be constantly vigilant against other people's attacks and possible retaliation. They tend to feel alienated from other people, misunderstood, and unloved. They are usually lonely people.

The placating or nonassertive style

Placaters always try to please and often attempt to ingratiate themselves. They apologize constantly, seldom disagree, and talk as though they could do almost nothing for and by themselves. They must always have someone else's approval. Placaters violate or simply ignore their own rights, their needs, and their feelings, and are

[20]*Peoplemaking*, Science and Behavior Books, Inc., Palo Alto, Calif., 1972.

unable to express them in a direct and forthright manner. When they do express their feelings or thoughts, they usually do it in a very apologetic and self-effacing way so that others often tend to disregard them. The basic message of nonassertion is that the placater does not really count and can be taken advantage of. And the message gets through: Placaters often *are* taken advantage of. They show lack of respect for themselves and, as a result, teach others not to respect them. The basic goal of placaters is to avoid conflict at all cost and to appease. Nonassertive supervisors, for example, have great difficulty saying "no" to their employees' requests and end up trying to please everyone, which in the long run pleases no one. They are afraid of hurting other people's feelings; they are worried that saying no or standing up for their own needs will cause other people to dislike them, or to think them foolish, stupid, or selfish.

The computing or intellectual style

Computers are people who tend to rely on intellectualizations to deal with interpersonal situations. The style requires an appearance of being calm, cool, and collected. Feelings are not allowed to show. A person using this style believes that emotions are best kept hidden inside since feelings distract from the work at hand. The style requires an emphasis on logic and rationality. People relying on this style are very distrustful of feelings and personal emotionality. "If people were only reasonable and used their heads, there would not be so many problems around here" is the motto. Intellectualizers often feel quite vulnerable and simply deal with their fears of inadequacy by presenting a distant and aloof front so no one can really get too close to them. They often choose professions which do not put them in much contact with other people, whom they find unpredictable and irrational.

The distracting or manipulative style

The distracting style is based on not dealing directly with interpersonal situations. Avoidance of threatening situations is the motto, and people using the style have developed all kinds of strategies to manipulate themselves out of unpleasant encounters. If the encounters themselves cannot be avoided, the style for dealing with people is characterized by distracting maneuvers, or by manipulating other people's feelings. Anger, hurt, and guilt are often used as manipulative devices to get others to do what is wanted. The supervisor who gets employees to work overtime by appealing to their potential guilt feelings will use verbal ploys such as, "How could you let me down after all I have done for you?"

The leveling or assertive style

Levelers are able to stand up for their rights and express feelings, thoughts, or needs in a direct, honest, straightforward manner. Messages are all congruent. Tone of voice, gestures, eye contact, and stance all fit the words that are spoken. Actions also match words, and the assertive people follow through on what they say they will do.

In the assertive style, standing up for one's rights is never done at the expense of another person's rights. There is respect for oneself, but also respect for others and room for compromise or negotiation. The basic message of leveling is "This is what I think, or this is how I see the situation" and does not imply domination or humiliation of the other people if they do not happen to think or see things the same way. Leveling involves respect, but not deference. The goal of leveling is communication and mutuality; and whenever conflicts of rights or needs arise, the attitude is to solve them together with the other people involved.

Although leveling and communicating assertively is no guarantee of getting your own way, it does have some very positive consequences. It usually increases your self-respect and results in greater self-confidence. If you can say what you feel and think without fear, you will feel good about having done it. Whether others agree with you or do what you want almost becomes incidental. You may not get a raise after asking for it; but if you explained honestly and directly the reasons why you feel you are entitled to one, you will feel good about having expressed yourself. You stood up for what you believed. If the supervisor heeds the request, so much the better. If not, at least you will have the satisfaction of having said your piece and you may, as a result, harbor less resentment toward the supervisor.

The placater who does not bring up the subject for fear of being turned down, the manipulator who complains constantly to others about the unfairness of management, the aggressive person who engages in heated and loud arguments with the supervisor, all may develop strong feelings of resentment in addition to not getting the raise.

A good deal of literature is now available if you want to read more on the assertive style of communication. Some sources are included in the bibliography.

The basic point about assertive communication is that it is the style which, in our opinion, is most likely to foster mutual trust, self-respect, and respect from others. Those are all vital ingredients for effective communication transactions on the job.

SUMMARY

Not everybody performs as well as everybody else. Much of this difference is related to motivation and management styles and techniques. In studying motivation you can learn from several different ways of looking at the reasons people are motivated and the theories about improving motivation. Abraham Maslow wrote about a classical series of needs which people have and which can be counted on to describe many behaviors. The arrangement of needs into a "hierarchy" or order of importance begins with physiological needs and continues with safety needs, social needs, esteem needs, and finally self-actualization needs.

David McClelland claimed that three basic motives can describe what makes people perform. In his theory he described needs for achievement, for affiliation, and for power. Frederick Hertzberg reports that motivating factors are related to satisfaction in job content and "hygiene" factors are associated with dissatisfiers including the company, supervision, salary, work conditions, and status. Hertzberg says that hygienic factors do not motivate, and managers must pay attention to the content of the job itself to improve motivation.

Michael Maccoby describes four managerial types based on character and emotional attitudes: the craftsman, the jungle fighter, the company man, and the gamesman. He describes the gamesman as the newest phenomenon in the field of management activities.

There are many ways to analyze motivation. Victor Vroom says you should look at the choices people make when they try to achieve their goals. He proposes that strength of motivation is conditioned by how intensely you see the goal as important, whether doing the job well will help you achieve the goal, and whether the goal is important. You make the decision. It is your own analysis of the situation which determines how you respond. Lyman Porter and Edwin Lawler believe that you will do whatever will result in a payoff to you. There are intrinsic rewards or payoffs which mean those feelings you have about the performance, and the extrinsic rewards which include the same factors in Maslow's hierarchy such as job security and status.

The path-goal theory says that managers will communicate clearly how a particular goal or satisfaction can be reached immediately or how doing something now will result in a later payoff. The manager helps the employee understand how the goal can be of value by reducing the uncertainties of the job.

Like many kinds of motivation, this system depends on trust. The study of trust is an issue in itself, which involves the kinds of situations in which trust can occur, how people develop trusting relationships, and how and when you decide to trust somebody. Defensive climates will induce people to act defensively. How you may be provoked into behaving defensively is an elaborate study, but it is possible to learn ways to reduce defensive communication and improve effectiveness.

Listening is a skill which can be taught and which can influence the relationships in an organization. One of the greatest gifts you may bestow on another is to listen attentively and empathically.

Styles of behaving with other people can also affect your management capabilities. Blaming, placating, computing, and distracting are nonfunctional kinds of behaviors. Leveling or assertive behaviors have much more chance of succeeding in your relations with others. Effective communication transactions depend on reducing the manager's reliance on only one style for all occasions, on the manager's ability to choose the appropriate style for the occasion, and to avoid getting in the rut of using only a limited range of responses for all situations.

PART THREE
THE PRACTICE OF MANAGING BY COMMUNICATION

Part Three deals exclusively with what we consider to be the practice of communication in organizational settings. What managers do through the exercise of their communication abilities is lead; make decisions, often in groups; and manage interpersonal and intergroup conflict. These activities, we contend, are accomplished through the vehicle of communication. In Part Three we claim communication as the methodology of management. This is what we mean by "managing by communication." To lead and exercise power, managers must relate to others. Leaders and followers are bound in communication transactions. Without followers there can be no leader. Chapter 7 deals with the concept of leadership—what leadership is, where it comes from. We survey the numerous approaches taken to understand such a pervasive phenomenon. Chapter 8 presents a study of group communication processes and how they affect decision making. Finally, in Chapter 9, we discuss conflict, how it is managed, whether it can be resolved, and how it can fruitfully be utilized to serve the organization's purposes.

CHAPTER 7

LEADERSHIP AND POWER

"Because of their transcendent practical importance, no successful leader has ever been too busy to cultivate the symbols which organize his following." Walter Lippmann

**APPLIED
LEADERSHIP**

Leadership has to do with the ability to influence others toward the achievement of common goals. Ever since mankind became an organized and interdependent system, people have been interested in the problem of who tells whom what to do and under what circumstances. Petr Kropotkin, in his book *Mutual Aid*, was critical of the Social Darwinists who proposed a social and economic system based on "survival of the fittest." Kropotkin's view was that even the lower animals survived better in organized, democratically run societies where interdependence was permitted by the integration of leader roles and supporting roles. This may be identified as an early precursor of the behavioral theories of management described in our first part of this book, exemplified by McGregor's Theory X and Y and Likert's Systems 1 through 4.

Even earlier, however, Quintilian (42–118) and Longinius (210–273), writing about the idealized state of human communication and rhetoric, believed that the "good man speaking well" could direct the fortunes of politics and commerce. They, along with Aristotle (384–322 BC) in his *Rhetoric*, proposed means of persuading others by ethical proofs, by logics, or by the use of emotion. All their principles, however, were directed at open discussion and honest purpose. Leading had to do with influencing others through communication.

Leading is based on communication. You communicate not only data or information but also, and very important, attitudes and assumptions. You communicate clearly what any course of action offers that may benefit your subordinates or others you wish to influence. In any leadership situation the values to be gained and the sanctions to be imposed if certain courses of action are not taken are either stated or implied. Leaders are persons who can articulate clearly to others the consequences of actions, policies, events, decisions, or solutions.

The literature on leadership is abundant. Much of it is confusing. In this section, let's look at three approaches to the study of leadership and highlight their implications for communication.

The Trait Approach[1]

There was a time when it was assumed that leaders were born to their roles. Historically, succession to power was determined by birth, as in a monarchy where the firstborn son becomes the crown prince and then the king. Political power went with the family name. Even today, a certain amount of economic and social power appears to be

---

[1]An excellent discussion of the trait theory and other developments in leadership studies can be found in R. M. Stogdill, *Handbook of Leadership*, The Free Press, New York, 1974.

inherited. A Ford or a Rockefeller, several generations removed from his ancestor who first became a leader of industry, still carries a responsibility, and perhaps a propensity, for leadership.

If you were asked to list traits that describe leaders, you might come up with characteristics such as intelligence, charisma, strength, integrity, decisiveness, and self-confidence. You would not be far off from the early trait research. The search for leadership traits which would distinguish leaders from nonleaders occupied leadership scholars for many years, but yielded many inconclusive results.

For one thing, few traits—among them intelligence, extroversion, self-assurance, and empathy—were discovered which truly distinguished leaders from nonleaders. But all the research shows is that persons who achieve and maintain leadership positions tend to have those traits. It does not say that people not in leadership positions do not have those traits also. In other words, leaders do not have a monopoly on intelligence or self-confidence.

In addition, personality traits are hard to define and to measure reliably. Much controversy exists, for example, about the meaning of intelligence and what exactly intelligence tests measure.

As a result of these difficulties, research on traits was pretty much abandoned during the 1950s. The greatest limitation to applying the trait approach, however, comes from the fact that traits do not operate one by one, independently, but get demonstrated in leadership transactions. Leadership traits not only interact with other traits in the leader, but, more important, are influenced significantly by followers' interactions. "In a land of the blind, a one-eyed man is king." A leader is a leader only in relation to followers. Other factors besides the internal makeup of a given person have to be considered to explain leadership behavior.

Communication implications

The trait approach views leadership as distinct from communication. When it does mention communication skills, it takes a rather static perspective of the communication process. The fundamental assumption of the trait approach is not trainable. Leadership does not depend on anything else but you. In communication terms, it is as though you believed that simply because you sent a message, it was necessarily received as you intended it. You know that communication is more complex a process, and that simply telling someone something does not necessarily generate understanding or compliance. The same goes for leadership. You may be very smart, very self-confident, very extroverted; but the situation may be one in which others may not wish to be led by you. Influence and leadership have to be communicated as a transactional process.

FIGURE 7-1

Task-functional behavior: Behavior of members which is necessary for a group to get its job done.

1. *Information seeking or giving:* Requesting or supplying factual material, objective data; seeking or giving relevant information about a group concern; asking and giving ideas, generalizations.
2. *Opinion seeking or giving:* Requesting or supplying opinions and beliefs; evaluating; helping the group find out what members think or feel about what is being discussed, particularly concerning its value rather than its factual basis.
3. *Initiating activity:* Starting the discussion; proposing tasks, goals, solutions; defining a problem or an aspect of a problem; suggesting new ideas, new definitions of the problem, or new organization of new material.
4. *Clarifying or elaborating:* Giving examples, illustrations; paraphrasing; interpreting; developing meanings; trying to envision how a proposal might work out; clearing up confusions; indicating alternatives and issues.
5. *Coordinating:* Showing relationships among ideas or suggestions; trying to draw together various trains of thought or effort of group members.
6. *Summarizing:* Restating information, opinions, or suggestions in concise form after a group has discussed them.
7. *Consensus testing:* Sending up a "trial balloon" to see if the group is nearing a conclusion or to identify points where agreement has not yet been reached; direct checking with the group to see how much agreement has been reached.

Source: *Adult Leadership,* 1953, 1, 8, 17–18.

The Functional Approach

Developed in the field of social science and group dynamics, this approach looked at the *functions* leaders perform or leader behaviors which assist a group to do its work and maintain order. You will note that the two general areas of functions essentially reflect the earlier behavioral theories about management which assert that you must pay attention not only to the production of workers but also to their human needs and motivation.

Lists of functions were developed and were clearly divided into three parts: *task functions* which moved the group to get the job done; *maintenance functions* which affect the behavior of members toward building and strengthening the organization as a working unit; and *nonfunctional* or *dysfunctional* behaviors which do not help the group in any way and even actually harm the organization and the work it is trying to do. These functions are listed in Figures 7-1, 7-2, and 7-3.

The Ohio State University and Michigan University studies

In this section we will review briefly the Ohio State University and the Michigan University studies, and the managerial grid which refined the functional approach to leadership. The Ohio State University Study and the Michigan University Studies[2] sought to isolate

[2]Stephen Kerr, C. A. Schriesheim, C. J. Murphy, and R. M. Stogdill, "Toward a Contingency Theory of Leadership Based upon the Consideration and Initiating Structure Literature," *Organizational Behavior and Human Performance,* pp. 62–82, August 1924.

1. *Climate making and encouraging:* Developing and maintaining a friendly, warm, relaxed, acceptive, and permissive atmosphere; seeking to reduce inhibitions; facilitating interaction; being responsive to others; praising others and their ideas; agreeing with and accepting contributions of others.
2. *Gatekeeping:* Attempting to keep communication channels open; helping others to contribute, participate, or "get into" the discussion by perceiving their nonverbal indications of a desire to participate.
3. *Harmonizing:* Reducing and reconciling misunderstandings, disagreements, and conflicts when possible; reducing tension or relieving negative feelings by jesting; "pouring oil on troubled waters"; "putting a tense situation into a wider content"; encouraging others to objectively study differences; mediating as a third party to hostile, aggressively competing sides.
4. *Compromising:* When the member's own idea of status is involved in a conflict, offering to compromise his or her own position; admitting error; practicing self-discipline to maintain group cohesion.
5. *Expressing group feeling:* Sensing the group's feelings or mood about an issue and expressing it; sharing own feelings; describing reactions of the group to ideas or solutions, seeking the group reaction, empathizing.
6. *Setting standards:* Expressing standards or criteria for the group to use in choosing its content or procedures; applying standards in evaluating group functioning and production.
7. *Evaluating:* Submitting group decisions or accomplishments against goals.

Source: *Adult Leadership*, 1953, 1, 8, 17–18.

FIGURE 7-2

Maintenance behavior: behavior of members which builds and strengthens the group as a working unit.

---

1. *Being aggressive:* Working for status by criticizing or blaming others; showing hostility against the group or some individual; deflating the ego or status of others.
2. *Blocking:* Interfering with the progress of the group by going off on a tangent; citing personal experiences unrelated to the problem; arguing too much on a point, rejecting ideas without consideration.
3. *Self-confessing:* Using the group as a sounding board; expressing personal feelings or points of view that are not oriented toward the needs of the group.
4. *Competing:* Vying with others to produce the most or the best ideas, talk the most, play the most roles, gain favor with the leader.
5. *Seeking sympathy:* Trying to induce other members to be sympathetic to one's problems or misfortunes; deploring one's own situation or disparaging one's own ideas to gain support.
6. *Special pleading:* Introducing or supporting suggestions related to one's own pet concerns or philosophies; lobbying.
7. *Horsing around:* Clowning; joking in an inappropriate or unnecessary manner; mimicking; disrupting the work of the group.
8. *Seeking recognition:* Attempting to call attention to oneself by loud or excessive talking, extreme ideas, unusual behavior.
9. *Withdrawing:* Acting indifferent or passive; resorting to excessive formality; daydreaming, doodling; whispering to others, wandering from subject.

*In using classifications like these, people need to guard against the tendency to blame anyone (whether themselves or another) who falls into "nonfunctional behavior." It is more useful to regard such behavior as a symptom that all is not well with the group's ability to satisfy individual needs through group-centered activity. Further, people need to be alert that what appears as "blocking" to one person may appear to another as a needed effort to "clarify" or "mediate."
Source: *Adult Leadership*, 1953, 1, 8, 17–18.

FIGURE 7-3

Nonfunctional behaviors: Behavior of members which does not help and sometimes actually harms the group and the work it is trying to do.*

several dimensions of leader behaviors. Their analyses yielded two broad categories of *initiating structure* and *consideration*, very basically the task and maintenance dimensions cited earlier.

Initiating structure refers to the ability of leaders to define and structure their roles in relation to their subordinates to achieve organizational goals. Initiating structure includes behaviors such as organizing work, making assignments, setting deadlines, and assigning specific tasks.

Consideration refers to the ability of leaders to develop relationships with others that are characterized by trust, respect, and regard for their feelings. Consideration includes behaviors such as helping people with their problems, being friendly, being open and approachable, and treating people as equals.

The studies[3] also yielded two basic dimensions of leadership behavior which were labeled "employee orientation" and "production orientation."

Both the Ohio and the Michigan studies sought to determine which leadership style was most effective. Both were somewhat inconclusive. The Ohio studies provided some data to support the idea that leaders who initiate structure a lot, and who are also high on consideration, are the most effective. Yet in some cases, leaders who initiate a lot of structure generate a lot of complaints and grievances on the part of the subordinates. The conclusions of the Michigan studies were that employee-oriented leaders were usually more effective than strictly production-oriented leaders.

The managerial grid A highly visual and descriptive system for looking at leadership has been used in research and training. Blake and Mouton's[4] managerial grid is very familiar to students and practitioners of leadership styles. It has been adapted to many management studies and teaching efforts and provides an excellent model for graphically showing different leadership styles. Whether you are an industrial manager, a schoolteacher, a parent, or a committee chairperson, this grid speaks to the concerns you may have for either people or for production. This relates again to the leaders' basic assumptions about people and how they fit into the world of work, decisions, actions, and events. Blake and Mouton assume that production and people are interdependent.

[3]R. Kahn and D. Katz, "Leadership Practices in Relation to Productivity and Morale," in D. Cartwright and A. Zander (eds.), *Group Dynamics: Research and Theory*, 2d ed., Harper and Row, New York, 1960.

[4]R. R. Blake and J. S. Mouton, *The New Managerial Grid*, Gulf Publishing Co., Houston, Tex., 1978; L. A. Klos, "Measure Your Leadership with the Managerial Grid," *Supervisory Management*, vol. 19, pp. 10–17, 1974.

Leadership styles reflect concerns for that relationship. Leaders, they assert, must be aware of both production and people and how they interrelate to form effective organizations. Performance is based on how a leader can influence the people and their production and make an appropriate balance. They propose a preferred style (located on the upper right quadrant of their grid, or numerically identified as 9,9 leader or manager) for most organizations. (See Figure 7-4, page 186.)

Briefly, the five divisions have been characterized as examples of leadership or management which reflect on the horizontal axis a concern for production or task and on the vertical axis a concern for people or process.

By identifying where you are on the grid, you can assess your own style of leading and figure out how you may move more toward Blake and Mouton's recommended quadrant of 9,9. Figure 7-5 describes briefly the typical leadership styles discussed by Blake and Mouton. However descriptive is the grid to permit your looking at optional styles of leadership, we must caution that the 9,9 leader may not always be most effective. As you will see in our section on the contingency theories, it is apparent that some structures may not need high concern with people to do an effective job. A rescue team from the fire department may be very concerned with their interpersonal relationships while resting in the firehouse; but once they get on the job, the task concern becomes nearly total. Groups whose total concern is for social interaction may not be interested in a task leader. For example, at an informal party a compulsive game player may unsuccessfully try to get guests involved in organized games: "C'mon everybody, we're going to play charades. . . ."

Concentrating on only one factor, leadership style, omits some important variables which are treated in the next section.

The problem with the studies discussed above is that they had little success in making consistent connections between leadership behaviors and group performance. Other factors besides the leader's behavior affect the outcomes of group work. However, the functional approach made three important contributions to the study of leadership.

Communication implications

First, it gives to scholars, analysts, and practitioners a very descriptive taxonomy of what is really going on in an organization. It describes what is happening. Some earlier views (trait theories, for example) had a tendency to prescribe, predict, direct, or order what *should* go on between leaders and followers. Functional analysis, more true to fact, permits us to watch the rise and fall of interactions as they occur.

A second contribution of this approach is in its emphasis on both

FIGURE 7-4

The managerial grid.
Source: **From Robert R. Blake and Jane S. Mouton, "Managerial Facades,"** *Advanced Management Journal,* **p. 31, July 1966.**

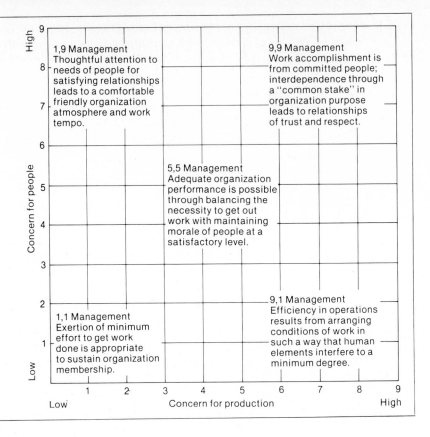

the task and maintenance (process) functions. Again there emerges the persistent reminder that organizations are composed of people as well as machines; that people will operate as emotional, psychological, and social creatures as well as physical or economic entities like cogs in a wheel of production.

A third important contribution is recognition that leadership may be trained for. When we believe that all leaders are tall, it is difficult to stretch a short person to be tall enough to lead others. The short person, therefore, cannot be eligible for leading. That view limits leadership to those whose traits already exist, and therefore limits maximum use of potential leadership resources in the society. On the other hand, if we believe functions make a person a leader, then there arises the possibility people can be trained to perform those functions. This is more true to the nature of what is going on in organizations. If you watch, you can see people learning how to handle certain activities, groups, assignments, teams, task forces, committees, or sections and thus emerging as leaders. If leading can be learned by on-the-job practice, it likely can be learned in special class settings or

(a) 1,1 at the lower left corner. This leader has low concern for people and low concern for production. "Don't let the first sergeant know your name" or "It ain't my job . . ." characterizes this leader. This leader tries to keep up just enough production to not be caught loafing and just enough interest in followers so they don't revolt or complain to superiors. Neither the production needs of the company nor the personal needs of workers can be trusted to this manager. This is the invisible leader by choice.

(b) 9,1 at the lower right corner. This leader believes in all work and no play, and considers it weak to be concerned about emotional or psychological needs of the subordinates. Any attempt to involve this leader with the followers is likely to be refused as a waste of time and "pampering of the help." Such a leader will take better care of the equipment and machines than of the people. This is a nose-to-the-grindstone leader.

(c) 1,9 at the upper left corner. This leader shows very high concern for people and low concern for production. "Keep a happy ship" is the motto. Even if the job never gets done, the friendliness and pleasures of the subordinates are most important. This leader has difficulty giving orders because they may elicit an unfavorable response from the followers. This is the popularity contest leader.

(d) 5,5 in the center. At first glance this leader may seem balanced and a good compromise because of a modicum of concern for production and for people. But in practice, this leader has to do a juggling act between production and people. The leader trades off a sometime emphasis on people with a spurt of task energy to get the work done. Followers find this most unsettling because the leader can't be depended on: one day a good guy, and the next a hard-driving bossy ringmaster. If you want help, you may or may not get it from this leader, depending on when you ask. This is the on-again-off-again leader.

(e) 9,9 in the upper right corner. Proposed as the most ideal style, this is a team leader with high concern for both production and people. This leader must motivate people for achievement of the task, and followers appear to find satisfaction in working with this leader because they believe the leader is interested in them as well as the job; and when the job is accomplished, then follower satisfaction is high. Although this leader must be aware of many factors to keep the people motivated and the job moving, it is possible to sharpen skills needed for this style by training and practice.

FIGURE 7-5
Blake and Mouton's leadership styles.

by persistent study. One can learn how to perform those functions of leadership needed in organizations.

Scholars associated with this approach include Tannebaum and Schmidt, Fiedler, and Hersey and Blanchard. What is stated in this theory is that how a leader should lead depends on (1) the leader's own characteristics, (2) the characteristics of the subordinates, and (3) the forces acting in the situation or environment. It is important to note that leadership theories have evolved from highly prescriptive ones which said "You should" to contingency ones which say "It all depends."

The Contingency Approach

One implication of this change is that our way of looking at leadership is more complex than before. We take more things into consideration. Also, we describe more realistically what is happening in an organization.

Another implication is that training people for leadership roles has consequently become more complex. Still another is that we have begun to recognize the matrix of communication which binds together all the elements of leading. For the purpose of this book, that last implication is most significant.

The Tannenbaum and Schmidt model[5]

The Tannenbaum and Schmidt model depicted in Figure 7-6 brings forth very clearly the role of communication in leadership. Each relationship described in the model must rely on messages from the leader to subordinates. Not all messages are given verbally, of course. Some are implicit or nonverbal in the relationship. Even those nonverbal signals and messages, however, are clearly transmitted and clearly understood if the organization is to function. As a communicator, you must be aware of the forces operating in the situation, in the followers, and in yourself. As we describe these, keep in mind how many of the factors relate to communication and to an ability to properly read, transmit, or analyze the effects of messages on the organization and its members.

[5]R. Tannenbaum and W. H. Schmidt, "How to Choose a Leadership Pattern," originally published in *Harvard Business Review*, 1958, vol. 36, no. 2, pp. 95–106. This article was updated and republished as an HBR Classic, in 1973, vol. 51, no. 3, pp. 162–180, with an additional diagram on p. 167.

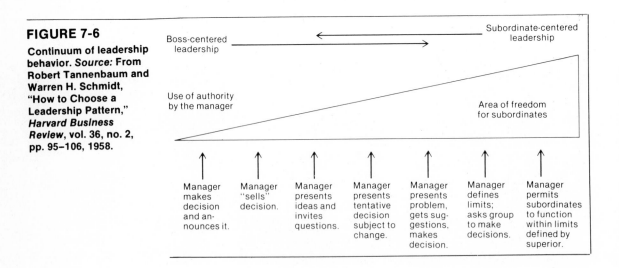

FIGURE 7-6

Continuum of leadership behavior. *Source:* **From Robert Tannenbaum and Warren H. Schmidt, "How to Choose a Leadership Pattern,"** *Harvard Business Review,* **vol. 36, no. 2, pp. 95–106, 1958.**

Situational factors.   What are the norms and values of your organization or your group? Do you have a system of communication already in operation such as memos, policy manuals, job descriptions, MBO documents, project proposals, budgets, orders, directives, projections of sales or production, statements of aims or purposes? How clear are the members about what the organization does? Does the group, unit, organization, class, company, or college have a record of effectiveness in getting things done? How do members as a group feel about themselves and their work? Are there special considerations of physical surroundings or hierarchies to be known? What is the immediate task? Can it be done in time? Can it be done by the subunit assigned to it? What other forces will need to be involved? Is there a need for immediate decisions and long-term implementation?

Although this does not exhaust the questions to be asked, let us emphasize that the situation and environment should be studied carefully for its implications of the total organization, tasks, time, and resources available for accomplishment.

Leader factors.   The leader has values, norms, attitudes, assumptions, tendencies, as well as information and intelligence. What this says is that to be effective as a leader, you should know yourself very well. Do you think workers should be ordered around? Should subordinates enjoy the experience of this task as well as get it done? Is this team capable of winning? Are they competent? How will you judge performance? Should you keep close charge of every part of the project? How much is good for them to know? How clear can you make your orders? How much time should you spend letting the questions arise? How much time do you have now to get the project under way as compared with how much time you can spare to keep checking on it? How much do you know about the project? How much do they know? Do you write better than you speak? Who are the key persons to involve? How much involvement is appropriate? How well do you know these key persons?

Follower factors.   That the rest of the organization is made up of human beings is a good point for a leader to remember. Each member of a team, class, group, company, or project is another person with internal needs for self-esteem, reward, motivation, etc. How much attention can be paid to the individual characteristics and personalities of the followers will depend on factors such as the group size, the expectations of both the leader and the followers, the time involved, the type of task, the situation. The leader must make a judgment about how to take into account the factors of task—disseminating information, orders, instructions, praise, blame, data—

and factors of maintenance—process, emotion. Are these followers accustomed to independence, or do they depend on receiving detailed orders? Are they convinced of the need to accomplish the task? Are there wide differences among them in their abilities, intellect, skills, needs, values, norms? How can those differences be accommodated? What are the followers' expectations about how a leader acts?

Interdependence of factors. Only a sampling of the factors is possible here. An alert, informed, articulate leader can help a group generate these questions which are most useful to the task being done, and can help arrive at answers. The individual factors of the leader, the situation, and the followers are complex by and of themselves. They do not, however, operate by and of themselves. They operate in relation to each other so that a change in one element may necessitate an adjustment in one or both of the others. There is little agreement among management experts on what is easiest to change—situations, leaders, or followers. What is evident, however, is that a good leader must be alert to all factors and capable of looking for better ways to respond to difficulties arising because of a change in any of the factors. For example, changes may occur in the timing of the situation which will have to be adjusted to. A leader alert to this factor will be able to renegotiate the task with followers and perhaps adjust his or her own manner of handling the event. One simple example is a class in which the instructor assigns a major term paper for a date in February, and just before it is due school has to be closed for three days because of snow and sleet. Does the instructor adjust the time? Does the class expect a reprieve on this assignment? Does the instructor ask the class if they want more time, or simply assume nobody has finished the assignment and therefore give another week to do it? What would be the reaction of students if the instructor imposed the deadline as it appeared in the syllabus without regard to the changed situation in the real world?

In another example of the interdependence of these factors, a committee is formed to recommend to the local school board a plan for summer school. A leader is elected. At the first meeting, subcommittee assignments are made by the leader, appointing members present to serve. At the second meeting, it is learned that only half of the persons appointed were present; but a new group of parents has appeared and wants to be included. How does the leader respond to a new group of followers, many of whom did not vote for that person to lead? What about reconstituting the subcommittees? Is there a problem with how much information the new people have to be given? More important, how welcome are they to join the larger committee? What feelings are going to be aroused by inclusion of new members? It is not improbable that the leaders may have to persuade the committee to form a new set of subcommittees or to use a different system entirely. It is also possible that the leader, elected by a group which is no longer identifiable, may have to gain a vote of confidence from the "new" group before proceeding.

What we are emphasizing is that leadership involves (1) knowing about how the factors of leaders, followers, and situations interact with each other, (2) being sensitive enough to recognize the forces in each of these factors as they rise and fall, and (3) being flexible and resourceful enough to respond appropriately to the needs of the three factors and their interrelationship.

Very influential in breaking away from the mechanistic approaches to leadership, Fiedler's theories are supported by his research and that of others. He contends that performance of groups or organizations is related to leadership style interacting with favorableness of the situation.

Fiedler's contingency model[6]

With this model, we have broken away from the "only one best way" argument for leadership. We have emphasized the "It all depends" concept which may be more difficult to study and to learn or adjust to, as well as making prediction of behaviors more difficult. But this model describes more factors, and seems to assist our adjustment to leading. Just as we earlier wrote that there is no one best way to look at organization and communication, we are now asserting there is no one best way to lead.

Fiedler contends that an appropriate leadership style (which may range from directive to permissive) should be chosen based on the three factors of (1) leader-member relations, (2) task structure, and (3) position power. A person who can analyze these factors and can, if he or she chooses, adapt to the needs of the situation and relationships will therefore be more effective. There is no one style of leadership which fits all occasions or all people. There is also no simple way to improve on these factors to make a leader more effective.

Leader-member relations. This factor includes the degree of confidence which followers have in their leader. Both the attractiveness of the leader and the loyalty of the followers (for whatever reason) are included. To improve on this factor, it is possible to make a leader more attractive by giving support or endorsements which improve his or her image. Another way to improve on this factor would be to reconstitute the followers so there are more compatible people working for the leader. A leader who chooses followers selectively has

[6]F. E. Fiedler, *A Theory of Effective Leadership*, McGraw-Hill Book Company, New York, 1967.

more chance of having good leader-member relations than one who has the followers imposed from some system outside the leader's control. If you can pick your friends to be in your group, you may do better than if you simply depend on volunteers. A caution: This factor does not operate in isolation, and what may be true for friends working together on a loosely structured social project may not be true for the same group assigned to accomplish a highly structured or demanding physical task.

Task structure.   Are the jobs to be done by followers routine, highly repetitious, structured, predictable in outcome and procedures, or are they ill-structured, undefined, creative, ambiguous, inconsistent, or unpredictable? Some change in task structure can be made by spelling out in detail the steps to be taken to accomplish the task. A committee referred to in the example above can have detailed agendas and very precise working by-laws for the subcommittees, or it can simply give the most general assignment. Some students are comfortable with a detailed syllabus for a course which spells out each day's assignments, the amount of credit for each quiz, elaborate grading systems, optional readings and the credit to be given for them, and what criteria the instructor will use in evaluating the work done. Other students do not seem to accommodate well to that system. If an instructor (the leader in a classroom setting) is having difficulty with students not turning in papers on time and arguing with grades and content of quizzes, more structure is needed, and the instructor might consider a more detailed syllabus. How much detail to provide becomes an important factor related to the needs of the followers. Structure will follow attention to specifics and detail.

Leader position power.   Inherent in the leader's position is influence or power. This includes the rewards or punishments associated with the leader's authority and title or position, as well as how much support the leader is perceived to receive from superiors or designated organization powers. Being given higher rank in an organization is one way of increasing this factor for the benefit of a leader. Announcing increased authority—by title or rank or increased span or budgetary responsibility—can be effective. Implicit in this action are more rewards to be given out, more sanctions to be imposed, more voice in evaluation of followers. All are designed to improve relations for the leaders. Figure 7-7 describes the findings from Fiedler's research.

Summary.   Besides asserting that there is no one best way of managing or leading, the Fiedler model suggests that it is possible to make changes in three factors to improve leadership effectiveness. We

FIGURE 7-7
Fiedler's contingency model.

Research findings: Findings from research on contingency theory indicate the following tendencies appear to prevail. Remember that *relationships* among the factors are as important as the factors themselves.

A *directive* (authoritarian, autocratic) style appears to have a good chance of succeeding in the following situations:

Leader-Member Relationship	Task Structure	Position Power
Good	Structured	Strong
Good	Structured	Weak
Good	Unstructured	Strong
Moderately poor	Unstructured	Weak

In other words, when the leader has good relations with followers under highly structured situations (as in repetitive work in a cohesive, small group), the leader can be very directive whether or not he or she has a powerful position in unstructured tasks, good member relationships and strong power are needed for the directive manager to be effective (as in compatible faculty group working together on a planning project under the direction of a popular dean). When leader-member relationships are not good, the task lacks structure and position power is weak; a very strong and directive style is needed to get anything done, and the leader risks little goodwill or slacking off of effort by being very directive.

A *permissive* (democratic, relational) style appears to have a good chance of succeeding in the following situations:

Leader-Member Relationship	Task Structure	Position Power
Good	Unstructured	Weak
Moderately poor	Structured	Strong

Good relationships may be capitalized on to lead a group through an unstructured task when position power is weak because the leader can encourage the group to develop its own activities. If the task is structured and the leader-member relationships are not good, then the leader with strong power or authority to accomplish the goal can successfully move a group with the nondirective or permissive style (as in a classroom under an unpopular but influential teacher, the group can accomplish its goals without much direction if there is high structure including detailed assignments, written syllabi, and carefully delineated roles).

Other situations under moderately poor relationships have only uncertain results so far and further study is needed. It is interesting to note that these research findings show more situations in which directive leadership is effective than situations favoring permissive leadership styles.

are not, therefore, limited to forcing leaders to change their ways to be most effective. It is possible to make changes in followers, or in the situation or task structure which may improve the total organizational mission. Selecting leaders for appropriate tasks or specific follower tendencies is another means of improving leadership. Leaders can be matched to followers and to structures more imaginatively than was customary in the past by looking at the behavioral characteristics of people and by predicting how situational variables may change or remain constant.

Life-cycle theory   Adopting the quadrants essentially like Blake and Mouton's managerial grid, Hersey and Blanchard developed a theory of leadership concerned with the "maturity" of a group or organization.[7]

They define *leadership* as "a process of influencing the activities of an individual or group in efforts toward accomplishing goals in a given situation" and *leadership style* as "the consistent patterns of behavior which you exhibit, as perceived by others, when you are attempting to influence the activities of people." They assert that improving group maturity levels is done by "(getting groups) to take more and more responsibility."

They suggest that the most effective leader should work to get the group or organization to operate as "maturely" as possible. Low-maturity groups need direction from a leader; high-maturity groups need little help on either their task or their maintenance factors. It therefore is important for a leader to relate his or her style to the needs of that group in response to where that group is in a life cycle of maturity.

In reference to Figure 7-8, life-cycle leadership theory, an immature group (one that cannot develop its own resources for work or interaction) needs high task efforts from a leader for the greatest probability of success. As a group is maturing, the leader must be careful to delegate responsibility carefully and to increase socio-emotional (process) support slowly. As a group continues to mature, the leader may use less task reinforcement and more relationship behavior. What is important here is reinforcing successive approximations; whenever task items are accomplished, even partially, then the leader should give socioemotional support for that task effort. Gradually the accomplishment of the task itself may become sufficient for the inner satisfaction of the followers. The leader offers reinforcement on the socioemotional level until the followers gain a level of confidence or self-esteem (maturity) so the leader can minimize both the task and relationship support (lower left quadrant).

Hersey and Blanchard's *tri-dimensional leader effectiveness model* depicted in Figure 7-9 is also based on the quadrants of task and relationship. It predicts which of the four tendencies will probably be most effective in which situation. Appropriateness of leadership style is stressed rather than "goodness" or "badness" or "rightness" or "wrongness" of the styles. A feature of this model is the assertion that

---

[7]P. Hersey and K. H. Blanchard, "Life Cycle Theory of Leadership," *Training and Development Journal*, pp. 26–34. May 1969; *Management of Organizational Behavior: Utilizing Human Resources*, 2d ed., New York: Prentice-Hall, Inc., 1972; "So You Want to Know Your Leadership Style?" *Training and Development Journal*, pp. 22–37. February 1974.

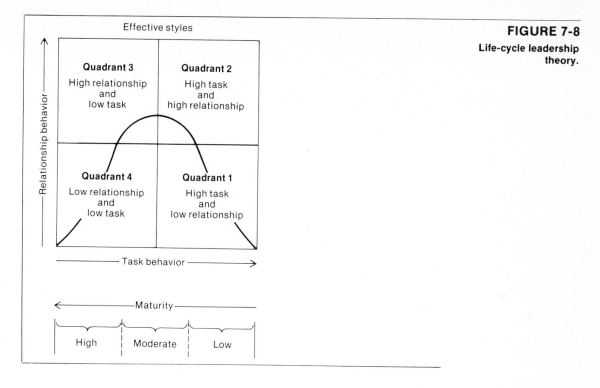

FIGURE 7-8
Life-cycle leadership theory.

an effective manager or leader who is faced with a variety of situations may need to be very flexible—capable of functioning in any of the four quadrants as the situation dictates.

What happens if you are not a flexible manager or leader? What if you choose to keep your style in one of the quadrants only? Are you lost to management or leadership? Not necessarily. This theory suggests that you should determine your range of styles and then try to function in those situations where your styles are most effective or appropriate. If you are a high-task, low-relationship leader and intend to remain so, then you should seek out assignments where task is paramount and the feelings of people are less significant.

In this way, rather than retraining all leaders to fit all categories, we can match leaders to types of challenges in leadership situations. Whether or not this approach will ever become universal, the thrust of the idea is that there are factors to manipulate besides sending managers off to learn how to manage differently. Look back at Fiedler's contingency model and see if those recommendations on altering a situation and followers (as well as changing the leader) seem to support the style range concepts of Hersey and Blanchard.

FIGURE 7-9

Tri-dimensional leader effectiveness model.

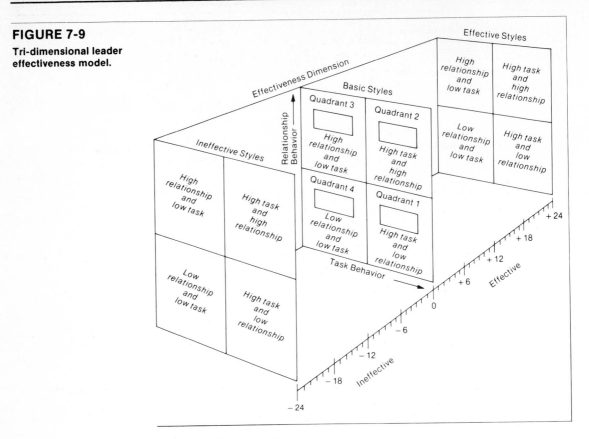

POWER

Whoever is leading an organization or a group is assumed to have some kind of influence over the behavior of the followers. Not all persons designated as leaders seem to be able to influence their subordinates in the same way or to the same degree. The relationship of leading and following appears to be reciprocal. It follows the transactional definition from Chapter 3, and must be restated here as: The power an individual has over others is largely dependent upon how that person is perceived, and the perceptions of a leader are dependent upon setting up the relationship so each participant understands who gives orders and who takes them. After reviewing three dimensions of the power relationship, we will review five bases of power.

What Is Power?

Power is a quality inherent in the relations between two or more people. Whenever people interact, a power relationship is implied. We are constantly aware of a power structure in our relations with others. Who calls the shots? Who gives in? Who can order whom around? Katz and Kahn[8] describe power in three dimensions: resources, dependencies, and alternatives.

Resources

A resource is something you have or own. Power is related to resources because we acknowledge ownership. In a society where no person has possessions or other resources, there is little basis for power. Resources may be as tangible as money, physical strength, skillful speech, or good looks, and as intangible as knowledge, ethics, information, contacts with important people, or charm. A resource permits its owner to control part of an environment. Hence, people in that environment are somewhat dependent on the owner for rewards or punishment. "Being in the know" is important for most people, and the person who has inside information has power. Being seen with celebrities is a desirable experience for some people, so someone who can introduce them to a motion picture star or a sports hero has a kind of power.

Dependencies

But mere possession of the resource is not enough. If you have a resource, I must be *dependent* on it for some reason to make it have power over me. I must want to know the information you have, or you have no power. Power exists only when the related resource is needed by someone. I may desperately want to know some information, but not the precise information you have, so the power relationship is not there—or I may be interested in meeting the conductor of the New York Philharmonic, but not the linebacker for the Cardinals, so your acquaintance with the linebacker will give you no power over me, even though you do own a potentially valuable resource of introduction.

Alternatives

The third dimension or variable is the *availability of alternatives.* Power is reduced for the holder of a resource by the number of other places a person can go to get the same or similar resource. In other words, I may want your resource, and I may be dependent on it; but if you try to hold me up too much, I may find another alternative. It may be giving up my requirement for the resource if the price of power is too high, or finding someone who can get me the same thing. I can go to

[8]D. Katz and R. Kahn, *The Social Psychology of Organizations*, John Wiley and Sons, Inc., New York, 1968.

another source of information if you exert too much power as a price for sharing that resource with me. If I have to buy season tickets to the football games just to meet one star whom you know, that may be more than I'm willing to invest. So you lose your power. If no alternatives exist, however, the dependency on the resource grants that holder great power.

Power is generally bestowed on a leader by consent of followers. If that consent is not engineered satisfactorily, it can be said that no power exists. Communication of the messages of power must be clear and unambiguous to be most effective. Whether you believe that power is assumed by persons in command (from the top down) or that it is granted by the followers to a leader (consent of governed), the crucial ingredient is the *communicated agreement* that the power differential exists.

Too extensive use of power may result in its loss if the followers decide that the resource of the leader is being used up in asserting power. For that reason, frequent reassessments of power relationships are important. In a family group the power patterns change as children grow up; but there remains an implied relationship of parents to children which, in some societies, persists strongly into several generations. Politicians who have lost their office in an election sometimes maintain their power, although perhaps for different reasons. While in office, the power resource of a politician may be the ability to provide services to a constituent; out of office, the resource may depend on charisma or hero identification.

The Bases of Power   The same person may have access to several types of power resources, or may depend on one resource to accomplish many power relationships. It is useful to identify some sources (resources) of power which people tend to accept and to apply to others. Five sources suggested by French and Raven[9] can be divided into two which are tangible, (1) reward and (2) coercion, and three which are intangible, (3) legitimacy, (4) reference, and (5) expertise.

Reward power   Reward power is based on the expectation of receiving praise, income, recognition, promotion, or other good things either tangible or intangible. You generally know who in the organization has the power to sign vouchers, to give raises, to know you did well and praise you.

[9]J. R. P. French and B. Raven, "The Bases of Social Power," in D. Cartwright and A. Zander (eds.), *Group Dynamics: Research and Theory*, Harper & Row, New York, 1968.

You seek reinforcement for doing well, and therefore this kind of power has great potential for good if it is handled objectively and judiciously.

Coercive power is based on fear. You can be punished if you do not accomplish the assignment, do the job right, or accede to the command given you. The same people capable of giving out rewards are identifiable as being able to give out punishment—if only by withholding the rewards. You work hard sometimes so you won't get in trouble. You want to avoid being reprimanded or demoted or scorned, so you grant coercive power to anyone whom you perceive as important enough to impress.

Coercive power

Legitimate power is assigned power. It comes from a person's title, rank, or assignment in an organization or in society. Parents are an example of this kind of power; even the laws of liberal societies create the power of parents over children as they assign responsibility. If you are elected to office, you acquire legitimate power. When you lose the election, you likely will lose that power resource. This kind of power rests on agreements—either by law or by social norms—that some persons are given rights over others, and it is possible to designate those offices or stations or ranks to whom this power is assigned.

Legitimate power

Referent power is related to attractiveness or appeal to others. It concerns our being liked and alike. It is belonging power. It is derived from wanting to be with others or to somehow be associated or identified with them. It is often linked to other kinds of power resources, as in the case of wanting to be like the favorite official of the organization or to be close to the person who controls the schedule or budget or promotion lists. It is an interesting kind of power because it can operate at a distance; your hero may not even be present for you to act in a way you assume that power figure would want you to act. This is the kind of power that instills patriotism, supports fan clubs, and elects charismatic politicians to high offices.

Referent power

Expert power is based on the "Knowledge is power" concept. What a person knows concerning a field or subject will give power because people prize information and knowledge as a resource. Knowing how to handle a problem is a kind of expertise, as is giving answers to

Expert power

questions that puzzle us. The consultant who helps the company improve its marketing program is an expert; but so is the psychologist who is expert in skills of listening and guiding a client. Some teachers believe their power comes from being experts in an academic discipline, but it is possible they derive much of their power from reward and punishment.

Summary

Is any one source of power best? As in choosing among leadership styles, it all depends. Power is only viable when it is accepted by both the power leader and the power follower. Unless a person depends on the power resource, it is not likely power will be established. More important, let us emphasize that unless all parties to a power structure see clearly the sources and identify the holders of power, there is no power structure.

Again, the argument for clear, precise, unambiguous communication arises. You can relate most appropriately to the power structures around you if the messages sent and received are clear; if your communication is accurate and adequate for the situation.

How Power Works

In this section, we will look at how power works and analyze the communication components involved in all power relationships. First we will discuss who wants power, then the relationship between power and dependency.

Who wants power

First of all, power is seldom equally distributed among members of an organization. Some people are indeed more powerful than others. The question of who wants power is related to individual needs and the value people place on getting and using power. People with a high power drive prefer jobs which give them both leeway in defining their role and their behaviors and control over others. People in power usually resist attempts at redistribution of power within the organization. A new department head will be reacted to cautiously when she comes into the organization until her relative place in the power structure can be figured out. How much influence will the new person yield? Whom does she know who is influential? What personal characteristics does she possess that will make her a power contender? All these questions and others have to be answered before the new person can be related to in a comfortable manner. Interpersonal communication may be cautious, distant, cold, or even downright unfriendly if the new person is perceived as a threat to the existing balance of power.

People threatened by power seekers may engage in intimidation rituals[10] designed to neutralize the contenders. Such rituals may range from accusing others of misunderstanding the situation ("If you really understood the situation, you would never suggest this rotation plan"; "If you'd been here as long as I have, you'd know this idea would never work here"); to isolation (assignment out of town, for example); to defamation ("Jones has been under a lot of pressure lately, no wonder he makes bad decisions"); to expulsion ("You are fired").

Power seekers usually attempt to get power individually. However, if their attempts are unsuccessful, they will resort to forming coalitions.

The power someone else has over you is directly related to how dependent you feel you are on that person. Power is in the eye of the beholder, since it is related to how you perceive your dependency. You define your relationships; and even when others appear to be in control of the definition of their relationship with you, you are still free to accept or reject their definition.

Power and dependency

If you feel you are greatly dependent on another person, then in essence *you give* power to that person and allow yourself to be controlled by implicit or explicit threats to withhold what you depend on.

Parental relationships are a mixture of dependency and power. The more dependent the child is on love, affection, or resources, the more power the parent can exert on the child. But the relationship holds only so long as the child defines his or her needs in a way which makes the parent the sole supplier of the coveted resource. The child is really free to decide (1) whether he or she needs that resource and (2) whether other persons besides the parent can supply it. The child can, and often does, redefine the relationship with the parent as an independent one. The parent is no longer given power.

Parental relationships are very much like working relationships on the job. If you possess highly marketable skills few people have, you have power. You have a scarce resource many people will seek. Many employers will be dependent on you; and as a result, you will find yourself in the enviable position of choosing among several options for a career. Regardless of the job you take, your boss— whatever his or her authority or status—will be dependent on you. Because you have many options available, it will be difficult for your boss to impose a lot of constraints on you. If you do not wish to comply

---

[10]R. O'Day, "Intimidation Rituals: Reactions to Reform," *Journal of Applied Behavioral Science*, vol. 10, pp. 373–386, 1974.

when you do not agree, there is very little the boss can do. If, on the other hand, you are easily replaceable and you know it, then you depend on the job and the people in authority, and as a result have much less power than in the previous example. In fact, if the employment market is bleak for people with your type of training, you may feel, and be, powerless because you are very dependent on that job for your livelihood.

The relationship between power and dependency explains, for example, why businesses attempt to diversify their sources of supplies. When they depend too much on any one supplier, they may place themselves at the mercy of that supplier and thus lose some degree of control on their operations. If you can take your business elsewhere, the supplier can no longer hold power or control you.

Communication implications

The communication implications of the relationship between power and dependency are clearly seen in business negotiations. Negotiators are keenly aware of the dynamics of power and generally attempt to figure how dependent the other side is on what their side can offer or withhold at the bargaining table.

Is power expandable or is it a fixed amount ("The more you have, the less I have")? The central question, however, is whether you are in a situation in which there is a *common interest* or a *conflict of interest*. As Katz and Kahn[11] point out, if the situation is one where there is a common interest, then using communication processes in the form of persuasion, rather than resorting to power struggles, is essential. In this sense, power is expandable. If you and I understand we are working for the same goals, we can be mutually influenced by each other's suggestions. The total amount of influence exerted in the relationship is greater than if either one just orders the other around. Productivity may also be greater when we mutually attempt to influence each other, and we both stand to benefit from the communicative processes at work.

However, if we have a conflict of interest, then you and I are engaged in a power struggle. In that case, the more you control the final decision, the less power I have—unless, of course, the situation can be redefined as one in which you and I have a mutual interest in a higher-level operation.

Conflicts of interest are a reality of organizational life and cannot be dismissed as the product of misperceptions. They cannot be resolved simply by believing that power is infinitely expandable. We

[11]Daniel Katz and Robert Kahn, *The Social Psychology of Organization,* 2d ed., Wiley and Sons, New York, 1978, p. 322.

will discuss the strategies for resolving conflict more extensively in Chapter 9.

SUMMARY

Leadership has been studied for many years, and most theories which are presently useful are based on communication. The earlier trait theory was based on static and personal determinants which had less to do with communication than did the later functional theory which claimed that certain functions needed to be performed by a leader. They involved task (getting the job done) and maintenance (building the group as a working unit). Certain styles of managing produced certain results, and these could be predicted by seeing what kinds of managerial behaviors succeeded. There was also the possibility that a manager could change styles by training.

The contingency approach claims that leadership methods should be based on (1) the leader's own characteristics, (2) the characteristics of subordinates, and (3) factors in the environment or situation that may affect the outcome. Robert Tannenbaum and Warren Schmidt also include the interdependence of all those factors. Fred Fiedler's contingency model is an elaboration of leader "position power" in relation to the factors mentioned above. The life-cycle theory of Paul Hersey and Ken Blanchard concerns the "maturity" of a group as a factor in determining the styles needed to manage effectively.

Power is a relationship which depends on three dimensions of resources, dependencies, and alternatives. The bases of power have been described as springing from (1) giving rewards; (2) handing out punishments; (3) having assigned, or legitimate, power; (4) having attractiveness or appeal; and (5) expertise or knowledge. Any conflict of interest among people encourages a power struggle. Power occurs when you see yourself as negotiating, dependent, or superior.

CHAPTER 8

GROUP COMMUNICATION PROCESSES AND DECISION MAKING

"A small group is defined as any number of persons engaged in interaction with one another in a single face-to-face meeting or series of such meetings in which each member receives some impression or perception of each other member distinctive enough so that he can, either at the time, or in later questioning give some reaction to each of the others as an individual person, even though it be only to recall that the other was present." Robert Bales

INTRODUCTION This chapter will attempt to answer some significant questions about groups and their usefulness. Why are groups important? How do people tend to behave in groups? How do groups do their work? Are groups effective? What keeps groups from doing their job well? There are many questions also which may seem trivial, but which have implications beyond their apparent content. How big should groups be? What is a group?

So much mythology exists about how people work together in groups—such as committees, task forces, families, teams—that most people have impressions or prejudices that are deeply rooted in their experience or in common aphorisms such as "Committees are groups which keep minutes and waste hours." "A camel is a horse put together by a committee." "There has never been a statue erected to a committee." "To kill a project, turn it over to a committee."

Rather than argue the truth of this "folk wisdom," this chapter will assume that much of your working energy and time will be spent in contact with others in what we call groups. Groups are a fact of life. Groups exist. Groups can either be effective or not, depending on factors which are controllable. This chapter will review means of making the best out of a world of group interaction.

DEFINITION OF GROUPS

Besides the quotation at the beginning of this chapter, we can suggest five characteristics which differentiate groups from simple collections of people waiting for a bus or attending a movie.[1]

1. Members of a group are in *interaction* with one another. They talk or engage in nonverbal interaction as they pay attention to each other.
2. Members share one or more motives or *goals* which determine the direction they will grow and move. The group must have a purpose—if only to have fun—in order to maintain the interaction.
3. Members develop *norms* which set the boundaries within which interpersonal relations may be established and activities carried on. Norms help regulate the achievement of goals.
4. If interaction continues, a set of *roles* becomes stabilized and this group becomes differentiated from other groups. Leadership and followership patterns are developed, and people relate to each other in those roles.
5. A network of *interpersonal attraction* develops on the basis of the likes and dislikes of members for one another. They share parts of themselves with each other and become involved in risk-taking behaviors not usually associated with persons outside the group.

We will define a small group, then, as a collection of two or more people in interaction, with identified goals and established norms, acting in role relations with each other with a network of interpersonal attraction. Although some scholars in small group research do not consider a dyad—or two people—a small group, we prefer to count any number above one as a potential group.

[1]This definition is based on P. Hare, *Handbook of Small Group Research*, The Free Press, New York, 1962, p. 10.

FACTORS IN GROUP GROWTH

Although the number of research studies may not be an accurate measure of the significance of a field, it is interesting that research in group dynamics has multiplied in great profusion in the fields of psychology, sociology, business, speech, journalism, and communication studies. Every decade since 1900 the amount of group research has increased at least ten times, so today it is estimated that there are several thousand research studies being reported for every one reported at the beginning of this century.

Not only has interest in researching groups increased, but the incidence of group activity and training programs involving group process has multiplied enormously. Recognition has grown that we spend much of our communicating time in groups. Below are some reasons for the growth in groups and group impact on organizations and communication.[2]

Complexity and Size of Society and its Problems

Every field of knowledge has expanded, and specialization is the present norm. No business executive can know all the details of the company's operations and must involve others in combined decisions by adding lawyers, comptrollers, tax experts, personnel directors, etc., to the corporate family. Institutions of all types have grown in size—not only industrial organizations but education, health care, government, services, etc.

Changed Attitudes toward Group Participation

There has been a growing awareness that members of a group will be more loyal and better employees if they are involved in some activity with the rest of the group. Member willingness to carry out assignments has been acknowledged to be a result of involvement and participation. The Hawthorne effect, discussed earlier, speaks to the usefulness of group participation as a function of production.

Distribution of Knowledge

Not only is there more to be known in every field, but there are more people knowing it. People are better educated, either through formal means (the rate of college attendance has skyrocketed) or through the mass media and especially television. The gap between those who know a lot and those who know a little has been narrowing. Each individual may possess information which some others may need, and the way to share it is through group interaction and communication.

[2]Discussion of these factors in growth of group discussion and group dynamics is based on our interpretations of D. C. Barnlund and F. Haiman, *Dynamics of Discussion*, Houghton-Mifflin, Boston. 1960; D. Cartwright and A. Zander, *Group Dynamics*, 3d ed., Harper and Row, N.Y., 1968.

There is less reliance today on the "authority" of tribal chiefs, great leaders, witch doctors, and accepting of dogma without some inspection or questioning. Controlled observations are shared, and verifiable data are checked with each other. Much testing of hypotheses across group lines is a characteristic of the more sophisticated institutions and their leadership.

Advance of the Scientific Method

More information is shared as a legitimate claim to knowing about what is going on in our institutions. Each person has a right to be respected, and that means each person has a right to ask opinions and bestow data as a resource. The traditional paternalistic convention "Children should be seen and not heard" has lost ground in all levels and ages of our society. Recognition that most people are worthy of being heard and have a right to know has increased.

Dignity of the Individual

As information about groups has grown, so has the ability to train people in how to improve their group skills. Organizations such as the National Training Laboratories (Bethel, Maine) have influenced several generations of managers, teachers, and political and social leaders to become aware of the impact of groups and of the capability of group leaders for learning improved effectiveness. The number of people trained in group processes multiplies significantly as theories about groups are tested and methodologies for applying those theories are put into practice.

Broadening of Knowledge and Skills in Group Dynamics

Related to the previous item but of special importance, is the idea that groups do not deal only with content, facts, decisions, or data. *Groups spend almost half their time dealing with the relations of members to each other*, to the leader, and to their environmental constraints. Researchers and methodologists began making people aware that the purpose of groups is divided between task (getting a job done) and process or socioemotional considerations (making it possible for us to work together as we get the job done). With this increased awareness of what really goes on in groups, teachers, trainers, researchers, managers, leaders all began to pay attention to many factors which were previously either ignored or given only passing attention by a few psychologically or socially oriented investigators or practitioners. The field of group dynamics grew from a rather sterile, limited emphasis on cognition, task, intellectual discourse, and Robert's Rules of Order to include the richness of nonverbal communication, emotions, motivations, caring, and the many dimensions of human relationships and group maintenance.

Awareness of Breadth of Group Interaction

Groups must take care of the intellectual, cognitive, and task needs of members, but they must also give significant attention to the socioemotional, personal, and maintenance needs of members. In reading about the types of groups in the next section, it is important to keep in mind the dual nature of group communication and dynamics.

TYPES OF GROUPS
People do not leave their emotions behind them when they enter a group. When people engage in discourse, however logically rigorous or intellectually demanding, they are still functioning human beings with a wide range of personal fears, joys, needs, hates, loves, prides, anxieties, etc. Any leader or group member who does not recognize the interfunctioning of task and process will miss much of what is actually going on in the group. The following categories should be placed on a continuum in an arrangement suggested by Barnlund and Haiman[3] and describe (rather than prescribe) types of groups. In other words, these types seem to exist in our society, either singly or in combinations; and the categories are not an attempt to tell you, the reader, what should be, but to call your attention to one system for looking at different kinds of groups based on their activities. Figure 8-1 summarizes the five different types of groups with their respective emphases on task and process communication.

Casual Groups
These can occur any place and any time. They grow up spontaneously. They contain almost no new information for people, but the verbal interaction may be predictable and mundane small talk. Yet casual groups are the backbone of informal lines of communication in

[3] Op. cit.

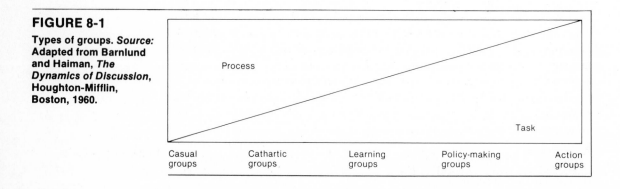

FIGURE 8-1

Types of groups. *Source: Adapted from Barnlund and Haiman, The Dynamics of Discussion, Houghton-Mifflin, Boston, 1960.*

organizations and the major way in which the grapevine functions. Whom you have coffee with often determines what you know about what's going on. In these groups, people attempt to (1) establish warm human relations, (2) lay the groundwork for more practical communication at other times, and (3) overcome or fill silence, or ward off loneliness or anonymity. Topics include weather, sports, TV shows. Casual groups are characterized by directionless talk without rigorous rules for testing the validity of remarks, exchange of personal experiences without an attempt to document them as though they were research reports, and opportunities to check the sentiments of others to learn what they think about your sentiments. The communication in these groups is low in content, or task, and high in process, or socioemotional. This is not to say casual groups are not important. They may be the main link between us and the society out there; they help set the personalities of individuals; their attraction is intimacy of human contact and opportunity for self-expression. These groups are not as well studied as some other kinds of work groups.

Cathartic groups tend to occur in situations where people are in close or intense contact: in college dormitories, in classes during exam periods, in industrial locker rooms, around water coolers, at union meetings, etc. Their purpose is to give vent to feelings or to serve as an outlet for tensions or irritation. Not too far from the casual groups in amount of content, their functioning is less random and less inclined to observe niceties of form in communication. There is a greater awareness of what drew the group together. Some examples of cathartic groups include Tall Girls Society, Left Handed Clubs, some labor negotiations meetings, and Human Relations Committees with specific causes to air. World War II "Grumble Clubs" in England served a very useful function in letting citizens gripe about wartime conditions. Results from these groups can be (1) reduction of hostilities or levels of anger, (2) better understanding of your own motivations and aims, (3) development of more mature social behavior and controlled reactions, and (4) incentives to know the self better and to improve either personal attitudes or circumstances. Informal groups in organizations often provide a safety valve that allows people to vent their daily frustrations on the job. Although "nothing" gets done in terms of actions, getting things off your chest can be valuable and can help you to feel better, even though the situation remains the same.

Cathartic Groups

Informally, learning groups occur whenever people get together to share information; formally, these groups include classes, seminars,

Learning Groups

schools, lectures, quiz groups, short courses, and pre-service and in-service training groups. A group working together to learn can (1) help each other assimilate the appropriate information, (2) develop the habit of evaluating ideas critically, (3) stimulate original thinking and innovative or creative ways of looking at ideas or information. As compared with the casual group and the cathartic group, the learning group reflects (1) a higher expectation of results from members, (2) clearer definitions of the problems and objectives to be met, (3) more shared information or general knowledge of the subject, (4) more specific preparation for the learning activity at times, (5) statements which are more relevant and better supported by data. Learning groups are usually associated with educational settings, conventions, conferences, sales meetings, hobby or study clubs, or other gatherings at which people can gain new insights, talk over common problems objectively, or compare ideas.

Some of the following results can be expected from participation in learning groups: (1) a clearer definition of a problem, event, activity, etc.; (2) added knowledge of a subject; (3) more skill in working with data; (4) more skill in working with people; (5) changes in attitudes or values. We want to emphasize that learning can occur along socioemotional dimensions as well as task or informational dimensions. People not only acquire added knowledge as a result of learning; they can also become more skilled at a task, more open, less prejudiced, and more sensitive. In brief, people can learn at a cognitive level, at a skills level, and at an affect or "gut" level. Learning groups are specifically available for all these types of learning—for example, lectures on nuclear energy for cognition, tennis lessons for skills, and assertiveness training for the socioemotional level. Most companies' in-service training fits the category of learning groups.

Policy-Making Groups

Policy-making groups usually are formed because something goes wrong in the environment or a change is in order. They are composed of people empowered to make decisions or recommend how things ought to be done. Democracy has been defined as "government by committee." Some groups are given authority over a problem or decision and are called "assigned groups." Others may take it on themselves to constitute a group; they move into the situation and assume control and are called "assumptive groups." These groups are expected to develop carefully worked-out recommendations which will get the support of those affected or those who are in position to make higher policy. Policy-making groups are more formal than the others we have discussed. They likely will have formal agendas and rules of procedures and will handle their affairs systematically, but will still take time for the socioemotional needs of members. External restraints may be imposed in the form of target dates to be met or a necessity for practicality in the decisions. As compared with the groups discussed earlier, the interaction and communication will be characterized by (1) a greater sense of responsibility, (2) seriousness of purpose, (3) controlled and purposive communication, (4) critical appraisal of ideas and others, (5) attention to external restraints. An additional outcome of experiences in policy-making groups is that the members often develop skills in decision making. They also may develop new techniques or systems for arriving at policy decisions as they creatively explore or review their own deliberations.

Action Groups

These groups differ from policy-making groups in the nature of their task assignment. The policy group may commit an organization to a direction or stand of some importance or permanence. The action group, however, must put the policy into effect or make some move which will have consequences. The group carries out the how and when of policy and suffers with the results. Action groups involve (1) many intricate issues involved in understanding and implementing policies or programs; (2) serious and lengthy discussions; (3) heavy emphasis on data, facts, objectivity, and task; (4) usually time pressure involving putting plans into effect or taking action before a deadline; (5) coordination with other agencies, or follow-up evaluations; (6) concrete, specific, and tangible decisions; (7) little attention to the personal needs of members or the maintenance functions of the group; (8) few digressions from the task. Some examples of action groups are a committee working to reorganize the curriculum of a university or to introduce a new product, the recruiting committee of a college, campaign workers for a politician, a team of medical personnel, or a sales staff.

Summary

Identifying the groups described above as separate, disparate types may be misleading. They may not exist in pure form except as we take them apart to study them. There is likely to be a merging of characteristics into shades of each type; a group may even shift from one emphasis to another. For that reason, it is important to view these types along a continuum and not as if they were in separate boxes or little packages.

Being able to identify the type of group you are working in, however, may be useful to you for these reasons: (1) It will help you determine the style of leadership which is most appropriate. (2) The kind and amount of interaction among members will be determined by the type of group. (3) It will help you establish an agenda appropriate for the group—none at all for the casual group but a very structured one for the action group. (4) Communication will be different in different types: random and unchallenged in the casual groups, but very terse, supported, probably written or recorded in the action groups. (5) Your own expectations of outcomes of the group can be adjusted so you will avoid frustration if the group does not perform up to your hopes. The casual group will do nothing to reform the activities of the university or company, just as the action group will do little for the socioemotional needs of members participating in the discussions.

WHEN TO USE GROUP DECISION MAKING

Groups are formed for reasons. Some groups (casual) form simply to prepare for future associations. Others (action) may form to carry out extensive activities. Decision making is one of the most frequent reasons groups get together. From the chapter on leadership, you remember that leaders must depend on the resources of followers if organizations are to function well. Groups are the basis of relationships among leaders and followers, and communication in the form of discussion is how groups reach decisions.

Leaders seldom reach decisions in isolation. Because decisions usually affect a number of people, not just the leader, it has been usual to involve others in all the identification, fact-finding, implementation, and evaluating activities of decisions. The leader who operates as a solitary decision maker may exhibit some characteristic which our society prizes—decisiveness, firmness, venturesomeness, conviction, strength of will—but may overlook two important aspects of groups: first, that groups have resources to offer a leader in arriving at good decisions, and second, that it has been demonstrated that followers will be more dedicated to carrying out decisions if they have been involved in the decision-making process.

The quality of leading is related to the quality of decisions made by the leader. Good leaders and good managers are those who make good decisions. The ability to tap the resources of followers—their knowledge, their judgment, their creative energies, their physical efforts, their time, and their goodwill—may distinguish the effective leader from the ineffective one.

Three factors dictate use of group decision making as discussion: forces in the leader, forces in group members, and forces in the situation. We suggest you review the contingency theories and the Hersey and Blanchard life-cycle theories (pages 191–196) and relate it to the following discussion of applications.

In a class setting, the leader is the teacher; in a business organization, the leader is the manager. (1) What is the leader's value system or attitude about groups and their ability to reach decisions? (2) Does the leader have confidence in the followers' abilities to contribute to a decision? (3) What are the leader's inclinations or tendencies on leading style? Authoritarian? Permissive? Flexible? (4) How secure does the leader feel in an uncertain situation of group discussion? (5) Is the leader willing to listen to group opinions even if some may not be popular or within the leader's biases or prejudices or beliefs? (6) What communication skills does the leader have?

Forces in the Leader

In a class setting, the group members are the students; in a business organization, they are the employees at various levels. (1) What personality characteristics are distributed among the members? (2) What are member expectations about how a leader should act? How groups can perform? (3) What needs do the group members have for knowing and for feeling involved? (4) Are members interested in this subject? Does it affect them? (5) What do members know about the subject? What is their level of knowledge or ability to acquire and understand the matter? (6) What do the members know or believe about the factors of task and process in group interaction? (7) What are the range and balance of communication skills among group members?

Forces in the Group Members

In a class setting, the situation includes the course itself, the university, etc.; in a business setting, it includes internal and external factors such as other elements of the larger organization, the economy, the suppliers, the customers, and the stockholders. (1) What type of organization is this now and what are its plans for the future? (2) How effective has this group been in previous situations and in relation to other parts of the organization? (3) What kind of problem is this? Is it amenable to solution? By this specific group? (4) What are the time limits? (5) What is the size of the group? (6) What physical settings will help or hinder interaction? (7) Are other resources available to the group such as predictive data, current reports, computer analyses, research results, comparisons with other actions, precedents, consultants, experts, authority figures?

Forces in the Situation

Although there appear to be adequate reasons for using groups to reach decisions, not all instances will prove group decisions or the

Individuals versus Groups

process of group decision making to be superior to individual efforts. For example, if there is a very limited time in which to arrive at a decision, an individual will have the advantage of making the decision more quickly. Groups take time. If there is not careful consideration of this factor, then expectations will not be adequately met. Groups can, however, bring more variety of resources to a discussion with the combined energies and know-how of the members. Also, an individual working alone has little chance to test out hypotheses or alternatives, whereas group members can check each other's recommendations or ideas for validity, objectivity, depth, clarity, judgment, etc.

Programmed and Nonprogrammed Decisions

In a later part of this chapter on "groupthink," we will develop some of the limitations and dangers in group decision-making. In considering a balance between individual and group decision making, it is important to call on a distinction made by Simon of *programmed* and *nonprogrammed* decisions.[4]

To the extent that decisions are routine, repetitive, and subject to handling by an established procedure or policy, they are considered programmed. Some events or situations occur with enough frequency to have initiated a "standard operating procedure" or set of steps to be followed when the organization faces occurrence. These decisions can (1) be handled by others than top management, (2) involve fewer than large groups of people in deep consultation, (3) be subject to limited interpretation by assigned areas or persons in organizations who specialize in deciding outcomes within a relatively narrow range of options. Programmed decision making appears to have been refined more than nonprogrammed through the use of mathematical systems or identifiable paths of selecting courses of action. In a college or university the admissions policies are set; but there are routine decisions to be made by an admissions director or committee limited to predictive scores on college success and other factors spelled out in the institution's catalog. Deciding that the college will accept SAT scores as well as ACT scores may be a nonprogrammed decision. Personnel decisions on matters of job reclassification may involve a few managers in a programmed decision, but a decision to establish a new R&D section is nonprogrammed.

Nonprogrammed decisions should be the main preoccupation of top management and should be resolved by general problem-solving processes, including creative or intuitive methods as much as mechanistic or mathematical systems. There obviously needs to be a balance

[4]H. Simon, *The New Science of Management Decision*, Harper & Row, New York, 1960.

between decisions made by top management and by middle managers. If the organization top leaders spend most of their time on programmed decisions which could be made by subordinates, there is likely to be difficulty in long-range planning, coordinated growth, or delegation of responsibilities when needed. In our own experience a useful rule is that decisions must be made at the lowest effective level of concern and authority. This practice (1) preserves a hierarchical appeal procedure, and (2) ensures the time of major leaders will be taken up with matters of a global (or nonprogrammed) nature while subordinate leaders may make programmed decisions by themselves and still participate in deliberations on nonprogrammed decisions.

To understand how groups (or, for that matter, individuals) make decisions, it is imperative that you consider the dynamic nature of decision making. One unfortunate attitude many people have about decision making is that it is like searching for the right answer. Goldberg and Larsen[5] caution us about the "accuracy myth" in trying to find the correct decision or to answer the problem correctly. They suggest that absolute decisions are not brought to groups to decide, but instead are researched from data, experience, experimentation, etc.

DECISION MAKING AS A PROCESS

Group members become frustrated when they encounter others with "right" answers or solutions different from theirs. They are living in an unreal world if they expect to turn up the *one right* solution, perfectly formed, with only positive consequences and with universal acceptance and permanent applicability.

What are you after, then, in group problem solving or decision making? You must see this as a process in which (1) people can confront a variety of ideas or solutions in open discussion, (2) judgments can be formulated and expressed in relation to those proposed solutions, (3) expressed judgments are not treated as accurate or inaccurate (true or false) but rather are evaluated for adequacy or appropriateness, and (4) a "best-fit" solution or decision can emerge from many competing ones because it compared well with opposing points of view.

Decision making, therefore, is that activity or process in which people confront others and their ideas in a flow of communication exchange. It is not a game of button-button-who's-got-the-button in which all members are competing to find the one, correct, true, accurate, preordained decision or solution to a problem. Decision making is a means, not an end.

[5] A. Goldberg and C. Larson, *Group Communication*, Prentice-Hall, Inc., Englewood Cliffs, N.J., 1975, pp. 142 et seq.

Next we will describe a sequence which can be useful in group decision making, and then we will predict some stages a group may go through in solving problems or arriving at decisions. Both of these sequences will be given a task dimension and a socioemotional dimension to indicate what a group leader may do to help the group move toward effective decision making.

Decision-Making Sequence

Ever since John Dewey[6] proposed a series of steps in reflective thinking, theorists have been developing refinements of that sequence. The six-stage proposal recommended here has its roots in Dewey's description of how he believed most people confronted problems or questions of choice of solutions: (1) People begin by recognizing the factors which constitute a problem. (2) Then they examine the problem to find out its nature and scope and implications. (3) Then they search for a possible solution or some potential ways out of the situation. (4) Then they compare the available solutions for best predicted outcomes. (5) Finally they select the solution, decision, or action which they believe will be best—if they are following this systematic treatment.

The sequence recommended below and summarized in Figure 8-2 includes an extra step, looping back to revise *at any step* in the entire process. With that understood, let us examine the steps as (1) defining the problem, (2) generating possible solutions, (3) evaluating and testing solutions, (4) deciding on the best solution, (5) performing implementation procedures, and finally, (6) evaluating and adjusting the results.

Step 1—clarifying and defining the problem

Figure out where the problem came from and what makes it important to the organization. See if you can state the problem clearly in simple, concrete terms and get group members to agree to the statement. Some members may suggest solutions at this stage, but that is premature. However right the solution sounds, unless the group has agreed on the

[6]*How We Think*, Heath & Co., Washington, D.C., 1910.

FIGURE 8-2	**Step**	**Task**
Decision making—six-step process.	1	Clarifying and defining the problem
	2	Generating solutions
	3	Weighing the solutions
	4	Selecting the best solution
	5	Implementing the solution
	6	Evaluating the results

definition of the problem, it will not likely be effective to propose solutions yet. When groups have trouble arriving at solutions in later stages, the best technique is to return to this defining stage which is almost surely the weak spot—very likely because solutions came more quickly than clarification of the problem. Absolutely avoid leaping to solutions even if you generate dozens of good ones. Some group members may accuse the leader of wasting time and may say, "We all know what the problem is . . ." but may have difficulty defining it. Such people are ventriloquists who speak for others who may or may not "know" what the problem is. There are times when definition of the problem comes from outside the group; and if that occurs (like orders from above, or a request from another group), be sure the group all have the same data, concur in definition of the problem or request, and have no questions about it. If clarification is needed, take time. Time spent in this stage will be a good investment even when members are anxious to get on with recommending solutions and actions.

Find all the solutions you can. This is a time for brainstorming. Spend no time here haggling over whether or not certain solutions can be accomplished; just get down on paper or a blackboard as many proposed solutions as the group can generate. Members should be free to suggest even "far-out" solutions without fear of ridicule or argument. No one needs to fight for his or her own pet solution at this stage. An effective group at this step is represented by members who feel free to suggest, but not compelled to justify.

Step 2—generating solutions

At this stage, people can defend their pet solutions. This is also the time to let go of your own ideas if you believe some other solution has more merit. Logic and data should be emphasized as the group considers, challenges, questions, probes, tests each other. An effective group at this stage is one which can operate nondefensively, which has a climate permitting people to support each other's ideas as well as their own. All members, however quiet, should be encouraged to speak their pieces. Avoid early voting or balloting on solutions. Seek consensus rather than testing by show of hands. This is done by discussing any doubts which are expressed, and by encouraging doubters to articulate their concerns—not to be railroaded or over-whelmed by advocates with big voices or high status. Avoid ballots which may result in split votes and split allegiance. Encourage understanding of the positive implications of preferred solutions as well as any uncertainties about their value.

Step 3—weighing the solutions

Make sure the "best" is in relation to the defined problem and the needs of the group, and not simply the most popular or the easiest to

Step 4—selecting the best solution

agree on. The kind of issue you are dealing with and the norms of the group will determine whether you vote or arrive at a consensus. In arriving at the best solution, make sure it is (1) understood by all the contesting members, (2) appropriate to the identified problem, (3) possible to implement, (4) within the authority and responsibility of this group, (5) arrived at by an appropriate and satisfactory means.

Step 5— implementing the solution

Decide with the group who is going to be responsible for carrying out the solution. Delegation of actions or duties at this stage is important. A group may, having agreed on a solution, simply assume, "Somebody will do it. . . ." That seldom happens without direct commitment. The same people who arrived at the solution should be involved in implementing it. Knowing that responsibility in advance helps sharpen choices of solutions and, also, after the choice is made will bring a group together as they directly share the outcome of the decision-making process. Not only the "who" of implementation is essential, the "when" and "how" should also be settled. A timetable and list of resources are required to complete the process of making and carrying out the decision.

Step 6— evaluating the results

There is a tendency at this point to simply evaluate the solutions. While they are important, it is also important to evaluate how well the group survived the other steps and how they participated. Some evaluation on improving group functioning is useful. If members have become discouraged or if they cannot pull together, look at the reasons. Your group must evaluate its own work through all the preliminary steps to see how the final solution worked. Modern systems for evaluating outcomes are available, and using a system like PERT (Program Evaluation and Review Technique) can be useful in setting up a sequence for implementation. Evaluation is an attitude as much as it is an activity. It requires a generous sense of openness to look at both the content of the group sessions and the socioemotional behaviors of the people who interacted, and especially the leadership functions.

The leader's role in decision making

As the catalyst, facilitator, director, or manager, the group leader will help steer a group through the above steps in a way which is consistent with his or her own abilities and needs as well as those of the group. In the rough-and-tumble of group interaction, the leader may be responsible for both the task accomplishment and the maintenance or socioemotional functions of the group process. It is not likely that all the task functions and the maintenance functions can be accomplished by the same person, even a skillful leader. But these functions must be taken care of, and an effective leader will exert influences to make sure they happen.

We have described the task-related steps with which a group may solve problems or make decisions. Most of the discussion about the six steps was in task terms. As the task assignments are being met, what is happening on the socioemotional level which needs taking care of? Below, in the same order, are some maintenance socioemotional functions which should be attended to as the task moves along. They are summarized in Figure 8-3.

Socioemotional Leading

Test for group cohesiveness. Involve all those who want to participate in talking about the problem. Avoid blaming or scapegoating in defining how the problem came about. Guide the group gently away from proposing easy or too-quick answers, and keep them discussing the problem without stifling participation. Seek *feelings* about the problem as well as facts. (Are members interested? Does the issue affect them? Are there moral or value issues involved which are difficult to talk about? What level of confidence do members have in each other and in their own ability to solve the problem once it is identified?)

Step 1

Draw members out all you can. Encourage a supportive climate to generate the greatest number of solutions. Reward creative suggestions. Do not support negative reactions to suggestions. Have one or more persons write solutions on a blackboard as they come up. Encourage spontaneity. Move quickly from one suggestion to the next.

Step 2

Test for resources: Who knows what? Who can do what? Do the solutions fit personal value systems as well as the organization purpose and structure? Encourage the group to look at the best possible fit of solution to problem rather than "the only" one. Assure members that they are not looking for the Holy Grail but only for the most adequate response to a felt need. Are members open in their reactions to each other and the issue? At this step, it is most important to have everyone free to comment.

Step 3

Check consensus. Direct attention away from voting. Discourage a show of hands or the taking of ballots. Draw out any quiet members

Step 4

Step	Socioemotional content
1	Testing for group cohesiveness
2	Encouraging supportive climate
3	Testing for resources
4	Testing for consensus
5	Encouraging public commitment
6	Evaluating results

FIGURE 8-3

Decision making—six-step process.

(silence may not mean consent at this step), and encourage expression of feelings as well as intellectual positions. Encourage discussion of psychological or social consequences as well as of economic or physical consequences.

Step 5

Encourage the group to make promises to each other, not just to the leader or some absent boss. Commitment must be made openly and before all other members. Avoid letting members sidle up to the leader after the meeting and promise to help. Be specific about names and dates and responsibilities. Check with those named to see that they understand. Do not assign responsibilities to absent members. Silent members are potentially nonsupportive; draw them into the action and get their testimony as they witness for the project.

Step 6

As recommended earlier, encourage members to evaluate the task without accusing each other of base motives. Evaluate the socio-emotional involvements as openly as the group norms will permit. Insist that the group acknowledge that both task and socioemotional activities were going on at the same time: "We generated solutions and agreed on a best one, but we also generated a lot of feelings about each other and the task as it went along." Can the group talk about the meeting with the hope of doing a better job together the next time?

Group Stages—Another View

Interventions by a leader during the decision-making process can be crucial to group dynamics. As we have seen in the life-cycle theories of Hersey and Blanchard (pages 194–196), the path-goal theory (pages 157–159), and Fiedler's contingency theory (pages 191–193), it is important to match leadership style to the stages of growth or maturity of a group. Rebstock[7] suggested four stages which a group may go through in analyzing a case or arriving at a decision. The following stages expand on his observations. Not all groups may go through all these stages; and they may also not proceed in a linear fashion, moving from one to the next in order. There may be looping back into previous stages as new members join, as new circumstances arise, or as progress seems to call for review. At best, this is our rough approximation of the predicted life cycle of a group in its attempt to make a decision. As groups become more proficient, they may not need the first two stages; as groups develop a history of interacting and communicating, they may compress stages into an abbreviated time span or energy expenditure. A group leader, however, who knows

[7]Eugene Rebstock, "General Semantics Training through Case Analysis," *ETC*, vol. 20, no. 3, 1963.

Stage	Process
1	Circling
2	Looking for quick and easy answers
3	Expressing frustration and blame
4	Exploring options
5	Finding solutions and resolutions
6	Implementation

FIGURE 8-4
Group stages.

what potential stages the group may go through and who has an indication of the recommended amount of task or socioemotional emphasis can be effective in helping the group. A summary of group stages appears in Figure 8-4.

Stage 1—circling

As the group prepares to work together, the emphasis is primarily socioemotional and is influenced by similar forces which drive a casual or cathartic group. Getting to know one another and taking the first cautious risks are preoccupations of members. The leader should press to get the task moving by discouraging members from establishing status positions and by making introductions or using other devices. The group can be asked to talk about the problem to be solved and, especially in subgroups or individually, to write out definitions of the problem to be shared with the rest.

Stage 2—looking for quick and easy answers

Now the group is trying to solve the problem before really having it stated clearly. "Here's what we should do . . ." is a characteristic statement, and the indirect form "Don't you think we should . . ." may also be heard. The leader should become task-oriented and should demand a thorough analysis of the problem in defined terms, probably written and agreed to. Avoid letting the group suggest solutions. The socioemotional focus should be on not stifling the enthusiasm of members about supplying solutions but on insisting the solutions will be sought later and will be most valuable.

Stage 3—expressing frustration and blame

Participants may complain they do not have enough data to analyze the problem or find a solution. The normal response is to form a committee—either to study the problem and its origins, or to come up with solution proposals. Members may believe they do not have clear instructions. The group may say it needs (1) more time, such as another meeting or more preparation time; (2) more people, such as more consultants or resource people, or different leaders, workers, researchers, recorders, secretarial help; (3) more information, such as data about the problem or solutions, followed by suggestions to form another committee or to set up research. On this last item, the leader may want to stress that we make decisions all our lives with incomplete data, and that there comes a time when we must stop collecting information and act. The group needs much socioemotional support from the leader at this stage, and together they may be able to see that avoidance of the task is not an unusual aim for groups, but with persistence and open communication the group can do its job.

Stage 4—exploring options

Among the options open to the group is to do nothing. As a group assembles a list of possible decisions, the arguments develop. The leader should exert strong task efforts at this stage. Objectivity should be prized. Time should be devoted to developing a thorough understanding of the history of recommendations and their implications. The problem came from somewhere, and its solutions will lead somewhere. Members should be encouraged to review the content of the decisions, their implications for the organization and the members, and how the decisions and their implications relate to needs of both the organization and the group. Much of the task effort may be spent on drawing out quiet members who may feel beaten down by more verbal members or may be pouting over treatment by others. The leader's socioemotional interventions should focus on keeping the climate open and on protecting less dominant members from being browbeaten into quick acceptance of ideas, but even those interventions are done in the spirit of task achievement.

Stage 5—finding solutions and resolutions

The group should select the best possible solutions and not the "right" ones. Decisions grow out of a realization that (1) the problems are complex; (2) the problems grew out of a historical background, they came from somewhere; (3) solutions are to be applied in the future, they are going somewhere; and (4) even the best solution is a compromise. The leader can back off and be nondirective on the task because by now the group knows its business and can also be neutral on socioemotional factors because by now the group has already developed some systems for dealing with feelings in working relationships and interpersonal contacts. The solution should be a group solution, and not one set up to please the leader or simply to reach adjournment. Whatever the leader can do to guide the group into that realization will help their task.

Stage 6— implementation

This is the stage at which people promise to follow through. They must make that promise to each other, and the leader should stay out of it except to guide that activity so there are witnesses to the members' intentions to do things and to report back. Only group members who have "bought into" the solution are going to work for its implementation, and the weakest commitment is likely to be to the leader who has not the time or resources to check on performance. Figure 8-5 gives a summary of manager interventions in group discussions.

If it is true that almost everybody belongs to groups, it is equally true that groups tend to have meetings. The settings for interaction between leaders and followers and among followers are referred to as meetings, conferences, seminars, discussions, round tables, or by a variety of special names adopted by organizations to describe the sessions, such as "the president's Monday staff meeting," "the dean's show-and-tell time," "a marketing confab," or "debriefing." Not only is the meeting a communication tool for management or leadership, but it is a useful learning and enhancement activity for employees or followers. Training for new leadership occurs in meetings as followers get a chance to observe leader models and to practice communication skills and learn from the results.

Much of what is decided at meetings depends on forces beyond the

MEETINGS AS COMMUNICATION

Stage	Task Activity and Manager Response	Socioemotional Activity and Manager Response
1. Circling	Ask the group to talk about the problem to be solved.	Discourage members from publicly establishing their status.
2. Looking for quick and easy answers	Require a thorough analysis of the problem in operational terms. Keep the group from suggesting solutions.	Do not stifle enthusiasm, but insist solution will come at a later stage.
3. Expressing frustration and blame	Do not let the group off the hook from deciding.	Help the group overcome frustration by stressing that decisions are always made on the basis of incomplete data
4. Exploring options	Review the content of decisions and their implications for the organization. Draw out quiet members.	Keep the climate open and protect less dominant members from being pushed into quick acceptance of ideas.
5. Finding solutions and resolutions	Back off. Be nondirective.	Help gently to explore the outcomes of any solution.
6. Implementation	Have members make a public commitment on their implementation of the decision.	Encourage members to talk about their feelings about doing the job.

FIGURE 8-5
Intervention style for managers.

meeting itself. Participants bring to the meeting their own personal assumptions about meetings and the group. Members sometimes have made outside commitments (or "deals") with others which intrude on the meeting, even if the other persons are not present. The results of a meeting will be carried out afterward—often by people not even attending. Decisions may affect people and events some distance away in time and space. Clear communication is essential for the conduct of the meeting itself and for the summary, review, implementation, and continued activities of the group.

Interaction between leaders and followers has been discussed earlier in this chapter and in Chapter 7 on leadership. In this section, we will concentrate on the meeting as an activity of organizational communication. Four factors will be emphasized (four P's)—planning factors, physical factors, procedural factors, and psychological factors. Greater detail on these factors can be obtained from a variety of sources. Bradford's how-to-do-it book titled *Making Meetings Work*[8] is an excellent treatment of ways to move beyond the traditional, and historically uninspired, methods of leading meetings. The same publishers, University Associates, have published many excellent articles, exercises, and references for handling meetings and training leaders. Keesey's *Modern Parliamentary Procedure*[9] is a valuable text for persons interested in formal procedures. It lives up to the preface statement by the founder of the American Institute of Parliamentarians, Robert English, that the book follows the principle "that parliamentary procedure should facilitate the transaction of business in an orderly, deliberative, democratic manner." We believe that meetings can be effectively guided by the democratic and generally unstructured system of group participation[10] without rigorously imposed bylaws, procedures, and unnecessarily interfering parliamentary forms. Only when groups need to subscribe to an agreed-upon system for settling the points of procedure do they need the structure of formal operating bylaws and Robert's Rules of Order. Under trained leadership, groups can function very well without such formal and often restrictive baggage.

Planning Factors

We already have discussed forces in the leader, the followers, and the situation (page 215) which determine when to use decision-making groups. Leaders must also ask themselves, before a meeting is scheduled, some of the following: (1) Is this meeting necessary? (2)

[8]L. P. Bradford, University Associates, La Jolla, Calif., 1976.
[9]R. E. Keesey, Houghton-Mifflin Company, Boston, 1974.
[10]See Bradford, op cit., p. 51.

Should this business be transacted by some other group or agency? (3) Are the correct people included? (4) Are the time and place appropriate? (5) Have the members received sufficient notice about what will go on and enough advance warning to prepare for the topics? (6) What do we intend to achieve? Will the meeting do it? (7) Are we prepared to follow up on or otherwise respond to whatever comes out of the meeting?

Group members preparing to attend a meeting should read previous minutes or other data to be discussed. Members can preview agendas or their own expectations in terms of knowledge, reports, and personal value reviews. Promptness is a courtesy to others, so schedule yourself to get to a meeting on time. Questions about how the group will work, why you are expected to be there, what time it will be over, and what you should bring should be asked in advance of the meeting, not after you arrive.

Physical Factors

Related to planning is the setting of a time and place, convenient enough and comfortable enough so members can concern themselves about making decisions rather than how hot or cold or remote or noisy the meeting place is. Duration of the meeting is a physical factor of great concern. A starting time should be set and held to, and so should the adjournment time, if possible. Groups usually pace themselves to fill the available time, and an open-ended meeting tends to achieve less than those set for a specified time. It has been a common idea that about two hours is as long as a meeting should run without a break. As our lives become more and more conditioned to the half-hour segments of television scheduling, thirty-minute and one-hour intervals take on greater significance. We encourage you to study proxemics and the nonverbal systems[11] operating in human communication. Many important features in the physical setting, such as the location of the room, the seating arrangements, the size and shape of tables, the time of day, and cultural differences about open and closed doors, can influence group interaction. In addition, visual aids or other special considerations of the setting can enhance the group's work. All such

[11]For a compendium of nonverbal factors see M. L. Knapp, *Nonverbal Communication in Human Interaction*, Holt, Rinehart and Winston, New York, 1972. A. Mehrabian, *Silent Messages*, Wadsworth Publishing Co., Belmont, Calif., 1971, is also useful. Two classics by E. T. Hall are *The Silent Language*, Premier Books, Doubleday & Company, Garden City, N.Y., 1959, and *The Hidden Dimension*, Anchor Books, Doubleday & Company, Garden City, N.Y., 1969. Excellent treatment of the "proxemic environment" is found in Chapter 3 of Dale Leathers' *Nonverbal Communication Systems*, Allyn and Bacon, Inc., Boston, Mass., 1976.

equipment or services should be planned in advance, thoroughly checked out or edited or prepared, and ready for the group to use or watch. Even more than what may be said by the leader, the physical setup may reflect how important the meeting is and how much care went into making sure the group could work well together. Interruptions are nonproductive either for the leader or members. Once the meeting starts, calls or visits from the outside should be held to emergencies. Other members are annoyed and distracted when one is called out to answer the phone, sign papers, or meet a visitor. Plan the location and other physical conditions to minimize interruptions.

Procedural Factors   Both leader and members are responsible for getting a meeting started on time. Members should be present and ready; the leader should call the group to order at the agreed-on starting time. If the group has a written agenda, it should be cleared with the participants so everyone understands the topics, their sequence, and essentially what the meeting is intended to cover.

Communication behaviors between leaders and members have been discussed earlier in this chapter and the previous one on leadership. In summary, it is the joint responsibility of the leader and members to see that the group moves its business along. Leaders must identify the members who have the useful data for certain decisions and must decide how to get the information from them. Who will lead the arguments for or against an issue and who will carry out a decision are matters to be worked out as the group proceeds. Recorders or reporters are essential in order to maintain control over what is decided. Not paying attention, interrupting, horseplay, or other forms of distraction should be controlled by the leader and the other members. Peer pressure is a useful deterrent to distracting behaviors by group members.

Business should be conducted *in the meeting* and not in the hallways or by cliques or subgrouping. Hidden agendas of members should be surfaced if possible. Norms established by the group will determine how authentic are interactions and how much trust and risk the members are willing to tolerate. Meetings of groups which habitually avoid decisions or use the group for personal motives are not productive and should be discontinued.

Procedurally, the meeting should begin on time. All members should know what is to happen and what each person's part will be. During the meeting, the leader (encouraged and assisted by members) makes sure that clear procedures are followed, summaries are made when needed, loose ends are avoided and decisions reached, and all persons who want to be involved have that opportunity. How to implement decisions should be settled immediately. All follow-up actions must be identified and commitment to actions sought from members. A summary of what was accomplished is useful, and the meeting should end at the agreed-on time with a clear indication of what is expected in the way of future meetings or actions.

Psychological Factors

Many interchanges of attitudes, emotions, and reactions are transmitted nonverbally by facial expressions, gestures, tone of voice, posture, and so on. A leader should be aware of the rich communication being exchanged nonverbally and should use nonverbal cues to analyze and support the verbal exchanges. People in meetings behave with all the motives and goals and needs associated with normal interpersonal relations. They do not suddenly become objective, scientific, and logical just because the meeting is called to order. The successful leader, therefore, will pay attention to psychological factors characteristic of human interaction, including not listening, displaying apathy, talking past or beyond one another, riding personal "hobby horses," and delivering self-serving lectures or speeches.

If socioemotional behaviors endanger the success of a meeting, the leader may want to identify the problem for the group, may want to draw out hidden agendas or personal motives in conflict with the group goals, or may simply take the means of inviting the group to solve the problem itself or remain ineffective. In the following section on "groupthink" and the dangers of group processes, we will discuss some more aspects of the psychological factors in meetings.

INEFFECTIVE GROUPS

Much of the mythology about the ineffectiveness of groups is based on the bitter experiences of people—leaders and followers—who have spent time in meetings or group settings and come away convinced there must be a better way. There usually is. But the better way may be simply running better meetings, changing our expectations of what groups can do, or altering in some way the factors which make normally efficient people suddenly become disruptive, disagreeable, bored, angry, frustrated, cynical, petulant, withdrawn, irrational, and inefficient.

Groups which work together need to take stock of their effectiveness. It is easy to meet simply for the sake of meeting. A leader should identify the kind of group (casual, cathartic, etc.) and determine whether that type serves the needs of the organization. Further, is the group working well? Referring to an unpublished training document by Jay Hall, Vincent O'Leary, and Martha Williams, we have developed our own questions to ask about a group to pinpoint where a group may

FIGURE 8-6

1. Do group members expect the group to function only as a task group and to ignore or deny existence of socioemotional factors?
2. Can members separate ideas from the person who expressed them or how the idea was presented? Can they avoid "personality-linked" judgments?
3. Are the topics relevant to the group and to group discussion?

   The following items are *relevant* for group decision making:
   a. Topics which require data from a number of group members for decision.
   b. Problems whose origins come from several group members or their concerns.
   c. Problems whose solutions will have to be implemented by members of the group.
   d. Problems whose solutions are capable of being implemented by other groups linked to this one, even if additional joint meetings with other groups will be required.
   e. Problems whose solutions require progressive deliberations, using the analytical skills of group members as well as information.

   The following items are *not relevant* for group decision making:
   a. Problems of concern to only a few members who can solve them in separate, one-to-one interaction.
   b. Problems of little significance or importance for the level of this group, and which could be settled by a lower echelon.
   c. Problems which should be solved by simply applying existing policies or regulations— in other words, situations where there is nothing new to decide.
   d. Problems for which there are incomplete data or which need additional research or staff study.
   e. Problems which are beyond the sphere of influence or control of the group to recommend solutions or to carry out recommendations.
   f. Problems which are trivial or even offensive to so many members that group interaction would destroy relationships or group confidence or sensibilities, or problems which are so trivial the group will not take them seriously.

4. Do you assume that silence means consent during deliberations?
5. Do you let the group vote prematurely, before all aspects of a problem have been probed? Do you check often for consensus to guide the group gently toward a decision and let them know where they are at every step?
6. Can the group tolerate conflict or disagreement? Or is the necessity for keeping everybody happy and having maximum agreement short-circuiting honest discussion?
7. Do you engage in tricks to settle arguments or get agreement? Tricks include flipping a coin; trading off with others (logrolling, "You scratch my back and I'll scratch yours"), forming coalitions, voting hastily, steamrolling, ridiculing deviance, name calling or labeling, pulling rank, flattery, shouting or walking out, not sharing information.
8. Do you adopt clear goals, set clear agendas, state problems clearly?
9. Do you encourage feedback on issues (task) and on feelings (socioemotional) among group members?
10. Do you change the rules to meet expediencies, or do you operate on a consistent set of procedures?
11. Do you encourage options (more than two solutions) or limit discussion to only two opposing alternatives?
12. Are you prepared to take time to work out decisions, and to insist that the group allocate appropriate amounts of time to the relative importance of the issues under discussion?

need help and to help leaders or consultants diagnose the dysfunctional behaviors of group members or leaders. These questions appear in Figure 8-6.

Groupthink

Adopting language from futuristic novels, the process of group decision making has been given a critical treatment by I. Janis as "groupthink."[12] Some of his formulations of how groups operate dysfunctionally are also presented in a film by the same name. Janis comments that "groupthink" always occurs in a *cohesive group* where members have strong positive feelings toward each other and want to remain members of the group. This sense of *solidarity* encourages the group to seek agreement and prevents it from seriously considering problems which might have consequences that "rock their boat"—the "boat" being a "happy ship." In this way, members of an overly cohesive group fail to use *critical thinking.*

Groups develop, according to Janis, an *illusion of invulnerability.* They become complacent and secure in their decisions. They also develop a scapegoating practice of identifying "we" and "they" as they feed their own cohesiveness by fixing a common enemy, aided by shared or *common stereotypes* about the adversary. Working together, the group can develop pooled *rationalizations* and support even the flimsiest excuses for their behaviors or decisions. They defend themselves with a cloak of *morality* as illusionary as their invulnerability; group support enables them to deny ethical responsibilities.

Groups which work closely together for too long a time become insulated to outside realities; and with *mind-guarding* practices, they can assure themselves that everyone else believes as they do. An *illusion of unanimity* is created inside the group, and members do not express doubts, which would be seen as disrupting the group oneness. Janis cites President John Kennedy's highly effective response to the Cuban missile crisis and recommends that outside experts be allowed to give opinions but that, more important, every member of the group be a critical evaluator. Every member must have freedom to explore all options, keep communication open, and come to an informed decision with a clear understanding of future responsibilities and risks.

SUMMARY

Common attitudes about how well groups work are not entirely favorable. Not every person in authority believes that groups and

---

[12]*Victims of Groupthink*, Houghton-Mifflin, Boston, 1972. "Groupthink," *Psychology Today*, vol. 5, no. 6. pp. 43–48, November 1971.

meetings are effective ways to make decisions or solve problems. In our interdependent society, however, it is imperative that people work in groups, and the existence of groups is a way of modern life. In addition, group work can be better than it has been for many people if those responsible for group behaviors—and this includes leaders and followers alike—will seek ways to improve group functioning. Leaders everywhere can make use of the growing volumes of data about group dynamics as well as the techniques and methodologies for improving group and leader communication skills. Subordinates in group situations are also capable of applying action principles in their roles. Techniques for working effectively in groups are becoming better and better known; but it will take persistent efforts of group leaders and members to bring the group communication processes to their potential of sophistication and effectiveness.

CHAPTER 9

MANAGING CONFLICT

"The mutual confidence on which all else depends can be maintained only by an open mind and a brave reliance upon free discussion."   Judge Learned Hand

It is not possible to understand the dynamics of communication without coming to grips with the notion of conflict. If communication is a transaction, then individual differences must be somehow mutually negotiated to develop common meanings. There cannot be differences without conflict.

THE TRADITIONAL VIEW OF CONFLICT

The idea that conflict is inevitable in interpersonal communication is, however, relatively new. Traditionally, conflict was viewed quite differently. It was considered both a sign of competence and a source of pride for people in organizations or other informal groups to boast about how well people got along, how few conflicts ever arose, or even to state flatly that the organization was totally conflict-free.

Traditional organizational ideas about conflict implied that conflict was bad, avoidable, and related to the behavior of a few undesirable individuals. Conflict was associated with anger, aggressiveness, physical and verbal fights, and violence—all basically negative feelings and behaviors. "Nice people don't fight," "It's better to get along," "Don't argue in front of the children," "If you loved me you would not argue," are familiar messages which teach that conflict is basically a bad thing. By that reasoning, only a bad person would disagree, feel angry, or fight. Of course, the potential negative effects of conflicts are very real. On a grand scale, wars among nations are expressions of conflicts at their worst. On a small but no less painful scale, divorces, separations, resignations, psychological withdrawals, and embattled relationships are examples of interpersonal conflicts and strife.

Although these traditional ideas about the inherent evils of conflict are still with us in many ways, a new view about conflict has emerged, and the solely negative view of conflict is no longer so widely held.

THE CONTEMPORARY VIEW OF CONFLICT

Joe Kelly[1] describes the new set of assumptions about conflict which are typical of the more recent approaches to the study of conflict processes. These newer approaches are based on the notion that conflict is inevitable, is often determined by structural factors in the organization, and is an integral part of the process of change. In fact, some degree of conflict is helpful.

This view recognizes that conflict is a natural part of any communication relationship. No matter how close you are to another

[1]*Organizational Behavior*, Richard D. Irwin, Inc., and The Dorsey Press, Homewood, Ill., 1969.

person, no matter how much you like or love another person, no matter how compatible you may be with another person or a group of people, there will always be times when your needs, thoughts, feelings, and actions will clash with those of others. No two people can ever be so alike as to always feel, think, and act identically. Conflict as a fact of life does not necessarily mean that organizations are doomed to experience harmful, dysfunctional, or destructive consequences. For what matters is, not so much the existence of conflict, but *how the conflict is handled*. Even though you may not be able to do anything about the existence of conflict, you may be able to change the way you approach conflict, deal with it, manage it, and resolve it.

Not all conflicts have the same outcomes. Some are destructive, others constructive.

POTENTIAL CONSEQUENCES OF CONFLICT

Conflict is potentially destructive in an organization when it consumes so much of people's energy that little is left for the work. Constant bickering and frequent disagreements often wear people out and decrease their motivation level. "Why expend effort to do something if it's only going to result in further arguments" may become the attitude of embittered department members. Conflicts can interfere with work and create so many interpersonal hostilities and antagonistic feelings that the people involved may simply become unable or unwilling to work with each other.

Destructive Outcomes

The example of June, an assistant vice-president at a large bank, will illustrate the point. June has been a supervisor in the trust department for the past five years. She is bright and very competent, and her supervisor has always been very supportive and has always sung her praises to other managers. She likes and respects him and enjoys the fact that he has given her a great deal of responsibility. Six months ago, however, her supervisor was transferred to another department. While she felt sorry to see him go, she was for a while hopeful that, given her experience in the department and her excellent track record, she would be asked to fill the position and be promoted. However, through the grapevine she heard that Alex, a young bank officer, would get the job and she would be passed over. Within a week and without official forewarning, Alex took over. At first Alex was friendly and eager to learn the ropes in his new assignment, but it became quickly apparent to everyone in the department that Alex and June simply could not or would not work together effectively. Although June knew intellectually that Alex was not himself responsible for the fact that she was not promoted, she was simply unable to deal with the resentment and anger she felt over the whole situation. She tried to be fair to Alex and help him, as she saw the need to work with him for the sake of the department, but she became increasingly more critical of his actions. Although she never openly criticized him in front of the employees in the department, her feelings were obvious to everyone. The situation escalated to the point where June found every excuse to avoid Alex. Because he simply did not know enough about the work to make decisions without her input, the whole department was in turmoil and June developed severe headaches and considered resigning.

This is a true story and not an uncommon one. As we will see later, however, it was not so much that conflict existed between June and Alex—which created problems for the department—but rather the way in which both chose to deal with it. We will come back to this point later as we discuss strategies for managing conflict.

Conflict can also lead to conservatism and conformity. As we discussed in Chapter 8, the groupthink phenomenon is based on the fear that open conflict will result in severe negative consequences such as public ridicule or blame. As a result, people feel pressure to agree with whatever they think is the "official" position, the safe idea, or simply the expected company line. As superficial consensus develops, people's fears are reduced; and although decisions may not be made very effectively, everyone is lulled into feeling that they all must be right since everyone agrees. Nothing is as comforting as the sense of validation that one derives from agreement with others. The price paid is often a reduction in the quality of the decisions made, since no unpopular ideas or new creative ideas are allowed to surface to rock the boat. Again, it is not so much conflict itself as the fear of conflict which is destructive.

Conflict can sometimes be so vicious and violent that it leads to the destruction or neutralization of opponents, particularly when the conflict situation is perceived in terms of mutually exclusive goals where one person can only win if the other loses. If the goals to be reached by both parties are extremely important to them, an all-out war can be started with all kinds of potentially destructive repercussions. This happens in organizations when two people compete viciously for the same job, the same resources, the same title, or the same sphere of influence.

Conflict can also lead to high turnover and absenteeism but mostly hinders group coordination and the implementation of tasks which require interdependent activities. In interdependent groups, cooperation may be the only way to get the job done; often, open or hidden competition between group members, or between different groups, will sabotage the effective accomplishment of the task. It is almost as though one person will prefer to lose just to make sure that no one else wins.

Frequently, conflict will lead to distortion of information, or even withholding of necessary information. In a highly competitive atmosphere, people are extremely vigilant and no one will knowingly give an advantage to others who are perceived as adversaries, competitors, or even enemies. The organization is not viewed as a whole, but rather as made up of competing entities where vested interests scramble for resources and influence and lose sight of the common goal for the common good. Conflicts often lead to duplication of effort when communication between competing groups or persons decreases—or disappears.

Positive Outcomes

When you consider the number of possible negative outcomes resulting from conflict, it is easy to understand why so much effort is often spent avoiding conflict or suppressing it. Yet, much benefit can also be derived from the existence of conflict or tension in organizations.

Tension and conflict often exhilarate, energize, and motivate people. Some people simply thrive on competition, and conflict is a strong mobilizer of their energies which otherwise might not be available for organizational activities. A person who has much to gain from successfully competing with others and winning will expend a tremendous amount of effort on attempts to win—effort which often benefits the organization. The supersalesperson who wants to be number one and works day and night to increase sales volume ultimately benefits the company.

Conflict can also lead to innovation, creativity, and change. If conflict is suppressed for the sake of conformity, uniformity, and security, few creative ideas are likely to emerge. Without new ideas for doing things, stagnation and routine may ultimately dominate the organizational climate. New ideas often are born in the midst of conflicting viewpoints which are openly shared and discussed. Encouraging individual self-expression can lead to better organizational performance and stronger habits of participation and commitment, and it ultimately improves intergroup coordination and information flow. Figure 9-1 summarizes criteria for judging whether a conflict is constructive and is being managed in a positive manner.

TYPES OF CONFLICTS

Though conflict used to be perceived as resulting from personal idiosyncrasies or the machinations of troublemakers, the contemporary study of conflict attributes it to a variety of factors. In fact,

FIGURE 9-1

Robbins' criteria for successful conflict management.

1. Does this conflict facilitate achievement of organizational goals?
2. Does this level of conflict work productively in the long run?
3. Are all relevant feelings and beliefs directly expressed?

Assael's characteristics of a constructive conflict.

1. Constructive conflict promotes inquiry into the efficacy of organizational or personal policies or values.
2. Constructive conflict results in improved communications between or among involved participants.
3. Constructive conflict results in a more equitable distribution of resources and power.
4. Constructive conflict results in the development and standardization of procedures of successful future conflict management.
5. Constructive conflict provides for restraint in the use of power by the dominant participant(s).

Filley's criteria for successful conflict resolution.

1. Is (are) the solution(s) reached acceptable to everyone involved?
2. Does (do) the solution(s) meet preestablished criteria for "goodness" and/or "appropriateness?"
3. Do participants focus on defeating the problem rather than each other?
4. Do participants avoid voting, averaging, and trading?
5. Do participants utilize facts, not "getting my way?"

there are many types of conflict, and each has roots in different levels of the organization structure.

In this section we discuss the different types of conflict: personal, interpersonal, and organizational.

Personal Conflicts

Personal conflicts occur within an individual who experiences (1) conflicting needs, desires, or values, (2) competing ways of satisfying a given need or want, (3) frustration from blocks which get in the way of satisfying a need, and (4) role discrepancies.

Conflicting needs. It is quite common to experience conflicting needs or desires. Our discussion of motivation in Chapter 6 pointed out that, at a given time, you may need to fulfill competing desires and sometimes these may appear to be mutually exclusive. The four different types of conflict of needs are summarized in Figure 9.2. In the *approach-approach conflict*, you may be attracted to two attractive goals, but only one can be reached; in the *approach-avoidance conflict*, you may want something that has both assets and liabilities. In the *avoidance-avoidance conflict*, you may face two possibilities, both negative. In the *double approach-avoidance conflict*, you may have two goals, but each has positive and negative aspects.

Approach-approach conflict. Should you go out with the "boys" or go out on a date? Should you spend a lot of time on project A to please your supervisor and get a promotion, or should you really concentrate on project B which is a lot more fun to do? Conflict often appears to be of the you-can't-have-your-cake-and-eat-it-too variety. Your need to be home as the children grow up may conflict with your need to get an education or to have a career. Your need to be independent, control your own life, and make your own decisions may also conflict with a need to be taken care of and be able to depend on someone. Some needs may truly be mutually exclusive, yet many apparent impossible contradictions can be resolved by defining the situation differently and by challenging the implicit assumptions which underlie the definition of the conflict itself. If you want to be a good mother, does it necessarily mean that you have to stay home all the time while the children grow up? Is it possible to define a "good mother" in some other way which might include the possibility of going to school or of working part-time or even full-time? Attitudes about such issues are complex and often deeply rooted. When such is the case, resolving the conflict by finding alternative ways to define the situation may be very difficult. Yet a patient spouse, or friend, or supervisor may often be of great help in assisting an employee to resolve such crippling personal conflicts. Sometimes counseling is needed to help a person sort out complex feelings and conflicting needs, and develop a satisfying course of action.

Approach-avoidance conflict.   Approach-avoidance conflict is frequently experienced in organizational settings where the accomplishment of a goal often has both attractive and repellent consequences. This type of personal conflict can become extremely crippling when the negative factors are just as strong as the positive ones, and the

---

1. *Approach-approach:* A person is attracted by two goal-objects at the same time, but only one can be satisfied.
   Example: The president of the company must decide whether to buy a Mercedes or a Jaguar.
2. *Approach-avoidance:* The goal the individual is striving for has both attractive and negative characteristics of equal strength.
   Example: A college student wants to go to graduate school to get that extra degree, but knows that he or she must put in two years of hard work.
3. *Avoidance-avoidance:* The individual is faced with two possibilities, both negative. This is the "lesser of two evils" syndrome.
   Example: An employee must choose between staying late at the office and coming in on Saturday to finish up late work.
4. *Double approach-avoidance:* A person faces two or more goal objects, for each of which the person has at least one approach impulse and at least one avoidance impulse.
   Example: An individual must decide whether to accept a new job with more prestige and higher pay, which would also use up a large amount of time now spent with the family.

FIGURE 9-2
The four types of intrapersonal conflict.

decision needed to solve the matter becomes very difficult to make. Examples of approach-avoidance conflicts are numerous. Do you take a job which is dull but pays well? Do you tell your supervisor that she or he made a mistake, and run the risk of making her or him angry? Do you finish your term paper tonight and turn it in on time, and thus let your girl friend down for the evening? If the negative consequences clearly outweigh the positive ones, the choice may be easy. If there is a clear difference between positive and negative outcomes, the conflict can be easily solved. When, however, the positive and negative outcomes are (1) hard to define or quantify, or (2) clearly balance each other out, then the choice is extremely difficult to make. The conflict can be, and often is, so paralyzing that people develop illness symptoms or can only withdraw physically or psychologically from the anxiety-provoking situation. Such conflicts are frequent in modern organizations and plague the life of executives. Stresses associated with positions which demand constant dealing with such decisions are intense. Statistics on the mental and physical health of executives indicate that such stresses do take their toll.[2]

Avoidance-avoidance conflict. Avoidance-avoidance conflict deals with equally unattractive options, and the choice requires deciding which is least unattractive. Do you stay late at the office or come in on a Saturday morning to finish up late work? In some cases, there is no way to avoid the situation, as not choosing one alternative automatically results in having to face the other. If you absolutely cannot stand your supervisor, but also cannot afford to be without a job, you are experiencing an avoidance-avoidance conflict. Staying in the company means putting up with the unpleasantness of your interpersonal day-to-day transactions with the supervisor; leaving means no job. Neither choice is satisfying, and you may be in the "lesser-of-two-evils" predicament until the job market looks better.

Conflict may also exist between a value that you hold and a behavior which is required of you. Conflicts of loyalty are frequently experienced by supervisors who have allegiances to several distinct groups in the same organization or who experience a clash between what they value dearly and the goals the organization demands. If you are an avid environmentalist, should you work for an industry which contributes heavily to pollution? If you value honesty, should you work in an organization which demands that you withhold information from consumers or from the public? If you are basically a cooperative person, do you stay in a company which rewards highly spirited competition? Do you become a party to illegalities, white lies,

---

[2]Ernest Dole and Lyndall Urwick, *Staff in Organization*, McGraw-Hill Book Company, New York, 1960.

and other practices which you consider shady? Such dilemmas are not always easy to solve.

Double approach-avoidance conflict.   You may pursue two goals, each with assets and liabilities. For example, will you accept a new job with more prestige and higher pay—one that would also cut out a large amount of the time you spend with your family?

Competing Ways to Satisfy Needs

As you set your goals, you often discover that there are many ways to achieve them. If you wish to perform a socially useful function, make money, and have prestige, which profession or career will you choose? If you want to be promoted quickly in the company, should you look for the kind of position where you will get a chance to stay in the same job for a while so that you can become an expert in that job; or should you go for the kind of position which will allow you to shift around laterally in the company for a while? Which of these positions will allow for a faster upward movement in the hierarchy? Which will allow you to climb higher?

Frustration from blocks.   Personal conflict often occurs when something gets in the way of reaching your goal. In the earlier example of June, the assistant vice-president at the bank, a block got in her way for her promotion; and Alex, the new supervisor, represented that block.

Psychologists long believed aggression to be the only response to frustration. It is evident, however, that frustration can lead to many other defensive mechanisms. In June's example, she responded in a number of ways to Alex. She first bent over backward to be fair and nice, what psychologists call *overcompensation*. Then she felt angry and simply would not help him learn what he needed to know, a hidden aggressive reaction. Then she withdrew physically and emotionally from the situation by avoiding him, by developing headaches, and finally by thinking about resigning from the bank.

Other reactions to frustration are possible, including *fixation*, stubbornly continuing to work toward an unattainable goal or doggedly pursuing a course of action which has proved to be doomed to failure. Another possibility is to seek *creative compromises* by redefining the frustrating situation or finding alternative ways to reach the goal. This alternative will be discussed in a later section.

Role Discrepancies

As mentioned in Chapter 4, role conflict is a common experience for managers who link different groups and who are expected to behave in ways appropriate to the values held by these different groups.

When the different groups hold similar values, there is little conflict. When they do not, there is tremendous pressure for the individual to be all things to all people—an impossible task. The first-line supervisor is often in that predicament. As the person in the middle between workers and management, the supervisor is expected to act in ways that will be found acceptable by workers, managers, and also other supervisors.

INTERPERSONAL CONFLICT

Interpersonal conflict occurs basically because of (1) individual differences and (2) limited resources.[3]

Individual Differences

As mentioned earlier in the chapter when we discussed the inevitability of conflict, the fact of individual differences is the very reason for conflict. Differences in age, sex, attitudes, beliefs, values, experience, and training all contribute to people's perceptual sets and thus to the way they see situations and other people. A young, aggressive, formally educated manager may see a situation differently from older managers with more seniority who came up through the ranks. Some men refuse to get along with or take orders from women managers. In social groups there may be some degree of choice about whom to associate with, but the same flexibility is unlikely to exist in the work environment. You work with certain people because they are there and because you were assigned to the job, the unit, or the department. Although you may have the ultimate choice of leaving the company, if you stay you don't really get to choose your associates. If they are much different from you, then some degree of conflict is inevitable.

Limited Resources

No organization ever has all the resources it needs. Financial resources, human resources, and technical resources are always somewhat limited. Choices have to be made, and wisely allocating valuable resources is one of management's critical tasks. Because of this fact of organizational life, constant choices must be made about who gets people, space, typewriters, equipment, budget allocations, information, power, etc. Competition is, in essence, built in when a system has scarce resources. Each person, or each group, competes to get a share of the pie. The smaller the pie, the more intense the

[3]James L. Gibson, John M. Ivancevitch, and James H. Donneley, Jr., *Organizations*, rev. ed., Business Publications, Inc., Dallas, Tex., 1976, pp. 166–168.

competition. Management's concern is to find the distribution of resources that will be most effective in permitting the organization to reach its goals. However, one group's or one person's idea of the most effective way does not always agree with everybody else's ideas. Each person in the organization may have a different idea of the "best way." The person who feels he or she is not getting a fair share often develops antagonism toward others who are perceived to get more, or toward those who are seen to be the cause of the unjust allocation. Such conflict can lead to a variety of dysfunctional behaviors which severely tax organizational effectiveness.

Role Differentiation

Interpersonal conflict often results from failure to agree on how relationships should be defined. In Chapter 4, we discussed at length what happens when one person refuses to accept the role definition implied in another person's actions. If you make a request, implying you have some authority over the other person, but the other person refuses to comply and, in essence, refuses to acknowledge or accept your authority, then a conflict about control exists. Who is in control and who defines the mutual roles? This type of conflict often occurs when two people basically agree about a certain course of action but one refuses to go ahead and do it because the other initiated the idea. A supervisor and employee may both agree that a project needs to be finished before a certain deadline; but if the supervisor mentions overtime, the employee may balk. The balking is not so much caused by the necessity to spend more time at work as by having to accept the supervisor's authority. Had the supervisor said nothing, the employee might have suggested overtime and volunteered to stay at work longer. In that case the decision would have been made by the employee who thus would have kept control. Conflict between people occurs frequently—not because they disagree on the content of an issue, but because they refuse to accept each other's definition of their relationship.

There is no end to what we can accomplish if it doesn't matter who gets the credit or who is in control.

ORGANIZATIONAL CONFLICT

In many cases, the potential for conflict comes from the structure of the organization itself. As organizations get bigger and more complex, they develop different hierarchical levels, as well as more complicated functions and roles. The potential for conflict is simply built in.

A member of the board of directors of a large corporation is unlikely to see things the way a worker does. The more hierarchical levels exist in an organization and the more they are insulated from one another, the less information people share and the less they know and understand one another. The perspectives, values, and goals of upper management are not usually the same as those of middle management, first-line supervisors, blue-collar workers, and clerical employees. In a small organization where there are few people at each of the levels, and where a great deal of communication occurs across levels, potential conflicts are minimized. In large organizations where levels are numerous, communication is more limited, and a worker may seldom see—let alone talk with—higher management, the potential for conflict is greater. Perhaps it is easier to fight with people you do not know personally. If you perceive management as the "enemy" and do not know the real people filling the roles, it is easier to fight them. The impersonal "they" of large corporations or bureaucracies do not have faces.

Functional conflict is also inevitable. Different parts of an organization simply have competing needs as a result of what they must accomplish. If the sales department must increase volume, salespeople may make promises about delivery schedules, discounts, etc., which will have repercussions for production, accounting, and advertising. Production may not be able to meet the delivery schedule because purchasing has not been able to get raw materials in on short notice. While salespeople might like to have large inventories available, production and finance are likely to resist building up stocks because of the cost of storage and of carrying unsold merchandise. If production is in the middle of union negotiations, it is likely to feel that this takes precedence over anything else. Sales, however, may feel under pressure from upper management to increase volume and is likely to feel that its concerns take precedence over anything else. In one hospital we know, severe conflict existed between the physical plant department and the nursing staff, simply because a new safety regulation from engineering stated that no small appliances were allowed on the floors because many of these would not fit new safety standards. Nurses, particularly those on night shifts, became very annoyed at engineering for preventing them from keeping coffeepots at their stations. They resented the interference with their working conditions by the engineers.

Conflicts between line and staff are typical and take many forms in different settings. University administrators are often pitted against faculty members. Medical and other hospital professionals are often at odds with hospital administrative personnel. Sales and production people frequently fight design engineers or accounting or research people. The uneven distribution of power, responsibility, and authority makes it almost impossible for conflict not to develop.

Each person in the organization has feelings about the fairness of work, influence, privileges, and rewards. Whether the differences are real or imagined makes little difference in how people react to others. If supervisors play favorites, likelihood of conflict is maximized.

Our main point throughout this discussion is that conflict is a reality of organizational life. It can be of great value to the organization when it prevents stagnation and when it stimulates exploration of new ideas and procedures. Conflict permits problems to be surfaced, discussed, and solved. Although conflict may appear dysfunctional or disruptive, it does have functional consequences when it permits the system to constantly adjust to its environment. Rigid organizational structures which suppress the "reality" of conflict by ignoring it often provoke violent conflicts. Organizations which are flexible and open and which allow for expressions of differences are not as likely to have strong manifestations of dissension. If conflict is faced and handled appropriately, it can be quite beneficial for the organization. If conflict is going to happen, then the question becomes: How can conflict be handled? What are some of the strategies for conflict management available to the manager?

CONFLICT MANAGEMENT STRATEGIES

Conflict management strategies can be classified into three general categories: (1) avoidance, (2) defusion, and (3) confrontation.[4]

Avoidance

Avoidance is often used in response to conflict or potential conflict. The basis for avoidance is the hope that somehow, if you don't look, the unpleasant situation will go away and you won't have to deal with it. It is tempting to believe in magic. Yet, pretending not to see a problem seldom results in making the problem disappear.

There are many different ways to avoid dealing with conflict, including withdrawal, denial, suppression, and smoothing over. Some people withdraw by walking out of a room, quitting a job, falling asleep at a meeting, or pretending to be very engrossed in some other activity. Others suppress the possibility of conflict by being constantly overworked and, as a result, have absolutely no time for potentially conflict-producing interpersonal relationships. Some people smooth over conflict and appear to be very accommodating in order to avoid conflict. Although the accommodator is indeed obviously bothered by something, he or she keeps pretending that everything is just fine. Other people deny conflict and change the subject of a conversation

---

[4]Robert Blake, H. Shepard, and Jane S. Mouton, *Managing Intergroup Conflict in Industry*, Gulf Publishing Co., Houston, Tex., 1964.

any time it gets close to something that might generate disagreement. Some constantly joke and distract others so nothing can really be taken seriously.

Avoidance strategies are used whenever people feel threatened by potential conflict and afraid they might not be able to handle it effectively. Avoiding conflict situations, of course, is unlikely to solve any problems. Conflict may simply recur in other forms. There is only a very slim chance it will go away.

Defusion

Defusion strategies are used when a person involved in conflict decides to buy time until tempers cool off and the intensity of the feelings subsides. In defusion strategies, people attempt to seek agreement on minor points of the issue and hold off or table the bigger problem until they gather more information, cool off, or have a chance to see things in a somewhat different perspective. Defusion strategies permit some level of agreement, but the bigger issues remain unsettled, sometimes for a long period of time. When this is so, the defusion tactic may only be a form of avoidance.

Confrontation

Confrontation strategies fall into three categories based on the outcomes of the confrontation: win-lose, lose-lose, win-win.[5]

WIN-LOSE OR POWER STRATEGIES

Win-lose strategies of confrontation are based on power. These common ways of managing conflict in organizational settings are based on the premise that for conflict to be solved, one person must win and the other must lose.

There are many different types of win-lose strategies. Managers who, by inclination or sheer power, operate in an autocratic fashion frequently use authority blatantly to overrule another person. A conflict between a manager and a subordinate is simply resolved by the use of authority on the part of the manager. Saying "I am the boss" is a way, at least on a short-term basis, to be on the winning side of the conflict or the argument. However, in the long run, the conflict may be simply postponed rather than solved. While pulling rank does win an argument or a battle, in the long haul it weakens a manager's position if employees feel they are being overruled solely on the strength of authority.

[5] Alan C. Filley, Robert J. House, and Steven Kerr, *Managerial Process and Organizational Behavior*, 2d ed., Scott, Foresman and Company, Glenview, Ill., 1976, pp. 166–167.

Sometimes the sheer show of authority represented by status and rank is not enough and a person may resort to mental or physical *coercion*. Disagreement or conflict with employees is simply resolved by threatening them with dismissal, demotion, a difficult assignment, or a dead-end job.

However, more and more managers are aware that they must not simply tell, but must sell, their ideas. As a result they may resort to another win-lose strategy, *railroading*. Railroading can happen through majority votes when discussion is stopped quickly and a call for a vote is taken before the issues at hand are thoroughly understood or discussed. If this happens too often and if the same group of people always end up in the minority, the losses come to be viewed as personal defeats and the majority rule can be destructive. Sometimes a small group of people who represent a minority can railroad their ideas in a meeting and win.

Interpreting silence as consent is a strategy which permits a small group or sometimes even one person to assume that everyone else agrees, thus preempting the need for open discussion of an issue.

A small minority may also agree ahead of time to present a strong united front on a given issue. A power-play like that intimidates the group into thinking that the idea has more support than it really has. Again, discussion is short circuited to the benefit of a small group which wins, while the others lose.

Filley and his associates[6] have summarized the characteristics of win-lose situations and suggest that in such strategies:

1. There is a clear-cut we-they distinction between the parties involved in the conflict.
2. Each party seeks total victory.
3. Each party perceives issues only from its own point of view.
4. Emphasis is on solutions rather than definition of goals, values, and objectives.
5. Conflicts are personalized and come across as personal attacks.
6. Conflict resolution is not planned.
7. Parties take a short-term view of the issues.

Typical win-lose situations include conflicts between supervisor and subordinate, labor and management, parent and child. Although competition can have functional consequences in an organization, win-lose strategies are often dysfunctional because they are based on the use of power and because someone always loses. In win-lose strategies, alternatives which might incorporate the mutual needs of

[6]Ibid., p. 167.

the two parties are ignored and creative problem solving is stifled. Although some agreement can exist that one party loses this time but will win the next time, ultimately the strategy creates bitterness and resentment which eventually surfaces in one way or another. People on the losing end may bite the bullet and wait until their turn comes when the balance of power shifts. Retaliation then can be vicious, and personal vendettas can drain the organization's energies.

Resorting to rules to solve a conflict is often another win-lose strategy. Such tactics are often a way to avoid direct confrontation by hiding behind company policy or regulations. A manager who does not want to take the responsibility, and the heat, for refusing a particular request may hide behind a regulation. "A rule is a rule, and we must enforce it." The other's loss is not the manager's personal responsibility. Naturally there are times when enforcement of rules and regulations is necessary and appropriate. However, when hiding behind regulations becomes a pattern to deal with unpleasant situations, conflicts are not resolved but simply avoided or kicked upstairs.

LOSE-LOSE OR COMPROMISE STRATEGIES

It seems at first glance that strategies in which everyone loses are not particularly useful ways of resolving conflict. They are, nevertheless, frequently employed. This approach to managing conflict can take several forms. Sometimes the parties agree to settle for a middle ground which may satisfy no one completely, but which at least does not give total victory or total defeat to either side of the controversy. If you want to eat at a Chinese place and your friend wants to eat at a French restaurant, you may finally agree to go for Mexican food. In this way, you do not win but neither does the other person, and you agree to compromise. Compromises are useful in the short run. However, if they become the customary way to settle differences, you may begin to feel that the other people are more anxious to prevent you from winning than to truly settle the issue.

Competing departments in an organization often negotiate allocation of scarce resources on that lose-lose principle. One department may agree to cut down on something if another department does too.

In bribery, another lose-lose strategy, one party may pay a high price to get the other to do something very disagreeable. A manager may offer you an important raise to do a very boring job, for example. Although on the surface it looks like a positive way to settle an issue, both of you may lose partially.

WIN-WIN OR INTEGRATION STRATEGIES

Characteristic features of win-win strategies of managing conflict are the two assumptions that:

1. Conflict is the symptom of a problem to be solved rather than a fight to be won.
2. Conflict can be managed so that no party has to lose.

Managing conflict through problem solving permits the integration of potentially opposite views and is a highly effective way of resolving differences. Face-to-face confrontation is imperative between the parties of the conflict. Emphasis is on solving a common problem rather than determining who is right, who is wrong, and who is to blame. Information needs to be openly exchanged in order to determine the facts which bear on the problem. Creative exploration of potential solutions should not start until the problem to be solved jointly has been carefully defined. What often appear to be mutually incompatible positions on the surface can often be redefined creatively as a larger problem in which all parties have a stake. Creative exploration of potential solutions to the problem through brainstorming techniques can be very useful in eliciting ways of managing the problem so that everyone has at least some of their needs met. It is important that most people involved in the conflict have a voice in suggesting alternatives for solving the problem. Many times an alternative course of action is discovered which none of the parties to the conflict would have identified alone. Through communication and participation, creative solutions can be developed and then tested and evaluated.

The outcome of a win-win strategy for managing conflict is frequently a better solution than either of the parties would have come up with. Greater trust, understanding, and respect are developed among those involved. This may sound naïve and unrealistic, yet a good deal of research has shown such strategies can be effective.

Naturally, problem solving and negotiated conflict management take time. When several people are involved and the issue to be solved is trivial or inconsequential, the time required to use a win-win approach may not be worth the effort. However, the more you rely on a method, the more proficient you become. Once you begin to think in terms of finding solutions to problems which meet apparently opposite needs, you learn to think differently and thus can deal with conflict differently. Rather than battling an enemy, you learn to solve a mutual problem with an associate. Much creative energy is released in the process.

In a win-win approach, the parties involved must define a common ground and their mutual interest. Unless the problem is perceived in terms of "we" rather than "us against them," little effort will be made to negotiate differences for mutual benefits. People involved need to understand that they do not have all the information required to solve the problem and that only through communication will more information be generated. Often neither party to a conflict is wrong or has erroneous data. Facts of a situation may be shared by all, yet the process allows people to get to know how others view the same facts and how each person's needs affect his or her perception of a solution.

In such problem-solving sessions, it is important that communications be orderly, that frankness and openness be encouraged and rewarded, and that people feel free to disagree without being attacked for doing so. Partial agreement may be necessary and should be acceptable as a realistic basis for decision making. Brainstorming should be used for generalizing alternative ways to solve the conflict. Brainstorming techniques are characterized by open and spontaneous communication among the people involved.

Defining the problem is clearly differentiated from generating solutions. Evaluation of the possible solutions occurs only *after* solutions have been generated. During the solution-generating phase of a brainstorming sequence, the emphasis is on supportive communication, free of critical judgments, and on the encouragement of originality and unusual ideas.

The win-win approach to conflict management means working together toward a solution which can satisfy all the parties involved. You need goodwill, creativity, and commitment to not imposing a solution that does not meet everyone's needs. If you have patience and

---

FIGURE 9-3

Filley's descriptions of personal styles.

9,1 *Win, lose:* "The tough battler." Seeks to achieve goals at all costs without concern for the needs or the acceptance of others. Losing means reduced status, weakness, and loss of self-image. Conflict is considered a nuisance which occurs only because others do not see the correctness of his or her position.

1,9 *Yield, lose:* "The friendly helper." Overvalues relationships and undervalues the achievement of personal goals. Conflict is thought to grow out of the self-centeredness of individuals and should be avoided in favor of harmony.

1,1 *Lose, leave:* Conflict is seen as hopeless, useless, and punishing. Rather than undergo the tension and frustration of conflict, the person will leave either physically or mentally.

5,5 *Compromise style:* Allows each side to gain something. Enjoys the maneuvering required to resolve conflict and will actively seek middle ground. May try to use rules or voting as a way of avoiding direct confrontation on the issue.

9,9 *Integrative:* "The problem solver." Does not see the two concerns as mutually exclusive. Sees conflict as natural and healthful, leading to a more creative solution if handled properly.
   1. Feels the attitudes and positions of everyone need to be aired.
   2. Evidences trust and candor with others.
   3. Sees everyone as having an equal role in the resolution.
   4. Does not sacrifice anyone simply for the good of the group.

time to keep working until such a solution is found, very creative answers to problems can usually be identified. Figure 9-3 includes Filley's description of personal styles for managing conflict.

Conflict is a reality of organizational life and of your personal life. Your view of conflict determines to a large extent how you will approach it and deal with it, and how successful you will be in managing it. If you view conflict as something bad which must be avoided at all costs, you may be tempted to respond with defensive maneuvers which may temporarily remove conflict from your awareness. You may even scheme with other people and pretend that everything is fine and you run a happy ship. The fact is that conflict and happiness are not necessarily opposites. Avoidance tactics may appear effective in the short run; they are usually unsatisfactory in the long run.

SKILLS FOR CONFLICT MANAGEMENT

It seems to us that, rather than burying your head in the sand and pretending that conflict does not exist or in some way minimize it, it is better to deal with it squarely. You need to develop or sharpen the skills that will permit you to handle conflict effectively. Handling conflict effectively, by the way, does not necessarily mean that you will solve every problem each time to your total satisfaction.

Conflict management skills are basically communication skills. They include (1) diagnosing the nature of the conflict, (2) initiating a confrontation, (3) listening, and (4) problem solving.

You may be familiar with the serenity prayer which became the Alcoholics Anonymous' motto:

Diagnosing the Nature of a Conflict

God, grant me the strength to change the things I can,
The patience to accept the things I cannot change,
And the wisdom to know the difference.

These words seem most appropriate as we discuss diagnostic skills in conflict management. When you encounter potential conflict or differences, you must ask yourself whether (1) the issue is one which affects you and has concrete consequences for you, (2) the conflict is caused by value differences or by differences in needs for which operational solutions can be found, and (3) the other party is willing and able to enter into a win-win negotiated approach. Some problems may simply not affect you directly. If you feel that smoking is an unhealthy habit and smoke bothers you, you may have to confront your chain-smoking office mate. If however, the chain-smoker's office is next door and you never meet in small, unventilated rooms, his or her smoking has practically no consequence for you. Initiating a confrontation about the other person's smoking habit may be inappropriate.

It is quite difficult to change a person's value system, and this may not always be necessary in order to negotiate interpersonal differences successfully. If your secretary does not value punctuality, it may not be useful to try and change her outlook on the value of time. The conflict here must be operationalized and you may need to confront her, not on her values, but on her behavior and how her behavior affects you.

Timing is important. If your supervisor is swamped, obviously worried about a lot of problems and rushed, do not go in expecting a leisurely discussion of a less immediate problem.

It is also important to state clearly and specifically (1) what the other person does and how it tangibly affects you and (2) what you wish the other person to do. If you do not know how the problem might be solved, it is useful to suggest that exploring the problem together may permit both of you to come up with a mutually satisfying decision. Don't just demand that your office mate stop smoking. State that the smoke bothers you and ask that you both sit down and figure some ways to solve the problem to meet both people's needs.

Listening

Truly effective communication does not occur without listening to what others have to say. As we mentioned in Chapter 6, listening requires that you not only attend to the content of what the other person is saying but also listen to the feelings involved and the emotional tone of the message. Empathic or active listening is a crucial skill in negotiating conflict. You must understand the needs of another person if you are to generate solutions that will potentially meet them. Listening is particularly difficult when you deal with problems and conflicts in which you are emotionally involved. You may be concentrating on defending your point of view rather than truly hearing the other person's arguments.

Problem Solving

In Chapter 8 we discussed extensively a typical problem-solving sequence. We firmly believe that application of the problem-solving sequence in conflict management is useful. You can gain much from treating conflict as a problem to be solved rather than as a fight to be avoided or won.

SUMMARY

While in the past people viewed conflict as bad and to be avoided, the trend now is to look at conflict as inevitable and manageable. As a reality of organizational life, conflict must be handled.

Not all conflicts have the same outcomes. Some may end up constructively and some destructively. If conflict consumes so much of everybody's time that not much else can get done, it is destructive. It can also lead to conformity and overconservative behaviors and decisions; it can freeze an organization into inactivity or cause so much turnover that the organization has no continuity. Communication in destructive settings becomes negative, duplicated, or non-existent.

Tension which goes with healthy conflict gives an air of excitement and action to the group. As a constructive force, conflict can mobilize the energies of participants, make them compete, bring out new ways of solving problems or winning, give a sense of team effort, and generally improve communication and information flow.

Conflict arises for many different reasons. Personal and organizational conflict are two obvious general categories. People's needs may be in conflict, or they may become frustrated when blocks are placed in their way. Conflicts over scarce resources and over roles to be played may also arise.

Strategies for handling conflict include avoidance, defusion, and confrontation. Under confrontation are the options win-lose, lose-lose, and win-win. Of these, win-win is possible in more instances than you may think, but people's habits have tended to lead them into the other patterns.

Among the skills for managing conflict are your own abilities to diagnose the nature of the conflict: (1) Does it affect me and have consequences for me? (2) Is it caused by a difference in values or needs? (3) Is the other party willing and able to negotiate a satisfactory management strategy such as win-win? Another skill is that of listening, particularly active listening as discussed in an earlier chapter. Still another skill is basic problem solving as discussed in Chapter 8, with the idea that conflict is a problem to be solved rather than a fight to be won, purposely lost, or avoided. There are many strategies for dealing with conflict and all are based on communication skills. The test of the effectiveness of conflict management strategies is not necessarily that conflict be resolved or made to disappear. In fact, sometimes creative conflict management may—for the short run—temporarily involve the escalation of conflict before its final successful resolution.

PART FOUR

THE SKILLS OF MANAGING BY COMMUNICATION

Throughout this book we have stressed that communication is the methodology of management. In Part Four we will examine two specific skills required of almost all managers in almost all organizational settings. In Chapter 10 we will take a look at oral presentations and the communication skills needed by managers who want to convey their ideas effectively and persuasively in small groups, in public, or in the media. Situations requiring effective oral presentations are numerous in organizations, and managers who communicate effectively in public are highly valued. In Chapter 11 we will examine another communication skill essential to the manager, interviewing. Interviewing situations are common in organizational life, and managers must frequently interview others to get information, to hire, to evaluate, to counsel.

CHAPTER 10

PRESENTATIONS

"Delivery should never get in the way of the message, but should project it, interpret it, deliver it clearly and cleanly, and leave it unobstructed for the hearer's consideration." Elton Abernathy

257

INTRODUCTION

By now you should have recognized our argument that communication is not random; it is full of purpose. Communication is controlled by speakers, listeners, and the situation in which they communicate. By this same argument, communication can be made better or worse by adjustment in those factors. To state the proposition another way: Communication in some situations, by some speakers (or writers), can have some effects on some audiences. If there are too many qualifiers in that statement, consider that you and I never have perfect control over others, over situations, and even over ourselves. Our presentations to others, therefore, are attempts to have something happen by controlling as much as possible the elements in the communication transactions.

Theory and Practice

We do not consider theory at all opposed to practice or skills. From the evident consuming interest in communication in our society, we believe that humans can use all the help they can get from theoretical bases and from skills training as well. Without ways of checking out the cause-and-effect relationships of human communication, the practice of communication depends on intuition, artistry, and hit-and-miss judgments that others are well-meaning or opportunistic. Much of this book has dealt with the development and testing of theories of human interaction in organizations. We are convinced that without such theoretical background, the student who approaches communication study may expect to obtain only skills training. Trick devices for special communication acts (such as selling techniques) are applicable in special situations and can be understood in relation to the principles of human communication which have been observed, reported, researched, probed, praised, or damned ever since early Greek philosophers. In fact, much of the subsequent study of rhetorical systems and ethics was stimulated in reaction to the teaching of the Sophists, whose results orientation offended other teachers. Our bias is that a good grasp of theory and underlying concepts of communication prepares a communicator for more options in a greater variety of situations. Learning *about* communication, we believe, is as important as learning the practices or skills of communicating, because the skills will thus become sharper, broader, more applicable, more adaptable, and on the whole improved. Communication learning will not be effective as only a cookbook of devices.

Effects of Presentations

Having just made a plea for understanding the development and theories of communication, we will move on to a serious skills application of what most of this book is about. From all you know and can do, you should select the most effective means to get the communication job done. In other words, you want something to happen when you communicate—if only to have someone pay attention. More often, your aim is for persuasion of another person or group, or to have it make a difference that you entered into communication by changing the relationship of the other participant(s) with themselves, their environments, or you.

Having something happen to a receiver, at first glance, seems to be a very effects-oriented statement. In light of the total interaction when that change of behavior occurs, you must remember that future courses of communication will be affected by that same change. To be simplistic, we will refer to the favorite statement of communication pragmatics, "You cannot not communicate."

The question remaining is: What can you actually do about communication? It follows, does it not, that if these forces in you, the other, and the situation are interacting, then something can be done about any or all of the factors?

The answer is that you are the only one who can, at that point, have any effect on the communication outcomes. What you do may have an effect on the other or on the environment, but only if the factors you can control have a consistent relation with the matters you don't control. It is a humbling thought that even your best efforts may not have the intended results if the intervening factors of the *other* and the *environment* have been predicted wrong, or if they change or fail to respond in an expected way.

Audience Focus

In this chapter, we will concentrate on the effects your communication can have on an audience. Your presentations are aimed at an audience. In this transactional scheme, there is no presentation without an audience, just as you cannot clap one hand. We will now look at your communication practices for different kinds of audiences and situations, including (1) awards and ritual occasions, (2) introductions and responses, (3) informational relationships, and (4) persuasive presentations.

To relate various audience situations to each other and to what you hope to do, we will concentrate on three factors which will determine whether your presentational efforts can, in some fashion, control the behavior of the receiver.

FACTORS AFFECTING PRESENTATIONS

We have stressed the interrelationship between the psychological forces in human interaction and the physical. For example, in the chapter on groups (Chapter 8), we distinguished between task

BOX 10-1   **FACTORS CONTROLLING PRESENTATIONS**

Factor A: Receiving (hearing)

Factor B: Believing (credibility)

Factor C: Acting (carrying out)

concerns and people concerns, or socioemotional concerns. Those concerns do not exist in a vacuum, nor do they exist without each other. Concerns for people and for task, we asserted, are active forces in the ongoing communication among participants; and they also are going on concurrently: The group did not do task only for a little while, and then shift to socioemotional activities. Each of those components was occurring in some participants all the time.

If your presentation is to have an effect on an audience, you must be aware of the psychological factors as well as the physical ones, and be able to exert influence over both and their interrelationships.

Check your awareness and skills in the following areas. Traditionally, six or eight separate components are listed as controllers of the presentational situation. We have condensed these into three factors which we believe are easier to learn, more inclusive of the described relationships in making a presentation, and easier to check.

Factor A— Receiving

An audience must be able to hear and understand your presentation. Physical components of this factor include your voice, the size and location of the audience, extraneous noise, and supporting materials.

Amplification devices are available in most presentation settings, and you should find out how they work, and whether they are working. You must also check out any mechanical or electronic devices you want to use to display either aural or visual materials. Are projectors threaded or loaded and tested for focus? Are recorders checked out? Do you know how to stop and start the equipment, or do you have an assistant or some help who know? Have you arranged to signal them? If it is important for you to be seen, where will you make your presentation and what physical objects will be available? Do you have a lectern? Is it lighted, in case you have to turn out the house lights to show slides, video, or movies? Are members of the audience going to be close or far away? Are they going to be comfortable? What might interfere with their interacting with you? Are very important people being taken care of by perhaps being given special seats?

Although those questions sound almost too basic to ask, a checklist of items in the physical setting can help you make the most of your presentation without interference from controllable factors. There are forces in the setting that you cannot control, so check carefully those which you can control.

Hearing and understanding you also involves the inclination of the audience to pay attention. What psychological barriers to their listening have you set up? Understanding you will be easier if you use language the audience can follow, and if you present your material in an order familiar to them. The topic itself may be interesting or not to an audience. If you make a presentation to a church board, topics of totally secular focus will not be relevant.

Listening is more than hearing. Hearing is a psychological reaction to wave stimuli; listening is a higher cognitive function involving the intellectual effort of a participant. After you have determined that your audience can hear your presentation, then you must make sure they listen. In the section below on presentation situations, there are some suggestions about getting an audience to listen.

Your presentation will succeed to the extent that the audience believes you are offering a legitimate payoff for their attention that is also compatible with their beliefs, needs, norms and values.

Factor B— Believing

How applicable is what you are telling a group? Do you present to a class of elementary school students a strongly worded plea to vote for a candidate in a public election? There is little payoff for these youngsters if they cannot go to the polls and participate, even though they may have some interest in a political race.

Asking people to go against their values or beliefs is difficult at best. You must give very strong inducements to have such an audience even listen to you.

For that reason, you must analyze your audience in terms of its known motivations. What do these people stand for? Are they consistent in their attitudes, or is there a wide dispersion of attitudes in the group? Your presentation must be tailored to the attitudes of the audience toward you and toward the topic.

Analysis of the audience should be done in advance. If you make a sales pitch to a chamber of commerce for support of a regional convention, you must be prepared to answer questions. You can certainly be more effective if you have anticipated the attitudes of the chamber toward the organization you represent, the convention group, the availability of hotel space, what business groups are represented on the chamber committee you are addressing, etc. You can ask friends who have confronted the same chamber for their advice. You can ask one or two chamber members whom you believe to be supportive of you how they analyze the members whom you will address.

Attitudes of audiences

Tailoring your presentation to the audience is such an obvious recommendation that we hesitate to take much time on the topic. You should use every means you have to find out, in advance, what the audience is like. Everything in an audience which affects the outcome of your presentation should be studied: age, social and economic level, education, interests, prior record of reactions, whether attendance is voluntary or not, competing events, political attitudes, and particularly what can be known about the audience attitudes about you and your appeal. If you know the audience is favorable, hostile, apathetic, or neutral, you can tailor your presentation accordingly.

Favorable audiences need reinforcing to an attitude they already hold. Hostile audiences can seldom be turned around by simple persuasive presentations; additional rewards or sanctions must be included with the communications to change hostile audiences. The best you can expect from a hostile audience may be simply neutralizing them or keeping them from being actively, overtly hostile.

Neutral audiences are worth your best efforts of persuasion or information giving. They have not made up their minds. They know about the material you are presenting, but are not committed to one stand or another. In contrast, the apathetic audience does not even know about what you are presenting and is, beyond that, probably not interested in finding out. An apathetic audience must be moved to attentiveness first, and then moved to interest and a direction.

In the example of the chamber of commerce presentation, you may find that group not interested in sponsoring your convention because they don't know anything about your organization or you. Their apathy will have to be challenged first by attention-getting devices like endorsements from famous people or from other business persons whose memberships will be meaningful to the chamber.

If the chamber group you are approaching is neutral, they are not either for or against your proposal; then you may use logical appeals to their own self-interest of improving the city image and income and creating additional future business.

A favorable audience needs little convincing, and you could make an error by being too long in your approach if you already have a strong support. In that case, your mission is to provide only the minimal material on which the chamber can justify its action to support you.

The hostile audience needs to be neutralized; and if you can divert their interest from what makes them hostile, your chance of getting support for your convention is increased. Perhaps they do not want a convention in the city at that time, so your argument must approach the advantages the timing will offer. Suggestions for handling audience situations will be treated in the later section of this chapter.

The audience must be able to act. They must be mentally, emotionally, or physically able to respond to your presentation—if only to pay attention to you. You can only ask for responses within the capability of your audience.

Factor C— Acting

When one of the authors was teaching a course to a maximum security group in the Canon City, Colorado, prison, he asked the group what form of presentation they would prefer for future courses. One lifer answered, "Field trips."

If you ask an audience to do something as a result of your presentation, they must have the power to do it as well as the inclination (as established in factor B).

You must look at your presentation in light of the relationship among the three factors: Can the group receive the message you are sending? Can they believe it? Are they capable of acting on it?

Interaction among the Factors

A person who is hungry will pay attention (factor A) to a message on television advertising food. If the message is attractively presented, she will believe it fits her needs (factor B). If she has money to buy it and the store is open and she has a way to get there (factor C), she can accomplish the "changed behavior" offered in the presentation.

In a committee meeting, the room is very large, the noise from outside is distracting, and members form little subgroups and whisper to each other while a presentation is being made for the adoption of a revised accounting system. The presenter is cutting himself off from factors B and C by not taking care of factor A: Can the group hear and understand?

An executive is explaining to a department the need for a new system for recording overtime and days off. As she talks, it becomes evident to the members of the department that the new system is being imposed without taking into consideration the executive's own policy of asking for extra work from them without giving compensatory time or pay. Even though the executive is speaking clearly and in precise words, she is not being believed at factor B, so it will ultimately be difficult to move the group to factor C's action stage.

You attend a lecture on mountain climbing. It is of intellectual interest to you, and you enjoy the pictures of Devils' Tower. When it comes to a presentation of the skill learning and techniques of rappeling down the face, the presenter no longer has your attention, even though the demonstration is well organized and visually interest-

---

BOX 10-2   **KINDS OF PRESENTATION SITUATIONS**

Awards and rituals: The most familiar and least rigorous.
Nickname: Noticing Each Other.

Introductions and responses: Often used; follows patterns loosely.
Nicknames: Who Are You? Who Am I?

Information and reports: Fairly common; usually structured and planned.
Nickname: Show and Tell.

Persuasion and decision: Less common; must be highly structured to be effective.
Nickname: Buy and Sell.

---

ing to others. You don't want to *do* anything about climbing, you simply want to be a spectator; so when levels of participation change in the presentation, you are no longer involved.

TYPES OF PRESENTATIONS

In the teaching of public speaking, there is a tradition of dividing the speaking activities into types by what the speaker expects to accomplish. These have been listed traditionally as speeches to inform, to persuade, and to entertain. Most listings of speech types include informational and persuasive, and then have more difficulty categorizing the rest, which are variously called consummatory, ceremonial, entertaining, eulogistic, and even "nonpurposive." The last term is offensive because all communication is purposive in the sense that something is expected to happen, and it is not random.

After setting up a nomenclature system, we will categorize presentations in order of (1) their familiarity; that is, how often we are likely to be doing the things involved in the type and (2) their general rigor as related to the settings in which they are likely to occur and their structure and meaningfulness to human behavior. We will call the presentation types (1) awards and rituals, (2) introductions and responses, (3) information and reports, and (4) persuasion and decision. The last two categories have been more recently labeled by some of our students as (3) show and tell, and (4) buy and sell—which may be appropriate, however flippant.

Awards and Rituals

We engage in presentation of awards and rituals frequently. Part of the ritual of transacting business is presentation of self in encounters, and much of how people will act toward each other is rigidly prescribed. When speaking to a clerk in a store, a waiter in a cafe, a teacher on a campus, a bus driver, a neighbor, or others in your less-than-serious encounters, there are communication patterns which you (1) know very clearly how to offer and (2) either use with great care or offend the others. Much of what goes on in casual encounters is prescribed and is so predictable and familiar that people greet others and part from them in a thoroughly satisfactory and balanced way.

Only in degree are ceremonial presentations different from those casual encounters. Ceremonial presentations—called here awards and rituals—are carefully prescribed and predictable. There is little room for innovation or creative altering of the ritual presentations; and if you stray from the expectations of audiences, it is likely the presentation will not be effective. People do not like to be surprised when they are attending a funeral, an awards convocation, a wedding, a Mother's Day service, a retirement dinner, or any ceremony which has a prescribed level of affection, seriousness, content, emotion, and affect. They will accept very dull and boring presentations, but not innovation.

Awards and rituals are the most familiar presentations; they occur very frequently. They are also not always recognized as a very significant form of presentation and occasion. Their importance lies in their wide use, and their impact on people's emotions rather than on their intellect. Included in this category are public ceremonies to honor personalities (retirements, swearings-in to office, inaugurals, recognitions of achievement such as twenty-five years of service, welcoming home heroes from battle, honoring athletic or philanthropic heroes, the presentation of honors by public agencies) or to commemorate events or places (groundbreakings, ribbon cuttings on new buildings, new programs, dedications, celebrations of holidays, anniversaries, citations of departments or companies, production milestones such as the millionth barrel of beer, goal achievement such as a United Way campaign kickoff and close). Many ritual presentations occur during the business meetings of clubs or other organizations when personal citations are read or public recognition is given to member achievements.

Much of what passes for information in regular meetings of clubs and other affinity groups is simply ritual. Reading of minutes and treasurers' reports in many organizations are occasions for team-building gestures or congratulatory strokes rather than for providing information on what went on at the last meeting or the financial shape of the club.

The purpose of ceremonial presentations is not so much to persuade or inform people as to give everybody a chance to admire, to be proud, or to participate in an important occasion. Proclamations are made by mayors, governors, or presidents and responded to by recipients. Not only are awards and rituals very familiar to us, but they seem to multiply and feed on one another; once a commendation or a citation is issued, it must be reacted to by more ceremony, thus creating an endless round of presentations. Such presentations are not to be either neglected or denigrated. They are important for our relations with one another, though not very important for the information or persuasion they contain. Socioemotional needs are taken care of by rituals and awards. People not only reinforce the memberships and dedications they have, but they can also selectively have new experiences and enjoy additional excitement, uplift, and feelings of belonging.

Awards and rituals follow an expected form which should not be violated, although presenters may adjust content and emphasis and may even make a pretense of going beyond the norms.

Awards and rituals (1) are more emotional than intellectual; (2) tend to make use of flowery language, metaphors, clichés, figures of speech, or other poetic devices; (3) tend to be optimistic in tone, positive, and supportive rather than argumentative or defeatist; (4) evoke our value symbol system with high abstractions such as integrity, religion, motherhood, patriotism, friendship, love, justice, success, and honor; (5) are usually given by prestigious people or chief functionaries or highly eloquent speakers, even if the presenter knows very little about the subject; (6) generally call for a response by a recipient or honoree or participant which, in turn, includes an enthusiastic agreement with the first presenter. However, if the event is honoring a person, a humble demurrer is called for from the honoree who says the success belongs to everyone in the team or group, and the recipient could not have done it without them.

If you are called on to make a ceremonial or award or ritualistic presentation, be full of praise and be generous in your use of abstract terms; but be very specific about the person or event so the audience can be sure the presentation was made up especially for that occasion. Be brief.

Factor analysis of awards and rituals

Relating to the three factors described earlier, this presentation has some difficulties in factor A. Physical settings are not conducive to good audience contact when events are held in places being commemorated—as when the ribbon is cut for a new library, a statue is dedicated to Audie Murphy, a speech is given at a cemetery on Memorial Day—or when they are held spontaneously in response to a success or the appearance of a celebrity—the team has just won the championship and the captain addresses the fans from the sidelines; the governor comes to the Fourth of July picnic in the municipal park; the ten-millionth visitor just bought admission tickets to Disneyland.

On the other hand, when award or ritual settings can be controlled in advance, such as the President's address to a joint meeting of

Congress honoring a senator who died, then the total array of visual and auditory technology can be concentrated on making sure factor A is optimized. Crews of technicians look after the physical arrangements, and many assistants, protocol experts, advisors, and consultants take care of the many considerations in the psychosocio-emotional realm. If the event can be planned ahead, much window dressing may be used: lighting, sound, visual aids, personal assistance of aides.

Factor B is at full strength on these occasions. Except for an occasional nonbeliever or dissenter picketing an event, most of the audience believes and is dedicated to hearing the message for support of its values or beliefs. People have come to be reinforced in what they already believe—the significance of the Alamo in winning freedom for Texas; the contribution made by the senior vice-president after twenty-five years of service to the firm; the glory of having a winning team; or the goodness of the late departed. The audience also believes that listening to the presentation is worth their time, although most presentations of awards or rituals do not strain the intellectual capabilities of listeners as much as they involve the emotional.

Factor C asks a minimum from this audience. Presentations of awards and rituals make no demand except reinforced belief or rededication to support. Can the audience perform what is asked? If they cheer or cry at the appropriate time or go away saying how great is that person or anniversary, they have met the needs of factor C.

Introductions and Responses

Perhaps more often than giving award or ritual speeches, you may be called on to introduce someone—if you include all the times you and others meet as strangers. Presentations range from highly personal contact when you bring a close friend home to meet your family to highly public when you are asked to introduce the keynote speaker at the annual convention before 3000 delegates. This range from formal to informal is only one reason that introductions take on different forms. Another reason is that they happen so often, people get so tired of hearing them sound all the same, but are still restricted to only a few liberties with form. The "roast" is a protracted introduction and response which is simply a form of comedy based on humorous or insulting presentations of a person to others.

When you make the introduction

Why are you making an introduction of this person? Finding an answer to that question will give you some options to choose from. Is this a visiting expert who has come to city council about the water potential? Is this a new member of the staff who should meet the rest of your organization? Is this a speaker at your club or at your rally?

In all the above cases, you want this speaker to have a favorable reception from some group. That's the reason for most public introductions. The person being introduced must be presented in the best possible light to be most effective with that public. Even if you take your steady date or intended spouse home to meet your parents, the introduction you make will be important to set the stage for acceptance into the family. You bring a stranger to have coffee with your close friends; the introduction you make will have an effect on how accepted the new person will be. The same is true of speakers or others whom you will have to introduce.

Some hints: (1) Do not overdo either length or content. Your introduction must be a minor part of the situation because the person being introduced is the main speaker, not you. The recitation of great accomplishments can be annoying to an audience if it goes on too long. The shortest introductions are given for people who need no buildup, and when no introducer has anything nearly as important to say as the person being introduced. The world's record for short introductions goes to the person who stands beside the podium and says, "Ladies and Gentlemen, the President of the United States!" (2) What does the audience need to know? If the speech is about bond issues, you will not help the audience to accept the speaker by listing incidental information like size of family, hobbies, or examples of expertise in foreign languages. On the other hand, how much association that speaker has had with bond sales, with financing, and with civic organizations and promotion will all be important. (3) Avoid cute references to your own private jokes or associations with the speaker. This is a common fault of amateur introducers. They mention with a smirk some ancedote or personal item known only to the speaker and introducer, thus excluding the audience from a private joke. Unless it is important, the audience does not need to know that you have fished together for twenty years; or that you went to the same high school ten years apart; or that your family also came from Poughkeepsie as did the speaker's; or you've admired this speaker for many years; or that you had a nice dinner together last night; or that you and the speaker both were in the Signal Corps. The audience wants to hear about the speaker, not about you; so avoid references to yourself as much as possible. (4) If the person's name is well known, it can be used sparingly. If it is not well known, you can help by using it (correctly pronounced, of course) at the beginning and end of your introduction and perhaps in the middle. Titles are as important as names. (5) Check with the speaker to find out what he or she wants included. What will be important to say about this speaker for this occasion *according to that speaker*? Most people know what they would like to have said about them in an introduction. Speakers will not usually tell you to brag about their accomplishments but will give you an idea of what they think is important for an audience to know in relation to the message to be given. You will generally get a pretty clear reply to your question. (6) In summary, tell the audience about the speaker, not about yourself; and tell them what the *speaker* thinks is important for that occasion.

Most speakers who do many public appearances have a biographical outline available. Such outlines include much more data than you should give an audience. The extra material allows you to adapt the information to that specific topic and group. You don't have to read it all to an audience; in fact, it is best not to *read* any of it. Marking up a few key items, alluding to the other many accomplishments without listing them, and using the biographical material for notes will help you give a better introduction.

One last warning. Don't rely on your own memory or on hearsay to get data to introduce a speaker. If you think the speaker attended Colorado State, check it; you may find out it was Colorado Mines. If you remember that the speaker was mayor of San Diego, check it; you may find out he was city manager. If you heard from a friend that the speaker played linebacker for Green Bay, check it; you may find it was another person of the same name. If you heard that the speaker is a native of Texas, check it; you may find out this is her first visit. Checking will save both you and the speaker the embarrassment that occurs when the opening line of the speech is a correction of something you said in the introduction—something which happens a lot. Listen for these slips which must be corrected by a speaker, and when they happen, remember it was because the introducer did not check.

When you are being introduced

Most of the above advice is good to keep in mind when you are being introduced. Know what your audience expects of you, and help your introducer to tailor a brief statement about you which will get the listeners ready to really listen.

Your best help will come from a biographical sheet (sometimes called a vita, or a résumé, or in the media slang, a "biog"). Include more than you need for any one occasion. Point out to your introducer those items which seem to you most relevant to that occasion and for that audience. Avoid inappropriate modesty. If you want this audience to accept you as a hero, let them know (through your introducer) that you are important to them. Your purpose is to do a good job, and the help of a well-designed introduction is important to any speaker.

Factor analysis of introductions and responses

When you introduce someone else, your audience is not planning to give you their undivided attention. They probably came to hear the person you will introduce. You may have to work at getting their attention and may not be able to make the introduction under the best conditions. That should not excuse a bad performance on your part, so the items you should check include: Is the public address system working? Can the audience hear you? Did you mumble the person's name, or did you deliver it with emphasis and clarity?

Factor B includes consideration of the way you manage to have the group eager to hear from the person you introduce. Your mission is to make this person important to the audience and thus to help make his or her speech acceptable. The factors discussed in the preceding section are issues to be aware of in getting an audience in a receptive frame of mind to hear the person you introduce, whether the audience is your bridge club, your parents, the chairman of the board, or the Kiwanis or Rotary Club.

Factor C requires the attention of the audience. What you want them to do is pay attention to the person you are introducing. The desired audience reaction is eager attentiveness, and you can make it happen or turn them off by the way you prepare them in your introduction.

On many occasions, a visitor or a guest lecturer is simply put up before the microphone and thus must present his or her own credentials to the audience. This practice is extremely bad-mannered on the part of the presenting organization, and forces the speaker to use equally bad manners. No organization who has invited a guest speaker should turn that person over to the audience without the best possible sendoff. When a speaker fails to reach an audience, there is some possibility that either a bad or an insufficient introduction so impaired that person's starting relationship that the presentation could not have succeeded. If nothing happened in the audience as a result of the guest speaker's appearance, the speaker may be to blame; but you should also check to see whether the introduction was a contributing factor.

Information and Reports

This type of presentation ranges from the simple answer to a question phoned to you by a friend ("What's the assignment for tomorrow in Calculus?") to an extensive presentation of the Federal Budget to Congress with speeches, accompanying documentation, and visuals. When you give information the purpose is to fulfill a need in the audience—a need to know more than it did, usually so it can do something about it (factor C again).

When your friend wants to know the assignment, you give the answer with the expectation that she will read the assigned pages, or at least have the information in case she wants to. When Congress receives the budget, the assumption is that the fiscal information will enable them to vote appropriate bills or otherwise conduct the business of the government another year.

Look at this category from the view of factor A—receiving. Much of the time the information to be presented is (1) new or revised, (2) difficult to understand, and (3) extensive or at least sufficiently complicated to require attention. A presenter can maximize the effectiveness of data by use of show and tell. Visuals can accompany verbal data to the advantage of both. A display of graphs may require some additional discourse by a speaker to make them relevant or to point out the most significant parts of very complete data. Your charts should be readable by all the audience for the same reason your voice should be heard.

Organizing is a significant aid to understanding. A random sheet of figures is meaningless, but the same statistics presented in comparative form (a succession of years and the relative changes, for example) can be effective in informing an audience of trends or reporting on the flow of money, resources, people, or ideas.

After you have decided what reaction you want from the audience, your first step in organizing your presentation is to find and organize the data themselves—what you want to report or to inform your audience about. You have already selected your purpose (to talk about solar energy, to report on the sales and marketing program results, to explain a new curriculum, to give directions on how to drive to your house), and so you need to decide what data you need and where you will get them. Your own experience and knowledge are all you have to explore for items of personal information; you don't need much library searching to fill out a form on when you were born, your address, your employment record, etc. You can direct a friend to your house without even having to consult a city map to look up street names. But if you want to report on the foraminiferal algae of the South Pacific atolls, you may have to consult many geology journals.

How much data you collect will depend on such factors as (1) how much time you have, (2) how extensive your report is to be, (3) how much the group needs or wants to know. Quality of the data as well as quantity will depend on audience characteristics. Is the material of interest and within their understanding? Is it something *you* are capable of explaining *to this particular audience?*

The physical means of collecting the data will depend on your own habits. One excellent approach is to write your collected data on 3 × 5 inch cards. You can rearrange cards more easily than you can reorganize pages of notes or information. Remember to note the source of your material so you can quote from your source or acknowledge credit for ideas or data.

After you have collected the data, you should organize the material in a way which will be effective for your presentation.

Knowing what your audience expects may help, but generally the data themselves will have a greater influence on the way you put them together.

If you are giving a historical development of a process or an organization (the history of our university, the evolution of chemical batch process, the development of communication theory), you may select a chronological or historical order.

When using a spatial organization, you arrange ideas, items, or events according to how they relate to each other in space.

You may organize your data by order of importance, by size or scope, or by category—for example, natural resources, rivers and streams, Cibolo Creek; or musical America, orchestras, string sections, violins, concertmasters.

Similarly, you may arrange your material in an order from simple to complex.

Causal order is useful when you want to show how some action developed from another—for example, an analysis of the admission changes in the university as a function of the lower birth rate.

From problem to solution is a useful organization plan when you make a success-oriented report on the progress of a new product or activity.

When you use an indirect sequence or withheld-solution order, you present first the arguments or possibilities or lists of options explored, then the one which the organization adopted, together with its consequences.

Leading up to a climax is another device that is useful in developing understanding of a presentation and support for its implications or future applications.

One of the most used devices for explanation is comparison or dichotomy—pointing out how the new thing you are explaining is like or different from the more familiar one. "An electron microscope operates very much like an optical system except that it makes use of magnetic fields instead of lenses made of glass. . . ."

These are just a sampling of the organizational arrangements available for preparing your presentation. You should be very certain that the system you use is clear to you and to your audience. It must reinforce your data and emphasize the items you want emphasized, rather than focusing on extraneous devices or data.

As you organize, you should outline. The two processes are complementary in good preparation. Data can be prepared for final presentation by simply jotting down items, then grouping them, and then putting the groups into the order you have selected for presentation. Again we remind you, cards are useful in grouping data.

This detailed description of factor A items is aimed at getting the audience to listen to and hence to understand your presentation.

Otherwise, the next two factors are of no consequence. One last reminder in this discussion of factor A: Your delivery will guide the audience into belief and action. You should practice your presentation to get experience and also to give yourself confidence that you know the material and can present it effectively, forcefully, directly, unhesitatingly, in the allotted time.

Besides providing information the audience can have confidence in, factor B should establish you as a creditable source and your information as honest and current and complete. Much has been written on source credibility or "ethos" as described by Aristotle in his *Rhetoric*. What gives you a relationship with an audience that will cause them to accept you and your ideas as authentic? Among the factors which are usually related to source credibility are: (1) How much of an expert is the presenter? (2) Is the presenter to be trusted? (3) Is the presentation dynamic as opposed to hesitant, cautious, apologetic, tentative? (4) Does the speech or report itself seem to be well-documented or well-researched? (5) Is the presenter fluent? Does the presenter use language and nonverbal support systems such as a paralanguage, gestures, facial expressions, and pacing to keep the audience involved? (6) Do the content of the speech and the movements of the presenter help to establish a common ground and association with the audience's values? The relationship of the presenter to the audience has been discussed in the chapter on motivation (Chapter 6) and will not be repeated here. We will only suggest that the presenter-audience transaction can be improved by judicious use of what you know about audience motives based on human needs.

Factor C was established as a purpose for the presentation before the first notes were taken; you wanted the audience to know something. To induce learning, acquisition of knowledge, and intellectual growth—all rather difficult to measure—may be a most noble purpose. Teachers have a feedback system for determining to some extent what students have learned; they use quizzes and exams. After most informational presentations you will not have that device available. Rather, you must depend on quizzical looks from the audience, questions, and challenging comments to find out how you did.

Another way of finding out how much your audience learned is to watch subsequent decisions. A company which wants to merge with another and collects prodigious amounts of data about the transaction will ultimately make a decision. The quality of that decision will depend to a great extent on the quality of the data collected and the efficacy of the presentation. The report should reflect the best possible research and organization of the material into a clear, honest, complete presentation.

Persuasion and Decision

In relating factors A and B to persuasive presentations, most of the points made above will apply. Information giving and report making are, in most cases, simply a passive form of persuasion and decision making. They are a precursor to persuasion or decisions in so many cases that the techniques recommended above will generally apply to persuasion as well.

On the other hand, the factor C stage of taking action is more imperative and more measurable in the persuasion presentation than in others. You want the action to take place. You may be opposed. You try to overcome the opposition and win approval for your view, your project, your candidate, your budget, or your cause. In an antagonist situation, the basic assumptions about human behavior have a very important role. Because you will act out your attitudes about humans and their motives and needs, you are not simply operating on the overt or action level. You carry with you, in your values and beliefs and attitudes, a basis for behaving in a certain way. To get others to react to you and to your arguments, you should remember Aristotle's description of rhetoric as making use of all the available means of persuasion. Those means include the techniques and devices for organizing an informational presentation as well as all the psychological resources you have read about in the rest of this book.

In the rhetorical approach to persuasion, let us say again, factor C requires some action from the audience. Only if factor B, believability, has followed the hearing and understanding of factor A will an audience be able to vote your way, follow your lead, change their minds, carry out your requests, or come to a decision favorable to your presentation aim.

The rhetorical approach suggests that you look at a combination of factors in the speaker, factors which we have already explored and will repeat here for emphasis. One factor is the "ethos" or source credibility of the speaker—charisma, magnetism, the unknown factor which makes one person more appealingly believable to an audience than others. A second rhetorical factor is "pathos" or the emotional appeals available to a persuader. Although presenters lean heavily on pathos in awards and rituals presentations, emotional appeals are considered inappropriate and perhaps even dishonest and unethical in attempts to persuade or inform. The fact is, emotion has no validity as data, although people do tend to respond emotionally in crises. Emotional appeals such as "tear-jerker" attempts or playing on sympathy are not highly regarded and are avoided by ethical speakers. Audiences nowadays have become rather sophisticated, and the more obvious "pathetic" appeals are less effective than they were once.

The appeal to "logos" or logics is most often associated with persuasion and decision making. As has been mentioned before, there is a myth in our society that decisions are made by coldly objective persons who sift through the most descriptive and pertinent data until they are able to select the one right decision. Most people hope that, in the most serious decisions affecting everyone, leaders will use such a logical and purposive and open system of problem solving and decision making. The fact is, however, men and women are not as rational as the mythology of logic tells us they should be. Decisions are made with incomplete data and for strongly biased and emotional reasons. Hasty or power-ordered decisions often prevail over better options. This seemingly cynical viewpoint on decision making is not intended to deter anyone from trying to use the logical processes in argumentation and in persuasive presentations. Logic has a higher rate of acceptance than other forms of persuasion when used well. When good evidence is gathered, organized in an orderly fashion, and presented dynamically and authoritatively, there is a good chance of acceptance. In giving you this recipe, we suggest that you be ethical—that is, accurate and honest—as well as enthusiastic about your cause.

Many persuasion systems are based simply on the manipulation of factors inherent in people and their relations to communication. The encyclopedia salesperson uses the stereotypical example of a "formula" persuasion presentation, taking advantage of the human need for belonging and other motives in a very successful system of sales. On the basis of corporate years of answering questions and parrying objections, the persuader is taught an entire script together with replies to most objections which may arise from the potential buyer. There have been serious abuses of consumers by such salespeople and some laws have been devised to protect citizens from door-to-door sales pitches, but the best defense is an informed body of consumers who will not listen to devious or unethical persuasion presentations.

We suggest you apply the principles of human behavior from this textbook in your reactions to persuasive presentations. We urge that you insist on ethical treatment from others, and that you be a model of ethical presentation yourself. In this way, anyone may help overcome a disadvantage most people have in communication dealings; we call it the "door-to-door sales syndrome." Remember that salespeople spend all their working hours figuring out how to sell you something, but you spend only a few minutes figuring out how to resist buying. In "buying and selling" presentations, we recommend you watch your participation as both a presenter and an audience.

SUMMARY

This chapter on presentations reviewed the relationship between the task assignment in communicating and the socioemotional factors which can influence your effect on the behaviors of others. Interacting with the situations are three factors, A, B, and C. Factor A is how the audience hears and understands a presenter, without which the message is neither delivered nor processed. Factor B is believability, or whether the audience sees the presentation as consistent with its beliefs, values, norms, and attitudes. In factor B, it is also important to remember that the presentation must offer a legitimate payoff for the audience. Factor C is the action stage, in which the capability and willingness of the audience to respond to the purpose of the presentation are tested or proved.

We have selected four kinds of presentations: (1) *awards and rituals,* (2) *introductions and responses,* (3) *information and reports,* and (4) *persuasion and decisions.* We have suggested ways in which you can evaluate your own presentations, and have also emphasized that within each of these types, people are involved in a wide range of informal and formal situations. Your personal life in your family and with your closest friends is one end of a complicated continuum of communication; the other end is large-scale presentations in industrial settings, conferences, national meetings, board sessions, and public appearances. The principles of presentation are very much the same in all those settings, leading to the conclusion that you are going to be using these types of presentations many times in your personal and professional life. Techniques suggested in this appendix can help you be more effective in your presentations, more ethical in your relations with others, and more attentive to your role of a recipient of presentations from others.

CHAPTER 11

INTERVIEWING

"The interviewer's questions must explore viewpoints as well as experiences; they must be as tough as the problems that will face the person who gets the job." S. G. Ginsburg

INTRODUCTION   Interviewing is such a common part of a manager's or supervisor's working life that it may be taken for granted. Interviewing takes on many different forms and represents much of the communicative behavior in organizations. As we will define interviewing, it is simply a highly specialized form of communication, but one which affects how people are hired for jobs, how they are appraised and told about it, and how they are able to work with others on the job. People not only find out what others think of them but also take the initiative in telling others what behaviors are appropriate and what are not.

Much of what you do, know, and feel comes from the interview sessions you are in. You depend on the interview to tell things, to find out things, to develop solutions, to foster agreement, and to pose problems. You depend on the interview to control how others behave and whether or not they get hired, promoted, or fired.

Here's a simple and direct definition of the interview: "An interview is a conversation, usually between two people, that is confined to a specific subject. The role of the interviewer is to seek information; that of the interviewee is to provide it."[1]

As with most communication, the interview has special characteristics which need to be understood before you can use this skill effectively. Also, as with other communication, the interview starts somewhere and brings along to the event itself many factors which may have an effect on the outcome. That brings us to a general description of interviewing as communication.

1. Interviewing is a special form of communication transaction. It is subject to all the weaknesses and strengths associated with human communication—including that meanings reside in people and not in words; that people have wide perceptual differences; that communication is transactional, which makes us confuse starting and stopping places, just to review a few. Very important, your own attitude about interviewing and the process of communication will have a serious effect on the interview outcome. The first characteristic of interviewing, then, is that *it is a specialized form of communication*, and unless you have basic communicative sensitivities and abilities you are not likely to be a very successful interviewer.

2. Interviewing is a carefully structured two-sided activity. In most cases, interviewing is a dyadic, or two-person, activity. Even in a news conference where a public official is being asked questions by a press corps of fifty newspeople, there are only two sides confronting each other although many more than two people are

[1]James M. Black, *How To Get Results From Interviewing*, McGraw-Hill Book Company, New York, 1970, p. 13.

involved. In other words, there may be exceptions in the numbers of humans involved, but you can identify the interview always as being two-sided and having a predictable form. This distinction separates the interview from the group discussion, panel, or round table where several views seem to each take a specific part. The interview is a simple them-us, dichotomous situation, as contrasted with many freewheeling conversations or loosely structured communication activities.

3. The roles of the interviewer and the interviewee are carefully prescribed. The interview is generally in control of the designated interviewer, who is usually responsible for setting the agenda, making the rules, running the show, and drawing out the others. Even in situations where an interviewee attempts to gain control of the communication, the interviewer is still responsible for keeping control, relinquishing it, or trying to get it back. Another way of describing this relationship is that most of the communication is designed and carried out by the person who has the interviewer role regardless of who called the pair together. If you phone up the dean's office, your boss, or your doctor and ask for an interview, you can still depend on having the position of interviewee.

4. Interviewing, like any common communication activity, relies on a constant and consistent stream of interactions between our verbal systems and our nonverbal systems. Paralanguage, gestures, body positions, object language, facial expressions, and all other rich and revealing nonverbal cues become part of the interview data as much as the content of the verbal messages. Both interviewer and interviewee become sensitive to the interplay of verbal and nonverbal communication as they move from the opening of the interview to the conclusion in a communicative waltz-step.

TYPES OF INTERVIEWS

There are many different ways to classify interviews. One way is by what is talked about: the content. In classifying by content, again there are many ways to divide up the different contents. Some writers have set up as many as ten separate categories while others have proposed as few as two categories.[2] Another familiar system divides

[2]Robert Goyer, Charles Redding, and James Rickey in their book, *Interviewing Principles and Techniques*, Kendall-Hunt Publishing Co., Dubuque, Iowa, 1968, pp. 7–8, described interview types as: (1) information getting, (2) information giving, (3) advocating, (4) problem solving, (5) counseling, (6) application for a job, (7) taking complaints, (8) giving reprimands, (9) conducting appraisals, and (10) stress interviewing. About the same time, Harold Zelko and Frank Dance in their book, *Business and Professional Speech Communication*, Holt, Rinehart and Winston, Inc., New York, 1965, p. 148, proposed two general classifications: (1) problem solving and counseling and (2) informative.

organizational interviews into: "intake" (when a person is entering the organization); "appraisal" (anything to do with job effectiveness); "interactive" (giving or taking orders, or solving problems); and "exit" (when a person is fired or leaves the organization). These classifications are based on an interaction rather than specific content, although the limits of the content are often implied by the occasion of the interview.

Our own system has three general headings with some subdivisions for specific purposes or contents. Distinctions between classes sometimes become blurred, and overlaps will occur. In the real working world, interviews will not always separate themselves so neatly as they do on paper or on a chart. Some mixing of content will occur. Some intertwining of purposes and relationships will make the actual interviews less sharply delineated.

Our three general types are: (1) information interviews, (2) problem interviews, and (3) professional interviews.

Information Interviews

In this general type are two predictable subdivisions: (1) *giving information*—telling how, teaching on a one-to-one basis, orientation, ordering, or giving instructions; and (2) *getting information*—finding out, probing, asking, researching, questioning, or clarifying.

Much of what goes on in a job interview falls into this category. Two people confront each other when one seeks employment and the other attempts to determine the suitability of the first for employment. So much attention is paid this form of interview that we have been tempted to assign it to the "professional" category. Personnel management is a highly developed profession in which skill in employment interviews is crucial, and there are also job seekers who become very practiced in the art of being interviewed for positions.

Because employment interviews are so important to corporations and to individuals, we will use job interview situations in many examples later in this section. In addition, some aspects of employment interviewing also apply to information interviews.

Information interviewing is designed to collect data. The interviewer probably already has some data about the applicant. The point of the interview, therefore, is to find out what kind of person the applicant (interviewee) is. This is a joint responsibility of the interviewer and the interviewee: One is seeking the best information possible, and the other is attempting to provide the most effective information and impression. Both interviewer and interviewee should prepare well for the event. (See Box A for suggestions on how to conduct an interview.)

CHECKLIST FOR AN INTERVIEW   **BOX A**

A. Decide or clarify the purpose of the interview.

B. Plan for the interview:
   1. Content of questions or data
   2. Sequence
   3. Structure
   4. Checklist or note system

C. Prepare the environment:
   1. Pay attention to comfort.
   2. Pay attention to privacy; avoid interruptions.
   3. Pay attention to proxemics.

D. Prepare the opening:
   1. Build rapport.
   2. Orient the interviewee, and clarify where you both want to go.
   3. Motivate the interviewee.

E. Carry out the interview sequence.
   1. Purposes:
      a. To establish and maintain rapport
      b. To orient the interviewee to the situation; to control the flow of the interaction
      c. To seek information
      d. To give information
      e. To summarize
   2. Talking
      a. Ask questions or make statements.
      b. Collect appropriate content.
      c. Use a sequence which moves the interaction along.
      d. Be flexible and sensitive to changes or new directions.
      e. Minimize your own talking; motivate the interviewee.
      f. Adjust to changing patterns of transactions; probe to fill gaps.
   3. Listening
      a. Watch answers or statements for:
         (1) Completeness
         (2) Information content
         (3) Accuracy
      b. Notice what is not said; pay attention to nonverbal communication.
      c. Inspect your own biases and prejudices as you listen to answers.
      d. Maintain an open mind.
      e. Check to see if the answers or data actually apply.
      f. Record accurately, completely, and clearly for later transcription.

F. The close should be appropriate to the kind of interview; check for yourself as well as for the interviewee.
   1. What can the interviewee expect to happen next?
   2. Who will follow through?
   3. When will it happen?
   4. Do you have everything you need?
   5. If anything is needed, clarify whose responsibility it is.

G. Write up your notes or your report, or get closure with the company or organization of the interview by filing it in the appropriate place.

Problem Interviews   Problem interviews occur because something needs to be done or fixed. The subdivisions include the following:

Complaints   When employees are not satisfied, they like to have an interview to see what can be done about the perceived problem. Not all complaint interviews are scheduled or formal; many may come about over coffee or in a casual meeting in the corridor. The complainer is the interviewee and is hoping something can happen as a result of sharing the problem with an interviewer who is seen as having some influence in getting the thing corrected. One very obvious complaint interview occurs in the department store complaint section, where it is the job of a paid problem interviewer to listen to customers who are dissatisfied with an article or service. Many special rituals and stereotypes have grown up about complaint departments, but they continue to be very real problem-interview situations in which many people become involved.

Confrontations   When expectations are not met in regard to salary, working conditions, promotions, etc., an employee may confront a supervisor in an interview situation. A teacher giving an unacceptable grade to a student may be confronted. Disagreement over terms of purchase, sale, or performance may result in confrontations.

Reprimands   A worker who fails to perform adequately or whose behavior results in danger or a costly error can expect to be involved in a reprimanding interview. A student who misses too many classes may be called in to speak with a teacher or counselor. If you do something wrong, you may be told to shape up. This is classed as a problem situation because something is in error and needs correction, and also because the reprimanding interview may often develop into a joint exploration of options between the interviewer and the interviewee. For example, the worker who is up for a reprimand may be given a chance to improve or may be put on warning or fired. The student with excessive absences may be dropped from a class or warned to start attending more regularly, or may develop with an instructor (the interviewer) a system for making up missed work.

Appraisals   Most people want to know how they are doing. Most people want to have praise for their successes, and will accept blame for their shortcomings. Setting goals and objectives early in the career of an employee gives some measures by which to judge progress. What is expected of the employee and how well is the person fulfilling the requirements for the job? For a student, there may be opportunities to discuss with a teacher the grades on exams or on term papers to see what expectations of the teacher are being met by the student's performance and what are not. Most people will perform better if they are given guidelines of what is expected of them; and then are told how well they are meeting those guides. A clear statement of expectations is crucial in this interview setting; and responsibility rests with both the interviewer and the interviewee to be sure they both understand what is supposed to be done by the interviewee as well as how progress is measured.

Decision making

This is a form of dyadic planning in which two people get together and pool their information and creative energies. Often it occurs between equals—two engineers solving a structural problem, two students doing an experiment together in a laboratory, husband and wife deciding to invest in a new home—although it may not be limited to co-workers. A teacher may call on a student to help develop a textbook selection system. The company auditor may seek assistance from the company comptroller to set up an innovative cost accounting system. An editor may consult a reporter on which news stories should be given attention by photographic support and other emphasis.

A system

In all these problem interviews, it should be apparent that some problem-solving system would be a most valuable tool. The pattern of reflective thinking proposed many years ago by John Dewey includes this sequence as applied to the dyadic interview:

1. Interviewer and interviewee should agree on a *definition of the problem*; unless there is understanding about what constitutes the problem, there is little chance of developing the next steps toward a solution.
2. *Analysis of the problem* should be jointly attempted. If one person (either interviewer or interviewee) gives a fast, off-the-cuff analysis without consultation, then the other should object or at least ask to have the analysis explained.
3. *Alternative solutions* can be suggested by either party. Again, it is important that both interviewer and interviewee have opportunities and freedom to suggest solutions and to talk them over.
4. *Solutions should be evaluated by both persons.* The evaluations should be based on logically derived and applied criteria rather than on the temptation in some dyads for one person to pull rank and say, "This is best because I'm boss."
5. *The preferred solution is chosen.* It should meet the requirements of reasonable chance for success and understanding and agreement between both parties, and it should relate directly to the problem as defined in the first step. At the same time, inverviewer and inter-

viewee should be intent on establishing a means of implementation of the solution, or should at least determine who is responsible for carrying out the solution.

**Professional
Interviews**

Besides personnel directors and employment specialists who, as we wrote earlier, may be in some senses considered professional interviewers, there are two distinct professional areas which make use of the interview: first, the so-called "helping" professions—medicine; law; and psychological, religious, and personal counseling—and second, selling.

Counseling

From the field of psychological counseling we have gained great insights into the ways people respond to both directive and non-directive questioning. Carl Rogers developed a model of the interview which sought to bring out the deepest concerns of the interviewee. Some medical schools now teach interviewing skills, on the assumption that pertinent data told to doctors by patients help in analyzing medical tests. Knowing what infomation to seek and how to seek it is important to lawyers who need to get details of their clients' problems Personal counselors and other social assistance interviewers must first find out about a person in order to help determine courses of action that will lead to better functioning or to obtaining necessary and rightful benefits. Nurses, dieticians, and family counselors are only a few people whose chief duties may include interviewing as much as providing services.

Selling

"Persuading" is the activity most commonly called in our society "selling." The salesperson who attempts to determine the customer's level of wants, ability to pay, and interest is engaging in a highly skilled interview system. The politician who delivers an appeal to voters is selling. The friend who tries to convince you to go to a movie is selling. Much of your communication interaction is either as "seller" or "buyer" in a persuading interview. And a large part of the economic and political worlds is populated by sales professionals.

**THE INTERVIEW
ITSELF**

We will look at the interview as a process which has a beginning, a middle, and a conclusion. It also has a history of what happened before the interview began, and it also will have an effect on the future of at least one of the participants—usually the interviewee. Our comments on the interview as a static situation should not mislead you into thinking the process begins or ends during the moments of actual contact. However, in order to help us talk about the interview, we will treat it as a start-middle-end sequence.

Interviews have content. They are about something. People exchange information. This is usually carried out by the verbal system of communication.

    Interviews also have clearly defined relationships. One person is in the role of asker, the other in the role of answerer. People exchange feelings and impressions and emotions, usually by nonverbal communication.

    People most often use words to tell each other about themselves. People usually use signals—voice inflections, gestures, mode of dress, where they sit, how they interrupt each other, who speaks first, and so on—to tell each other which of the two is superior or subordinate, to indicate the relationship between them.

    In the interview, both parties should pay close attention to both verbal and nonverbal factors. Much communication would be lost if only one of these systems existed. Both systems are going on at the same time, all the time. An alert interviewer and interviewee will pay attention to both, will observe both words and moves with great interest. One warning: In trying to pay attention to the wealth of information coming from both these systems, don't be trapped into (1) overanalyzing the meanings of words or gestures, making them into things they really could not mean, or (2) taking either the words or the moves out of context so they are interpreted as isolated tokens of communication exchange. Words and gestures are meaningful only within the flow of the communication transaction and within the context of the particular interview relationship.

Verbal and Nonverbal Components

Again, we want to emphasize that an interview may not start when you enter the room. It may have a history dating back to some move you made as a potential interviewee. You phoned for an interview with a lawyer or doctor; you received a notice to come to the dean's office; you answered an ad in the newspaper by sending your credentials to an employment office; you have been thinking about buying a new coat and have walked into your favorite clothing store. You had been a person for many years before you came to this situation. The other person has also existed in some places for some time. Both of you bring your past lives, experiences, prejudices, hopes, and expectations with you to the interview.

Sequence of an Interview

This stage establishes the relationship between persons. It should also orient both to the content of the interview—its purpose and the way things will happen. Remember, both nonverbal and verbal systems are operating as you (the interviewee) enter the room. How do you move? How do you shake hands? Do you sit right away? Where? Who is in charge? How do you find that out? After you and the

The beginning

interviewer size each other up in the first few seconds of the encounter, something will be said as greeting.

A greeting should be appropriate to the situation. If the interviewer is calling in a subordinate for a reprimand, the greeting will be different from that when a salesman approaches a potential customer. Few employees appreciate a phony friendly greeting from the boss who is getting ready to put them on notice, bawl them out, or fire them. On the other hand, when you walk into a store prepared to make a purchase, you feel better if the salesperson greets you in a friendly way and perhaps even engages in some pleasantries before starting to sell.

Establishing the reason for the interview is part of the opening. You probably already know why you are there. Seeking a job, hearing an argument, getting advice, and considering a purchase are all clear-cut reasons for an interview. If there is any doubt, however, the reasons should be clearly expressed early in the interaction. If the boss calls you in, you should have an idea of why. If you are asked to stop in and talk to your instructor, is it because your grades are low, you've missed a few classes, or you're being asked to help with some special assignment? If you call a doctor, some questions are usually asked about purpose (symptoms, severity, personal data); then when you arrive at the interview and the social amenities (if any) are over, you may be asked, "Now, tell me what seems to be the trouble. . . ."

Related to the purpose is clarifying what is to be covered in the interview. It is clear that when you go to see the doctor, you do not intend to talk about buying a car. On the other hand, there are so many items of information or concern you could share with a doctor that very early in the discussion you will probably both set limits on your topics. In a job interview, both parties will want to be certain what position you are talking about because some interviewers may be interviewing for several jobs at once. An effective interviewer will often outline for the interviewee what to expect during the session.

Employment interview: "I'd like to ask you a few questions about your background first, and then we can spend some time on what you may want to ask about the company." Persuasion interview: "Let me show you the brochures on these new cars, and as we go through them, you'll get an idea of what is available." Appraisal interview: "I will review for you the responsibilities of your job as I see them; then I will let you know my evaluation of your performance in those areas. After that you can tell me what you think about my assessment, and we can arrive at an understanding of where you are in the company." Dietician counseling: "Tell me what you have for each meal of the day during a typical week. Then we can develop a better picture of how to adjust your diet based on what you like and don't like."

An interviewee should be told what will be done with the results of the interview. Who will see records of it or hear about it? Another piece of information which ethically should be shared with the interviewee is what can be expected to happen as a result of this interview. If the job interview will be reported in detail to another office, that should be said. Telling the interviewee what is going on and how the results will be used can assist both parties in deciding what to tell or ask, and how to conduct themselves. It helps avoid guessing games about each other's role and the interview itself.

Employment interview: "You've already given us a written résumé, and I want to clarify a few items in it so as to be able to pass those along to the department you'd be working in." Sales interview: "I need to know something about your price range, if that is not too personal, so we can get you the best buy." Appraisal interview: "What I'm talking to you about will be summarized by me and put in your file. You will have a chance to see my notes and to make written comments on them. Of course, nobody but you, me, and your immediate superior will see these records." Dietician counseling: "What you tell me about your present eating habits and your tastes will help us develop a long-term plan for your diet. It is imperative that you let me know all you can so we can balance your weight and medication. The doctor will look at my record of your present diet and prescribe changes which you and I can then talk over so you can understand their importance."

An interviewee should also be given a clear understanding of what role to play in the interview. That can be set at the same time the interviewer is giving an outline of the sequence. Who is going to do the talking and in what order and who interrupts whom are easy to establish with a few words: "In this appraisal of your work, I want to give you the total evaluation and then ask for your comments; please don't interrupt, but make your own notes carefully and I'll be pleased to go over anything a second time if you don't understand it." "I want you to tell me all you can remember about the sequence of events leading up to the time the man grabbed your purse, starting when you walked into the store." "Let's start this interview with my explaining a little about the job and about how we see it fitting into the total organization. Although I don't want to do all the talking, it is important that I give you a full picture before you ask any questions."

In summary, the interview opening should be appropriate for the kind of interview and for the intended relationship between the parties. It should be both realistic and consistent with what is to follow. Confusion and ill will are generated by false openings; and an interview which gets off to an uncertain, ambiguous, misleading, and false start will not go anywhere.

The middle

The purpose of the interview will determine how the persons interact during the main part of the interview. Other determinants are the amount of information held by each party and the personal style and strategies used by each. There is no cookbook for interviews, and listing "ten sure-fire steps" won't work. There are, however, some methods which—with maximum flexibility and attention—can help to develop a successful interview. As a give-and-take transaction, the interview will depend on the motivations and skills of both participants in a moving and changing interaction. Not all people are good at all kinds of interviewing. Counseling interviews require different strategies than sales or persuasion interviews. A meeting between equals brings together different motivations and needs than a meeting between superior and subordinate. The interviewer, nonetheless, has a responsibility to get the interviewee to participate as fully and appropriately as possible or as the situation requires.

What motivates a person to answer questions? A skilled interviewer knows the general theories about motivation and tries to discover the specific motivations of the interviewee. Generally there are two kinds of motivational forces assisting the interview. First is the person's *internal* motivation to be liked, paid attention to, included, catered to, listened to, and seen as a person of some importance. Second is the *external* motivation to get the job or to use the interviewer as a means to achievement, success, recognition, more money, or promotion. Within each interviewee is a balance of these forces, and within the content of the interview the balance may be moving or changing. Willingness or reluctance to answer questions openly and completely will change as motivations change. The skilled interviewer is alert to changes and adjusts strategies of questioning to fit.

Let's explore now what may inhibit adequate replies, what makes a person "hold back." Then we will develop some suggestions of useful strategies for drawing out the interviewee if inhibitions occur.

Reasons a person will hold back include the following:

1. The interviewee may not want to be there. Someone called in to face an angry boss is not likely to be very chatty. An annual appraisal review may be an uneasy situation for some employees. Or if you have been sent to apply for a job for which you are not prepared or feel unqualified, or for which you think someone else has already been selected, it is not a time for easy conversation.
   Suggested corrective: The interviewer should probe to find out why the person does not want to be there, in case the interviewee has wrong assumptions about the session. In case of a reprimand, however, the interviewer should simply acknowledge the unpleasantness of the situation and not pretend that it is fun for either

participant. Appraisal interviews usually have some pleasant sides which may be used to help place the interviewee at ease.

2. The person may fear or distrust the interviewer or the setting. "Would you buy a used car from that man?" "Doctors always scare me."

   Suggested corrective: Sensitivity to the internal motivations of the person faced with a frightening or distrusting situation is the first step for the interviewer. Openly facing the fear or distrust may be possible in some settings. More time to build confidence and trust is indicated in this situation. A longer warm-up may be helpful.

3. The questions may be very personal or private, or may touch on something the interviewee cannot talk about easily. In this category are taboo topics, "telling on" others, and being asked to divulge information about income or love life which the interviewee considers to be nobody else's business and unrelated to the situation. In other words, the person does not see why the interviewer needs to know.

   Suggested corrective: An interviewer who senses answers are being held back for these reasons may try to get at the same data by asking for general impressions rather than specific questions about the interviewee. Hypothetical questions about how other people feel about the topics sometimes can get at the interviewee's own attitudes. It may be necessary to explain to the interviewee why the information is needed: "If we are to talk about your salary needs with our company, it is helpful to talk about your earning record." "If we are going to develop a program for you in prelaw we need to know some attitudes you have about law, ethics, morality, and some record of your outside activities."

4. The interviewee may not understand what is expected. Asked to tell about schooling, the person may tell only the degree programs involved and omit significant short courses, seminars, and training sessions successfully completed. Asked about parents, the respondent may tell about what they did for a living and not how they behaved toward each other or toward their children.

   Suggested corrective: Be ready to rephrase the question if you find the interviewee not replying with clarity. You can return to the question later if you think rephrasing will embarrass the respondent. Simply repeating the question is a very direct technique and may be appropriate.

5. The interviewee may not have the information or may not recall. Asking for names and dates and specific courses or incidents may tax anyone's memory. A request for statistics, earning records, or other technical details may not get a satisfactory answer because the person did not know at the time or has forgotten.

   Suggested corrective: Check your own expectations of what needs to be recalled from memory. Give the respondent a chance to think about it; and if there is still no recollection, invite a later reply or skip it. If you are sure the interviewee can get the data, ask that it be sent to you. If there is no reason to expect the interviewee to either obtain or recall the data, then be prepared to accept an approximation rather than an exact figure. "About how many hours of credit did you have in laboratory sciences—not the names of courses, but an approximate number of credits?" "How many people have you had working under you at any one time—maybe just those in the first level below yours?"

6. Interpersonal tensions may develop between parties, tensions may be built into the situation if either person dislikes the kind of situation or the purpose of the interview. Many signals for this tension are given nonverbally. Mannerisms, physical appearance, speaking voice, and grammar are only a few cues on which interpersonal likes depend. In addition, the tensions may have less to do with the present situation than with previous associations. Someone who looked like this interviewer or sounded like that interviewee may have caused a problem. Dislike of a person can be based on resemblances to others as much as on how the person actually behaves.

   Suggested corrective: Be aware of your own prejudices and what turns you off to another person in an interview situation. If you are against smoking, then as an interviewer you should indicate that you do not approve, and you should not have ashtrays handy. When someone gets on your nerves, ask yourself whether the characteristics that bother you are important for the situation you are in and also whether you are judging this person unfairly because of some other experience. If you sense the other person reacting negatively to you, consider which features of your person or your communication seem to interfere with the conduct of the interview and, if possible, minimize that factor. One employment interviewer gave up a habit of doodling on the margins of application papers when a nervous and apprehensive interviewee mentioned that he had made an effort to prepare a neat application and wondered if he was to get that copy back or if others in the company would judge him by the doodles.

7. An interviewee may feel one-down, or inferior, and there is a good chance the result will be holding back. When someone's self-esteem or ego is being put down, the person tends to withdraw. Much information about being above, equal to, or below others is communicated nonverbally. Inflections of voice, eye contact, and body movements are only a few indicators of how people feel about each other, and most people are quick to sense those signals and to respond.

Suggested corrective: Learn to control your voice and moves and to be aware of when you seem to be giving signals which can inhibit the other person. If your job is to get the appropriate data from an interviewee, you cannot enjoy the luxury of acting superior or trying to put the other person down.

8. An interviewee may disagree with the purpose of the interview. Some employees do not think appraisal interviews are worth anything and will suffer through a session only because it has been scheduled and they cannot avoid it. Advising sessions are sometimes resented by students who are first compelled to wait and then to sit through long painful deliberations with their faculty advisors. *Suggested corrective:* Let the other person express opinions and be heard. Acknowledge the difference of opinions about the usefulness of the particular interview but suggest maybe something can be salvaged from the encounter—as long as you both have to do it. Further explanations of the purpose may be helpful if you sense the interviewee does not have good data on reasons for the interview, or has been given bad information from others.

The close

Just as the interviewer and the interviewee used the beginning of the interview as an opportunity to tell each other what was going to happen, the close or ending should tell something. There are two important issues to be dealt with at the end of the interview.

1. First you must review and check back to the beginning. Whatever you promised the other person at the start, you need to get back to at the end. You need to develop "closure," consisting of two parts:
   a. Review the content of what you talked about. You said at the beginning that you would, for example, describe the job and then give the other person a chance to ask questions. You did that, and you must at this final stage of your encounter review the fact that you did. "As I mentioned at the beginning of our interview . . ." is a good way to start telling the other person that you have come to the end and are in the process of reviewing the interaction. Included in the content is what you talked about: If it is employment, you need to say that you mentioned the job responsibilities, the pay, the working conditions, the relations with other sections, etc. If it is persuasion, you want to make sure the points you made were clearly understood and will register on the other person. "Let me summarize my points, then . . ." is an apt beginning in this instance. In a problem interview, you need to develop a summary of all sides of an argument or the data presented. "Both of us agreed that we would . . . and then you made the point of . . . and I said . . ." is a good summary form. The content summary at the close is a time to tell each other what

happened; the main responsibility for this is on the interviewer who is in charge of closing out the interview.

b. Review your impressions and feelings. Often these are expressed only indirectly, but it is important to develop closure on the relationship as well as on the content. The job applicant must be reminded that he or she was given courteous treatment. A persuasive situation will end on a note of action—"Are you willing to . . . ?"—which indicates continuance to a satisfactory conclusion. An appraisal interview will usually end on a positive note but sometimes on a negative and resentful note. The interviewer must attempt to end positively if at all possible. Closure with an interviewee is not pleasant if both parties are angry; they will carry away many unsolved problems and unresolved animosities. Even if the parties do not agree, there must be a recognition of that fact so some feeling of being finished with each other can be accomplished. "We ended up disagreeing, but I think you know how I feel" is a better closure than both parties pretending they have no feelings toward each other and toward the interview.

2. The second issue to be dealt with is direct attention to a next step. Where do we go from here? If some specific items are helpful in the beginning of an interview, they are imperative at the end.

a. Who will be in touch with whom? The interviewee wants to know what will happen as a result of the interview. You must be able to say whether you will be in touch, deliver the product you just sold, send the report to others, or carry through. If you are not the person to take the next step and your job is ended with this interview, the interviewee ought to be told who is the next responsible person.

b. By what means will the other person find out what happens as a result of the interview? Will you write a letter? Telephone? Have your secretary send a check? Should the interviewee come back and report personally to a certain desk or office? The actual means of notification of the result is very important for an applicant or an interviewee.

c. When will the results be available? A vague statement like: "Well, we'll be in touch . . ." is a devastating close to an interview. How and when are imprecise, and to say "we" when you mean "I" or a named person is vague. Time is usually important after an interview. A person who is buying or being employed or evaluated is interested in hearing the outcome. "When" is more important to the interviewee than it usually is to the interviewer. Once you've sold the item, delivery to the customer is less of an issue to you than it is to the buyer. Once you have checked personally on the applicant for a job, there are others for you to see and time is less significant to you than it is to the person who has applied for the position. Once you have finished an appraisal interview, you are going to file the results or pass them along; but time is less significant to you than it is to the subject of the appraisal, who needs and deserves to know when the appraisal will land in a file or on some official's desk. A promise to do something at the end of an interview is a serious one, and you should be prepared to live up to it. If you tell a job applicant that you will send notification by mail in the next week, then you have a real obligation to do what you promised.

In summary, the close of an interview is like the act of putting signatures on a contract. It is the final, binding act to an important interaction and must be taken very seriously by the interviewer because the interviewee takes it very seriously. The interview is not complete without a good ending. It should be positive in tone and complete in content and data summary, and it should specify precisely who will do what by what means and when.

THE INTERVIEWER

When you are in an interviewer role, a great responsibility rests on what you do. You must make correct decisions which involve not only the interviewee's career, well-being, use of a product, or some other factor but also affect the company or organization you work for. You have not helped your company if you recommend an incompetent for hiring, nor have you helped the person who is hired for an unsuitable job.

Characteristics of a Good Interviewer

What makes a good interviewer? Different writers and analysts have suggested traits which good interviewers should have.[3] For our purposes, we will suggest three broad categories of traits: intellectual abilities, communicative skills, and affective or psychological traits or sensitivities.

[3]For a few such references see these books: Richard A. Fear, *The Evaluation Interview*, The American Management Association, New York, 1969, p. 14; James Menzies Black, *How To Get Results from Interviewing*, McGraw-Hill Book Company, New York, 1970, p. 14; Felix M. Lopez, *Personnel Interviewing*, 2d ed., McGraw-Hill Book Company, New York, 1975, pp. 57, 65.

**Intellectual
abilities**

Knowledge, or intellectual abilities, includes how much you know about the firm or organization you work for and how much you know about its policies and practices or a product if you are selling. You need to know about human motivation such as what makes people work well at a job, buy a product, answer questions, or not answer questions. In an employment interview, you need to know data about the person being interviewed and about the job to be filled. Most of this knowledge can be obtained from other people; from records, job descriptions, tech manuals, policy manuals; from formal training about motivation and personal needs; and from job résumés or by checking references for a job applicant. Your information should be (1) accurate, (2) organized, (3) clear, and (4) readily available either in memory or in printed form if it is to be shared with others. Knowledge is a powerful tool for you in the interview when you have it, but a real source of embarrassment when you don't.

**Communicative
skills**

An effective communicator has been described in many parts of this book. We believe that just having knowledge is not good enough. You must be able to put it to work in a communicative sense. An ability to use language effectively is first. That includes being careful of meanings, organization, and aware of feedback. You must know that both the verbal and nonverbal systems are operating at the same time in a communication transaction, and you must have the skill to do your part in communicating on both of those "channels," as well as being able to interpret the other person's verbal and nonverbal communication. Communication consists of both speaking and listening. In the interview, perhaps as much as in any communication, the process of listening is crucial.

**Empathy or
affective traits**

A flexible attitude and an open mind are crucial. Closed-mindedness is a great deterrent to good interviewing as it leaves no room for new ideas or innovative replies. A part of sensitivity to feedback is empathy, or the ability to sense another's needs and to share concern and interest. Definitions of empathy usually include the ability to feel along with another person, or to understand how you might react if you were in the other person's spot. It is easy to understand that an effective interviewer must be able to "assume the other person's role." We must caution, however, that empathy is not the same as sympathy; that it is a very complex characteristic; that even the most current research does not shed much light on when it is acquired, by whom, and for what purposes; and especially that not much is known about how to train for it. The empathic interviewer can understand the feelings or motives of another without showing the same feelings or getting overly involved (feeling too much sympathy). You can observe that the other person is nervous, but you don't have to get nervous too to understand the dynamics of nervousness and what is making the other person nervous. If the interviewee is angry, you can understand what worked on his or her feelings, but you don't have to get angry too just to prove you understand.

Training for Interviewing

Some interviewer abilities are trainable; others may not be. Although empathy is complex and not easily trained for, knowledge is more easily obtained, and the habits of collecting, storing, and retrieving data can be trained for fairly easily. Communication skills, we believe, can be trained for—including the much-neglected and vital skill of listening.

One author suggests the following qualities for a good interviewer: (1) a warm, engaging manner; (2) sensitivity in social situations; (3) reasonable intelligence; (4) critical and analytical judgment; (5) adaptability; and (6) maturity.[4] Suggestions on how to train for those qualities include the standard sequence of (1) telling, (2) demonstrating, (3) supervised practice, and (4) evaluation and critique. For some qualities it makes sense to use a training program; but for some of the characteristics (social sensitivity, intelligence, and maturity, for example) training seems to be a rather long shot.

Our contention is that proper selection of potential interviewers may be more important than extensive training in an attempt to develop those traits or qualities which may not be directly or quickly trainable. We believe that identifying potential interviewers who possess a quality of empathy has more chance for success than trying to train for it. That is also true for intelligence, and certainly for flexibility and adaptability which are significant traits needed in interviewing. There is also no agreement among authorities that "warmth" is a good trait, even if it is trainable. Some observers say that too much warmth gets confused with weakness; and although warmth is fine for a friend to have, the necessity to make decisions on hiring, appraising, or selling may not leave much room for that trait.[5]

Problems in Interviewing

Our experience with interview training shows that the source of interview problems is usually the interviewer, although the level of expectations of the interviewee seems to have a significant effect on the outcome.

[4]Fear, op. cit., p. 32.
[5]Milton Mandell, *The Employment Interview*, American Management Association, New York, 1961, p. 15.

After making some 500 tape recordings of interviews, John D. Drake[6] reports that professional interviewers make the same mistakes as amateurs in interviewing. The errors consist primarily of these four items: (1) talking too much and listening too little, (2) jumping to conclusions, (3) communicating to the applicant how to give the "correct" response to questions, and (4) failing to translate the facts heard in the interview to prediction of on-the-job performance. Ten years earlier, a study of some 273 firms and employment interviewers had much the same results.[7] The three most common shortcomings of interviewers were: (1) poor interviewing techniques, (2) too much talking, and (3) making "snap judgments." These shortcomings usually lead to failure to get all the essential facts from an applicant and, therefore, weaken the effectiveness of the interview as a communication act. Nearly half of the companies surveyed also reported that their interviewers were biased. Among interviewer prejudices were matters relating to age, sex, race, religion, and appearance, as well as the deep-seated personal characteristics or personality traits of the interviewer or supervisor.

In working with interviewers and interviewees, our own conclusions are similar. Interviewers do not conduct interviews as well as possible for a variety of reasons. Most errors are the fault of the interviewer and that person's training, personal abilities, and individual communicative and empathic skills.

Interview errors and correctives

We suggest the following shortcomings of interviews are worth watching for and—in a negative way—can serve as a guide to interview errors and how to overcome them.

1. Using untrained interviewers or persons unprepared to take on the situation. Selecting Joe and Sally to conduct interviews because they have time and private offices may not be appropriate. Interviewing is too exacting a process to turn over to whoever is available at the moment. Interviewers should be selected for their traits and potential trainability.
2. Lack of interviewer preparation. A plan should be developed to include answers to the following questions:
   a. What is the purpose of this interview? What is supposed to happen as a result of it?
   b. What content should be covered? What data should be exchanged?

---

[6]*Interviewing for Managers*, New York, American Management Association, 1972, p. 14.

[7]Mandell, op. cit., p. 12.

      c. What structure and setting will accomplish the desired ex-
change of data?

      d. What sequence will be most likely to produce good data and a
satisfactory relationship?

      e. What will happen to the interviewee when the session is over?

      f. What will happen to the data after the session is over?

3. Insufficient or inappropriate content.

      a. This usually occurs when the interviewer does not plan the
questions and the sequence and, therefore, wanders around
with the questions. Answers will lack continuity and focus.

      b. Interviewers are likely to ask questions about their own
interests rather than asking what is needed for the situation or
getting data from the interviewee. A list of questions or set of
statements and their organized sequence can help avoid this
problem.

      c. Interviewers sometimes settle for *any response* instead of an
acceptable one. The interviewer should be alert to whether the
question asked is actually answered, rather than some other
question which may not have been asked. It takes skill to probe
for replies rather than just letting the answers flow along.

      d. Failing to ask the same questions of each applicant in a series of
interviews will result in poor comparative data. Again, a
preplanned interview list and sequence can avoid this vari-
ability in data.

4. Unwillingness to confront an interviewee or to probe when poor
data or weak answers are given. An interviewer must first be able
to sense whether a reply is clear, accurate, and precise. When it is
not, a confrontation is needed and probably even expected by the
interviewee.

      a. Direct confrontation can be achieved by: (1) Repeating the
question: "My question was. . . ." (2) Asking about subpoints
to get more extensive replies: "Maybe the question was too
general about what you eat for breakfast; let me ask if you
usually eat cereal? How about toast?" (3) Clarifying by
example: "When I asked where you had worked, I was interested
in not only the company, but in which department such as
assembly, research, sales, or which?" (4) Pointing out the
contradictions or evasive or incomplete answers. Be as polite
or direct as you feel the situation may call for: "It is not clear,
evidently, what kind of answer I was asking for . . ." or "That's
an indirect reply, but let's see if we can try it again. . . ."

      b. Indirect confrontations can be achieved by using nonverbal
communication. (1) Both persons in the situation must be
sensitive to subtle cues or the indirect confrontation will not

work. (2) Silence is an excellent device. A skilled interviewer can "wait it out" with a tension of silence which an interviewee may be forced to fill. (3) A neutral comment from the interviewer such as, "Tell me more about that . . ." may help. (4) A reflective comment such as, "That seems to be a strong feeling in you, right?" may elicit more information. (5) An internal summary of what had been said before may help point out gaps in the information or an unsatisfactory reply.

5. Guiding the answers. Some interviewees are very skillful in detecting what answers the interviewer expects. When you "tip your hand" in this way, the answers you get will not reflect the interviewee's information or opinion but rather will be a clever recitation of the answer you supplied. This quality is so well developed in some people that it appears to be a mindreading act. Your questions, and very important, your tone of voice and your manner, should not give away the answers you expect or hope for. Otherwise, you will simply get a mirror reflection of your own expectations and not data from the interviewee. Careful planning of your questions and their sequence will help avoid this problem.

6. Doing all the talking. If your job is to give information or conduct training, then it is proper to do most of the talking. In employment interviews and most other settings, however, you as the interviewer should attempt to get data from the other person. One of the most common errors occurs when an interviewer tries to sell a job applicant on the company before any data have been generated. In an appraisal interview the same thing happens if the superior simply bawls out the subordinate instead of allowing time for response or for comments on planning improvements or setting goals. If you suspect you may be talking too much in the interviewer role, you should tape record your next interview (with the permission of the interviewee) and check on the proportion of time you are speaking. Videotape recording is another good feedback device, as is the observation of a third party who is alerted to watch for your verbal output.

7. Jumping to conclusions. As the interview gets rolling, you begin to anticipate answers. You may fall into the trap of "thinking you hear" an answer just because you are expecting it. You may leap ahead of your questions and not listen for the answers, thinking that the silent interviewee actually did respond.
   a. Be aware that you have some preconceived ideas about the person facing you, and you may assume that certain replies mean something they do not.
   b. Be careful to pay very strict attention to answers, not to be so preoccupied with keeping the questions rolling that you don't really hear the answers.

c. Check yourself to find out whether you are reading more into a reply than was intended. If you have doubts, ask again or probe for clarification or more data.

8. Poor listening. This may be the most important error committed in interviews. Look back through the first seven items in this list and check how many times poor listening is implied as a factor. Listening as a communicative act is so vital to interviewing that the first characteristic of an interviewer should be the ability to listen. Either that trait should be highly developed in the person selected to interview, or extensive training should be accomplished before an interviewer is ever sent forth to work.

9. Inadequate setting. So much depends on how people relate to each other during the interview that distractions can cause interview errors.

a. Interruptions by telephone or people coming into the interview room can damage the flow of the interview.

b. Noise from any source can be distracting.

c. Privacy is of great importance to most interviews. The student who discusses a grade with a teacher while others listen is not in a good position; neither is a job interviewee very comfortable talking about past experiences or future plans with others able to hear.

d. Time is part of the setting and a critical factor. Being hurried in giving replies may upset an interviewee, and weak or incomplete answers will result. Having too much time can also be damaging if the participants run out of items to talk about before the scheduled session has ended. Experience is needed on how long each kind of interview should take. In addition, scheduling too many sessions for one interviewer without a break can be unproductive.

e. The location of the furniture in an interview setting (see the discussion of proxemics in the text) can have an effect on how the participants relate to each other and on the quality of information exchanged.

10. Recording and reporting error. Failing to follow a form or a logical sequence can produce a weak interview report. An interviewer has much to do and much to pay attention to during the session, and is handicapped by having to take extensive notes or otherwise spend a lot of time and energy out of direct contact with the interviewee.

a. It helps to develop a checklist for some kinds of information.

b. Good interviewers are able to judge which items should be recorded and which can be passed by.

c. Many interviewers who do not know the formal systems of shorthand develop their own versions for notetaking.

   d. It is important to transcribe the notes or make a report very soon after the interview is ended. If you have a series of interviews and are unable to write up a report after each one, there is danger of blurring your impressions from one to the other.
   e. Try to put as much data in your report as you think will be needed. Some interviews will not require extensive record keeping, but others must be carefully described and a transcription kept for legal reasons or simply out of fairness to the persons involved. Personnel are more protected by law today than ever before, and the interview situation is a potential source of legal action if it is not properly conducted and properly documented.

SUMMARY

We have concentrated on the interviewer and his or her responsibility and role in interviewing. The interviewee also has responsibilities—to be prepared and to respond accurately and succinctly.

The section just preceding this summary is devoted to "errors" in interviewing which dramatically point up what you should watch for in your interviewing. Within each section dealing with errors is some specific advice on how to be alert for and how to avoid those errors.

Good interviewing is less dramatic than bad. It results in a satisfactory match between an employer and a potential employee; in a sale of goods or services; or in an evaluation clearly explained to an employee with a resulting change in work behaviors; or in collection of data which guides the future healthy, productive life of a client or patient.

Bad interviewing accomplishes the opposite. Employees become unproductive, unhappy, and then unemployed. Buyers may purchase an item and then complain or become dissatisfied or angry, or sales may be lost. Appraisals of employee performance may turn into shouting matches or bitter blasts of ill will between superior and subordinate. In medical and psychological interviews, a person's health or mental and emotional stability is at stake.

It is imperative that interviewers be chosen for their personal and professional characteristics. Some characteristics can be trained for and some cannot. Training should be constant and extensive for those skills needed to supplement the inherent traits found in potentially good interviewers.

Three basic principles of interviewing apply.

1. Interviewing is essentially a dyadic communication transaction and therefore is subject to all the strengths and weaknesses of human communication behavior.

2. The interviewer assumes primary responsibility for the total interview and must gain and retain control without so overwhelming the interviewee that poor responses result.
3. The interviewer's primary responsibility is to get information (or sometimes to give it) and should effectively move the interview along so the data given by the interviewee most nearly represent what is needed in the situation as well as clearly representing what the interviewee believes or needs to tell.

BIBLIOGRAPHY

ADAMS, STACY J.: *Interviewing Procedures, A Manual for Survey Interviewers,* University of North Carolina Press, Chapel Hill, 1958.

ALBERTI, ROBERT E., and MICHAEL L. EMMONS: *Your Perfect Right,* Impact, San Luis Obispo, Ca., 1970.

APFELBAUM, E.: "On Conflicts and Bargaining," in L. Berkowitz (ed.), *Advances in Experimental and Social Psychology,* Academic Press, New York, 1974.

ARGYLE, MICHAEL: *The Psychology of Interpersonal Behavior,* Penguin Books, Baltimore, 1967.

ATHANASSIADES, J. C.: "Investigation of Some Communication Patterns of Female Subordinates in Hierarchical Organizations," *Human Relations,* vol. 27, 1974, pp. 195–209.

AYERS, J.: "Techniques for the Study of Communication in Organizations," in *Communication in Organization,* J. L. Owen, P. A. Page, and G. I. Zimmerman (eds.), West Publishing Company, St. Paul, Minn., 1976, pp. 290–295.

BACH, GEORGE, and HERB GOLDBERG: *Creative Aggression: The Art of Assertive Living,* Avon Books, New York, 1974.

BACHARACH, S. B., and M. AIKEN: "Communication in Administrative Bureaucracies," *Academy of Management Journal,* vol. 20, 1977, pp. 365–377.

BARBARA, DOMINICK: *The Art of Listening,* Charles C. Thomas, Springfield, Ill., 1958.

BARNARD, CHESTER I.: *The Functions of the Executive,* Harvard University Press, Cambridge, Mass., 1938.

BEM, DARYL J.: *Beliefs, Attitudes and Human Affairs,* Brooks/Cole Publishing Co., Belmont, Ca., 1970.

BENNIS, WARREN R.: "Interpersonal Communication," in *The Planning of Change: Readings in Applied Behavioral Sciences,* Warren G. Bennis, Kenneth D. Benne, and Robert Chin (eds.), Holt, Rinehart & Winston, New York, 1961.

BENNIS, W., E. SCHEIN, F. STEELE, and D. BERLEW: *Interpersonal Dynamics: Essays and Readings on Human Interaction,* 3d ed., The Dorsey Press, Homewood, Ill., 1973.

BERNE, ERIC: *Games People Play,* Grove Press, New York, 1964.

BERSCHEID, E., and E. H. WALSTER: *Interpersonal Attraction,* Addison-Wesley, Reading, Mass., 1969.

BINGHAM, W.: *How To Interview,* Harper Brothers, New York, 1959.

BIRD, CAROLINE: *Born Female: The High Cost of Keeping Women Down,* David McKay Co., New York, 1968.

BLACK, JAMES M.: *How to Get Results from Interviewing,* McGraw-Hill Book Company, New York, 1970.

BLAKE, R. R., and J. S. MOUTON: *The Managerial Grid,* Gulf Publishing Co., Houston, 1964.

BLAU, P. M.: *Exchange and Power in Social Life,* John Wiley & Sons, New York, 1967.

BLAU, PETER, and J. RICHARD SCOTT: *Formal Organizations,* Chandler Publishing Company, San Francisco, 1962.

BLOCK, JEANNE HUMPHREY: "Conceptions of Sex Role," *American Psychologist*, vol. 28, no. 6, June 1973.

BLOOM, LYNN, KAREN COBURN, and JOAN PEARLMAN: *The New Assertive Woman*, Delacourt Press, New York, 1975.

BOWER, SHARON, and GORDON BOWER: *Asserting Yourself—A Practical Guide for Positive Action*, Addison-Wesley, Reading, Mass., 1976.

BOYD, B., and J. M. JENSEN: "Perceptions of the First-Line Supervisor's Authority: A Study in Superior-Subordinate Communication," *Academy of Management Journal*, vol. 15, no. 3, 1972, pp. 331–342.

BRIEF, A., and M. WALLACE: "The Impact of Employee Sex and Performance on the Allocation of Organizational Rewards," *Journal of Psychology*, vol. 92, 1976, pp. 25–34.

BURKE, R. J., and D. S. WILCOX: "Effects of Different Patterns and Degrees of Openness in Superior-Subordinate Communication on Subordinate Job Satisfaction." *Academy of Management Journal*, vol. 12, no. 3, pp. 319–326.

BURTON, JOHN W.: *Conflict and Communication: The Use of Controlled Communication in Internal Relations*, Macmillan & Co., Ltd., London, 1969.

CHAPMAN, J.: "Comparison of Male and Female Leadership Styles," *Academy of Management Journal*," vol. 18, no. 3, 1975, pp. 645–650.

COLLINS, B. E., and H. GUETZKOW: *A Social Psychology of Group Processes for Decision-Making*, John Wiley & Sons, New York, 1964, pp. 214–215. Reprinted by permission.

CONRATH, D. W.: "Communications Environment and Its Relationship to Organizational Structure," *Management Science*, vol. 20, pp. 586–603.

CUSHMAN, D. P.: "The Rules Perspective as a Theoretical Basis for the Study of Human Communication," *Communication Quarterly*, vol. 25, 1977, pp. 30–45.

CUSHMAN, D. P., and G. C. WHITING: "An Approach to Communication Theory: Towards Consensus on Rules." *Journal of Communication*, vol. 22, 1972, pp. 217–238.

CUSHMAN, D. P., and R. T. CRAIG: "Communications Systems: Interpersonal Implications," in *Explorations in Interpersonal Communications*, G. R. Miller (ed.), Sage Publications, Beverly Hills, Ca., 1976, pp. 37–58.

CUSHMAN, D. P., and W. B. PEARCE: "Generality and Necessity in Three Types of Theory about Human Communication, with Special Attention to Rules Theory," *Human Communication Research*. vol. 3, 1977, pp. 344–353.

DAVIS, MURRAY: *Intimate Relations*, Free Press, New York, 1973.

DAVIS, K.: "Management Communication and the Grapevine," *Harvard Business Review*, vol. 31, 1953, pp. 43–49.

DELBECQ, A. L.: "The Effectiveness of Nominal, Delphi, and Interacting Group Decision Making Processes," *Academy of Management Journal*, vol. 17, April 1974.

DeRISI, WILLIAM J., and GEORGE BUTZ: *Writing Behavioral Contracts*, Research Press Co., Champaign, Ill., 1975.

DEUTSCH, M.: *The Resolution of Conflict: Constructive and Destructive Processes*, Yale University Press, New Haven, 1973.

DOWNS, CAL W., DAVID M. BERG, and WIL A. LINKUGEL: *The Organizational Communicator*, Harper & Row, Publishers, New York, 1977.

DRAKE, JOHN D.: *Interviewing for Managers*, American Management Associations, New York, 1972.

DRUCKER, P. F.: *Management: Tasks, Responsibilities, Practices*, Harper & Row, New York, 1973.

FARACE, R. V., P. R. MONGE, and H. M. RUSSELL: *Communicating and Organizing*, Addison-Wesley, Reading, Mass., 1977.

FARACE, R., J. TAYLOR, and J. STEWART: "Review and Synthesis: Criteria for the Evaluation of Organizational Communication Effectiveness," in *Communication Yearbook, II*, B. Ruben (ed.), International Communication Association Press, 1978.

FARRELL, W.: *The Liberated Man*, Random House, New York, 1975.

FAST, JULIUS: *Body Language*, M. Evans, New York, 1970.

FEAR, RICHARD A.: *The Evaluation Interview*, 2d ed., McGraw-Hill Book Company, New York, 1973.

FENSTERHEIM, HERBERT, and JEAN BAER: *Don't Say Yes When You Want To Say No*, Dell Publishing Co., New York, 1975.

FILLEY, A. C.: *Interpersonal Conflict Resolution*, Scott, Foresman & Co., Glenview, Ill., 1975.

FISHER, B. A.: *Small Group Decision Making: Communication and the Group Process*, McGraw-Hill Book Company, New York, 1974.

FRANKLIN, J.: "Down the Organization: Influence Processes across Levels of Hierarchy," *Administrative Science Quarterly*, vol. 20, no. 2, 1975, pp. 153–163.

FRENCH, J. R. P., and BERTRAM RAVEN: "The Bases of Social Power," in *Studies in Social Power*, Dorwin Cartwright and Alvin Zander (eds.), Ann Arbor Research Center for Group Dynamics and Institute for Social Research, 1959.

FROST, JOYCE HOCKER and WILLIAM W. WILMOT: *Interpersonal Conflict*, Wm. C. Brown Company Publishers, Dubuque, Iowa, 1978.

GABBARD-ALLEY, ANNE, and ERIN M. PORTER: *An Interpersonal Approach to Business and Professional Speech Communication*. American Press, Boston, 1977.

GARRETT, A.: *Interviewing, Its Principles & Methods*, Family Welfare Association of America, New York, 1942.

GIBB, JACK R.: "Defensive Communication," in *Interpersonal Dynamics: Essays and Readings on Human Interactions*, rev. ed., Warren G. Bennis, Edgar H. Schein, Fred I. Steele, and David E. Berlew (eds.), The Dorsey Press, Homewood, Ill., 1968.

GIBBIN, JAMES: *Effective Managerial Leadership*, AMACOM Executive Books, 1978.

GOFFMAN, ERVING: "On Face-Work: An Analysis of Ritual Elements in Social Interaction," in *The Self in Social Interaction*, vol. I, Chad Gordon and Kenneth J. Gergen (eds.), John Wiley & Sons, New York, 1968.

GOFFMAN, ERVING: "The Presentation of Self to Others," in *Symbolic Interaction*, Jerome G. Manis and Bernard N. Meltzer (eds.), Allyn & Bacon, Boston, 1972.

GOLDHABER, G., H. DENNIS, G. RICHETTO, and O. WIIO: *Information Strategies: New Pathways to Corporate Power*, Prentice-Hall, Englewood Cliffs, N.J., 1979.

GORDON, RAYMOND L.: *Interviewing: Strategy, Techniques & Tactics*, The Dorsey Press, Homewood, Ill., 1969.

GORNICK, VIVIAN, and BARBARA K. MORAN: *Woman in Sexist Society*, Basic Books, New York, 1971.

GOYER, ROBERT W., W. C. REDDING, and JOHN T. RICKEY: *Interviewing Principles and Techniques*, Kendall/Hunt Publishing Company, Dubuque, Iowa, 1968.

GUETZKOW, H.: "Communication in Organizations," in *Handbook of Organizations*, J. G. March (ed.), Rand McNally, Chicago, 1965, pp. 354–413.

GUSTAFSON, D. H., A. L. DELBECQ, and A. VAN de VEN: *Group Techniques for Program Planning*, Scott, Foresman & Co., Glenview, Ill., 1975.

HAGE, G. R.: *Organizational Communication and Control*, Interscience-Wiley, New York, 1975.

HALL, EDWARD T.: *The Silent Language*, Doubleday, New York, 1959.

HALL, EDWARD T.: *The Hidden Dimension*, Doubleday, New York, 1966.

HAMACHEK, DON E.: *The SELF in Growth, Teaching, and Learning*, Prentice-Hall, Englewood Cliffs, N.J., 1965.

HAMACHEK, DON E.: *Encounters with the Self*, Holt, Rinehart, and Winston, New York, 1971.

HARITON, THEODORE: *Interview! The Executive's Guide to Selecting the Right Personnel*, Hastings House, Publishers, New York, 1970.

HARRAL, STEWART: *Keys to Successful Interviewing*, University of Oklahoma Press, Norman, 1954.

HARRIS, T.: *I'm OK—You're OK*, Avon Books, New York, 1969.

HARVEY, J. B.: "The Abilene Paradox: The Management of Agreement," *Organizational Dynamics*, vol. 3, 1974, pp. 63–80, © 1974 by AMACOM, a division of American Management Associations. All rights reserved. Excerpted by permission of the publisher.

HASTORF, A. H., D. J. SCHNEDIER, and J. POLEFKA: *Person Perception*, Addison-Wesley, Reading, Mass., 1970.

HELLRIEGEL, D., and J. W. SLOCUM: "Organizational Climates: Measures, Research, and Contingencies," *Academy of Management Journal*, vol. 17, 1974, pp. 255–280.

HIGGINSON, M. V., and T. L. QUICK: *The Ambitious Woman's Guide to a Successful Career*, American Management Associations, New York, 1975.

HUNT, R. G., and C. LICHTMAN: "Role Clarity, Communication and Conflict," *Management of Personnel Quarterly*, vol. 9, no. 3, 1970, pp. 26–36.

HUSTON, T. L.: *Foundations of Interpersonal Attraction*, Academic Press, New York, 1974.

JACOBSON, WALLY D.: *Power and Interpersonal Relations*, Wadsworth Publishing Co., Belmont, Ca., 1972.

JANIS, IRVING: *Victims of Groupthink*, Houghton-Mifflin Co., Boston, 1972.

JOHNSON, B.: *Communication: The Process of Organizing*, Allyn & Bacon, Boston, 1977.

JOHNSON, ROBERT G.: *The Appraisal Interview Guide*, American Management Associations, New York, 1979.

JONES, E. E., D. E. KANOUSE, H. H. KELLEY, R. E. NISBETT, S. VALINS, and B. WEINER: *Attribution: Perceiving the Causes of Behavior*, General Learning Press, Morristown, N.J., 1972.

JORGEWAD, D.: *Everybody Wins: Transactional Analysis Applied to Organizations*, Addison-Wesley, Reading, Mass., 1973.

JOURARD, SYDNEY M.: *The Transparent Self*, D. Van Nostrand, Princeton, N.J., 1964.

JOURARD, SYDNEY M.: *Disclosing Man to Himself*, D. Van Nostrand, 1968.

KAHN, ROBERT LOUIS: *The Dynamics of Interviewing: Theory, Technique, and Cases*, John Wiley & Sons, New York, 1957.

KAHN, R. L., and CHARLES CANNELL: *The Dynamics of Interviewing*, John Wiley & Sons, New York, 1958.

KATZ, D., and R. KAHN: *The Social Psychology of Organizations*, 2d ed., John Wiley & Sons, New York, 1978.

KNAPP, M. L.: *Social Intercourse: From Greeting to Goodbye*, Allyn & Bacon, Boston, 1978.

KORDA, MICHAEL: *Power! How to Get It, How to Use It*, Random House, New York, 1975.

KOTTER, JOHN P.: "Power, Dependence, and Managerial Success," *Harvard Business Review*, July–August, 1977.

LAING, R. D.: *The Divided Self*, Penguin Books, Baltimore, 1965.

LAING, R. D., H. PHILLIPSON, and A. R. LEE: *Interpersonal Perception*, Perrenial Library, Baltimore, 1966.

LAWLESS, DAVID J.: *Effective Management: Social Psychological Approach*, Prentice-Hall, Englewood Cliffs, N.J., 1972.

LAWRENCE, P. R.: *The Changing of Organizational Behavior Patterns*, Harvard University Press, Boston, 1958.

LAWRENCE, P. R., and J. W. LORSCH: *Organization and Environment: Managing Differentiation and Integration*, Harvard University Press, Boston, 1967.

LAWRENCE, P., and J. LORSCH: *Organization and Environment*, Richard Irwin, Homewood, Ill., 1970.

LAWRENCE, P., and J. LORSCH: *Studies in Organization Design*, Richard Irwin, Homewood, Ill., 1970.

LECKY, PRESCOTT: *Self-Consistency: A Theory of Personality*, Island Press, New York, 1945.

LIBERMAN, ROBERT, LARRY W. KING, WM. J. DeRISI, and MICHAEL McCANN: *Personel Effectiveness*, Research Press, Champaign, Ill., 1975.

LIKERT, R.: *The Human Organization*, McGraw-Hill Book Company, New York, 1967.

LIKERT, R., and D. BOWERS: "Organizational Theory and Human Resources Accounting," *American Psychologist*, vol. 24, 1969, pp. 585–592.

LOPEZ, FELIX M.: *Personnel Interviewing Theory and Practice*, McGraw-Hill Book Company, New York, 1975.

LUFT, J.: *Of Human Interaction*, National Press Books, New York, 1969.

LYNCH, E. M.: *The Executive Suite—Feminine Style*, AMACOM, New York, 1973.

MACCOBY, E. E., and C. N. JACKLIN: *The Psychology of Sex Differences*, Stanford University Press, Stanford, Ca., 1974.

MacDONALD, D.: "Communication Roles and Communication Networks in a Formal Organization," *Human Communication Research*, 1976, pp. 365–375.

MAHL, G. F.: *Psychological Conflict & Defense*, Harcourt Brace Jovanovich, New York, 1971.

MANDELL, MILTON M.: *The Employment Interview*, American Management Associations, New York, 1961.

MARROW, A., D. BOWERS, and S. SEASHORE: *Management by Participation*, Harper & Row, New York, 1967.

McCLELLAND, DAVID C.: *The Achieving Society*, Princeton, N.J., 1961.

McGREGOR, D.: *Human Side of Enterprise*, McGraw-Hill Book Company, New York, 1960.

MEAD, GEORGE HERBERT: *Mind, Self, and Society*, The University of Chicago Press, Chicago, 1934.

MEHRABIAN, A.: *Nonverbal Communication*, Aldine-Atherton, Chicago, 1972.

MEHRABIAN, A.: *Public Places and Private Spaces*, Basic Books, New York, 1976.

METCHER, K.: *Creative Interviewing*, Prentice-Hall, Englewood Cliffs, N.J., 1977.

MILLER, G. R., and H. W. SIMONS: *Perspectives on Communication in Social Conflict*, Science Research Associates, Chicago, 1975.

MILLER, G. R., and M. STEINBERG: *Between People: A New Analysis of Interpersonal Communication*, Science Research Associates, Chicago, 1975.

MUCHINSKY, P. M.: "Organizational Communication: Relationships to Organizational Climate and Job Satisfaction," *Academy of Management Journal*, vol. 20, 1977, pp. 592–607.

NATIONAL CENTER FOR HEALTH STATISTICS: *A Summary of Studies of Interviewing Methodology*, U.S. Department of Health, Education, and Welfare, Publication No. (HRA) 77-1343, Rockville, Md., 1977.

NICHOLS, RALPH, and L. A. STEVENS: *Are You Listening?*, McGraw-Hill Book Company, New York, 1957.

NIELSEN, W., and J. KIMBERLEY: "Smoothing the Way for Organizational Changes," *Advancement Management Journal*, vol. 41, no. 2, 1976, pp. 4–16.

NIERENBERG, G. I.: *Creative Business Negotiating*, Hawthorn Books, New York, 1971.

NIERENBERG, GERARD L., and HENRY H. CALERO: *How to Read a Person Like a Book*, Cornerstone Library, New York, 1971.

NISBERG, JAY N., and DANIEL SPURR: "Getting the Facts: How to Set Up a Communications Framework for Interviewing," *Management Review*, vol. 66, April 1977, pp. 13–17.

NYE, ROBERT D.: *Conflict among Humans: Some Basic Psychological and Social Psychological Considerations*, Springer Publishing Co., New York, 1973.

O'REILLY, C. A., and K. H. ROBERTS: "Information Filtration in Organizations: Three Experiments," *Organizational Behavior and Human Performance*, vol. 11, 1974, pp. 253–265.

PEARCE, W. B.: "The Coordinated Management of Meaning: A Rules-Based Theory of Interpersonal Communication," in *Explorations in Interpersonal Communication*, G. R. Miller (ed.), Sage Publications, Beverly Hills, Ca., 1976, pp. 17–35.

PESKIN, DEAN B.: *Human Behavior and Employment Interviewing*, American Management Associations, New York, 1971.

PHILLIPS, G., D. PEDERSEN, and JULIA WOOD: *Group Discussion: A Practical Guide to Participation & Leadership*, Houghton-Mifflin Co., Boston, 1979.

PIETRI, P., H. HALL, R. HARRY, K. VAN VOORHIS, and D. PORTERFIELD: "Organizational Communication: An Historical Survey," *Journal of Business Communication*, vol. 11, 1974, pp. 3–24.

PORTER, L., and K. ROBERTS: "Communication in Organizations," Technical Report #12, Contract #N00014-69-A-0200-9001, NR151-315, Office of Naval Research, Washington, D.C., July 1972.

PRAZAK, J. A.: "Learning Job-Seeking Interview Skills," in *Behavioral Counseling. Cases and Techniques*, J. D. Krumboltz and C. E. Thoreson (eds.), Holt, Rinehart and Winston, New York, 1969, pp. 414–428.

PYE, R.: "Office Location and the Cost of Maintaining Contact," *Environment and Planning*, vol. 9, 1977, pp. 149–168.

READ, W.: "Upward Communication in Industrial Hierarchies," *Human Relations*, vol. 15, 1962, pp. 3–15.

REDDING, W.: "Communication with the Organization," Industrial Communication Council, New York, and Lafayette, Ind.: Purdue Research Foundation. 1972.

REIF, W., J. NEWSTROM, and R. MONCZKA: "Exploding Some Myths about Women Managers," *California Management Journal*, vol. 17, no. 4, 1975, pp. 72–79.

RICHARDSON, S. A., et al.: *Interviewing: Its Forms and Functions*, Basic Books, New York, 1965.

RICHETTO, G.: *Organizational Communication Theory and Research: An Overview. Communication Yearbook I*, Transaction International-Communication Association, New Brunswick, N.J., 1977, pp. 331–346.

RICHETTO, GARY M., and JOSEPH P. ZIMA: *Fundamentals of Interviewing*, Science Research Associates, Chicago, Ill., 1976.

ROBERTS, K., and C. O'REILLY: "Measuring Organizational Communication," *Journal of Applied Psychology*, vol. 59, 1974, pp. 321–326.

ROBERTS, K., C. O'REILLY, G. BRETTON, and L. PORTER: "Organizational Theory and Organizational Communication: A Communication Failure?", Technical Report #2, Contract #N000314-69-A-0222, Washington, D.C., Office of Naval Research, May 1973.

ROGERS, E., and AGARWALA ROGERS: *Communication in Organizations*, Free Press, New York, 1976.

ROGERS, L., and R. FARACE: "Analysis of Relational Communication in Dyads: New Measurement Procedures," *Human Communication Research*, vol. 1, no. 3, pp. 222–239.

SALANCIK, G. R., and J. PFEIFFER: "Who Gets Power and How They Hold on to It: A Strategic Model of Power," *Organizational Dynamics*, vol. 5, no. 3, 1977, pp. 2–21.

SATU, U: *Peoplemating*, Science & Behavior Books, Palo Alto, Ca., 1972.

SCHEFLEN, ALBERT E., and ALICE SCHEFLEN: *Body Language and the Social Order*, Prentice-Hall, Englewood Cliffs, N.J., 1972.

SCHEIDEL, T., and L. CROWELL: *Discussing and Deciding*, Macmillan Publishing Co., New York, 1979.

SCHEIN, E. H.: *Organizational Psychology*, 2d ed., Prentice-Hall, Englewood Cliffs, N.J., 1970.

SCHELLING, T. C.: *The Strategy of Conflict*, Harvard University Press, Cambridge, Mass., 1963.

SCHERMERHORN, J.: "Openness to Interorganizational Cooperation: A Study of Hospital Administrators," *Academy of Management Journal*, vol. 19, no. 2, 1976, pp. 225–236.

SCHINDLER, RAINMAN E., and R. LIPPIT with JACK COLE: *Taking Your Meetings Out of the Doldrums*, University Associates, LaJolla, Ca., 1977.

SCHUTZ, WILLIAM: *The Interpersonal Underworld*, Science and Behavior Books, Palo Alto, Ca., 1966.

SHOSTROM, E.: *Man the Manipulator*, Bantam Books, New York, 1967.

SIDNEY, ELIZABETH: *The Skills of Interviewing*, Tavistock Publications, London, 1966.

SOMMER, R.: *Personal Space: The Behavioral Basis of Design*, Prentice-Hall, Englewood Cliffs, N.J., 1969.

STEELE, FRED I.: *Physical Settings and Organization Development*, Addison-Wesley, Reading, Mass., 1973.

STEINFATT, T. M.: "Communication and Conflict: A Review of New Material," *Human Communication Research*, vol. 1, 1974, pp. 81–89.

SURVEY RESEARCH CENTER: *Interviewer's Manual*, Institute for Social Research, Ann Arbor, Mich., 1969.

TAYLOR, C. W.: "Organizing for Consensus in Problem Solving," *Management Review*, April 1972, 61.

TEDESCHI, J. T., B. R. SCHLENKER, and T. V. BONOMA: *Conflict, Power and Games*. Aldine, Chicago, 1973.

TERSINE, R. V., and W. E. RIGGS: "Delphi Technique: A Long-Range Planning Tool," *Business Horizons*, April 1976, 19.

THAYER, L.: *Communication and Communication Systems*, Richard Irwin, Homewood, Ill., 1968.

THOMPSON, V.: "Bureaucracy and Bureaupathology," in *Organizational Behavior and the Practice of Management*, D. Hampton, C. Summer, and R. Webber (eds.), Scott, Foresman and Company, Glenview, Ill., 1973.

TORONTO, R.: "A General Systems Model for the Analysis of Organizational Change," *Behavioral Science*, vol. 20, no. 3, 1975, pp. 145–156.

TORTONIELLO, T. R.: *Communication in the Organization: An Applied Approach*, McGraw-Hill Book Company, New York, 1978.

TOULMIN, S. E.: "Rules and Their Relevance for Understanding Human Behavior," in *Understanding Other Persons*, T. Mischell (ed.), Basil Blackwell, Oxford, 1974, pp. 185–215.

TURABIAN, KATE L.: *Student's Guide for Writing College Papers*, The University of Chicago Press, Chicago, Ill., 1976.

WALTON, R. E.: *Interpersonal Peacemaking: Confrontations and Third-Party Consultation*, Addison-Wesley, Reading, Mass., 1969.

WATZLAWICK, PAUL, JANET HELMICK, and DON D. JACKSON: *Pragmatics of Human Communication*, W. W. Norton, New York, 1967.

WEICK, K.: *The Social Psychology of Organizing*, Addison-Wesley, Reading, Mass., 1969, p. 33. Reprinted by permission.

WILMOT, WILLIAM W.: *Dyadic Communication: A Transactional Perspective*, 2d ed., Addison-Wesley, Reading, Mass., 1978.

WOFFORD, J., E. GERLOFF, and R. CUMINS: *Organizational Communication: The*

Keystone to Managerial Effectiveness, McGraw-Hill Book Company, New York, 1977.

ZALZENIK, ABRAHAM, F. R. MANFRED, and KETS de VRIES: *Power and the Corporate Mind*, Houghton-Mifflin, Boston, 1975.

ZELKO, HAROLD P., and FRANK E. X. DANCE: *Business and Professional Speech Communication*, Holt, Rinehart and Winston, New York, 1965.

LABORATORY MANUAL

CHAPTER 1

COMMUNICATION AND ORGANIZING

ACTIVITY 1
GETTING ACQUAINTED

Purposes: 1. To help students in a new class break the ice, interact, and get to know one another.
2. To set the norm of student participation and active learning in a laboratory setting.
3. To assess students' initial expectations and the resources of the group.

Class size: Up to fifty. Best with thirty to thirty-five.
Time required: Depends on group size. Group of fifteen: 45 minutes. Group of thirty: 60 minutes. Group of fifty: 75 minutes.
Materials needed: Newsprint or notebook paper, felt-tip pens, masking tape.
Physical setting: A large room with movable tables and chairs so that an open space can be set up in the center of room.

INTRODUCTION

This activity is designed to shorten the time usually required for strangers to get acquainted. It also permits you to learn something about this group and other students' expectations about the class.

PROCEDURE

Step 1: 15 Minutes

The instructor will lead a discussion with the class to generate and record on the board items you think should be included in signs you will make and wear for the rest of this class session.

At least three items must be included on the signs:

1. Your name
2. A brief statement of what you hope to get out of this course
3. The personal skills or talents you bring to the class which are relevant to the learning objectives of the class as you understand them now

Other items might include any or all of the following:

4. Marital status
5. Number and age of children, if any
6. Occupation
7. Educational background
8. Hobbies and interests
9. Five words that describe you
10. Your greatest asset
11. Your greatest liability
12. The three most important people to you
13. Place where you feel most at home

The class will suggest items to be included on the signs; eight to ten items are sufficient. A general format for the signs should be agreed upon. The instructor will then ask you to prepare your sign and to tape it on your chest.

Step 2: 15 to 30 Minutes

Clear an open space in the room and mill around, looking at other students' signs. When you see someone you would like to talk to, stop, talk for a few minutes, then move on. Ask people to explain or talk about what they wrote on their signs. Meet as many students as you can.

Discussion questions:

1. Do you feel you know something about many other students in the class after this activity?
2. What are the most cited expectations for the course?
3. What kinds of skills and resources are shared in this group?
4. Does the process of disclosing something about yourself help you get to know others?
5. Why is it often hard to get acquainted in a group of strangers?

ACTIVITY 2
MAKING AN INTRODUCTION

Purposes: 1. To help students in a new class break the ice, interact with one other person, and get to know something about each other.
2. To set the norm of student participation and active learning in a laboratory setting.
3. To give students a chance to practice interviewing, to make a presentation in front of the group, and to publicly introduce a person to a group.

Class size: Up to thirty.
Time required: 50 minutes.
Materials: Paper, pencil.
Physical setting: Regular classroom.

INTRODUCTION

As a professional, you will often be called upon to introduce a colleague or a guest speaker to a group of people. You need to know how to interview that person to get the information needed for an effective introduction. This activity will help you to sharpen your interviewing skills. It will also permit you to get to know one other person in the class and to get on your feet to talk for a minute in front of a class.

PROCEDURE

Step 1: 20 Minutes

Select one person in the class you do not know or do not know well. Find a comfortable place to sit together. Decide who will interview the other first.

As an interviewer, you have 7 minutes to ask your partner any question which will contribute information you need to introduce him or her to the class. Your partner is free to answer or to pass.

The remaining 5 minutes are used to organize your notes and get ready to introduce your partner to the class. You will have one minute to actually make the introduction.

Step 2: 30 Minutes

Each student in turn introduces his or her partner. Students should stand up and face the whole class when making the introduction.

Step 3: 15 Minutes (Optional)

Discuss with the whole class the following questions:

1. How did you feel during the interview phase? As an interviewer? As an interviewee?
2. Did anyone pass on some of the questions asked? Why?
3. How did you feel when you stood up in front of the class and introduced your partner?
4. How did you feel when you were being introduced?
5. What did you learn as a result of this activity:
   a. about yourself?
   b. about others in the class?

Note: If the class has an odd number of students, the instructor may volunteer to make up a pair with one student. In this case, this pair should go first during the introduction round. Another alternative is to have one group of three students. That group will spend only 4 to 5 minutes on the individual interviews.

ACTIVITY 3
COMMUNICATION IN THE ORGANIZATION—A SIMULATION

Purposes: 1. To simulate a hierarchy in an organization and learn how information travels through the various levels of the hierarchy.
2. To experience firsthand information flow in a simulated organization.
3. To provide a common ground for students to use when illustrating principles of information transmission in organizations.
4. To explore the differences between one-way and two-way communication.

Class size: Any size. Entire class is to be divided into teams of no fewer than five and no more than nine students. The number of teams to be created depends on the number of Tinker Toy sets available.
Time required: 1½ hours.
Materials: Tinker Toy sets. Special instructions on what should be included in each set appear in the Instructor's Manual, along with instructions for building a model.
Physical setting: A large room, preferably with a separate table for each team. Access to a private area where transmitters and observers can look at the instructor's original model; this area must be hidden from everyone else's sight.

INTRODUCTION

1. The instructor may want to preface this activity with a short lecture on information transmission in organizations. The class may be asked to say what they think might be typical barriers to communication and suggest some ways to overcome them.
2. The instructor goes over the directions for the activity with the class and explains that an object has been constructed from Tinker Toys. The objective of each team is to duplicate the construction of this object as closely as possible. Each team will subdivide itself into four groups: Workers, Runners, Transmitters, and Observers. The actual construction of the object will be done by the Workers, who will not see the original model during the activity. Workers are dependent on information transmitted to them by the Transmitters via the Runners. There must be at least one team member in each of the four groups.

PROCEDURE

The object of the simulation is to reproduce the original model which can only be seen by the Transmitters.

Step 1: 15 Minutes

Each team will meet at its table for 15 minutes to go over the simulation instructions and to plan its operations. During planning, each team is to decide who will play what roles and how they intend to complete the task. The team may develop any code or system they wish, provided they abide by the general rules of the game, which appear below.

GENERAL RULES

Only the Transmitters and the Observers may see the original constructed object. The Transmitters may not watch the process of duplication by the Workers. The color of Tinker Toy parts may not be mentioned in any description or conversation. This is a timed exercise requiring you to expedite activities in order to complete the task. You are competing with the other teams.

TRANSMITTERS

The purpose of your group is to examine the construction of the object, decide how you want to describe it, and finally describe it to the Runners. The construction should be described so that it may be reconstructed by the Workers. You may *not* use colors in your descriptions. You may *not* use gestures in your descriptions. You may *not* use any written form of communication in your descriptions (nor diagrams, nor pictures). Do *not* allow the Runners to see the object.

RUNNERS

Your objective is to communicate information between the Transmitters and the Workers. You may *not* verbally communicate with the Transmitters for the first 10 minutes of the exercise. You may *not* at any time see the original model.

WORKERS

Your group will attempt to duplicate the construction of the original model from the information provided by the Runners. *All* forms of communication may be utilized within the Worker's group. You may *not* communicate verbally with the Runners for the first 10 minutes of the exercise. Only Workers can participate in the construction.

OBSERVERS

You will observe the entire process of solving the problem and completing the task. Write down any comments you may have on the way the groups in your team worked together. Be specific in your comments. Please refrain from any conversation with members of the groups during the exercise. Be prepared to speculate on why the team succeeded or did not succeed at its task. Specific items you might consider are included in the Instructions to Observers.
Note: After the first ten minutes, Workers will be allowed to communicate with Runners, and Runners will be allowed to communicate with Transmitters.

Step 2: 20 Minutes

The actual simulation is run. During the first 10 minutes, communication flows only one way: from Transmitters to Runners to Workers. After 10 minutes the instructor will signal to start using two-way communication. Everyone can talk to everyone (except Observers). At the end of Step 2, the instructor will end the simulation and gather all models to compare them with the original.

Step 3: 10 Minutes

Observers report their observations to the whole class.

Step 4: 20 Minutes

Class discussion focuses on the following questions:

1. What were the major barriers to communication?
2. How were they overcome? How did they affect the teams' performance?
3. Which role was hardest to fill and why?
4. What did it feel like to be:
   a. A Transmitter?
   b. A Runner?
   c. A Worker?
   d. An Observer?
5. Who had the most important job to do? Why do you think that way?

INSTRUCTIONS TO OBSERVERS

Please observe the group in terms of how it structures its task. Try to answer the following questions:

1. How were the Transmitters, Runners, Workers, and Observers selected? What criteria were used? Were any special qualifications required of Transmitters, Runners, Workers? What reasons were used to justify the number of Transmitters, Runners, and Workers?
2. If more than one Runner was used, how did they divide up the job? How did they organize their jobs? Did they do any planning beforehand, or did they jump into the assignment?
3. Was there any attempt during the initial period, before the Tinker Toy pieces were seen, to set up some kind of code or system among the three role representatives?
4. Did you notice any indications of leadership attempts by particular persons?
5. What assumptions were made about the parts?
6. What assumptions were made about language? Did anyone try to use technical language with people who did not understand it? Did everyone assume that words meant the same to everyone? Were there differences in terminology in describing the parts of the object?

7. Was too much or too little information at a time being transmitted?
8. Were there any problems associated with not following the instructions or in reinterpreting them?
9. How would you describe the morale of the group?

ACTIVITY 4
ONE-WAY AND TWO-WAY COMMUNICATION*

Purposes: 1. To demonstrate the differences between one-way and two-way communication.
2. To explore the advantages and disadvantages of both systems.

Class size: Any size.
Time required: 30 or 40 minutes.
Materials: Two diagrams from the Instructor's Manual for the demonstrator, or any geometrical diagram made up by the instructor. Pencils.
Physical setting: Regular classroom.

PROCEDURE

Step 1: 20 Minutes

1. The instructor may wish to discuss various ways to look at communication in the organization, in terms of content, direction, networks, etc. The instructor will indicate to the class that this activity will demonstrate directional aspects of the communication process.
2. The instructor asks for a volunteer or selects a class member to be the demonstrator. The class is told that the demonstrator will give directions to draw a series of squares. Class members may neither ask questions nor give audible responses. Students are instructed to draw the squares exactly as they are told to. Students are asked to get a pencil and two sheets of paper while the demonstrator studies the first diagram of squares.
3. While the demonstrator studies the diagram, the instructor places the following chart on the board:

---

*This activity can be substituted for Activity 3 if (1) the class is too large, (2) there is not enough time, or (3) there is no way to secure the appropriate number of Tinker Toy sets.

One-way communication		Two-way communication	
Time _____		Time _____	
Estimated Accuracy	Actual Accuracy	Estimated Accuracy	Actual Accuracy
5 _____	_____	_____	_____
4 _____	_____	_____	_____
3 _____	_____	_____	_____
2 _____	_____	_____	_____
1 _____	_____	_____	_____
0 _____	_____	_____	_____
Median _____	_____	_____	_____

4. The instructor asks the demonstrator to turn his or her back to the class and to tell the group what to draw as quickly and accurately as possible.
5. The time it takes the demonstrator to complete the instructions is recorded on the board.
6. Class members are asked to estimate the number of squares they drew correctly. The number of students who estimated five correct squares, four correct squares, etc., is recorded on the board.
7. The demonstration is repeated. This time the demonstrator faces the class, uses diagram 2, and is allowed to reply to questions from the group.
8. The instructor again asks students to estimate the number of correct squares they drew on this round. The time taken to complete this second demonstration is also recorded on the board.
9. The instructor computes the median for estimated accuracy for the two rounds and records the figures on the board.
10. The instructor shows the class the diagrams and asks students to determine their actual accuracy on the two rounds. The median of actual accuracy is computed and recorded on the board.

Step 2: 10 to 20 Minutes

The class discusses the following:

1. How do one-way and two-way communication compare in terms of time, accuracy, and level of confidence?
2. Can students think of examples of one-way and two-way communication from their own lives?

3. When is it important to use two-way communication? What are its costs?
4. When is one-way communication sufficient or necessary?
5. How can the disadvantages of one-way communication be overcome or minimized?

ACTIVITY 5
DESIGNING AND BUILDING A THREE-DIMENSIONAL SYMBOL

Purposes:　1. To help students in a new class break the ice and interact with one another in a semicompetitive atmosphere where creativity and resourcefulness will be at a premium.
2. To set the norm for student participation and active learning in a laboratory setting.
3. To begin sharpening observation skills of communication behaviors as they occur in small groups.

Class size:　Any size. Class is to be divided into teams of no more than six people.
Time required:　1½ hours.
Materials:　Construction paper, glue, scissors, paper clips, tape.
Physical setting:　A large classroom with movable table and chairs.

PROCEDURE

Step 1: 45 Minutes

The class is divided into teams. The instructor will appoint two judges and one observer per team. Special forms for judging and observing are given below.

Task

Your team is charged with designing and constructing a three-dimensional model of a symbol for the hundredth anniversary of University General Hospital. (The organization need not be a hospital. The task can be geared to any other organization of the instructor's choice.) The trustees have commissioned a sculpture which will be permanently displayed in the lobby. The unveiling of the sculpture will take place during the anniversary ceremonies.

Use imagination and fantasy to fashion something appropriate for the occasion. A kit of supplies is provided for the activity. You may use any or all of the supplies listed under Materials above, plus any other materials you wish to use.

You have 45 minutes to complete the assignment. You are competing with other teams. The completed models will be judged by impartial judges (students selected by the instructor and the instructor).

Criteria for judging will include:
1. Size　　　　　　　　　　20 points maximum
2. Aesthetic appeal　　　　20 points maximum

3. Sturdiness   20 points maximum
4. Appropriateness for the occasion 20 points maximum
5. Creativity   20 points maximum
                                    ─────────────
                                     100 points

The model awarded the most number of points will be selected by the trustees.

Step 2: 15 Minutes   Observers report their observations to the class as a whole.

Step 3: 30 Minutes   Class discussion on the following:

1. What are the factors most related to the teams' effectiveness?
2. Would the teams have functioned differently if the members had known each other? What difference does knowing each other make in group performance?
3. Is the morale of the group related to group performance? If so, in what way does the relationship work?
4. How can you measure communication effectiveness?

SYMBOL DESIGN AND CONSTRUCTION
Judges' Evaluation Form

Assign from 0 to 20 points for each criterion.

	TEAM			
	1	**2**	**3**	**4**
Size	_____	_____	_____	_____
Aesthetic appeal	_____	_____	_____	_____
Sturdiness	_____	_____	_____	_____
Appropriateness for the occasion	_____	_____	_____	_____
Creativity	_____	_____	_____	_____
Total	_____	_____	_____	_____

SYMBOL DESIGN AND CONSTRUCTION
Observers' Form

1. You are to observe and record significant behaviors of team members during the design and construction phases of this activity.
2. You will give an oral report of your observations after the judging to the entire class.
3. You should be observing the team as a whole as well as individual team members on a number of communication dimensions:

a. *Amount of communication:* Is participation widespread or is there a wide variation among members? If the latter is the case, who participates most? Least? How can you explain these differences? Is participation constructive, or are members simply going through the motions? Are there any alliances among certain team members? How do participation and amount of communication relate to the team's effectiveness?

b. *Communication climate:* What is the general climate of the team? Are members cooperative, friendly, or hostile? Are they supportive of each other's contributions or critical of others' ideas? Does the climate change during the activity, or does it remain the same?

c. *Conflict:* Do you notice any conflict during the team's activity? Is conflict related to ideas about the project itself or is it more related to members' personalities and how they relate to each other? How are conflicts resolved in this group?

d. *Involvement:* Are members involved and interested in the task? How much interest do they show and how do they show it? Was the general interest level of the team high or low? To what can this be attributed? Lack of understanding of the assignment? Lack of involvement with other team members? The nature of this particular project? Other dynamics having to do with the course itself, the personality of the team members, the team mix, etc.? Is the level of involvement related at all to the team's effectiveness?

e. *Leadership:* Who emerges as the leader of this team? How does that happen? Does someone run the group or are leadership and influence more evenly spread among the team members? Does someone appear to dominate clearly? What are other members' reactions to the leader of the group? Do they accept his or her leadership or resist it? What is the influence of the leader based on? Expert knowledge of design, construction ability, high verbal patterns, personal charisma, creativity, etc.?

f. *Decision making:* How are decisions made in this team? Majority votes? Consensus? Unanimity? Single-handed decisions of one member? Factions? Are decisions accepted or resisted? Are differences in degree of acceptance based on who makes the decisions or how they are made?

g. *Effectiveness:* How far did the team go with the task? Was it completed? Was their symbol rated high by the judges? In your opinion what contributed the most to team effectiveness or lack of effectiveness?

INSTRUMENT
COURSE EXPECTATIONS SCALE

Purposes: 1. To examine students' expectations for this course.
               2. To communicate these expectations to the instructor.

Class size: Any size.
Time required: 10 minutes.
Materials needed: None.
Physical setting: Regular classroom.

PROCEDURE

Step 1: 10 Minutes

Students usually expect to derive something of value from a course. In terms of your personal expectations, put a check mark on each scale to show how you would rate the importance of the following outcomes: (Turn in to your instructor. Names are optional.)

By the End of this Course I Will:	Unimportant to Me	Mildly Important to Me	Important to Me	Extremely Important to Me
1. Gain new knowledge about communication in business organizations	_____	_____	_____	_____
2. Meet a requirement for my major	_____	_____	_____	_____
3. Gain self-confidence	_____	_____	_____	_____
4. Gain an understanding of how people behave in organizations	_____	_____	_____	_____
5. Improve my communication skills in one-on-one interactions	_____	_____	_____	_____
6. Gain an understanding of myself as a communicator	_____	_____	_____	_____
7. Improve my communication skills in small groups	_____	_____	_____	_____
8. Improve my skills in making presentations to large groups	_____	_____	_____	_____
9. Improve my interviewing skills	_____	_____	_____	_____
10. Obtain a good grade for the course	_____	_____	_____	_____

**Step 2: 20 Minutes
(Optional)**

At the next class period, the instructor may elect to report to the class a tabulation of the results and to discuss the course's objectives and how they might fit in the class' expectations.

CASES
SUGGESTIONS FOR CASE ANALYSIS

Cases are designed to help you sharpen your analytical skills. The strongest way to analyze a case is to apply a variation of the scientific method. The scientific method of analysis is simply a logical approach that has been used in many fields of study. The method usually includes seven steps:

1. Clearly and completely identify the fundamental problem, issue, or question.
2. List all the facts related to this problem, issue, or question.
3. List alternative courses of action.
4. List advantages and disadvantages of each alternative.
5. Review all the above.
6. Draw conclusions and make recommendations or decisions.
7. Follow up and evaluate.

**Step 1:
Problem Definition**

A case seldom involves one clear-cut problem. Rather, it presents a complex situation with more or less obvious "symptoms." Your task is (1) to determine the symptoms which require immediate attention and (2) to identify the fundamental issues and causal factors giving rise to those symptoms. *It is important to separate the immediate problems from their more basic sources.* For example, an immediate problem may be a high rate of absenteeism, while the more fundamental issue may be a poor motivational climate.

How you define a problem in a large measure determines how you go about solving it. A short-term solution for absenteeism is likely to be different from solutions which attempt to deal with motivational climate.

Note: Defining problems implies that you have conceptual tools available for diagnosing the situation. Such conceptual tools are absolutely necessary for intelligent case analysis and should be specifically identified in your written case analysis. These conceptual tools are provided in the readings and in class discussions. For example, there is no way to identify a span of control problems if you do not know what the concept refers to. Preparation is imperative if this step is to be more than a cursory, shallow treatment of the problems.

**Step 2:
Justification for
Problem Definition**

A perennial complaint of students working on cases is "We don't have enough facts to solve the problem; we don't know enough about the situation."

Managerial decisions are always based on limited information. No manager ever has all the facts. No one can wait to know everything about a situation before doing something about it. In fact, most practicing managers find that most of their decisions have to be made quickly on the basis of very incomplete information.

Rather than throwing your hands up in the air and giving up, this is the step where you need to review what information you do have. You may need to make some inferences to fill in the gaps. Clearly label what is inference and what is factual. Do not be afraid to assume, but clearly state the assumptions you are making. You should make your assumptions on the basis of your knowledge of what normal typical managerial practices are like, and they should be consistent with the facts you do have about the case.

In this step, you need to explain how you arrived at your diagnosis of the problem.

One way to do this is to support your definition of the problem with (1) relevant facts from the case, (2) pertinent assumptions you made on the basis of these facts, and (3) interpretations of events and processes you think are justified. This is where you tie in conceptual material to case events.

**Step 3:
List Alternative
Courses of Action**

Be creative. Brainstorm ideas and jot them down as they come to you. Write down as many ideas as you can, without evaluating them or censuring anything. Include even those that seem foolish, outlandish, or silly. You can always cross them out later. The point here is to let your imagination take over.

**Step 4: Evaluate
Alternatives**

Look critically at the alternatives you came up with in step 3. List advantages and disadvantages of each alternative in terms of criteria that seem appropriate. Some criteria might be:

1. How well does the alternative meet management's objectives?
2. How much time and what organizational resources are needed to implement the alternative?
3. Does the alternative conform to personal and organizational values for equitable and responsible behavior?
4. What is the probability of success?

List the criteria you want to use and then proceed to evaluate the alternatives.

Step 5: Review

Read all your notes and think. This may be a good time to let the case sit for a while. Get back to it later when you have had a chance to digest all the data.

Step 6: Draw Conclusions, Make Recommendations/ Decisions

Select the alternative(s) you would recommend and explain/justify your choice. Be sure to include the reservations you may have about the choice (no choice solves everything) and the limitations of the recommended action.

Be sure to include specifics about the implementation of your recommendation: who should do what, when, and how.

Step 7: Follow Up and Evaluate

You cannot implement your recommendation and evaluate its actual impact. However, you can, in this step, describe how you would set up an evaluation procedure. Suggest a timetable and methods for the evaluation process. State who should do the evaluating.

CASE 1
SOUTHERN UNIVERSITY*

Courtney had been secretary for the Student Union Program Office at Southern University for almost a year. She prided herself in her work and on the respect she had gained from her numerous co-workers. Among her many duties was typing correspondence for the twenty officially recognized organizations on campus—a job which she enjoyed because it gave her a chance to work with students. In fact, she felt very lucky to have such a delightful job; at least she had felt that way until last week. Now, she was thinking of quitting.

Daniel was at Southern University on a full scholarship and had just been elected an officer of student government. He prided himself on maintaining a 3.9 grade point average and still having the time to be active in the student lawmaking body on campus. He enjoyed the popularity and leadership that went along with the office and felt he was doing an excellent job. In fact, he was very happy with his college

*Case written by Courtney Westerman for a class assignment. Reprinted by permission of the author.

life; at least he had been until last week. Now, he was thinking of resigning from student government.

The trouble began for Courtney and Daniel the week before, when Daniel brought in a letter to be typed. He told her he wanted one letter to go to Mr. Grant and four copies to go to four people whose names he gave her. When he returned to pick up the typing, he found an original to Mr. Grant and four carbon copies. He became furious and told Courtney she had done it completely wrong. He had wanted five original copies of the letter, no carbon copies. He told her she would have to redo the letters immediately. Courtney, however, told Daniel she couldn't do it until the morning because it was five o'clock, time for the office to close. She then stormed out of the office leaving Daniel fuming.

No sooner had Courtney finished typing Daniel's five letters the next morning than Daniel appeared with more work. This time he wanted fifteen copies of a bylaw to be individually typed. Courtney suggested using the new multilith copy machine. She would type one original copy of the bylaw and then reproduce fourteen copies that looked beautifully typed. Daniel, however, said he didn't care what kind of newfangled machine they had; he knew there was only one way to get copies that looked individually typed, and that was to type them individually. They argued for a few minutes and then Daniel stomped off toward her boss's office. Courtney, seeing this, assumed he was going to complain to her supervisor. She was so worried and upset that she couldn't work efficiently for the rest of the week.

Since that time Courtney has done other work for Daniel. It isn't her best work, but she doesn't care, for she feels he doesn't have faith in her anyway. She thinks he's like all the other big-shot officers— a know-it-all who only cares about himself. She feels her job is threatened when he is around so she avoids him at all costs. She hasn't heard from her boss yet, but wonders whether she should go ahead and quit before Daniel gets her fired.

On the other hand, Daniel feels threatened by Courtney. She is just like all young secretaries—lazy and inefficient. Furthermore, he doesn't trust her; he's afraid she'll tell lies about him to the other students and get him ousted from his office. He fears he should resign before he has to face the embarrassment of being asked to leave.

CASE 2
COMPUTER DEPARTMENT*

Sandy worked for a local utility company in computer operations. Recently she observed a situation which caused many ill feelings and could have easily been avoided. Two departments in her company were involved. The first was the maintenance department, which worked on the hardware of the computers. The other department involved software personnel, who took care of the programming of the machine.

The problem began with a routine Sysgen, which is a complete reprogramming of the entire system. Computer operations, maintenance, and software personnel are all involved in a Sysgen. In the past all problems that had occurred during Sysgen had always been traced back to software errors. The recent Sysgen, however, appeared to have hardware malfunctions.

Sandy notified maintenance and software of the existing problems. Maintenance insisted it must be another programming error. When Sandy told them that the problem had all indications of being a maintenance error they became very angry with Sandy and the programmers. Maintenance said that since the system was running perfectly up to the Sysgen that there was no way the problem could be blamed on them. Instead of everybody pitching in and working together on the problem, each group was blaming the other for the trouble and nothing was being done to correct the errors. In the final analysis the problem was traced back to a hardware malfunction. It was purely coincidental that this error occurred precisely at Sysgen time.

CASE 3
THANKS TO ROTARY FROM JOE

Joe, a student at the local college, is selected to give a 15-minute speech to the local Rotary Club to thank the club for its annual gift to the scholarship fund at his college. Joe puts together a speech telling why people who have money should support those who do not. He tells the club members that adults are obligated to help young people who want to go to college or get started in business. He ends up speaking for nearly 45-minutes because he strays from his notes to talk about

*Case written by Marilyn Elliott for a class assignment. Reprinted by permission of the author.

his own personal experiences on campus and in the community. He talks at length about his efforts to maintain a satisfactory grade point average and belong to campus clubs at the same time.

ASSIGNMENT 1
ESTIMATE OF MYSELF AS A COMMUNICATOR

Your own communication experiences have provided you with a wealth of information about yourself in your communication with others. How you see yourself as a communicator affects a great deal what you do.

For this assignment you need to reflect about your communicative behaviors in three different settings:

1. In a one-to-one situation (communicating with one other person)
2. In a small group (a committee, work group, buzz group, etc.)
3. In a large group (speaking in front of a class, speaking to a group of fifteen or more people)

Think of yourself in each of the three settings and answer the following questions in writing:

1. What do I do that makes me an effective communicator?
2. What do I do that makes me less than effective in my communication?
3. What would I like to learn to do better?

It is essential that you write from your own point of view how you see yourself and not how you think other people see you. Do not ask others to estimate your effectiveness.

Be prepared to share some of your notes with the rest of the class or to make an oral summary of your answers in front of the class.

ASSIGNMENT 2
INTERVIEW: THE MANAGER'S JOB

Make an appointment to interview a practicing manager in any work organization to determine the following:

1. The manager's estimation of the time spent on the job in communication with people (percentage of total day's work):

  a. Face-to-face
  b. In writing
  c. Over the telephone
  d. By other media (dictaphone, TV, etc.)

2. The manager's list of the people he or she interacts with most frequently (not by name but by position or function, e.g., "my secretary," "my assistant," "my boss," "another department head at my level," etc.)
3. The manager's description of the most common communication problems, hassles, and barriers encountered daily and ways to cope with them
4. The manager's evaluation of how he or she finds out what is going on in the department

Write a short paper to summarize your findings. Be sure to include the actual title and position of the manager you interviewed, as well as the organization. Also include the approximate number of people directly responsible to this manager.

Be prepared to discuss your findings in class.

ASSIGNMENT 3
THE COMPANY MAGAZINE

Secure six different company magazines, newletters, or internal publications designed for employees. Analyze the topics covered and the relative value and interest these topics have for most employees.

Present your findings orally to the class.

DISCUSSION QUESTIONS

1. What roles do reports play in the communication of information?
2. What are some specific methods for communicating information up the line?
3. Employees in the 1980s need and want to be better informed than their counterparts fifty years ago. What factors in our society account for the change?
4. Of the three directions of internal communication (up, down, and lateral), which do you think is generally least efficient? Why?
5. Should management communicate about all aspects of the company's activities to employees? List possible topic areas which management should inform employees about.

CHAPTER 2

ORGANIZATIONAL THEORIES AND THEIR COMMUNICATION IMPLICATIONS

ACTIVITY 1
SIMULATION: DIVISION OF WORK*

Purposes: 1. To demonstrate the managerial functions of planning, organizing, leading, and controlling.
2. To explore differences in managerial styles and their effect on motivation and performance.
3. To demonstrate the effects of division of labor on performance and the role of communication in managerial action.

Class size: Minimum twelve, maximum fifty. Students are to be divided into companies of six students each.
Time required: 1½ hours
Materials needed: Three sets of ten cards for each company; 3 × 5 cards or computer cards are appropriate.
Physical setting: Regular classroom.

PROCEDURE

Step 1: 5 Minutes

1. The instructor selects three students from the class to be production workers and gives each a set of cards numbered from 0 to 9. The cards represent capital equipment. Students are not to communicate with each other in any way nor to look at each other's cards.
2. The instructor gives the following instructions to the workers: "You are the production workers of a company. Each card is a machine. When I write a number, each one of you puts up any card you wish from 0 to 9 *simultaneously without communicating with the other workers.* The total of the numbers on the three cards must equal the number put on the board." Then the instructor writes a number between 0 and 27 on the board.
3. Ten trials are run, each time using a different number from 0 to 27. The instructor records the number of correct or incorrect responses.

Step 2: 45 to 50 Minutes

1. The instructor tells the workers they are inefficient. If they were a real company they would be out of business. What they need is a management team. The instructor selects three other students to be the management of the company and divides the rest of the class into companies of three workers and three managers each. Students not in a company will serve as observers. Workers and managers of the same company must sit facing each other.
2. The task of management is to formulate a strategy and communicate it to the production teams. They have 10 minutes. The production process will be identical to step 1.

*Adapted by Michele T. Myers and Gail E. Myers from an activity widely used in training programs. We have been unable to identify the originator of this exercise.

3. The instructor runs another ten trials, records the correct and incorrect responses, and notes increases in productivity.
4. At this point you may want to introduce some complicating factors:
    a. The following wage rates for associated skills must be charged:
        1. Multiplication and division are highly skilled tasks. Labor costs for employees using these skills are $12 per hour.
        2. Addition and subtraction are semiskilled tasks. Labor costs for employees using these skills are $8 per hour.
        3. Pattern recognition is unskilled work and is paid at the rate of $4 per hour. (For example, if a light flashes, a button is pushed; if it does not flash, the button is not pushed.)

        Since the companies are highly competitive, it is management's task to cut down on labor costs as much as possible.
    b. The companies are in a very old industry. The cards represent capital equipment which is old and wearing out. Management must eliminate as many cards as possible, but must retain three cards to be shown and added together. Management has 10 minutes to formulate a strategy for dealing with the complications and to communicate it to employees.
5. Another series of ten trials is run, and again correct and incorrect responses are recorded. Companies are asked to figure out labor costs and number of cards from the set used. Data are posted but strategies are not revealed.
6. Management teams get another 5 minutes to refine their strategies.
7. Another series of ten trials is run.

Step 3: 30 Minutes   Class discussion could center around the following:

1. How many in the class would choose a career like the workers' job? For $10,000 a year? For $25,000 a year? For $50,000 a year? For $100,000 a year? For $1 million a year? Ask why so few would do it unless highly paid? How did workers feel about their jobs? Discuss feelings.
2. Why is the workers' task so uninteresting? Why is there so much repetition?
3. How did management relate to workers? How did management behave? Did they immediately discuss strategy with workers or did they keep the discussion among management only? How did workers feel about their management teams? If differences are noted, explain what accounts for them. Was there congruence between how students think managers should behave and how they actually behaved? Use Theory X and Theory Y to explore the assumptions and behaviors of managers.

4. What is appropriate subordinate behavior? What is appropriate managerial behavior?
5. How does management motivate workers to perform well on repetitive and boring tasks?
6. Was it more fun to be a manager or to be a worker in this simulation? Why? Is there a tradeoff between the advantages of division of labor and the boredom and monotony which results for workers?
7. Who had the best ideas during strategy sessions? Management? Workers? How were the ideas communicated? Were workers consulted?

ACTIVITY 2
WORDS-IN-SENTENCES COMPANY*

Purposes: 1. To experiment with designing and operating an organization.
            2. To compare production and quality outputs and communication under different organization structures.

Class size: Any number ranging from five to fifteen members each.
Time required: 1½ hours.
Materials: None.
Physical setting: Movable chairs or separate rooms if groups are large; tables are helpful, but not essential.

INTRODUCTION   In this exercise each group of students will form a "mini-organization" and will be competing with other companies in the industry. The success of your company will depend on: (1) your objectives, (2) planning, (3) organization structure, (4) quality control, and (5) communication. It is important, therefore, that you spend some time thinking about the best design for your organization.

DISCUSSION QUESTIONS

1. How do classical and contemporary theories of organization differ in their treatment of organization structure, design, and communication?
2. How would you classify the technology of a WIS company? Why?
3. What would theory predict to be the best or most appropriate structure for a WIS company? Why?
4. What reactions did you have throughout this activity?

   *Douglas T. Hall, Donald B. Bowen, Roy J. Lewicki, and Francine S. Hall, *Experiences in Management and Organizational Behavior,* © 1975, St. Clair Press, Chicago. Reprinted by permission of John Wiley & Sons, Inc.

PROCEDURE

Step 1: 5 Minutes

Form companies and assign workplaces. The total group should be subdivided into small groups of comparable size. Since the success of any one group will not be dependent on size alone, do not be concerned if some groups are larger than others. Each group should consider itself a company.

Step 2: 10 Minutes

Read the directions below and ask the instructor about any points that need clarification. Everyone should be familiar with the task before beginning step 3.

DIRECTIONS

You are a small company that manufactures words and then packages them in meaningful (English language) sentences. Market research has established that sentences of at least three words but not more than six words each are in demand. Therefore, packaging, distribution, and sales should be set up for three- to six-word sentences.

The "words-in-sentences" industry is highly competitive; several new firms have recently entered what appears to be an expanding market. Since raw materials, technology, and pricing are all standard for the industry, your ability to compete depends on two factors: (1) volume and (2) quality.

Group Task

Your group must design and participate in running a WIS company. You should design your organization to be as efficient as possible during each 10-minute production run. After the first production run, you will have an opportunity to reorganize your company if you want to.

Raw Materials

For each production run you will be given a "raw material word or phrase." The letters found in the word or phrase serve as the raw materials available to produce new words in sentences. For example, if the raw material word is "organization" you could produce the words and sentence: "Nat ran to a zoo."

Production Standards

There are several rules that have to be followed in producing "words-in-sentences." If these rules are not followed, your output will not meet production specifications and will not pass quality-control inspection.

1. The same letter may appear only as often in a manufactured word

as it appears in the raw material word or phrase; for example, "organization" has two o's. Thus "zoo" is legitimate, but "zoonosis" is not. It has too many o's and s's.

2. Raw material letters can be used again in different manufactured words.
3. A manufactured word may be used only once in a sentence and in only one sentence during a production run; if a word—for example, "a"—is used once in a sentence, it is out of stock.
4. A new word may not be made by adding "s" to form the plural of an already used manufactured word.
5. A word is defined by its spelling, not its meaning.
6. Nonsense words or nonsense sentences are unacceptable.
7. All words must be in a dictionary of the English language.
8. Names of people and places are acceptable.
9. Slang is not acceptable.

Measuring Performance

The output of your WIS company is measured by the total number of acceptable words packaged in sentences. The sentences must be written in legible handwriting on no more than two sheets of paper.

Delivery

Delivery must be made to the Quality Control Review Board 30 seconds after the end of each production run.

Quality Control

If any word in a sentence does not meet the standards set forth above, all the words in the sentence will be rejected. The Quality Control Review Board (composed of one member from each company) is the final arbiter of acceptability. In the event of a tie vote, a coin toss will determine the outcome.

Step 3: 15 Minutes

Design your organization using as many group members as you see fit to produce your words-in-sentences. There are many potential ways of organizing. Since some are more efficient than others, you may want to consider the following:

1. What is your company's objective?
2. How will you achieve your objective? How should you plan your work, given the time allowed?
3. What division of labor, authority, and responsibility is most appropriate, given your objective, your task, and the technology?
4. Which group members are best qualified to perform certain tasks?

Assign one group member to serve on the Quality Control Review Board. This person may also participate in production runs.

Step 4: 10 Minutes—Production Run 1

1. The group leader will hand each WIS company a sheet with a raw material or phrase.
2. When the instructor announces, "Begin production," start manufacturing as many words as possible and packaging them in sentences for delivery to the Quality Control Review Board. You will have 10 minutes.
3. When the group leader announces, "Stop production," you will have 30 seconds to deliver your output to the Quality Control Review Board. Output received more than 30 seconds after production is stopped does not meet the delivery schedule and will not be counted.

Step 5: 10 Minutes

1. The designated members of the Quality Control Review Board review output from each company. The total output should be recorded (after quality control approval) on the board or easel.
2. While the board is completing its task, each WIS company should discuss what happened during run 1.

Step 6: 10 Minutes

Each company should evaluate its performance and organization. Companies may reorganize for run 2.

Step 7: 10 Minutes—Production Run 2

1. The group leader will hand each WIS company a sheet with a raw material word or phrase.
2. Proceed as in step 4 (production run 1). You will have 10 minutes for production.

Step 8: 10 Minutes

1. The Quality Control Review Board will review each company's output and record it on the board or easel. The total for runs 1 and 2 should be tallied.
2. While the board is completing its task, each WIS company should prepare an organization chart depicting its structure for both production runs.

Step 9: 10 Minutes

Discuss this exercise as a total group. The instructor will provide discussion questions. Each company should share the organization charts it prepared in step 8.

INSTRUMENT
SUPERVISORY ATTITUDES: THE X–Y SCALE*

DIRECTIONS   The following are various types of behavior which a supervisor (manager, leader) may engage in in relation to subordinates. Read each item carefully and then put a check mark in one of the columns to indicate what you would do.

         Before you take the test, make a guess on where you think you will appear on the scale under Scoring Instructions by marking an "x" somewhere between 10 and 40 as your initial score.

If I Were the Supervisor, I Would:	Make a Great Effort to Do This	Tend to Do This	Tend to Avoid Doing This	Make a Great Effort to Avoid This
1. Closely supervise my subordinates in order to get better work from them.	_____	_____	_____	_____
2. Set the goals and objectives for my subordinates and sell them on the merits of my plans.	_____	_____	_____	_____
3. Set up controls to assure that my subordinates are getting the job done.	_____	_____	_____	_____
4. Encourage my subordinates to set their own goals and objectives.	_____	_____	_____	_____
5. Make sure that my subordinates' work is planned out for them.	_____	_____	_____	_____
6. Check with my subordinates daily to see if they need any help.	_____	_____	_____	_____
7. Step in as soon as reports indicate that the job is slipping.	_____	_____	_____	_____
8. Push my people to meet schedules if necessary.	_____	_____	_____	_____
9. Have frequent meetings to keep in touch with what is going on.	_____	_____	_____	_____
10. Allow subordinates to make important decisions.	_____	_____	_____	_____

*The X–Y Scale was adapted from an instrument developed by Robert N. Ford of AT&T for in-house training of supervisors. Ten items were taken from the longer instrument, and the selection was based upon their application a wide variety of training enterprises. Reprinted from J. W. Pfeiffer and J. E. Jones (eds.), *The 1972 Annual Handbook for Group Facilitators*, University Associates, San Diego, Calif., 1972. Used with permission.

SCORING INSTRUCTIONS

1. For items 1 to 3 and 5 to 9 the scoring is:

Do	Tend to Do	Tend to Avoid	Avoid
1	2	3	4

2. For items 4 and 10 the scoring is reversed:

Do	Tend to Do	Tend to Avoid	Avoid
4	3	2	1

3. Total the numbers you circled on the inventory and locate your score on the scale which appears below. Compare your initial score (where you positioned yourself on the scale before you scored the inventory) with your final score on the inventory. Is there any discrepancy? If so, in what direction does the discrepancy occur? What does this mean to you?

```
Theory X  +----------+----------+----------+  Theory Y
         10         20         30         40
```

CASE 1
PROMOTE THE PARIAH?*

The notice of the opening for assistant foreman had been on the bulletin board for just 20 minutes, but Sy Franklin was already beginning to worry. Stan Bianchi was obviously the best-qualified person for the job—he had been with the company longer than any of the other people on the line, his work was always satisfactory, and he was usually on time—but Sy couldn't imagine that Stan would be able to do the job well.

The basic problem with Stan was that the other people in the department didn't get along with him. Behind his back they made fun of him, calling him "Stan the bland" and saying that he wasn't smart enough to come in out of the rain. Stan wasn't really dull, but he did have problems communicating with other people. Sy could see the tension building every time someone had to deal directly with Stan.

"Well, worrying about it won't do me any good," Sy thought to himself. "I just hope Stan doesn't apply for the job."

"Excuse me, Sy. Could I talk to you a minute?" Harry Fenlow had caught Sy daydreaming. Harry had compiled a fine work record in the

18 months that he had been on the job. Harry was the antithesis of Stan; he got along well with just about everybody.

"Sure, Harry, come on in." Sy led Harry into his office. After exchanging pleasantries, Sy asked Harry to come to the point.

"So, what's up, Harry?"

"Well, I was wondering about the assistant foreman's job. I'd like to apply for it."

"That's great, Harry. I think you'd be perfect for it. I can't tell you anything definite, of course, but I would say you have a good shot at it."

Harry thanked Sy and went back to his work station, feeling very pleased with himself and very optimistic about his chances of getting the job. But not 10 minutes later, Stan was standing in the doorway of Sy's office, his face red with anger.

"I hear you're giving Fenlow the assistant foreman job instead of me," Stan mumbled.

"Now, Stan, let's calm down and talk this over sensibly."

"Fenlow is shooting off his mouth about how you said the job was his."

"First of all, I didn't promise Harry the job. I said he has a good chance of getting it—which he does."

"And what about me?"

"I just don't believe," Sy said haltingly, searching for the right words, "that you have the necessary leadership characteristics for this job. To put it bluntly, you don't communicate well with the other people, and you don't get along with them."

"Hey, Sy," Stan said, shaking his head, "you never said anything to me about 'communication.' All you ever pushed was 'performance, performance, performance'."

"Sure, Stan, performance is important, but. . . ."

"Don't bother with excuses, Sy. I've already decided to apply for the job. I'm not going to back out and make it easier for you. You're going to have to come up with a better reason than that for not promoting me," Stan said loudly as he slammed the office door.

Sy worried that he'd made a bad situation worse. As it stood now, Stan didn't even believe he was telling the truth.

Consider these questions and ask your own:

1. Did Sy do the right thing in admitting to Stan that he felt Stan was unqualified for promotion?
2. In effect, Sy is saying that Stan will probably never be promoted. How can he continue to motivate Stan in light of this?
3. Does Sy "owe" Stan a chance at the assistant foreman's job because of his good work record? Explain.

CASE 2
EQUAL TIME*

"Good afternoon, Dumbo Children's Wear," said Liz through a mouthful of tuna salad. "I'm sorry he's out to lunch right now. May I take a message?"

Most of the people in the office had left for lunch, as was the usual around 12:30. Liz Kaplan, a new employee, was on hand to answer the phones while everyone was out. After seven years of being a full-time mother, Liz had finally been able to get out of her housewife-and-mother role and go back into the job market, bringing some needed income into the household. Still, she wanted to be home when her children returned from school. So, instead of taking a lunch hour and a 15-minute coffee break like the rest of the employees, she stayed at her desk, and Cliff allowed her to leave at 3:45.

Although the day was a little tiring with no break and no chance to get outside for a while, the office did calm down a bit when most people were out to lunch, and Liz was very happy with the arrangement. Cliff Feldman, the office manager, was pleased with the arrangement, too, since having Liz around to answer the phones prevented him from losing any business during lunchtime.

Liz had been at Dumbo about a month when six employees approached Cliff late one afternoon. "Cliff, we'd like to talk to you if you have a minute," Arnold said.

"Sure, Arnold. Come into my office, everyone. What can I do for you?"

"The six of us have decided that we would like to forfeit our lunch hours and coffee breaks as Liz does, so that we can leave at 3:45 every day. A lot of companies are allowing their employees to make this kind of decision; it's called flextime."

"I know what it's called, Arnold, but I'm afraid it's out of the question. I can't afford to shut the entire office down at 3:45 each day. I'd be losing one/eighth of my business."

"You let Liz do it, so why can't we?"

"I just told you why. And I thought you all understood about Liz. She's got two little kids and has to be home by four. Please, people, have some compassion for the woman."

"We do," said Emily. "But I have kids, too, and, Cliff, I wouldn't mind being home for them either you know."

*Reprinted by permission of the publisher, from "Let's Get Down to Cases," *Supervisory Management*, January 1979, © 1979, by AMACOM, a Division of American Management Association. All rights reserved.

"Emily, your kids are in high school; you really can't make a comparison."

"Well," said Emily, "I think I can, and that's not really for you to judge. The point is that we all have things we would like to take care of at that time of the day. Whether it's children or beating the rush hour, what's fair for one should be fair for the rest of us."

"Think about it, won't you Cliff?" Arnold asked. "It really isn't fair to play favorites."

The group left his office, and Cliff quickly shut the door. He could not believe how unsympathetic his staff was being to Liz or imagine what he should do about it. He was thankful, at least, that they had waited until Liz had left to drop their bombshell.

Consider these questions and ask your own:

1. Should Cliff allow his workers to go on flextime, even though he feels it would jeopardize the business?
2. Should Cliff revoke the early-leave privilege he gave Liz and tell her that she'll have to make other arrangements about her children?
3. Is Cliff justified in allowing Liz to leave early?
4. Discuss how a system 1, 2, 3, or 4 manager might handle the situation and relate to the people involved in the case.

CASE 3
THE "STAR"*

"Greg, I'd like you to meet Owen Wilson. He'll be working with your engineering team on the Devbo project. Introduce him around and make him feel at home," said Janice Levine, engineering manager.

Janice had just hired Owen from another firm where he had established himself as a fine troubleshooter and superb engineer. She was confident that he would be a tremendous asset to the team project, and he had seemed eager to be a part of it. She returned to her office satisfied that she had handled another management decision effectively.

There were six men and women working on the Devbo project. Greg called a meeting of the team members, introduced Owen, and

*Reprinted by permission of the publisher, from "Let's Get Down to Cases," *Supervisory Management*, March 1979, © 1979, by AMACOM, a division of American Management Associations. All rights reserved.

discussed the progress the team had made so far and the workload he saw ahead. He explained that since the project was such an important one to the company, the group had worked out a system whereby the same assignment was given to three members of the team. A common deadline was set, and on that date, the team would submit written presentations to the group. A few days later, at a meeting, the team would go over the three solutions and pick the best idea. What usually happened was that a compromise solution was agreed upon.

Owen was fairly quiet during the meeting; he smiled politely when told his assignment and that it would be due in three weeks.

During the next three weeks Owen stayed pretty much to himself. At project meetings he listened to the others carefully, offering his opinion only when asked.

When the time came for Owen's assignment to be discussed at the project meeting, Owen did not show up until the meeting was almost over.

"Owen, where have you . . ." Greg started to ask.

"Well, people, have you all agreed on my findings?" Owen interrupted. "I've already taken the liberty of typing up the memo to the Devbo supervisor. I'll just need your countersignature, Greg—under mine, of course."

Greg and the rest of the team members were floored. "Just a minute, Wilson," said Amy Snyder. "We've been discussing all three presentations here. You were expected to present your case, but that doesn't really matter now. We've just about decided on a compromise of all three plans. Your 'memo' is just a bit premature, don't you think?"

The other members of the group nodded in agreement with Amy, all talking at once, and all complaining that Owen was extremely "out of line."

"Calm down everybody," said Greg. "Perhaps Owen didn't fully understand how we work here. Is that the problem, Owen?"

"Listen, I'm sorry if I've offended you," said Owen. "But I have gone over these plans very thoroughly and I am convinced that mine is the most efficient way to handle the matter. Janice Levine hired me for my expertise. I'm sure she doesn't expect me to work as just one of the team." And with that he left the room.

Greg and the team members looked at one another in disbelief. After the initial shock was over, Greg picked up the phone and called Janice. "Janice, we have a bit of a problem here—and his name is Owen Wilson." Greg continued to explain the problem to Janice. In the end, he handed over the entire matter to her. All of a sudden her effective management decision had taken on new dimensions.

Consider these questions and ask your own:

1. What can Janice do to straighten Owen out on his role in the engineering project?
2. How can the relationship between Owen and the rest of the team members be smoothed?
3. Should Owen continue to work with the same group, or would a change in project assignment be better?
4. From a communication standpoint, what could have helped prevent the situation?

ASSIGNMENT 1
ORGANIZATION CHART

Draw a detailed organization chart for your college or university. Be sure to represent all areas of the college, academic as well as administrative. You will need to talk to several people from the administration of the college to determine what their various functions are and how they are related to one another.

What inferences can you draw from the chart?

1. Is the organizational structure flat, tall, centralized, decentralized?
2. Who has authority and makes decisions? Who reports to whom?
3. Are there other bodies in the university which have decision-making power and yet do not appear on the chart?

Turn in the chart to your instructor and be prepared to discuss your inferences out loud.

ASSIGNMENT 2
ORGANIZATIONAL ANALYSIS: LIKERT SYSTEMS

Select an organization in which you have been a member for some time. Describe the organization in terms of its purposes and structure (an organizational chart will be helpful) and indicate your position in the structure. What function do you perform in the organization?

Analyze the organization in terms of Likert's four systems of management. You may want to check your perceptions with other members of the organization. Be sure to address all the variables Likert describes. Give specific examples to support your analysis.

DISCUSSION QUESTIONS

1. What are the advantages and disadvantages of a hierarchical structure?
2. Does decentralization increase or decrease the control of the chief executive?
3. How many subordinates can a manager effectively manage? Discuss the question in terms of communication behaviors.
4. Can you give examples of nonbureaucratic organizations? In what way do they differ from bureaucratic ones?
5. How much does an organization chart say about the lines of communication in an organization? About the lines of authority and decision making?

CHAPTER 3

COMMUNICATION THEORIES AND THEIR ORGANIZATIONAL IMPLICATIONS

ACTIVITY 1
RUMOR CLINIC

Purposes: 1. To demonstrate serial information transmission.
2. To demonstrate the distortions that alter serial information transmission.
3. To observe firsthand how rumors are transmitted.

Class size: Any size. Six volunteers will be needed for the demonstration.
Time required: 45 minutes.
Materials needed: Rumor Clinic Story and Observer forms for all class members except volunteers. Pencils.
Physical setting: Regular classroom.

PROCEDURE

Six students are asked to volunteer for the rumor clinic. All but one are sent out of the room and asked to remain there until they are called in one at a time. Other class members will function as observers and are given the Rumor Clinic Story and the Observer form.

The instructor reads the story aloud to the first volunteer. (Volunteers must not take notes.) The second volunteer is called in, and the first volunteer repeats the story from memory. The third volunteer is called in, and the second volunteer tells the story from memory, and so on until all the volunteers have heard the story. The sixth volunteer, the newspaper reporter, is asked to write a brief story based on the information transmitted by the fifth volunteer.

The story written by the reporter is then compared with the original Rumor Clinic Story. Class discussion can center on the sources and distortions, inferences made by each volunteer, additions of information, deletion of information, etc. Discuss with the class what can be done to reduce errors in serial transmission. The instructor can ask students to give examples from their own experience about rumor transmission and distortions involved in the process.

SAMPLE RUMOR CLINIC STORY

Joe Smith, age 12, walked into the emergency room of University General Hospital at 9:30 A.M. on Saturday morning, March 5, with his friend, Pete Jones, age 11. Joe demanded that he receive care for a cut on his head. He had some pain, but he did not feel dizzy, and he had no trouble walking about. However, the cut looked messy and he wanted it taken care of.

The nurse explained that he could not be admitted without his parents' or guardians' permission. When asked where his parents were, Joe said they were sleeping and he did not want to bother them. Besides, they had told him not to play football.

With this comment he walked out of the emergency room, followed by Pete.

"RUMOR CLINIC"
OBSERVER FORM

Directions

Observers are to note on the form below any changes made by volunteers as the story is repeated. Record all changes which modify, in any substantive way, the original story given to you.

Volunteer	Changes in the Story When Repeated
1	
2	
3	
4	
5	

Newspaper
reporter

ACTIVITY 2
CRITICAL INCIDENT: WHO STARTED IT ALL?*

Purposes: 1. To demonstrate the process of labeling situations and of sequencing events by assigning a beginning to a chain of events.
2. To illustrate the concept of the hen-and-egg dilemma in communication and the personal ways in which each person determines the causes and effects in a chain of events.

Class size: Any size.
Time required: 45 minutes.
Materials needed: Two chalkboard erasers, chalk, a Chapstick.
Physical setting: Regular classroom.

ACTIVITY 3
WHERE THE MONEY GOES

Purposes: 1. To explore the relationship between meaning and decision making.
2. To observe communication in a small group setting, and to sharpen diagnostic skills and recording skills.

Class size: Any number. The class is to be divided into groups of six students.
Time required: 45 minutes.
Materials needed: A copy of Where the Money Goes for each student; a copy of the Observers Report form for each observer.
Physical setting: Regular classroom with movable chairs so students can sit in circles in their small groups.

PROCEDURE

Step 1: 15 Minutes

The class is divided into groups of six students, and the instructor assigns one observer for each group. The groups should have a copy of Where the Money Goes. The observers should have a copy of Where the Money Goes and an Observer Report form.

Groups complete the assignment. All the money must be allocated. If not, note the amount left unallocated.

Step 2: 15 Minutes

Observers are asked to report observations of communication behaviors noted in the small groups.

*From Instructor's Resource Manual to accompany *Interpersonal Communication, Roles, Rules, Strategies and Games,* Dennis R. Smith and L. Keith Williamson, © 1977, Wm. C. Brown Company Publishers, Dubuque, Iowa. Reprinted by permission.

Step 3: 15 Minutes   General class discussion can focus on:

1. What did each organization mean to each student?
2. Did these personal meanings affect students' attitudes about supporting the organizations?
3. How did personal experiences with these organizations influence students' attitudes toward them? Ask for examples.

INSTRUCTIONS   Your group is a committee responsible for distributing funds—a total of $10,000 collected from community donors—among several community organizations. Only a small amount of the money is specifically earmarked: Mr. Minter gave $500 to the general fund with the clear commitment that it would all go to Cancer Center, and an anonymous donor gave $200 specifically for the Child Abuse Council. Other funds are not earmarked. The committee must decide in one meeting how to allocate the total amount. The agencies making appeals, together with the amounts they are requesting, are listed below. Notice that the total they are asking for is several thousand more than you have available to distribute.

Child Abuse Council: An agency that assists in the detection, prevention, and education of parents who abuse children, and provides medical aid for abused children. Asking for $6,000.

Cancer Center: A center for detection of cancer and referral to treatment organizations. This center itself does no treatment. Asking for $3,500.

Boy Scouts: This organization has local chapters active in all city areas including the inner city. Asking for $2,500.

Girl Scouts: Like the Boy Scouts, this organization serves all areas of the city. Asking for $1,500.

Symphony Society: Membership drives of this society have recently not produced enough funds to keep their best musicians employed. Asking for $2,000.

Drug Central: A center that offers advice and referral to addicts as well as conducting education programs for citizens of all ages. The center distributes some medications but is primarily a referral center. Asking for $2,000.

Crisis Center: A telephone system that offers advice and counseling to persons who are in trouble or emotionally disturbed, and serves as a center for suicide prevention and psychological referral. Asking for $1,500.

Aid to the Aged: An information center for elderly citizens that offers advice about legal rights and pensions, and would like to expand its service to include recreation. Asking for $3,500.

How do you distribute your $10,000? How would you respond to the members of these organizations who asked you why their request was cut? What does each of these organizations mean to you? Do your personal feelings affect your attitude about supporting them?

OBSERVERS REPORT FORM

Which members of the group exhibited the following communicative behaviors?

	Never	Seldom	Often	Frequently
Work Roles				
1. Initiating ideas or actions	1	2	3	4
2. Facilitating introduction of facts and information	1	2	3	4
3. Clarifying issues	1	2	3	4
4. Evaluating	1	2	3	4
5. Summarizing and pulling together various ideas	1	2	3	4
6. Keeping the group working on the task	1	2	3	4
7. Taking a consensus; asking whether the group are near a decision	1	2	3	4
8. Requesting further information	1	2	3	4
Participation Maintenance Roles				
1. Supporting, encouraging others	1	2	3	4
2. Reducing tension	1	2	3	4
3. Harmonizing; keeping peace	1	2	3	4
4. Compromising; finding a common ground	1	2	3	4
5. Encouraging participation	1	2	3	4
Blocker Roles				
1. Expressing hostility	1	2	3	4
2. Seeking recognition	1	2	3	4
3. Avoiding involvement	1	2	3	4
4. Dominating the group	1	2	3	4
5. Nitpicking	1	2	3	4

INSTRUMENT
PLANNING AND GOAL SETTING

OBJECTIVES OF THE ACTIVITY

1. To increase understanding of the nature and role of goals in personal and organizational endeavors.
2. To experience an explicit goal-setting process, personally and organizationally.

3. To determine the factors which are most relevant in making the goal-setting and planning process effective.
4. To get insight into the relationship between personal and organizational goals.

DEFINITIONS

1. *Goal:* A generic term including purposes, missions, targets, what you want to achieve. Can be stated in terms of outcome.
2. *Objective:* An operational goal. What you must *do* to achieve a goal. A behavior, an action.
3. *Goal area:* A category of related goals. Examples of goal areas are

> Career
> Personal relationships
> Status and respect
> Learning and education
> Spiritual growth and religion
> Material rewards and possessions
> Leisure

4. *Measure of performance:* What must be done to evaluate goal achievement.

A. PERSONAL GOAL SETTING

1. Before working on specific objectives, it is important to get a general idea of what you would really like your life to be. Write a description of a successful "you." Jot down your first thoughts. Don't worry about polished sentences. Think in terms of outcomes and results rather than activities (e.g., attaining a bowling average of 180, earning a certain level of income, becoming president of a medium-sized company). One way to get to your own fantasies is to imagine that you are writing your own eulogy, or the kind of letter of recommendation you would want from an esteemed colleague fifteen or twenty years from now.

2. Refine the ideas you expressed in item 1 by listing the important *goal areas* and the *goals* in each area. Indicate in the right-hand column the importance of each goal according to the following scale:
High   Compared with my other goals, this goal is very important.
Medium   This goal is moderately important.
Low   A lot of other goals are more important than this one.

Goal Area	Goals	Importance
_____	_____	_____
	_____	_____
	_____	_____
	_____	_____
_____	_____	_____
	_____	_____
	_____	_____
	_____	_____
_____	_____	_____
	_____	_____
	_____	_____
	_____	_____
_____	_____	_____
	_____	_____
	_____	_____
	_____	_____
_____	_____	_____

3. Determine priorities for your listed goals. Select the goals that seem most important to you at this time (across all goal areas). Rank-order them in terms of their importance to you. Select no more than five or six goals. Indicate both the goal area and how you will measure performance and/or judge results. Be as specific as possible while recognizing that not all indicators can be quantified.

Rank	Goal	Goal Area	Performance Measure
_____	_____	_____	_____
_____	_____	_____	_____
_____	_____	_____	_____
_____	_____	_____	_____

4. For each of your ranked goals write several objectives for a relatively short time period (a year or less). What actions will you take? What will you *do* to get closer to the goal? In writing objectives, be careful to state a *behavior* or *action* to be performed. You must also include dates, frequency, and a timetable for each objective.

In the right-hand column, indicate how easy implementing the objectives appears to be, according to the following scale.

High   Compared with my other objectives, I can easily implement this objective.

Medium   I can implement this objective with moderate ease.

Low   It will be very difficult to implement this objective.

Goals	Objectives	Timetable	Ease of Implementation
_____	_____	_____	_____
	_____	_____	_____
	_____	_____	_____
	_____	_____	_____
_____	_____	_____	_____
	_____	_____	_____
	_____	_____	_____
	_____	_____	_____
	_____	_____	_____
_____	_____	_____	_____
	_____	_____	_____
	_____	_____	_____
	_____	_____	_____
_____	_____	_____	_____
	_____	_____	_____
	_____	_____	_____
	_____	_____	_____

5. Review items 1 through 5. Do any of the goals conflict with one another? Are the various goals in some way interrelated? Will working on one goal detract from working on another goal—or will it help? Which goals are mutually supporting and which are mutually exclusive?

List potential conflict areas in order of their importance.

6. Select one goal you want to achieve in the next six months. State it here and list the objectives that must be implemented to reach the goal.

   a. How important is it that you achieve this goal?

   b. What conflicts are there with other goals? How will you manage the conflicts?

   c. How will you feel when you achieve the goal? (Try to imagine yourself having achieved the goal. What are you feeling?)

   d. How will you feel if you do not achieve the goal?

e. What are your chances of succeeding? What will happen if you succeed?

f. What will happen if you fail?

7. Planning: You must examine four basic issues:
   a. What personal shortcomings will keep me from achieving my goal?

   b. What obstacles in my environment will keep me from achieving my goal?

   c. What can I do to eliminate or lessen the effects of a and b?
   Obstacle: What I can do about it:

   Shortcoming: What I can do about it:

   d. Who can help me with achieving my goal?
   Specific persons: What will I ask of them?

CASE 1
ANN JONES*

**PRINCIPAL
CHARACTERS**

Jim Taylor—Head computer operator, third shift; age 25; technical school graduate of a twelve-month course in programming; employed by the company for eighteen months; desires a job as a programmer.

Ann Jones—Age 22, employed as beginning programmer; has a B.S. in mathematics; has had one programming course in college; first woman programmer to be employed by the company.

Bob Nelson—Head computer operator of first shift on the weekends; age 35; employed by the company for seven years; a nice guy whose main ambition is to do an adequate job and earn his paycheck.

Company—A large defense contractor with large computer installation. Within the computer department, each programmer is responsible for the successful running of his or her programs. If anything goes wrong which is not covered in the program instructions, the head operator of the shift is instructed to attempt to contact the programmer for instructions.

After Ann had been on the job for three months, she was given the responsibility of a group of programs which were scheduled to be run Sunday from 1 to 8 A.M. The programs had many different tape and card inputs and required strict adherence to written instructions which frequently changed as additions and refinements were made. The first few weeks everything seemed to go smoothly, then one Sunday morning, Jim called Ann about 6:30 A.M. to say the programs were not running and asking for instructions. After asking a few questions, Ann was able to determine the problem over the phone and Jim finished running the group of programs.

The next Sunday morning, Jim called at 4:30 A.M. saying the programs wouldn't run. Again Ann asked several questions. When she could not determine the problem over the phone, she agreed to make the twenty-minute drive to the plant. Upon arrival, Jim informed her that he had solved the problem by himself. Ann could not determine exactly what had gone on, but since the problem was solved, she left.

The following Sunday Jim called at 3:30 A.M. Ann again could not determine the cause of the problem over the phone. She asked Jim if there were other programs which could be run at that time. When he said there was plenty of other work to be done, she said she would come to the plant during the day to work out the difficulty. After Bob came on duty at 8:00 A.M. Ann called Bob to discuss the problem with him.

*Case written by Marilyn Elliott for a class assignment. Reproduced by permission of the author.

He said he had tried to run the programs already but was having trouble. He suggested that he try one more time to run them setting up the entire operation himself before Ann made the trip to the plant. When Bob set up the programs, they ran beautifully. He called Ann and told her to forget coming in. He said that Jim had just neglected to follow her written instructions. He also said that the first time he tried to run the programs, Jim had done all the setup work. Ann thanked Bob for his effort and hung up the phone.

On Monday morning, Ann arrived before Jim finished his shift. She told him she was furious and that he had better not call her again at home unless there actually was a problem which could not be solved by reading her written instructions. Jim replied that the programs were her responsibility and he would call her any time he felt like it. He then slammed the door and went home.

CASE 2
THE PERRY COMPANY*

Upon receiving her master's degree in English, Linda Weldon went to work for the Perry Company, a wholesale jeweler. It was not the sort of work Linda had envisioned for herself; she had planned in graduate school to complete a doctorate in English literature and find a college teaching position. But a year of graduate work and the paucity of college teaching jobs for English Ph.D.s convinced her she was not dedicated enough to go to school for three more years, only to end up unemployed. She stopped school upon completion of the M.A. and interviewed for several management training positions; she was discouraged by interviewers who told her they were hiring women only to fill government-demanded quotas. Linda moved back to the city where she had gotten her B.A. since many of her friends still lived there; but she was further discouraged in her job hunting pursuits as professional employment agencies informed her an M.A. in English qualified her for nothing. After spending the summer making minimum wages as a secretary, Linda finally accepted a job at the Perry Company.

Her interviews with Bob Perry, president of the small, family-owned company, were promising. Bob recognized Linda's potential and told her he needed someone to begin an advertising program for the company and to develop some training seminars for the retailers who bought jewelry and flatware from the Perry Company. Although

*Case written by Sandy Ragan for a class assignment. Reprinted by permission of the author.

her job was to be a created position, Bob was enthusiastic about its possibilities and about having Linda on his payroll. She was intelligent, articulate, attractive, and verbally skilled—qualities Bob felt would upgrade the company. Bob did inform Linda, however, that the present need of the company was for an office manager, as the secretary-receptionist had suddenly resigned. Linda was offered a job at the Perry Company but was asked to fill secretary-receptionist responsibilities on a temporary basis. Bob explained that she could "work into" advertising and training this way and that, in the meantime, he could sell the new position to the other officers in the company.

Linda accepted the job offer—mostly because no other employment loomed on her horizon but also because Bob was charming and flattering and appeared an amiable boss; too, the promise of advertising and training looked most appealing. However, her misgivings about the job were several: she felt overqualified for and belittled by secretarial work; her salary was deplorable for her level of education, she thought; and Bob had given her no concrete date about when she could expect to assume only advertising and training functions. She soon discovered that she was one of the few employees of the company with a college education; the other women were employed in shipping, sales, and accounting and were physically removed from her reception area. Her lunch hours were either spent alone or with women whose educational and socioeconomic backgrounds differed vastly from hers. The three executive officers of the company were men; of these, only Bob and the company's vice-president, John Turner, had earned B.A.s. Bob's nephew, Bill, was the company's treasurer and was adept at managing its finances without benefit of a formal education.

During the first month, Linda worked hard in her job as office manager, a position which was actually far more challenging than she'd imagined as it involved filling the secretarial needs of all three officers. She used her organizational skills to revise the office's filing system and to manage the seasonal volumes of correspondence more efficiently. She worked well with all three of her bosses but especially enjoyed her working relationship with Bob, who treated her with respect and admiration. After the first month, Linda was challenged by and pleased with her job; she was also encouraged by Bob's continued reminders of his desire to work her into advertising and training. Her only real disappointment was a feeling of not fitting into the company and not developing any social relationships with its employees. Her work area was physically closer to the officers than to any of the other employees, and her interests and education were also more compatible with theirs, but status and sex precluded more than a formal business exchange.

During the second and third months of her work, Linda continued to feel fairly pleased with her job. Her feeling was enhanced by a very positive three-month appraisal interview with all three of the company's officers. They rated her "excellent" in all performance categories, expressed enthusiasm with her work and her future at the company, and gave her the highest percentage raise the company awarded with promises to increase her salary by several increments at the next evaluation period. Slowly, Bob began to assign Linda some of the advertising and training functions she had hoped for: she wrote copy for several magazine ads, published a Christmas letter for the company's retail customers, and traveled out of town with Bob to help him conduct a training seminar for retailers. Bob praised Linda highly for the professionalism she lent the company; however, she continued her functions as secretary-receptionist as well. As Linda assumed more responsibility and gained more respect from Bob, she became increasingly irritated by the tedious clerical jobs she still performed. She was especially aggravated when Paul treated her like a menial employee by asking her to cash his personal checks and purchase his health foods on her lunch hour. Too, she began to resent some of his office habits: his 10 A.M. arrivals, his inefficient handling of correspondence, his blundering with valued customers. More than once, Linda had heard office gossip that Bob was president only by virtue of being the oldest son and that Bill, the treasurer, actually kept the company alive.

After four months of employment, Linda discovered, because she had access to employee salaries, that Jeff, the newest male employee of the Perry Company, made $200 more a month than she did. This fact discouraged her, especially because she felt Jeff was incompetent and knew he'd had only two years of college. She did not discuss her growing resentment with Bob. The next week, Bob surprised Linda by hiring a new receptionist, a young woman Linda could train as her assistant so that she would be freer to pursue more advertising and training. This delighted Linda, although Bob still discussed no concrete plans for enlarging her new functions. Two weeks later, Bob called Linda into his office and explained that he had conferred with the other officers and that they had advised him to "slow down" with Linda; they couldn't see how advertising and training could benefit the company at that time, and they feared that their high praise of her would make her too ambitious; she might even leave the company as a salesman recently had. Bob told Linda not to give up her ambitions but to be more patient until he could convince the other officers of her potential value to the company. In the meantime, she could continue as office manager, but her new assistant would give her time to pursue some other responsibilities Bob had in mind.

Linda was enraged by their conversation but acquiesced without argument; two weeks later, she gave notice to a stunned Bob, telling him she had accepted a job that would better suit her abilities. Linda left the Perry Company feeling a great deal of bitterness toward it.

ASSIGNMENT 1
WHO IS TO BLAME?

Find two people who have recently had an argument (husband and wife, boy friend and girlfriend, student and teacher, roommates, etc.).

Interview the two separately to get their separate versions of the events. When did the fight or argument begin? Who started it? By doing what? What followed? Get a sequence of events from the perspective of each person. Compare the two versions to determine whether there were differences in the way events were sequenced and as a result labeled.

If you were to help the pair settle their argument, how would you go about it?

ASSIGNMENT 2
RELATIONSHIPS

What is a "relationship"? What role does communication play in building a "relationship"? Do you and those with whom you have a relationship play by "rules"? If so, what are the rules?

Keeping your answers to the previous questions in mind, what do you think are the differences in your relationships with the following people:

1. A fellow student of the opposite sex
2. A fellow student of the same sex
3. A male professor
4. A female professor
5. A dean
6. The kids you went to high school with who are not going to college
7. Your parents
8. The man who interviews you for your job
9. Your female supervisor

Why are there differences in these relationships? Can you generalize about relationships? What concepts from the text can you use to analyze the relationships mentioned above?

DISCUSSION QUESTIONS

1. If we believe that meanings are in people and not in the words we use, what are the implications for our understanding of messages?

2. What are some examples of "feedback" in your physical environment? The thermostat in a house is the most common example. Can you think of others?

3. Can you think of instances in which communication does not occur? Compare the statement "You cannot not communicate" with the question "When a tree falls in the forest where nobody can hear it, does it make a sound or not?" It may be helpful to talk about your definitions of "sound" and "communication" during this discussion.

4. What is the origin of the expression "hen-and-egg"? Why do we use it to describe the punctuation, or starting points, of our communication transactions?

5. In what circumstances would the bull's-eye view of communication be applicable? What about the ping-pong theory? How does the transactional view take in more issues and events than other views?

CHAPTER 4

COMMUNICATION TRANSACTIONS

ACTIVITY 1
ROLES

> *Purposes:* 1. To focus on the concept of roles and the communication dynamics through which roles are established, defined, and maintained.
> 2. To identify the sources of expectations regarding an individual's roles and for pinpointing the nature of conflicting role demands present in any situation.
>
> *Class size:* Any number of participants.
> *Time required:* About 45 minutes.
> *Materials:* Role worksheet.
> *Physical setting:* Regular classroom.

PROCEDURE

Step 1:
5 Minutes

On the role worksheet pick a role you would like to explore. It could be your role as a student, a son or daughter, a spouse, a friend, a date, an employee, a supervisor. It should be a role you do play at one time or another. Once you have identified the role you wish to consider, list a variety of persons who are in some way connected to you when you play that role. You may list as many people as you can think of.

Step 2:
10 Minutes

The next step is to list the expectations each of these people has about how you should perform the role. Be as specific as possible when you list role expectations.

ROLE WORKSHEET

Role: _____

People I come in contact with when in the role:

1. _____

2. _____

3. _____

4. _____

5. _____

6. _____

7. _____

8. _____

9. _____

10. _____

Specific expectations about my role performance from:

Person 1. _____

Person 2. _____

Person 3. _____

Person 4. _____

Person 5. _____

Person 6. _____

Person 7. _____

Person 8. _____

Person 9. _____

Person 10. _____

Step 3   Students who have chosen similar roles should be formed into groups and then asked to compare their lists with each other. No more than six students should be in a group.

Step 4   Group discussion with the class should focus on similarities and differences noted in role expectations by students. Within each student's list, were there conflicting expectations from the various sources listed by the students? How would students go about resolving conflicting role expectations? In the short term? In the long term?

ACTIVITY 2
ENVIRONMENT

Purpose: To highlight for discussion the intrapersonal communication processes involved in gathering information about one's physical environment.

Class size: Up to fifty participants. Class is to be divided into groups of six students.
Time required: About 30 minutes.
Materials needed: Paper and pencil for each student. Newsprint, markers, and tape for each group.
Physical setting: Regular classroom.

PROCEDURE   Students are to move around the classroom as freely as they like without talking to each other. They should observe as much as they can about their environment, including the people in it. They should use as many senses as they can.

After ten minutes of milling, each student is to sit down and make a list of the things observed.

Groups of six students are then formed. Each group lists on a large newsprint sheet all the things they have observed.

Lists should be posted for all to see.

Class discussion should focus on similarities and differences about things observed. What seemed to appear on all lists? What was noticed by only a few? What came from the physical environment? What came from the social environment? How was the environment defined? Was it limited to the classroom walls? Did it include stimuli from outside? From the street? From a hall? From another classroom? From the internal environment? How observant of your environment are you? Is it important to be attuned to the environment? If so, why?

ACTIVITY 3
AGREE/DISAGREE LIST ON SEX ROLE EXPECTATIONS

Purposes: 1. To explore students' attitudes about sex roles and sex role stereotyping.
2. To analyze the implications of sex role stereotypes for the opportunities of women in the business environment.

Class size: Any number. Class is to be divided into groups of five to six members.
Time Required: 45 to 60 minutes.
Materials needed: A copy of the Agree/Disagree List and a pencil for each person.
Physical setting: Regular classroom.

PROCEDURE

Step 1

Every member fills out the Agree/Disagree List individually. About five minutes is allotted for this step.

Step 2

Groups of five or six members are formed. The instructor can decide whether the groups should be mixed or segregated by sex. Groups are asked to discuss each item of the Agree/Disagree List and to reach consensus. The instructor must emphasize that consensus does not mean voting nor necessarily complete endorsement of the item. It means that you are willing to accept that item even though the endorsement may represent less than 100 percent of your convictions.

Discussion must be continued if disagreements are deep. If consensus cannot be reached, the group should go on to the next item. Thirty minutes should be spent on this step.

Step 3   Each group should report its consensus items. The class as a whole can then discuss the implications of the answers for the professional roles of men and women. About twenty minutes is allotted for this step.

AGREE/DISAGREE LIST ON SEX ROLE EXPECTATIONS

	Agree	Disagree
1. Women need to perform better than men in order to be promoted over a man.	_____	_____
2. Women are paid about the same as men in similar positions.	_____	_____
3. It would be difficult for a woman to supervise a group of men.	_____	_____
4. Women's opinions are given the same credibility as men's in a predominantly male committee.	_____	_____
5. If a woman had an income substantially greater than her husband's, she would feel uncomfortable.	_____	_____
6. If a woman earned an income substantially greater than her husband's, the husband would feel uncomfortable.	_____	_____
7. It is easier for women to perform for men managers than for women managers.	_____	_____
8. In work situations women tend to restrain themselves from outperforming men.	_____	_____
9. Men are more logical than women, generally.	_____	_____
10. Men are more mechanically inclined than women.	_____	_____
11. Men are more competitive and aggressive than women.	_____	_____
12. Women have more intuition than men.	_____	_____
13. Women are more emotional than men.	_____	_____
14. Women really want to be taken care of by a man.	_____	_____

	Agree	Disagree
15. A woman's place is at home taking care of her husband and children.	_____	_____
16. Children of working mothers develop more emotional problems than children of mothers who stay at home.	_____	_____

INSTRUMENT
INTERPERSONAL COMMUNICATION INVENTORY*

This inventory offers you an opportunity to make an objective study of the degree and patterns of communication in your interpersonal relationships. It will enable you to better understand how you present and use yourself in communicating with persons in your daily contacts and activities. You will find it both interesting and helpful to make this study.

DIRECTIONS

The questions refer to persons other than your family members or relatives.

Please answer each question as quickly as you can according to the way you feel at the moment (not the way you usually feel or felt last week).

Please do not consult anyone while completing this inventory. You may discuss it after you have completed it. Remember that the value of this form will be lost if you change your answer during or after this discussion.

Honest answers are very necessary. Please be as frank as possible, since your answers are confidential.

Use the following examples for practice. Put a check (√) in one of the three blanks on the right to show how the question applies to your situation.

	Yes (Usually)	No (Seldom)	Sometimes
1. Is it easy for you to express your view to others?	_____	_____	_____
2. Do others listen to your point of view?	_____	_____	_____

*Copyright 1971, Millard J. Bienvenu, Sr. Reproduced with permission of the author.

The Yes column is to be used when the question can be answered as happening most of the time or usually.

The No column is to be used when the question can be answered as seldom or never.

The Sometimes column should be marked when you cannot answer definitely Yes or No. Use this column as little as possible.

Read each question carefully. If you cannot give the exact answer to a question, answer the best you can but be sure to answer each one. There are no right or wrong answers. Answer according to the way you feel at the present time. Remember, do not refer to family members in answering the questions.

	Yes (Usually)	No (Seldom)	Sometimes
1. Do your words come out the way you would like them to in conversation?	————	————	————
2. When you are asked a question that is not clear, do you ask the person to explain?	————	————	————
3. When you are trying to explain something, do other persons have a tendency to put words in your mouth?	————	————	————
4. Do you merely assume the other person knows what you are trying to say without your explaining what you really mean?	————	————	————
5. Do you ever ask another person to tell you how he or she feels about the point you may be trying to make?	————	————	————
6. Is it difficult for you to talk with other people?	————	————	————
7. In conversation, do you talk about things which are of interest to both you and the other person?	————	————	————
8. Do you find it difficult to express your ideas when they differ from those around you?	————	————	————
9. In conversation, do you try to put yourself in the other person's shoes?	————	————	————
10. In conversation, do you have a tendency to do more talking than the other person?	————	————	————

	Yes (Usually)	No (Seldom)	Sometimes
11. Are you aware of how your tone of voice may affect others?	_____	_____	_____
12. Do you refrain from saying something that you know will only hurt others or make matters worse?	_____	_____	_____
13. Is it difficult to accept constructive criticism from others?	_____	_____	_____
14. When someone has hurt your feelings, do you discuss this with him or her?	_____	_____	_____
15. Do you later apologize to someone whose feelings you may have hurt?	_____	_____	_____
16. Does it upset you a great deal when someone disagrees with you?	_____	_____	_____
17. Do you find it difficult to think clearly when you are angry with someone?	_____	_____	_____
18. Do you fail to disagree openly with others because you are afraid they will get angry?	_____	_____	_____
19. When a problem arises between you and another person, can you discuss it without getting angry?	_____	_____	_____
20. Are you satisfied with the way you settle your differences with others?	_____	_____	_____
21. Do you pout and sulk for a long time when someone upsets you?	_____	_____	_____
22. Do you become very uneasy when someone pays you a compliment?	_____	_____	_____
23. Generally, are you able to trust other individuals?	_____	_____	_____
24. Do you find it difficult to compliment and praise others?	_____	_____	_____
25. Do you deliberately try to conceal your faults from others?	_____	_____	_____
26. Do you help others to understand you by saying how you think, feel, and believe?	_____	_____	_____
27. Is it difficult for you to confide in people?	_____	_____	_____
28. Do you have a tendency to change the subject when your feelings enter into a discussion?	_____	_____	_____

	Yes (Usually)	No (Seldom)	Sometimes
29. In conversation, do you let the other person finish talking before reacting to what he or she says?	_____	_____	_____
30. Do you find yourself not paying attention while in conversation with others?	_____	_____	_____
31. Do you ever try to listen for meaning when someone is talking?	_____	_____	_____
32. Do others seem to be listening when you are talking?	_____	_____	_____
33. In a discussion, is it difficult for you to see things from the other person's point of view?	_____	_____	_____
34. Do you pretend you are listening to others when actually you are not?	_____	_____	_____
35. In conversation, can you tell the difference between what a person is saying and what he or she may be feeling?	_____	_____	_____
36. While speaking, are you aware of how others are reacting to what you are saying?	_____	_____	_____
37. Do you feel that other people wish you were a different kind of person?	_____	_____	_____
38. Do other people understand your feelings?	_____	_____	_____
39. Do others remark that you always seem to think you are right?	_____	_____	_____
40. Do you admit that you are wrong when you know that you are wrong about something?	_____	_____	_____

Total Score

SCORING KEY AND NORMS

Instructions

Look at how you responded to each item in the ICI. In front of the item write the appropriate weight from the table on this page. For example, if you answered Yes to item 1, you would find below that you get three points; write the number 3 in front of item 1 in the inventory and proceed to score item 2. When you have finished scoring each of the forty items, add up your total score. Then you may wish to compare your score with the norms listed below.

	Yes	No	Sometimes		Yes	No	Sometimes
1.	3	0	2	21.	0	3	1
2.	3	0	2	22.	0	3	1
3.	0	3	1	23.	3	0	2
4.	0	3	1	24.	0	3	1
5.	3	0	2	25.	0	3	1
6.	0	3	1	26.	3	0	2
7.	3	0	2	27.	0	3	1
8.	0	3	1	28.	0	3	1
9.	3	0	2	29.	3	0	2
10.	0	3	1	30.	0	3	1
11.	3	0	2	31.	3	0	2
12.	3	0	2	32.	3	0	2
13.	0	3	1	33.	0	3	1
14.	3	0	2	34.	0	3	1
15.	3	0	2	35.	3	0	2
16.	0	3	1	36.	3	0	2
17.	0	3	1	37.	0	3	1
18.	0	3	1	38.	3	0	2
19.	3	0	2	39.	0	3	1
20.	3	0	2	40.	3	0	2

MEANS AND STANDARD DEVIATIONS FOR THE ICI

Age Groups	Males	Females
17–21	Mean 81.79 SD 21.56 N 53	Mean 81.48 SD 20.06 N 80
22–25	Mean 86.03 SD 14.74 N 38	Mean 94.46 SD 11.58 N 26
26 and up	Mean 90.73 SD 19.50 N 56	Mean 86.93 SD 15.94 N 45
All age groups	Mean 86.39 SD 19.46 N 147	Mean 85.34 SD 18.22 N 151
All age groups; males and females combines	Mean 85.93 SD 19.05 N 298	

CASE 1
THE SHORT FUSE*

Irma Berger had been the bookkeeper at Craftsman Woodworking for twelve years. She knew the books inside out, and no one dared to question her records. That is, no one until Eugene Flax. Eugene had been brought on board as office manager. He was the only person in the shop with a college education, and he seemed to get pleasure in tossing his degree around. After about a month at Craftsman, Eugene decided to tackle Irma's books to determine whether he could improve her bookkeeping in any way.

Word got around the shop fast that Eugene had requested that Irma give him some time to go over her books. While the carpenters grudgingly agreed that most of Eugene's improvements in their work schedules had worked out well, they were anxious to see if Irma would cooperate with Eugene. Sam Kastle, shop foreman, decided to give Irma a little teasing on the subject.

"Well, Irma, it looks like your time has come," said Sam.

"I don't know what you're talking about," snapped Irma.

"Sure you do. Eugene is going over your books, right? Well, when he's done you can bet he'll have a whole slew of 'improvements' for you to make. He learned how in college."

Although she had been the only woman in the business for twelve years, Irma was still very bad about taking ribbings from any of the guys. She bristled with irritation, and threw Sam out of her office shouting, "I think that both you and he have a lot to learn, Sam Kastle. Now get out of here so I can get some work done."

For some time after Sam had left, Irma was upset about what he had said. Whereas before she had turned her books over to Eugene confidently, she now feared that he would try to upset her system of recordkeeping. She had been keeping the books for twelve years, and the thought that somebody could just tell her that she was doing it wrong made her blood boil. She tried to calm herself down, but the more she thought about Eugene the angrier she became. Her anger became so intense that her hand shook when she reached for her coffee cup. She was simply not about to listen to any changes that Eugene might have. The business was running just fine as it was, and she didn't need him to help her.

Meanwhile, Eugene had been examining Irma's books and had

*Reprinted by permission of the publisher from "Let's Get Down to Cases," *Supervisory Management*, September 1979, © 1979 by AMACOM, a division of American Management Associations. All rights reserved.

found them to be in excellent order. Every payment and credit had been accounted for, and the totals were always perfect. He realized how lucky Craftsman Woodworking was to have such an efficient bookkeeper. The only fault that he could see was that Irma had been using a very small record book. He felt that if she were to use a larger one, it would be easier for her to keep the records neat, and for others to read whose eyesight might be bad.

He brought Irma back her books, along with a brand new recordbook, which he hoped she would be pleased with. "Irma," he said, "I've gone through your records, and I'm very pleased with them. I have just one suggestion—that is, for you to use this new book for your records. It will make it easier for you to write and to read entries."

Irma had worked up so much resentment inside that she barely heard a word of what Eugene said. Upon hearing the word "suggestion," she lost her temper and when Eugene had finished, she said, "I don't need any of your suggestions. For 12 years I've done my job correctly. If that's not good enough for you, with your college degree, then I quit." With that outburst she picked up her bag and rushed out of the building, leaving Eugene with his mouth hanging open.

Consider these questions and ask your own:

1. What is the first step Eugene should take to find out why Irma has flown off the handle?
2. What can Eugene learn from his experience with Irma?
3. How can Eugene improve his relationships with the employees at Craftsman Woodworking?

CASE 2
TO TELL THE TRUTH*

Michael Canfield was the supervisor of training at the Tropic Manufacturing Company. When the company added a new product line, it was decided the training function should be separated from within the personnel department. At the same time senior management gave approval for a series of supervisory development programs to be started, and also authorized four new training positions. These were in addition to the three technical instructors who had been in the company for several years.

As Michael took up his new task, he found that he had two major priorities: to set in motion a training needs analysis to determine what type of supervisory course was needed and to recruit, interview, and hire four new instructors.

As the year passed Michael found that the time he had spent in selecting the four new instructors was paying off. Each of them had excellent performance records, and all seven instructors worked at their own personal growth and were better instructors than they had been twelve months ago. Michael was satisfied that his efforts at frank communication and the time spent with each instructor on a regular basis had led to the very strong group loyalty among his instructors.

Since his own personal world was so orderly, it came as a shock to him when he heard some of the other supervisors saying that the new product line was a complete failure. It seemed that the market had been overestimated. To salvage as much capital as possible, the company would probably reduce expenditures across the board. The supervisors mentioned that it wouldn't be just programs cut; it probably would be people, too.

The next day Michael's boss called him in and covered much of the ground that the other supervisors had discussed. But his boss went on to say that the training section would have to lay off two instructors and that the rule "Last in, first out" would apply. Also, she added that the losses were so severe that a total of four instructors might have to be let go. The final decision would be made within the next five days, and until it was, she asked Michael to keep their talk confidential and not take any action.

Michael returned to his office to find that all of his people had heard the rumors about the layoff. They implored him to tell them what the boss had said.

Kurt spoke up. "If we are to be laid off soon, we need all the advance notice possible. I have a family to support, a mortgage, and a monthly car payment. I can't be out of work very long!" Michael hedged by saying that he didn't have definite information, but Tanya exclaimed, "Come off it. You've always been straight with us before. Now is no time to start playing games. What's going on? We need to know!"

To tell the truth or not was suddenly Michael's dilemma. If he told them, everyone would probably start looking for a new job—and by breaking his boss's confidence, he might end up joining them on the unemployment line. If he didn't tell them what he knew, he would be cutting short the time available for the newest instructors to update their résumés and start job searching. Michael also knew that if he withheld information now, everyone would know it later on and his rapport with his own people would be seriously damaged.

Consider these questions and ask your own:

1. Should Michael tell all that he knows and ask his staff members to keep it among themselves?
2. Should he take aside the two instructors who are destined to be laid off and suggest that they begin looking for employment?
3. Is it Michael's duty to remain silent until he is given clearance from his boss to talk to his staff?

CASE 3
FINISHED BEFORE YOU STARTED*

J. Thorndyke had called a staff meeting—and as always his staff made certain that they were all present and accounted for at the specified time and place. Thorndyke was a stern taskmaster in running the accounting firm of Thorndyke, Fuller, Perkins, Smith and Sussman, and while his employees were a little fearful of his wrath, they generally respected his judgment.

"I'd like to announce some changes that will be taking place over the next month or so," said Thorndyke. "Elizabeth Hubbins will now be reporting directly to Stuart Nelson; and Janet Friedman will take over Elizabeth's responsibilities with those clients whom Robert Calhoun handles."

The changes came as a surprise to no one. Thorndyke had discussed the changes with all parties involved prior to the meeting. He explained that they were needed to improve work distribution.

The staff responded to his announcement with polite murmurings, and the meeting disbanded.

That afternoon Stuart Nelson received a message from Thorndyke's secretary to report to his office at 3:30 for a brief meeting.

Wondering what more Thorndyke had to say about the reorganization, Stuart knocked on Thorndyke's large oak door at exactly 3:30.

"Come in, Stuart," said Thorndyke. "I'd just like to make one other point about the reorganization—but, first, perhaps I should ask how you feel about supervising Elizabeth Hubbins."

*Reprinted by permission of the publisher from "Let's Get Down to Cases," *Supervisor Management,* August 1979, © 1979 by AMACOM, a division of American Management Associations. All rights reserved.

"I don't have any problems with it, Mr. Thorndyke, although I am a little concerned about whether she will be able to handle my clients. You know how touchy some of them are."

"Hmm," he answered. "I was afraid that was your attitude. Listen, Nelson, Elizabeth Hubbins is a very bright young woman, and she must be given every chance to succeed with our firm. I have a hunch about her, and my hunches are usually right. I'm going to be watching her development very closely, and I don't want to see her stifled. I hope that I'm making myself clear."

"Yes," gulped Stuart. "This is a bit of a surprise to me, Mr. Thorndyke. I have never had any complaints from my subordinates about my stifling them; I really try to give them every chance to grow. I assure you that you have no reason to be concerned about Elizabeth Hubbins."

"Well," Thorndyke said with a raised eyebrow, "as long as you understand the situation, that's all, Nelson."

Stuart was fuming as he left Thorndyke's office—but then most people would have been under those circumstances. He decided, however, to ignore the accusation and handle the reorganization in the same manner that he had intended to—fairly.

But, as fate would have it, and as big a hunch as Thorndyke had had, Elizabeth got off to a bad start in her new position. She offended three of the clients and made a costly error in another's payroll. Stuart had no other choice but to reprimand her and warn her that another mistake or client complaint could mean serious trouble for her.

Stuart had been expecting some kind of defensive reaction from Elizabeth—but he was in no way prepared for what she said.

"You can't talk to me that way," she exclaimed. "Johnny promised me—I mean Mr. Thorndyke told me I should learn as much as I can and not worry if I make a few mistakes."

Johnny?!! Stuart felt sick to his stomach upon hearing the familiar way she spoke of the dominating J. Thorndyke. He quickly ended the meeting with Elizabeth so that he could think about the situation in private.

Consider these questions and ask your own:

1. How should Stuart handle Elizabeth now that he is aware of her relationship with his boss?
2. What can Stuart do to protect his clients from Elizabeth's mistakes?
3. Should Stuart seek advice from any of his peers, or would he be better off handling the problem himself?

ASSIGNMENT 1
NONVERBAL INFERENCES

Have you ever been in a situation in which you inferred from nonverbal behavior a message that was not intended? What was the result? How did you check your inference?

ASSIGNMENT 2
NONVERBAL PROFILE

Visit an organization of your choice. Observe as many nonverbal cues as you can for a period of time. Develop a nonverbal profile for the organization. How are nonverbal factors used in the organization to communicate status, hierarchy, morale, atmosphere, climate, etc.? What does the organization look like (environmental factors, location, appearance of building, offices, hallways, etc.)? Write a paper to describe your findings, and present your interpretations to the class orally. This assignment lends itself well to the use of slides, pictures, and other visuals.

ASSIGNMENT 3
INTERPERSONAL PERSPECTIVES

Select an issue and a person who has interacted with you on that issue. Draw your side of the interpersonal perspective model, representing your position on the issue and your perception of the other person's position. Interview the other person and have him or her draw his or her side of the model. Analyze areas of agreement, understanding, and realization. What have you learned from completing this assignment?

DISCUSSION QUESTIONS

1. Communication transactions depend on "mutually and simultaneously" taking each other into account. Are there times when you are observing others and not being observed? Under what circumstances does this occur? How do you feel about it? What happens if you are looking at someone and suddenly they "catch you" looking at them? How do you feel when you turn around and find someone staring at you?

2. Is it possible to carry on communication transactions *only* at the content level, or do you invariably involve the relational level at the same time?

3. Discuss the different words you would use in talking with a person who is not your equal. Do the words change because the other person is seen by you as subordinate to you or superior to you? What other "hints" would you use in a conversation with another person to indicate that person is superior to you in your estimation? What hints do you give when the other person is subordinate to you?

4. What are the implications of "punctuation" or telling when a transaction starts and ends—the hen-and-egg question? Are you likely to be effective with another person if your ideas differ about when the communication transaction actually began?

5. Why is it easier to diagnose and possibly solve a communication problem at the level of agreeing or disagreeing on issues (first level) than it might be to deal with problems on the other two levels?

6. Identify eight to ten features of your classroom context which affect the communication that takes place there. Did you pick mostly verbal or nonverbal factors?

7. Describe a communication situation in which two people punctuate and sequence their interaction differently (do not use examples from the text). What are the consequences of different sequencing and punctuating for the relationship between the two communicators?

8. Cite examples of nonverbal communication in a work setting. In what ways does nonverbal communication help define role relationships?

CHAPTER 5

INFORMATION AND FLOW

ACTIVITY I
LUTTS AND MIPPS: GROUP PROBLEM SOLVING*

Purposes: 1. To study the sharing of information in a task-oriented group.
               2. To focus on cooperation in group problem solving.
               3. To observe the emergence of leadership behavior in group problem solving.

Class size: Any number. Class is to be divided into groups of six to eight.
Time required: About 45 minutes.

Materials needed: 1. A copy of the Lutts and Mipps Instructions Form for each participant.
                      2. A set of Lutts and Mipps Information Cards for each group (twenty-six cards to a set).
                      3. A copy of the Lutts and Mipps Reactions Form for each participant.
                      4. Paper and pencil for each participant.

Physical setting: A classroom large enough to allow members of each group to be seated in a circle.

PROCEDURE

1. Lutts and Mipps Instructions Forms are distributed.
2. After participants have had time to read the instruction sheet, the instructor distributes a set of Lutts and Mipps Information Cards randomly among the members of each group. Participants begin their task.
3. After about twenty minutes, the instructor interrupts and distributes the Reactions Forms, which are to be completed individually.
4. The instructor leads a discussion of the problem-solving activity, focusing on information processing and the sharing of leadership in task situations. Group members are encouraged to share data from their reaction forms. The solution to the problem appears in the Instructor's Manual.

LUTTS AND MIPPS INSTRUCTIONS FORM

Pretend that lutts and mipps represent a new way of measuring distance and that dars, wors, and mirs represent a new way of measuring time. A man drives from town A through towns B and C to town D.

     The task of your group is to determine how many wors the entire trip took. You have twenty minutes for this task. Do not choose a formal leader.

     You will be given cards containing information related to the task.

     Reprinted from J. W. Pfeiffer and J. E. Jones (eds.), A Handbook of Structured Experiences for Human Relations Training, vol. II, (revised), University Associates, San Diego, Calif., 1974. Used with permission.

You may share this information orally, but you must keep your cards in your hands throughout the task.

LUTTS AND MIPPS REACTIONS FORM

1. Whose participation was most helpful in the accomplishment of the task?

2. What behavior was helpful?

3. Whose participation seemed to hinder the accomplishment of the task?

4. What behavior seemed to be a hindrance?

5. What feeling reactions did you experience during the problem-solving exercise?

6. What role(s) did you play in the group?

ACTIVITY 2
UPWARD COMMUNICATION: YOUNG MANUFACTURING COMPANY*

Purpose: To explore organizational communication and decision-making processes.

Class size: For the multiple role play: Six to eight groups of five. For the demonstration: One group of five.
Time required: Both options last from 1 to 1½ hours.
Materials needed: None.
Physical setting: For the multiple role play: Ideally, two or three small meeting rooms each accommodating two groups of five; or a very large room that can allow all groups to role play without getting in each other's way. For the demonstration: A table in front of the class or in the middle of the room.

INTRODUCTION

The Young Manufacturing Company is a role-play exercise of a meeting between the president of a small company and four of his subordinates. Each character's role is designed to recreate the reality of a business meeting. Each character comes to the meeting with a unique perspective on a major problem facing the company as well as some personal impressions of the other characters developed over several years of business and social association.

THE CAST OF CHARACTERS

Bob Young, the president, is the principal owner of Young Manufacturing, a small fabricator of automotive replacement parts. The firm employs 500 people, and during its nine years of operation has enjoyed better profits than its competitors because of a reputation for high-quality products at a modest cost. Recently, however, competitors have begun to overtake Young Manufacturing, resulting in declining profits for it. Bob Young is expending every possible effort to keep his company comfortably at the top.

Roy Gray, manager of quality control, reports directly to Young. He has held this position since he helped Young establish the company nine years ago.

Don Blue, production manager, also reports to Young. He has been with the firm seven years, having worked before that for one of the "big three" auto firms in production management.

Tim Green, supervisor of final assembly, reports to Don Blue. He came to Young Manufacturing at Blue's request, having worked with Blue previously at the same large auto firm.

*Douglas T. Hall, Donald D. Bowen, Roy J. Lewick, and Francine S. Hall, *Experiences in Management and Organizational Behavior*, Chicago, St. Clair Press, © 1975. Reprinted by permission of John Wiley & Sons, Inc.

Fran Gold, supervisor of subassembly, also works for Don Blue. Gold was promoted to this position two years ago. Prior to that time, Fran had gone through a year's management training program after receiving an MBA from a large urban university.

Today's Meeting

Bob Young has called a meeting with these four managers in order to attempt to solve some problems which have developed in meeting production schedules. Young must catch a plane to Detroit in half an hour; he has an appointment to negotiate a key contract which means a great deal to the future of Young Manufacturing. He has only 20 minutes to meet with his managers and still catch the plane. Young feels that swinging the Detroit deal is absolutely crucial to the future of the company.

The meeting will begin when you receive instructions from your instructor. It will last for exactly 20 minutes.

PROCEDURE

Step 1: 5 Minutes— Both Options

Review the Introduction.

Step 2: 5 Minutes— Both Options

The instructor will divide the class into five equal-sized groups and designate a meeting place for each group. The members of each of these first groups will all prepare to play the same character later in the role play—that is, the members of one preliminary group will all concentrate on Bob Young, another on Don Blue, a third on Roy Gray, and so on.

After the five groups have assembled, the instructor will tell each group where to find the role instructions for the role they are to play.

From this point on, until you receive instructions from the instructor to the contrary, you are not to share any details of your role with people playing other characters. Stay in the role until you are explicitly instructed to stop role playing. Do not let the other managers hear your planning or see your role instructions. Share your thoughts about how your character will feel or behave only with people who have been assigned the same role.

Step 3: 10 Minutes— Both Options

With the assistance of others assigned the same role, prepare to play the part of your character. Ask yourselves questions such as the following: What does it feel like to be this person? What does it feel like to be in the situation of this character? How would your character react to the other characters in the role play? What are the implications of your position in the organization for your behavior? What will you try to get out of the meeting? What outcomes will you try to avoid?

Talk about these questions and develop perspectives on the role with others assigned to the same role.

It is not necessary that everyone play the role in exactly the same way. The point is, given the role, how would you play it? What do the others assigned to this role think of your approach?

Step 4: 20 Minutes— Option One

Following the instructor's directions, meet in a five-person group with the four others assigned to play the roles of the other managers. Start the meeting only when told to proceed by the instructor. Remember: Stay in role even if you should happen to finish before 20 minutes have elapsed. At the end of the meeting, go on to Step 5, "Both Options," below.

Step 4: 20 Minutes— Option Two

During the preliminary meeting, members of the group select one person to play the role. The role players meet in an "office" set up in the front or middle of the room. Remember: Stay in role even if you are not chosen to play the part. Remain in role even after the end of the role play. The designated role players hold the meeting, ending in exactly 20 minutes.

Step 5: 5 Minutes— Both Options

Fill out the "End-of-Meeting Questionnaire." Stay in role while filling in the questionnaire. When finished, give the questionnaire to the instructor.

Step 6: 15 Minutes— Both Options

Discuss the exercise, using the "Discussion Questions" below. Stay in role until after question 1 has been discussed.

DISCUSSION QUESTIONS

1. How does Bob Young see the situation right now? What is the problem? The solution? How does Bob Young feel about the other characters? Have they helped or hindered Bob Young in trying to solve the problem? (Note: When all the Bob Youngs have shared

their views on these questions, the characters may finally drop their roles and share the role instructions they received).

2. What factors operated to create the kind of communication you saw in the Young Manufacturing Company? Can anything be done to improve communication?

3. Discuss the tabulated questionnaire data. What does it mean? Do the results in your group match those for other groups?

4. What are the central variables operating to affect communication at Young Manufacturing Company? What effect do they have?

5. What might Bob Young do, by way of a long-term solution, about the typical difficulties found in the Young Manufacturing Company?

END-OF-MEETING QUESTIONNAIRE

1. Bob Young in your group was played by:

2. The character you played was:

3. Indicate how your feelings about each of the other characters changed during the course of the meeting. Use the scale provided to describe the change in your feelings. Do not include your role in this rating.

   Scale: 1 = My esteem for him decreased substantially.
   2 = My esteem for him decreased somewhat.
   3 = No change.
   4 = My esteem for him increased somewhat.
   5 = My esteem for him increased substantially.

Characters	**Rating**
Bob Young	_____
Roy Gray	_____
Don Blue	_____
Tim Green	_____
Fran Gold	_____

4. Rate the group on the following dimensions. Circle the one number that comes closest to your perceptions of how the people in the group behaved.

Everyone was working at cross purposes.	1 2 3 4 5 6	Everyone was trying to solve the problem.
Most members kept their goals secret.	1 2 3 4 5 6	Most members revealed their goals.
I kept my goals secret.	1 2 3 4 5 6	I revealed my goals.

ROLE OF
BOB YOUNG,
PRESIDENT

As you enter the meeting, you are thoroughly annoyed that delivery dates are not being met consistently—and that when they are met there have been increasing customer complaints about defective parts. These problems are relatively new to Young Manufacturing, but you want to resolve them once and for all, today. If the company's reputation begins to slip, it could jeopardize the contracts you are negotiating for the firm.

You have not been able to determine what conditions have led to this problem, or who is responsible. In order to try to find out, you have called this meeting. You are determined to resolve the problem before you leave.

You have some private feelings about each of your subordinates—perceptions you have developed in day-to-day dealings over the years:

Roy Gray, manager of quality control, is an old personal friend as well as a long-time business associate. He has served the firm faithfully since its founding. Lately, however, he seems preoccupied, as though something were bothering him and taking his mind from his work. About three years ago, he was pushing Don Blue to hire his son, but Blue chose Fran Gold instead, which was a good move because Fran was obviously better qualified, what with an M.B.A. and all. Don and Roy still work well together, so it doesn't appear that there are any lingering hard feelings.

Don Blue, production manager, is probably your most valuable employee. He deserves the lion's share of credit for Young Manufacturing's success; he knows production, keeps costs down, maintains quality, and trains bright young workers. If the company expands, you are planning to make Don a vice-president and eventually to put him on the board of directors.

Tim Green, supervisor of final assembly, seems to be slipping lately. In the past, if there was a quality problem, final assembly could either rework the parts or catch the bad ones before shipping. Now, however, bad parts are getting through, and on top of it all, deliveries are running behind schedule. But Tim Green's men aren't working overtime, and—when the president strolled past the final assembly area yesterday—they didn't even look busy. People were horsing around as though they didn't have any work to do. You are wondering how long Don Blue will wait before he speaks to Green.

Fran Gold, supervisor of subassembly, looks like a bright young supervisor with a great future at Young Manufacturing. Don Blue has brought Fran along well, and although Fran occasionally makes the mistakes of impetuous youth, you are willing to put up with a few bad decisions if Fran continues to learn from them.

The meeting you are going to hold will last only 20 minutes. Begin by representing the problem to your subordinates. Be sure to get the situation straightened out before you have to leave to catch your plane. Find out what information your subordinates might have which is relevant to solving the problem before making any decisions or issuing any instructions.

ROLE OF DON BLUE, PRODUCTION MANAGER

What a fix! If Bob Young finds out about that defective gasket material, it will be my head—and probably Tim's and Fran's too. A million units of the crummy junk got through receiving inspection somehow, and 800,000 of them are still in the warehouse. I had a feeling that changing our ordering procedure was a mistake, but I wanted to reduce our inventory carrying costs. I never should have tried to cover up the situation after we saw what happened.

But what else could we do? Roy has always been Bob's buddy. If I blame Roy, it would be like doing in the crown prince. Roy has been with Young since they started the company, and they are thick as thieves on weekends, too.

And I didn't have much choice, anyway. When that shipment came in, we were down to less than two days' supply in subassembly. Fran Gold would have had to shut down completely if the lot had been rejected, and, at first it looked like Fran and Tim could adjust the assembly procedures fairly easily to compensate for the defects. A shutdown would have put Young Manufacturing out of business for good. Customers aren't going to wait for late deliveries anymore.

As it turned out, things were worse than I thought: Subassembly inspection began to find defects and held up several lots before they could get to Tim Green for final rework. Normally, I would work something out with Roy, but I can't do that this time. Roy hates Fran's guts, and he is just waiting for a chance to see Fran hung. This would be the perfect setup to make Fran the scapegoat. Roy never got over Fran's getting the job that Roy's kid wanted.

Well, somehow I'm going to have to keep the plant operating. It would sure help if Bob Young would ease up the pressure for output and learn to rely on me the way he does on Roy Gray.

ROLE OF ROY GRAY, MANAGER OF QUALITY CONTROL

That Fran Gold is the problem. Smart-aleck young college whiz kid, ambitious as hell, and sneaky to boot. If Bob Young had only listened to me a couple of years ago, he could have hired Al, my son, and had a faithful employee instead of this brash little sneak.

Blue was leaning toward Al, but he was afraid of what Young would say if he hired Al instead of Gold, just because Fran Gold had an M.B.A. and Al didn't. Don Blue is a good guy, generally able in his work, and, thanks to the exceptional quality control process we operate, has earned a reputation for running a high-quality plant. Don and I have gotten along well for several years, and I would like to keep a good working relationship with him. We solve most quality problems on our level without involving Bob Young, and that makes both of us look good.

But dammit! Why doesn't Don wake up to how Fran Gold is trying to push all the crappy work through inspection? I'd like to tell him, right now, but that would cause problems too. It would embarrass Don in front of Bob Young, and to make things even worse, Blue seems to think that Fran Gold can do no wrong. Every time Gold is criticized, Don blows his top and defends Fran to the bitter end.

ROLE OF FRAN GOLD, SUPERVISOR OF SUBASSEMBLY

Looks like the chickens are finally coming home to roost. This organization has been living on luck for nine years now, and now they are about to find out what a bunch of amateur managers they really are. Not one of them knows the first thing about inventory management, so here we are, stuck with a million defective gaskets and nothing we can do but try to rework them to where they will get by.

Don Blue made the first mistake in not ordering at the right time, then, when they got past Roy Gray's inspectors, ol' Blue compounded his error in not telling Bob Young what had happened. He asked Tim Green and me to rework them and try to slip them through inspection. Fat chance that Roy Gray would give us any help; if Roy wasn't so buddy-buddy with Young, he'd be pushing a broom in the shop instead of running quality control.

ROLE OF TIM GREEN, SUPERVISOR OF FINAL ASSEMBLY

Well, loyalty has always been my trademark. Maybe this time I've gone too far, though. Sure, I owe my job to Don Blue, and he has always been a good boss. He sure goofed on this one though. Don should have reordered the gaskets months and months ago. But no, to keep inventory costs down he waits till the last possible minute, orders a million units, and then gets defective material.

The plan to rework the material in subassembly and final assembly seemed like the only sensible solution when Don first proposed it. The problem turned out to be tougher than anyone had expected, but what the hell, it was better than letting the company go under. Too bad that Don and Roy Gray were in no position to tell Young what had happened. Guess they want to save their jobs, too, though.

Can't blame them. It would sure be a terrible time for me to be out of work. Martha is going back into the hospital for another operation next week (hope they find it this time!), and the college tuition bills for the twins have to be paid by the end of the month. Besides, it isn't easy for a 50-year-old guy to find a job like this one.

Well, guess I'll just have to continue to try to talk quality control into releasing the defective lots for rework so that something gets out the door. Hope we can begin to catch up on some of those delivery promises. Bob Young looks mad, and there's no telling what he's likely to do next. But then Bob Young seems to like to surround himself with mediocrity—look at these other clowns.

One of these days (maybe today!) Don Blue or Roy Gray is going to make a mistake so obvious that even Bob Young will know the difference. When that happens, they might be looking for a bright M.B.A. with some new ideas to run this show. Better play it cool and be ready when the time comes. Meanwhile, as long as I am in the clear, I'll just sit back and watch Don and Roy talk their way out of this one.

CASE 1
THE FISCAL CRISIS*

The end of the fiscal year brings pressure to many businesses—and Centennial Insurance was no exception. Randall Nesbitt, senior underwriter, was particularly harried this year. He was feeling extra pressure from the top because a new vice-presidential position had opened up, and he hoped to be considered for the job. This time, he wanted all the reports completed, on time, with no mistakes.

Randall was confident that his chief underwriters would be able to get their reports in on time, with the exception, perhaps, of Lois Landers. Lois had recently been promoted to chief underwriter of automobile policies and was still getting used to all the added responsibility. Randall had noted her progress and was pleased to see that some of the more experienced people were helping to explain things to her. Just to make certain she received all the help she needed in preparing the reports, he called Fred Olson, chief underwriter of life insurance, into his office.

"Fred, I'd like to ask for your help with something," Randall said. "I've been working with Lois Landers to teach her how all the fiscal reports are done, and she seems to be catching on. I would really appreciate it, though, if you would pay some attention to what she's doing, and see if she needs any help."

Fred was a little surprised at his boss's request. Automobile insurance was totally out of his area, but he told Randall he would see if there was anything he could do. Later, Fred asked Lois if she would like to have lunch with him the next day.

At lunch, Fred and Lois discussed the various reports that had to be completed, and Fred explained to Lois some easier ways to calculate costs than she had been using. It seemed to Fred that Lois was still confused about all the reports, and he told her to ask for help if she needed it.

As the week continued, the group got further involved in data gathering. Once she got over her initial shyness, Lois was asking Fred's help regularly—to the point where Fred was falling behind in his own work. Fred had a particularly heavy workload, but since he'd been in his position for five years now, he knew that he'd be able to get his reports in on time.

Thursday afternoon, Randall called a meeting of the department supervisors. At the meeting, Randall reminded his people that their reports were due on Monday and asked each of them to submit a progress report to him by the end of the day. Fred's report read that, with steady work, he saw little problem in completing his reports by Monday morning.

The next day, Randall visited Fred's office. "Excuse me, Fred," he said, "I received your progress report and I just wanted to congratulate you on handling the task so well."

"No problem," Fred answered.

"Yes. Well, I only wish Lois were doing as well with her reports as you are. I had really hoped you would help her out."

Fred began to sense trouble coming on. "Wait a minute, Randall. It's not fair to blame me for her mistakes. I helped her as much as I could, without neglecting my own work."

"I know," Randall replied. "It's just that Lois doesn't seem to be able to handle the reports. I'm sorry but I'm going to have to ask you to take on some of her load this weekend. Those reports have to be in on Monday, or it'll be my neck."

Fred was furious. Lois had been on his back all week with those reports, and he was not about to let her ruin his weekend too. "I'm sorry, Randall," he said. "If it's your neck that'll be in trouble without Lois's reports, then it's up to you to do them. I have plans for this weekend."

Consider these questions and ask your own:

1. Was Randall wrong in asking Fred to help Lois with the reports, considering that they were not his responsibility?

2. Should Randall complete Lois's reports himself? Or should he work with Lois on them?
3. How should Randall handle the situation with Fred?

CASE 2
A SIMPLE PROBLEM OF COMMUNICATION*

Chicago Chemicals is one of the three largest producers of chemicals in the United States. Due to the size of the organization and the nationwide scope of its activities, Chicago Chemicals relies on a regional system for recruiting future personnel. Each regional office is responsible for locating, screening, and hiring all persons to be employed in that area. Depending on the part of the country, this may include engineers, production staff, and marketing personnel, in addition to those persons employed in other supporting departments. The North Central Regional Office is responsible for recruiting in Wisconsin, Illinois, Michigan, Indiana, Ohio, and Pennsylvania. In addition to the North Central office, there are seven smaller district recruiting offices that in turn, employ sixty-seven full-time recruiters.

Thirty-five persons currently work in the regional office under the management of Richard Thompkins. The office itself is composed of four departments: administration and personnel; scheduling; advertising and publicity; and recruiting operations. (See the Organization Chart in Exhibit 1.)

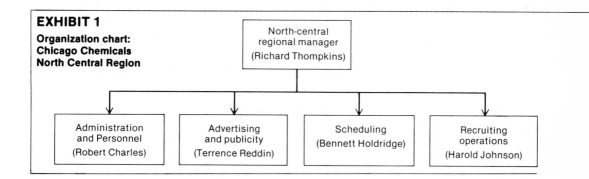

EXHIBIT 1

**Organization chart:
Chicago Chemicals
North Central Region**

North-central regional manager (Richard Thompkins)

| Administration and Personnel (Robert Charles) | Advertising and publicity (Terrence Reddin) | Scheduling (Bennett Holdridge) | Recruiting operations (Harold Johnson) |

*From Donald D. White and H. William Vroman, *Action in Organizations: Cases and Experiences in Organizational Behavior*. Copyright © 1977 by Holbrook Press, Inc., Boston. Reprinted with permission of Allyn and Bacon, Inc.

DEPARTMENTAL RESPONSIBILITIES

The director of the administration and personnel department is Robert Charles. The department is responsible for coordinating activities at the regional office, designing and printing all recruiting materials, and developing specific programs for all recruiting activities in the region. In addition, the department maintains a reporting and control system and initiates security checks on potential employees when necessary. The department is responsible also for selecting and training all recruiters and for assigning them to individuals.

The advertising and publicity department, under Terrence Reddin, directs the advertising and publicity program for the regional office in support of its recruiting function. Members of the department provide guidance and assist recruiters on special projects. Mr. Reddin has initiated a high school education information program and a widely based public relations program in the region. These two programs are not directly related to activities of the individual recruitment offices. An internal information program for the region has been initiated by the department.

The scheduling department is a small but powerful unit under the direction of Bennett Holdridge. Holdridge's department prepares, maintains, and monitors all contracts and contract agreements for office space, vehicle rental and maintenance, and other forms of intra/interregional transportation. The time frames for all recruitment trips must be cleared through the scheduling department. In addition, the scheduling department provides staff assistance to the regional director and to each recruitment office supervisor.

Work in the scheduling department often is exacting and requires a considerable amount of detailed paperwork. Staff members find it necessary to be thorough and deliberate when completing assigned tasks. An expansion at the Chicago office which took place one year ago drained off many of the "older hands" from the department. Therefore, existing members of the department average a little over two years' experience in their jobs. (See Exhibit 2.) The department received a rating of "excellent" in the last regional office evaluation. Some of the group norms are: Strive for accuracy. Pay attention to detail. Do the job right the first time.

Recruiting operations, under Harold Johnson, is responsible for a wide range of activities. Principally, it directs the development of plans and programs pertaining directly to personnel selection. The department, under Harold Johnson, establishes policies and carries out plans from the Chicago office to achieve personnel procurement objectives. Johnson's staff formulates and initiates recruitment programs and policies for the region. Evaluation of the performance of individual recruiters is handled by the department, and certain personnel programs, such as a recent incentive awards program and a safety program, were initiated there. It is not unusual for Johnson or individual department members to recommend additions, changes, and/or new programs to other departments or to Mr. Thompkins himself.

No serious problems have ever arisen between recruiting operations and the other departments. However, some members of other departments have complained of interference from the operations department. For example, all divisions are required to make staff assistance visits into the field. Recruiting operations often exhausts its travel money before the end of the quarter. The department claimed that there were numerous unanticipated changes in requirements. On the other hand, many persons outside the department suggested that the difficulty was the result of poor planning. Additional travel funds eventually were obtained from Chicago, and the matter was dropped.

A final function of the department is to analyze district operations and investigate "slow employment areas" or unduly large numbers of unsuccessful placements. Reports concerning these investigations are forwarded directly to the regional manager.

The members of the department averaged over eleven years' experience and each had served in the field for up to three years as a recruiter. (See Exhibit 2.) In fact, their appointment to the recruiting operations department was based on outstanding performance as recruiters. Department members take pride in their appointments. They are a cohesive group and often socialize off the job. Norms of the operations group include: Keep the recruiters in the field well informed. Delays hamper accomplishment.

PERSONNEL PROBLEMS AT HOME

In recent months, word of conflict between the recruiting operations and scheduling departments filtered up to Mr. Thompkins. Symptoms of conflict were numerous and varied. For example, he noted that members of each department seemed to avoid having conversations with one another whether on or off the job. On more than one occasion, he had observed a group of employees from one of the two departments quickly disperse when members of the other department entered the discussion. Moreover, activities of the two departments have been marked by a noticeable lack of communication. On three separate occasions during the last six months, directives from the operations department to local recruiters in the field have instructed those recruiters to move out of old facilities and into new ones before the scheduling department had finished the paperwork on the move. On another occasion, field offices were instructed by the operations department to have additional telephone lines installed in their offices before approval had been received from scheduling. Scheduling had an extremely difficult time justifying them after the fact, since expenditures of this nature were closely scrutinized by the Chicago office.

Richard Thompkins decided that steps must be taken to discover the underlying cause of the interdepartmental difficulties. After talking with members of each of the two departments on an informal basis, he began to make some notes to himself about the conversations. His findings were summarized as follows:

1. No one really wants to talk about the other department; most do not complain readily.
2. Members of each department believe that they are doing their job, but they claim that the other department hinders their work.
3. Attitudes of scheduling and personnel about the operations department are best summed up in a comment of the scheduling supervisor: "Those guys just seem to me to be pushy and self-centered. They're too much rah-rah and go-go-go. Who do they think they are, anyway?"
4. Operations department members describe the scheduling department as "slow as hell." "They never want to cooperate with us." "We really care about this recruiting operation, but those guys just don't seem to understand the importance of getting to these people (potential employees) the fastest with the most!"
5. A comment from Harold Johnson: "My men know the importance of their job, and I think they have real company loyalty. To tell you the truth, I can't say the same for the fellows in some of the other departments."

After reading over the list a couple of times, Thompkins leaned back in his chair and smiled knowingly. Later that day he called into his office the two department heads. He began his discussion by saying, "Bennett, Harold, I think we have a bit of a communication problem here. It's as simple as that."

EXHIBIT 2 **DEPARTMENT MEMBERS (RECRUITING OPERATIONS AND SCHEDULING)**

		Age	Years of Experience on the Job
RECRUITING OPERATIONS DEPARTMENT			
Department manager	Harold Johnson	52	18
Staff	Gerald Thomas	34	8
Staff	James Lawson	38	7
Staff	Betty Jennings	36	3
Staff	Richard Horn	44	14
Staff	Joe Sutton	46	11
Staff	Gene Maddox	46	14
Staff	Gordon Edwards	49	14
Staff	Tom Campbell	36	7
SCHEDULING DEPARTMENT			
Department manager	Bennett Holdridge	48	9
Staff	Gary Ford	22	New employee
Staff	John McGee	34	4
Staff	Robert Webb	35	3
Staff	Barbara Peterson	24	2
Staff	Jan Owens	21	New employee

ASSIGNMENT 1
COMMUNICATION LOG

Maintain a log of your communication activities at work or at school (conversations; phone calls; meetings; written materials read, sent, or received; etc.) for one week.

1. Specify the amount of time spent on each activity using the following scale:
   a. Less than 3 minutes
   b. 3 to 15 minutes
   c. 15 minutes to one hour
   d. Over 1 hour

2. Evaluate the information derived through your communication activities by using the following scale (more than one item can be checked):
   a. Useful

    b. Important
    c. Satisfactory
    d. Timely
    e. Accurate
    f. Excessive
    g. Not enough

ASSIGNMENT 2
LOAD

In spite of last semester's good resolutions to pace yourself better and manage your time more efficiently, you find yourself one week away from finals with a lot of work to do. You have two major papers to write, twenty-five books to read, and 200 pages of notes to go through to get ready for your finals.

You are taking a 15-hour course load and have attended class fairly regularly throughout the semester. You are working as a teacher's assistant ten hours a week and must continue work until the end of the semester.

During this last week, classes will be mostly review for finals in three of your courses, but new material will be presented in two others.

How will you cope with this load? Develop some strategies and evaluate their potential effectiveness.

ASSIGNMENT 3
INFORMATION LOAD IN ORGANIZATIONS

Interview several managers in an organization you are familiar with in terms of their level of information load. How do they manage their load? Their time? How related is each manager's load to other departments' output? Does overload in one department create overload in another? Underload? Summarize your findings and present them to the class.

DISCUSSION QUESTIONS

1. Is it true that preemptive messages (called "phatic communion" by Malinowski) are a waste of time and carry no information? Why does "small talk" have such a bad name in business circles when it seems to be used a lot?

2. Whose responsibility is it to get the message faithfully across: (*a*) the sender, writer, or speaker or (*b*) the listener or reader?

3. What are the effects of "load" on communication? Is underload a more difficult problem than overload? If you have to have one or the other in an organization you know, which would it be? Why?

4. Which kind of information flow seems to you to be easiest to carry out with fidelity: upward, downward, or lateral? What affects accuracy in each type?

5. What relation does structure in an organization have to the movement of messages? Are some structures better than others for communication effectiveness up, down, or across?

6. How are communication flow and organizational structure related? Give examples.

7. In organizations, information is used to monitor performance and control activities. Give specific examples to support this statement.

8. Give some common examples of problems with upward communication. How can they be overcome?

CHAPTER 6

MOTIVATION AND INFLUENCE

ACTIVITY 1
UNDERSTANDING WORK MOTIVATION—AGREE/DISAGREE LIST*

Purpose: To uncover the many practical dimensions of motivation.

Class size: Any size. Class to be divided into groups of six to eight members.
Time required: 30 minutes.
Materials needed: A copy of the Agree/Disagree List and a pencil for each participant.
Physical setting: Regular classroom.

PROCEDURE

Form groups of six to eight members. Go through each of the questions and draw upon your experience to accept or reject the statement.

Underlying each statement is an assumption about human nature. In some cases, the question implies that people are basically lazy. In other questions, the assumption is that people are essentially motivated and are only stopped from working hard by bad supervisory practices and too-simple jobs. Try and determine the assumption in each question and check them against your answer. Go through this process as a group. There is no need to reach consensus or to make a group decision on the items in the list. Simply share your views with one another and discuss them.

AGREE/DISAGREE LIST

Motivation

Please read each statement carefully and place an "X" by it to indicate whether you agree or disagree. Please mark only *one* answer for each statement.

	Agree	Disagree
1. Work that an employee considers interesting is an important source of motivation.	_____	_____
2. The opportunity to experience achievement on the job is an absolute necessity if a person is to be motivated at work.	_____	_____
3. To be a good supervisor, it is more important to be a good designer of work than to be skillful at human relations.	_____	_____

*From Donald D. White and H. William Vroman, *Action in Organizations: Cases and Experiences in Organizational Behavior.* Copyright © 1977 by Holbrook Press, Inc., Boston. Reprinted with permission of Allyn and Bacon, Inc.

	Agree	**Disagree**

4. Shorter work hours (for example, the four-day week) is one good motivational tool. _____ _____

5. Incentive pay plans, if tied directly to individual productivity, are an effective motivational tool. _____ _____

6. Improved two-way communications can greatly enhance job satisfaction of employees. _____ _____

7. Plans that push decision-making responsibility down in an organization will be met with resistance by most employees. _____ _____

8. Improved working conditions often affect employee attitudes significantly and contribute to their level of job satisfaction. _____ _____

9. Excessive absenteeism may be due to poor supervision, inadequate pay, or boring work, among other things. _____ _____

10. Elimination of the sources of job dissatisfaction, whatever they may be, will result in improved job satisfaction and motivation. _____ _____

11. A major responsibility of supervisors and managers is to motivate their people to achieve. _____ _____

12. In most cases, extending more decision making to employees involves more risk than gain. _____ _____

13. One effective way to reduce employee dissatisfaction is to see that people are informed about the reasons for decisions that affect them. _____ _____

14. Employees on routine or repetitive jobs are often more motivated and satisfied with their jobs if they understand how their work contributes to the overall company goals and objectives. _____ _____

15. One of the most common sources of dissatisfaction at work is personality clashes and disagreements. If these conflicts can be minimized, job dissatisfaction will be reduced but employee motivation and interest in the work will probably not improve. _____ _____

16. A supervisor's or manager's task is best defined as that of providing his people opportunities for achievement so that they will become motivated. _____ _____

17. Most employees would prefer to have their supervisors take over the more complex and difficult tasks in their jobs as long as their pay would not be reduced. _____ _____

18. Boring, uninteresting work may make some employees more demanding about such things as pay, working conditions, and holidays. _____ _____

19. Most employees would prefer not to have their work identified because they do not want to receive feedback on their errors. _____ _____

20. Indicators of status and/or longevity such as well-furnished offices, privileges of various kinds, and service awards are very important to some employees and provide a strong source of motivation and job satisfaction. _____ _____

ACTIVITY 2
ACTIVE LISTENING: A COMMUNICATION SKILLS PRACTICE*

Purposes: 1. To identify the emotional messages that are often hidden in communication.
          2. To gain practice in active listening skills.

Class size: Any size. Class is to be divided into dyads.
Time required: Approximately 1½ hours.
Materials needed: Two copies of the Active Listening Worksheet, one copy of the Active Listening Feedback Sheet, and a pencil for each participant.
Physical setting: An area large enough to allow each dyad to talk without disturbing the others.

PROCEDURE

1. The instructor gives a short lecture on active listening skills, emphasizing that people communicate much more than words or ideas and that strong feelings often lie behind words. The instructor then points out the confusion that often results from the difference between "think" and "feel" and talks about the nonverbal cues that can reveal feelings that are not verbalized.
2. The instructor divides the group into dyads and directs that each dyad is to identify one member as the employee and the other as the supervisor.
3. After giving a copy of the Active Listening Worksheet and a pencil to each participant, the instructor goes over the instructions and tells the participants that they will have twenty minutes in which to complete the activity.
4. After twenty minutes, the instructor calls time, distributes a second copy of the Active Listening Worksheet to each participant, and directs the participants to reverse roles and repeat the activity with different members playing the supervisor and the employee.
5. After twenty minutes, the instructor calls time, reassembles the total group, and gives each participant a copy of the Active Listening Feedback Sheet. The instructor goes over the suggested responses with the participants. Any questions are discussed by the group. (10 to 15 minutes.)
6. The instructor asks class members to write on the back of the Active Listening Feedback Sheets their observations about the

*Reprinted from J. W. Pfeiffer and J. E. Jones (eds.), *A Handbook of Structured Experiences for Human Relations Training,* vol. VII, University Associates, San Diego, Calif., 1970. Used with permission.

experience and conclusions about how active listening skills can help or hinder effective communication. (5 minutes.)

7. After encouraging the class to share their observations and reactions, the instructor leads a discussion on the application of active listening skills.

**ACTIVE
LISTENING
WORKSHEET**

Instructions

People communicate much more than words or ideas. Behind the words often lie feelings. These *feelings* often are communicated through nonverbal means, even while conflicting *ideas* are communicated verbally. Trying to look and listen for feelings, write an active listening response for each situation and message on this sheet.

The employee will begin by reading statement 1, and the supervisor will give an active listening response. The supervisor will then read statement 2, and the employee will give an active listening response. This process will continue, with the employee reading all odd-numbered statements and the supervisor reading all even-numbered statements.

As each member gives a response, it should be noted in the space provided.

Example

Situation and Message

The supervisor sets a policy that he or she will sign all letters.
The employee says: "I want to sign my own letters. I wrote them, didn't I?"

Active-Listening Response

The supervisor responds: "You feel frustrated (resentful) when you are not allowed to sign letters that you have written."

Situation and Message

1. The supervisor says a report is not thorough enough.
The employee says: "Now I have to write this report over. You never tell me what you expect until it is written."

2. The supervisor must meet a report deadline.
The supervisor says: "We have got to be better organized."

3. The employee is not implementing the supervisor's ideas.
The employee says: "I was on this job long before you came here. I don't need you to tell me how to do it.

4. The regular staff meeting never starts on time.
The supervisor says: "I get tired of waiting for some people every week before we can start these meetings."

Active-Listening Response

The supervisor responds:

The employee responds:

The supervisor responds:

The employee responds:

Situation and Message	Active-Listening Response
5. The supervisor has just made a project-team assignment. The employee says: "I don't want to work with Bill on any more assignments. He never meets his deadlines."	The supervisor responds:
6. The employee has not turned in the last two monthly progress reports. The supervisor says: "Can't you be as professional as the rest of the staff and turn in your report on time?"	The employee responds:
7. The supervisor has initiated a new work procedure. The employee says: "We tried something like this three years ago and it didn't work then."	The supervisor responds:
8. The supervisor recognizes that some employees' talk is so loud it is interfering with other employees' writing a report. The supervisor says: "Can't you be more considerate while others are trying to work?"	The employee responds:
9. The supervisor has passed on a change in work priorities from the top office. The employee says: "You give us too much unscheduled work. I never can get it all done."	The supervisor responds:
10. The employee has refused to work overtime on a project. The supervisor says: "Young people today are lazy!"	The employee responds:

ACTIVE LISTENING FEEDBACK SHEET

This sheet provides some possible responses for each situation; it is not intended to identify "correct" responses. A response may well be influenced by the way in which you perceive the situation and the intonation that accompanies the verbal message you receive. In some of these situations, the speaker appears to be more defensive than in others. If the listener resists evaluative statements or solutions, active listening and observation skills can be used effectively to deal with such interactions.

SAMPLE ANSWERS

1. *a.* You are uncertain and puzzled about what is expected.
   b. You probably feel frustrated or discouraged about revising this report.
2. *a.* You are concerned about finishing the report by the deadline.
   b. You are feeling bogged down by all the work.

3. *a.* You are frustrated when I offer suggestions because of your experience with this job.

   b. You think that I distrust you when I give ideas on how to do your job.

4. *a.* You feel irritated that our meetings always start late.

   b. You are anxious to start our meetings on time.

5. *a.* You feel that Bill will not do his share if he is assigned to this project.

   b. You feel disappointed that I did not consult with you before the assignment.

   c. You feel afraid that your performance might be jeopardized as a member of this team.

6. *a.* You think that I am not responsible when I do not turn in my progress reports.

   b. You are irritated when my progress reports are late.

7. *a.* You are concerned that this new procedure will not work.

   b. You feel impatient when procedures that failed once are implemented again.

8. *a.* You are angry that our talking is disturbing others.

   b. You are afraid that our talking will keep others from doing their work.

9. *a.* You feel frustrated when your work load appears to change constantly.

   b. You feel discouraged because there is too much to do.

10. *a.* You are angry because you think that young people today are not as dedicated as you are.

    b. You feel discouraged about the lack of interest in this project.

ACTIVITY 3
WIN AS MUCH AS YOU CAN*

Purposes: To compare cooperative and competitive techniques in problem solving within the context of intra- and intergroup relations. To illustrate the impact of win-lose situations.

Class size: Any size. Class is divided into groups of eight students and subdivided into dyads.
Time required: Between 45 minutes and 1 hour.
Materials needed: A Win-as-Much-as-You-Can Tally Sheet for each dyad; pencils.
Physical setting: A room large enough to accommodate clusters of eight sitting in the formation shown in Figure 6-1.

PROCEDURE

1. The class is divided into groups, or clusters, of eight. Any students who are not in a group will be process observers and will help the instructor throughout the exercise.
2. Each cluster is subdivided into dyads.
3. Each student is instructed to study the Tally Sheet for 3 minutes. At the end of the 3 minutes, the dyads are asked to share their understandings of the exercise with each other.
4. The instructor reads aloud the following directions:
   a. The title of this exercise is "Win as Much as You Can." You are to keep this goal in mind during the next twenty minutes.
   b. There are three key rules:
      (1) You are not to confer with other members of your cluster unless specifically given permission to do so. This prohibition applies to nonverbal as well as verbal communication.
      (2) Each dyad must agree upon a single choice for each round.
      (3) Each dyad must ensure that the other members of your cluster do not know your choice until you are instructed to reveal it.
   c. There are 10 rounds to this exercise. During each round you will have 1 minute to mark your choice for the round. You may now mark your choice for round 1. Remember the rules.
      (1) (After the lapse of 1 minute.) If you have not marked your choice, please raise your hand. (Make sure that everybody has completed the task before you go on, but keep them moving.)
      (2) Share your decision with the other members of your cluster.
      (3) Score according to the chart on the tally sheet.

*Developed by William Gellerman in J. W. Pfeiffer and J. E. Jones, *Handbook of Structured Experiences for Human Relations Training*, Vol. II, University Associates, 1970. Reproduced with permission.

    d. Continue the exercise as follows:
       (1) You have one minute to mark your decision for round 2.
       (2) Has everyone finished?
       (3) Share and score.
    e. Continue the exercise in round 3 as before.
    f. Continue the exercise in round 4 as before.
    g. Round 5 is a bonus round. You will note that the tally sheet indicates that all amounts won or lost will be multiplied by 3. Before I ask you to mark your choice for this round, I will allow you to discuss this exercise with the other members of your cluster. After the group discussion, you and your partner will have one minute to discuss your decision as before. You will have three minutes for group discussion. (Stop discussion after 3 minutes.) You and your partner now have one minute to mark your decision for round 5. Remember the rules are now in effect. (After the lapse of 1 minute.) Has everyone finished? Share and score.
    h. Do round 6 and 7 as you did rounds 1 to 4.
    i. Round 8 is the same as round 5 except that the bonus value has now increased from 3 to 5 times par.
    j. Do round 9 as you did rounds 1 to 4 and rounds 6 and 7.
    k. Round 10 is the same as rounds 5 and 8 except that the bonus value has now increased to 10 times par.
    l. Compute the net score as a cluster from the four dyadic scores. For example: +18, −21, +6, and +2 = +5, etc. The maximum possible score for each cluster is +100 (e.g., +25, +25, +25, and +25, if they all choose "Y," the collaborative option on each round).

5. The instructor opens a discussion of the process and its implications. The key points to be raised are:
    a. Does the "you" in "Win as much as you can" mean you as a dyad or you as a cluster?
    b. Competition versus collaboration models are considered in relation to how the cluster's net score compares to a possible net score of 100.
    c. How does this exercise relate to other intra- and intergroup situations?

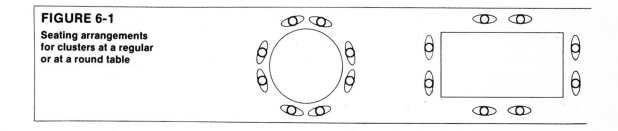

FIGURE 6-1

Seating arrangements for clusters at a regular or at a round table

FIGURE 6-2

Win-as-Much-as-You-Can Tally Sheet

Instructions: For ten successive rounds you and your partner will choose either an X or a Y. Each round's payoff depends on the pattern of choices made in your cluster.

PAYOFF SCHEDULE

4 X's	Lose $1 each
3 X's	Win $1 each
1 Y	Lose $3
2 X's	Win $2 each
2 Y's	Lose $2 each
1 X	Win $3
3 Y's	Lose $1 each
4 Y's	Win $1 each

You are to confer with your partner in each round and make a *joint decision*. In rounds 5, 8, and 10 you and your partner may first confer with the other dyads in your cluster before making your joint decision, as before.

SCORECARD

	Round	Your Choice (Circle One)		Cluster's Pattern of Choices		Payoff	Balance
	1	X	Y	___X	___Y		
	2	X	Y	___X	___Y		
	3	X	Y	___X	___Y		
	4	X	Y	___X	___Y		
Bonus Round: **Payoff × 3**	5	X	Y	___X	___Y		
	6	X	Y	___X	___Y		
	7	X	Y	___X	___Y		
Bonus Round: **Payoff × 5**	8	X	Y	___X	___Y		
	9	X	Y	___X	___Y		
Bonus Round: **Payoff × 10**	10	X	Y	___X	___Y		

INSTRUMENT 1
ASSERTIVENESS INVENTORY*

The following questions will be helpful in assessing your assertiveness. Be honest in your responses. All you have to do is draw a circle around the number that describes you best. For some questions the assertive end of the scale is at 0, for others at 4. Key: 0 means *no* or *never*; 1 means *somewhat* or *sometimes*; 2 means *average*; 3 means *usually* or *a good deal*; and 4 means *practically always* or *entirely*.

1. When a person is highly unfair, do you call it to his or her attention?   0   1   2   3   4
2. Do you find it difficult to make decisions?   0   1   2   3   4
3. Are you openly critical of others' ideas, opinions, behavior?   0   1   2   3   4
4. Do you speak out in protest when someone takes your place in line?   0   1   2   3   4
5. Do you often avoid people or situations for fear of embarrassment?   0   1   2   3   4
6. Do you usually have confidence in your own judgment?   0   1   2   3   4
7. Do you insist that your spouse or roommate take on a fair share of household chores?   0   1   2   3   4
8. Are you prone to "fly off the handle"?   0   1   2   3   4
9. When a salesman makes an effort, do you find it hard to say "no" even though the merchandise is not really what you want?   0   1   2   3   4
10. When a latecomer is waited on before you are, do you call attention to the situation?   0   1   2   3   4
11. Are you reluctant to speak up in a discussion or debate?   0   1   2   3   4
12. If a person has borrowed money (or a book, garment, thing of value) and is overdue in returning it, do you mention it?   0   1   2   3   4
13. Do you continue to pursue an argument after the other person has had enough?   0   1   2   3   4
14. Do you generally express what you feel?   0   1   2   3   4
15. Are you disturbed if someone watches you at work?   0   1   2   3   4
16. If someone keeps kicking or bumping your chair in a movie or a lecture, do you ask the person to stop?   0   1   2   3   4
17. Do you find it difficult to keep eye contact when talking to another person?   0   1   2   3   4
18. In a good restaurant, when your meal is improperly prepared or served, do you ask the waiter/waitress to correct the situation?   0   1   2   3   4
19. When you discover merchandise is faulty, do you return it for an adjustment?   0   1   2   3   4
20. Do you show your anger by name calling or obscenities?   0   1   2   3   4

21.	Do you try to be a wallflower or a piece of the furniture in social situations?	0	1	2	3	4
22.	Do you insist that your landlord (landlady, mechanic, repairman, etc.) make repairs, adjustments, or replacements which are his or her responsibility?	0	1	2	3	4
23.	Do you often step in and make decisions for others?	0	1	2	3	4
24.	Are you able to express love and affection openly?	0	1	2	3	4
25.	Are you able to ask your friends for small favors or help?	0	1	2	3	4
26.	Do you think you always have the right answer?	0	1	2	3	4
27.	When you differ with a person you respect, are you able to speak up for your own viewpoint?	0	1	2	3	4
28.	Are you able to refuse unreasonable requests made by friends?	0	1	2	3	4
29.	Do you have difficulty complimenting or praising others?	0	1	2	3	4
30.	If you are disturbed by someone smoking near you, can you say so?	0	1	2	3	4
31.	Do you shout or use bullying tactics to get others to do as you wish?	0	1	2	3	4
32.	Do you finish other people's sentences for them?	0	1	2	3	4
33.	Do you get into physical fights with others, especially strangers?	0	1	2	3	4
34.	At family meals, do you control the conversation?	0	1	2	3	4
35.	When you meet a stranger, are you the first to introduce yourself and begin a conversation?	0	1	2	3	4

INSTRUMENT 2
ASSERTIVENESS CHECKLIST

Answer each of the following questions "Yes" or "No." To be more precise, you might use the terms "Always," "Often," "Sometimes," and "Never." Then circle the answers that indicate that you have a difficulty in assertion; try to write a sentence after those circled answers which explains your problems with assertion in your own words.

1. Do you buy things you don't really want because it is difficult to say no to the salesman? _____
2. Do you hesitate to return items to a store even when there is a good reason to do so? _____
3. If someone talks aloud during a movie, play, or concert, can you ask him or her to be quiet? _____
4. Can you begin a conversation with a stranger? _____
5. Do you have trouble maintaining conversations in social situations? _____
6. Do people act as if they find you boring? _____
7. Are you satisfied with your social life? _____
8. When a friend makes an unreasonable request, are you able to refuse? _____
9. Are you able to ask favors and make requests of your friends? _____
10. Can you criticize a friend? _____
11. Can you praise a friend? _____
12. When someone compliments you, do you know what to say? _____

13. Is there someone with whom you can share your intimate feelings?   _____
14. Would you rather bottle up your feelings than make a scene?   _____
15. Are you satisfied with your work habits?   _____
16. Do people tend to exploit you or push you around?   _____
17. Can you be open and frank in expressing both tender and angry feelings
    to men?   _____
18. Can you be open and frank in expressing both tender and angry feelings
    to women?   _____
19. Do you find it difficult to make or accept dates?   _____
20. Are you spontaneous during sex play and intercourse?   _____
21. Are you satisfied with your progress in your career?   _____
22. Do you find it difficult to upbraid a subordinate?   _____
23. Are you (or would you be) a good model of assertiveness for your
    own child?   _____

CASE
THE PLAN THAT BACKFIRED*

Danny had been thinking for quite some time now that he should put some of the management principles he had been reading about into practice in his department. That night, he finally decided to stay late and work on a job enrichment plan for everyone on the staff. The way clerical services was presently set up, each employee had one specific task to do. Whether it was typing, filing, collating, processing orders, or covering the switchboard; each employee was considered on an equal level, and salary differed according to seniority rather than job.

Danny hoped that by reassigning responsibility so everyone would work on all the different jobs instead of doing the same thing constantly, he would eliminate some of the tedium the staff felt, making it a happier and thus more productive group.

The next day he called a meeting of his six-person staff. Laura, Bert, Sal, Ellen, Toby, and Morton said very little when he told them of the new work arrangement, but Danny attributed that to their surprise about the new system. He encouraged them to ask him for any help they might need, and tried to win their support for the job redesign.

During the next few days, clerical services worked according to the new plan. Except for an occasional difference of opinion about who would type what letter, the staff seemed to be adjusting very well to the new work arrangement, and Danny was extremely pleased with how things were working out. He was just considering writing a memo to his boss, Timothy Lesser, about his job enrichment program,

*Reprinted by permission of the publisher, from "Let's Get Down to Cases," *Supervisory Management*, July 1979, © 1979 by AMACOM, a division of American Management Association. All rights reserved.

when Bert, Laura, and Morton appeared at his door. "What can I do for you?" Danny asked.

"We want to talk to you about this new work system," Bert replied. "We don't think it's fair that you ask us to do more work but continue to pay us the same salary."

Danny hadn't counted on this happening, but still he didn't panic. After all, he had a reasonable explanation. "Bert, I thought all of you understood the purpose of the new system. You aren't being asked to do more work—just different work. I had hoped it would help make your jobs more interesting—make the day go quicker."

"Are you serious?" asked Bert sarcastically. "What makes you think we care whether our jobs are 'interesting' or not? If you really want to help us, why don't you get us more money! Money is what we happen to be interested in, Danny."

"Do you three know if Sal, Ellen, and Toby feel the same way as you do about this?" Danny asked.

"Of course they do," said Morton. "We all feel that this new program of yours is just another way to get more work out of us for the same pay. We think we should either go back to the old system or be given more money."

Danny was literally speechless. How could he tell people that they couldn't find satisfaction in their work if they were interested only in their paychecks? The management books he'd been reading hadn't told him what he should do about something like this. The case studies he had read always ended with more satisfied, more productive workers. Now what was he to do? Was his carefully planned job enrichment program a waste of time?

1. Should Danny abandon his new plan and go back to the old work system?
2. How could Danny have introduced the job enrichment program so that his staff would have felt more positive about the change?
3. Can Danny now convince his staff that the enrichment program is really for its benefit? How?

ASSIGNMENT 1
INTERVIEW A

Interview a professional person (physician, lawyer, psychiatrist, psychologist, social worker, teacher, executive, administrator, policeman, etc.) who spends a great amount of time talking and listening to people. In the course of your interview try and find out this person's view on the importance of listening in his or her job, the kinds of problems that result from poor listening in this field, and some of the ways the problems can be overcome. Take notes and report your findings to the class.

ASSIGNMENT 2
INTERVIEW B

Interview a manager or supervisor about the motivation techniques he or she finds effective on the job. What conclusions do you draw about the manager's perceptions and assumptions about employees?

ASSIGNMENT 3
MEANING OF WORK

What is the meaning of work for you? What other values do you hold that might conflict with your work values? How do you plan to resolve the potential conflicts? Write a two-page essay summarizing your thoughts on these questions.

DISCUSSION QUESTIONS

1. Compare Maslow's hierarchy of needs with McClelland's three basic motives which make people perform. Does one of these systems reflect your own ideas of what motivates people more accurately than the other?
2. Do you agree with Maccoby's ideas that character and emotional attitudes are strong determinants in motivation? Do his four types fit your own experience with managers?
3. If people will make their own choices of which goals to attempt, how do they know about the rules for getting there and what the payoff will be? Is communication the important factor in articulating the potential rewards and the means of achieving them? Can you motivate toward goals without some form of communication?
4. Discuss the tendencies to trust which you have observed in yourself or some other person. If you do not trust, is developing some defensive strategies the only option?
5. What is your opinion of leveling or assertiveness as a useful style for the manager? Is leveling or assertiveness always the best means of dealing with interpersonal problems or solving external issues? Explain.

CHAPTER 7

LEADERSHIP AND POWER

ACTIVITY 1
TRADING CARDS: A POWER SIMULATION*

Purposes: 1. To experience the consequences of conflict between group goals and goals of individual members.
  2. To experience intergroup and intragroup competition.
  3. To identify patterns of competition and cooperation among group members in a stressful situation.
  4. To identify how group and individual strategies affect the group's attainment of a goal.

Class size: Ten to twenty-eight. Class is to be divided into two to four equal-sized groups of at least five members each.
Time required: Between 1½ and 2 hours.

Materials needed: 1. A copy of the Trading Cards Rule Sheet for each participant.
  2. A copy of the Trading Cards Score Sheet for each group.
  3. One set of five trading cards (one yellow, one green, one pink, one blue, and one white) in a large envelope for each participant. (Index cards or equal-sized pieces of colored construction paper can be used.)
  4. A name tag containing a name or a geometric symbol for each member of each group. (Each group's name or symbol is different from those of the other groups.)
  5. Newsprint and a felt-tipped marker.

Physical setting: A large, open area, allowing free movement of all participants.

PROCEDURE

1. The instructor tells the participants that structured experiences can be used to evoke real responses to simulated situations, and encourages them to focus their awareness on their behaviors and feelings in the forthcoming experience.
2. Participants are arbitrarily divided into two to four equal groups of at least five persons each. Each member is given a large envelope containing five trading cards and a name tag showing the name or symbol of his group. Members are instructed to wear their tags on their chests.
3. After giving each participant a copy of the Trading Cards Rule Sheet, the instructor goes over the rules and explains that there are two kinds of winners, individual and group. The individual winner is the person or persons whose cards have the highest point value at the end of the final round of play. The group with the highest total of individual scores at the end of the final round of play is the group winner.

* Reprinted from J. W. Pfeiffer and J. E. Jones (eds.), *A Handbook of Structured Experiences for Human Relations Training*, Vol. VII, University Associates, La Jolla, Calif., 1970.

4. The instructor gives a copy of the Trading Cards Score Sheet to each group.

5. The instructor announces the beginning of the first six rounds of trading. (5 minutes.)

6. At the end of the round, the instructor announces a 5-minute scoring period.

7. Five more rounds are conducted, with a scoring period after each round. After the scoring of rounds 2 and 3, the instructor announces that the teams have five minutes in which to discuss their strategies for the next round. After the scoring period for round 4, the instructor announces that groups *may* consult with each other for five minutes if they wish to do so.

8. At the end of the final round, the teams' final totals are tabulated. Each team reports its total score, its individual high score, and the name of the team's individual winner. These are listed on newsprint by the instructor.

9. The instructor gives a short lecture on power and competition and their impact on team functioning (fifteen minutes), and then asks the participants to discuss how they feel about the experience. The participants should discuss their strategies and styles of interaction, including which behaviors (cooperative or competitive) got them what they wanted, which behaviors did not, and what effect this had on the groups. The instructor asks the participants how they decided whom they would trade with and what they would trade. After the discussion, learnings from the experience are summarized and applied to other situations.

TRADING CARDS RULE SHEET

Trading is governed by the following rules:

1. Each trading round lasts 5 minutes.

2. Participants who wish to bargain must hold hands.

3. There is absolutely no talking except while holding hands.

4. Once players join hands, a legal trade must be made, i.e., two cards of different colors must be swapped.

5. Only one-card-for-one-card transactions are legal.

6. Players may indicate that they choose not to trade by folding their arms across their chests.

7. A player may not show his or her cards to anyone, with the exception of the one card being traded to another player.

Scoring

At the end of each round, each team gathers to calculate its individual and team scores. The score is the total number of points for the cards actually held by each player.

> Yellow card = 50 points
> Green card = 25 points
> Pink card   = 15 points
> Blue card   = 10 points
> White card = 5 points

In addition, bonus points are awarded for holding three or more cards of the same color.

> Three cards of same color = 10 points
> Four cards of same color = 20 points
> Five cards of same color   = 30 points

For example, the score of a hand of three blue cards and two yellow cards is 140 points:

> 3 blues @ 10   =   30
> 2 yellows @ 50 = 100
> Bonus   =   10
> _____
>   140

TRADING CARDS SCORE SHEET

Group symbol: _____

Individual Members	ROUNDS					
	1	2	3	4	5	6
1	_____	_____	_____	_____	_____	_____
2	_____	_____	_____	_____	_____	_____
3	_____	_____	_____	_____	_____	_____
4	_____	_____	_____	_____	_____	_____
5	_____	_____	_____	_____	_____	_____
Totals						

ACTIVITY 2
TINKER TOYS: STYLES OF LEADERSHIP

Purposes: 1. To demonstrate different styles of leadership:
    a. Autocratic
    b. Laissez-faire (permissive)
    c. Democratic
    2. To develop comparisons among participants on how groups respond to those styles in terms of:
    a. Productivity—doing a good job; the task itself
    b. Satisfaction—feeling good about the job and others
    c. Leader relationship—how the group feels about the leader's effectiveness

Class size: Any size. Ideally, class should be divided into at least three competing groups of about five to seven members each.
Time required: Between 1½ and 2 hours, including discussion time.
Materials needed: One large set of Tinker Toys for each two groups, divided so that the two groups have approximately the same numbers of spools, sticks of various lengths, and accessory parts. A Product Judging Sheet and a Participation Reaction Sheet for each participant. Pencils. Chalkboard or large sheet of paper.
Physical Setting: A large table allowing each group to sit close together so they can work together on construction.

OPTIONS

With a small class of fewer than fifteen persons, the exercise should be carried out as suggested in Procedure A. With larger classes of fifteen or more, Procedure B should be used. Both situations will generate discussion of the different outcomes from different leadership styles, although the small-class exercise has a more limited competitive experience.

PROCEDURE A (SMALL CLASS)

The instructor serves as leader. A collection of Tinker Toy pieces large enough to allow construction of a fairly large item, such as a tower, is placed in the center of each of two large tables.

Half the group sits at one table, half at the other table. Each table will be instructed in turn. The two tables should be far enough apart so they cannot easily hear or see each other. The instructor tells table 1 to wait until he or she finishes with table 2.

The instructor addresses table 2, adopting a laissez-faire attitude, "You have a few minutes to build some kind of construction which makes use of different pieces. Final products will be judged on the bases of height, stability, and beauty. That's all the help I'll give you, and you are on your own. I'll let you know when time is up and we will judge the results. You may work as a group in any way you want to."

The instructor then goes to table 1 and says, "You will build a tower from the Tinker Toys according to my specific instructions. All of you will work together. When we get done, we will judge whether yours is better than the other group's—based on height, stability, and beauty. Now listen carefully; I want no questions or argument. Make a square of the pieces, using four knobs and four of the blue pieces. On opposite corners place the longer green pieces, each with a knob on top of it. Link them together with a piece of the appropriate length."

The instructor continues to give autocratic orders, noting sharply the errors which some group members make and suggesting that if members would only listen carefully, they could make a better construction. After about 10 minutes, the instructor calls time on both tables and asks the students to respond individually to the questions on the Participation Reaction Sheet.

When the individual responses are completed, each table is asked to compute average ratings. The class then rates the products on the Product Judging Sheet. The ratings are tallied on a chalkboard or a large chart on the wall.

Discuss the implications of the choices and the reactions of both tables. (Discussion questions can be adapted from the list following Procedure B.)

PROCEDURE B (LARGE CLASS)

The class is divided into at least three groups of five to seven members, and a leader is selected for each group. The instructor tells each leader how to conduct the group task. If there are three groups, one leader will use an autocratic style, one a laissez-faire or permissive style, and one a democratic style. If there are more than three groups, the styles of leadership should be distributed as evenly as possible. Experience has shown that dramatic effects are achieved by comparing the autocratic and permissive styles. If there are four groups, two should be autocratic, one permissive, and one democratic. If there are five groups, two should be autocratic, two permissive, and one democratic. If there are six groups, two should be autocratic, two permissive, and two democratic.

Here are typical instructions to give the different group leaders:

1. *Advice to autocratic leader:* You will determine what the group will do in putting together the Tinker Toy project. Get the attention of the group and tell them they must follow directions exactly. The goal is to build a tower which will be judged highest, most stable, and most beautiful by a student vote. Give very specific instructions. Do not hesitate to criticize anyone who gets out of line or fails to listen or follow directions. Accept no questions, suggestions, or argument. It is your model they will build, and any difficulties they have are their own fault.

2. *Advice to permissive leader:* You will let the group work completely on its own in putting together the Tinker Toy project. Simply tell them that the goal is to make a construction as tall, stable, and beautiful as possible in a short time. Do not make suggestions or even respond to questions or suggestions from group members. If anyone asks you a direct question, the answer should always be, "Whatever you want to do will be fine." Do not amplify the description beyond saying that the final judgment will be made on the bases of height, stability, and beauty. It is the group's model entirely and should not reflect any of your ideas as leader.

3. *Advice to democratic leader:* Your job will be to help the group make democratic decisions on putting the Tinker Toy project together. Explain that they are in competition with the other groups to make the best tower, and the members will work together. Do all you can to stimulate interaction among group members and to have them share ideas and efforts. When ideas come up or suggestions are made, help the group react either by taking a vote or by getting a consensus on how to proceed. The finished product should be a result of the group's combined and cooperative efforts guided by your leadership.

JUDGING AND REACTIONS

At the end of the building session, the constructions will be placed together and each member will fill out a Product Judging Sheet. The combined totals will be scored and the results entered on a Scoring Form copied on a chalkboard or a large sheet of paper on the wall. Each member will also be asked to fill out a Participation Reaction Sheet. These will be tallied by each group and the results posted on the Scoring Form for everyone to see.

PRODUCT JUDGING SHEET

Using a scale of 1 (poor) to 10 (superior), give each product a grade.

	Group 1	Group 2	Group 3	Group 4	Group 5	Group 6
Height	_____	_____	_____	_____	_____	_____
Stability	_____	_____	_____	_____	_____	_____
Beauty	_____	_____	_____	_____	_____	_____
Total	_____	_____	_____	_____	_____	_____

PARTICIPATION REACTION SHEET

Circle the appropriate number.

Not Satisfied   **Highly satisfied**

My reaction to the leader:

| 1 | 2 | 3 | 4 | 5 | 6 | 7 | 8 | 9 | 10 |

My reaction to my own participation:

| 1 | 2 | 3 | 4 | 5 | 6 | 7 | 8 | 9 | 10 |

My reaction to my group's product:

| 1 | 2 | 3 | 4 | 5 | 6 | 7 | 8 | 9 | 10 |

SCORING FORM

	Group 1	Group 2	Group 3	Group 4	Group 5	Group 6
Total Product Points	_____	_____	_____	_____	_____	_____
Reaction to Leader	_____	_____	_____	_____	_____	_____
Reaction to Participation	_____	_____	_____	_____	_____	_____
Reaction to Product	_____	_____	_____	_____	_____	_____
Leader Style (Autocratic, Democratic, Laissez-faire)	_____	_____	_____	_____	_____	_____

DISCUSSION

Based on the results of the scoring and recorded data, the instructor begins discussion by asking for student analysis of the leadership styles. This is the time to clarify the different styles by reviewing the instructions and to ask each group how they perceived the leader—whether the laissez-faire leader was appropriately permissive, the autocratic leader properly imperious, the democratic leader sufficiently egalitarian.

Other discussion topics could include:

1. How did the leaders feel about their roles? Were the roles easy to assume?
2. In judging the products, did people always vote for their own? How did their feelings about the task and the leader affect the judging of the constructions themselves?
3. A leader can affect the performance of a group. What seemed to

occur in these groups which could be related to leadership style?

4. A leader can affect the satisfaction felt by group members. What reactions by the group members can be traced to feelings generated by the different leadership styles?

5. Which groups felt best about their products? Can they tell why?

6. Which groups felt best about their own personal contributions to the construction task? Can they tell why?

7. Which groups did the "best" job of building? Why?

8. Which groups seemed most satisfied with themselves and their leader? Why?

9. If the groups had had more time to get to know one another and had not had the time pressure, would they have behaved differently?

10. If the groups had had more time to do the job, how would they have reacted to the various leadership styles? Would the leaders have acted the same way all during the time a group was together if they had been a longer-term group?

11. What did you learn in this exercise that is applicable to other situations?

12. What set of "general rules" about leadership styles can you develop as a result of this exercise?

ACTIVITY 3
COOPERATIVE SQUARES

Purposes: 1. To analyze certain aspects of cooperation in solving group problems.
2. To become more sensitive to how your behavior may help or hinder group problem-solving.

Class size: Any size. Class is to be divided into groups of five members. Extra students will function as observers.
Time required: Thirty to 35 minutes.
Materials needed: One set of cooperative squares per group. (Instructions on how to make the sets are included in the instructor's manual.)
Physical setting: Regular classroom with tables far enough apart to allow groups of five to work together without too much interference from other groups.

The Cooperative Squares exercise may sound somewhat elaborate, but it is worth the effort. This exercise has been used for many years in psychological experiments and in group work. It is perhaps one of the most dramatic ways to demonstrate covert attitudes and levels of sensitivity.

PROCEDURE

1. The class is divided into groups of five and instructed to sit at tables or on the floor. The members of each group should be sitting close to one another, and the groups should be fairly far apart.
2. A set of five envelopes containing the squares and an instruction sheet are distributed to each group. The instructor should state clearly that the envelopes are to be opened only on signal.
3. Discuss with the class the meaning of "cooperation." The groups should then discuss what is essential for successful group cooperation. The instructor may list suggested requirements for cooperation on the board, and should then introduce the Cooperative Squares exercise by telling the groups that they will have a chance to test their suggestions. The requirements for cooperation listed may include:
   a. Each individual must understand the problem to be solved.
   b. Everyone needs to believe he or she can help and contribute to the solution.
   c. Each individual should be aware of the potential contributions of the other members.
   d. Each individual should recognize the problems of other individuals in the group in order to help them make their contributions.
4. After the discussion, the instructor reads the instructions aloud and allows a few minutes for questions from the class to make sure instructions are understood.

INSTRUCTIONS

When the instructor signals to begin, an envelope is given to each group member who then empties out the contents of the envelope onto the table. Each person then starts to form a square, following these three simple rules:

a. No member of the group may speak to another member.
b. No member may take a piece away from another member or in any way signal that he or she wants it.
c. Any member may give one or several pieces to any other member.

   The task will not be complete until each individual has formed a complete square of the same size as those formed by the others.

Remember

You may give, but you may not take a piece that is not offered to you.

5. The instructor gives the signal to begin working.
6. Observers are given the following instructions:

As an observer, you may want to look for some of the following:

a. Who is willing to give away pieces?
b. Did anyone finish his or her own square and then stop communicating with the group? Is there anyone who continually struggles with his or her pieces, yet is unwilling to give any or all of them to others?
c. How many people are actively engaged in putting the squares together?
d. Is there a turning point at which the group starts cooperating?
e. Are the rules violated?

7. When all the groups have completed their squares, the instructor leads a general discussion with the whole class about their reactions to the exercise, about cooperation, about their feelings as they worked on the puzzles. If the groups who finished first were allowed to circulate and observe the ones still working, ask whether this had any effect on the level of frustration experienced by those still trying to put pieces together.

Notes

Observations must be solicited from both observers and the participants. The instructor asks such questions as:

1. How did you feel when someone held a piece and did not see where it would fit?
2. What was your reaction if you saw someone build a square and then sit back without seeing that his or her solution prevented others from solving the problem? Did many members "sit" on their squares, unwilling to break them even though they were made of the "wrong" pieces? Do we tend to "sit on our squares" in other situations?
3. How did you feel when you finished a square, then saw you would have to break it up and give away some pieces?
4. How did you feel about the person who was slow at seeing the solution?
5. If you were that person, how did you feel?
6. What happened that helped or hindered the group?

The instructor should point out cases in which the rules were violated. Usually the rules are broken when the frustration level rises. The instructor should point out also the tendency to "blame the system" when the group is unsuccessful. Most group members probably checked their envelope many times to make sure pieces were not missing. They may even have told the instructor that they could not complete the problem because pieces were obviously missing.

INSTRUMENT
LASI QUESTIONNAIRE*

Situation	Alternative Actions
1. Your subordinates are not responding lately to your friendly conversation and obvious concern for their welfare. Their performance is in a tailspin.	a. Emphasize the use of uniform procedures and the necessity for task accomplishment. b. Make yourself available for discussion but don't push. c. Talk with subordinates and then set goals. d. Intentionally do not intervene.
2. The observable performance of your group is increasing. You have been making sure that all members were aware of their roles and standards.	a. Engage in friendly interaction, but continue to make sure that all members are aware of their roles and standards. b. Take no definite action. c. Do what you can to make the group feel important and involved. d. Emphasize the importance of deadlines and tasks.
3. Members of your group are unable to solve a problem themselves. You have normally left them alone. Group performance and interpersonal relations have been good.	a. Involve the group and together engage in problem solving. b. Let the group work it out. c. Act quickly and firmly to correct and redirect. d. Encourage the group to work on the problem, and be available for discussion.
4. You are considering a major change. Your subordinates have a fine record of accomplishment. They respect the need for change.	a. Allow group involvement in developing the change, but don't push. b. Announce changes and then implement with close supervision. c. Allow the group to formulate its own direction. d. Incorporate group recommendations, but you direct the change.
5. The performance of your group has been dropping during the last few months. Members have been unconcerned with meeting objectives. Redefining roles has helped in the past. They have continually needed reminding to have their tasks done on time.	a. Allow the group to formulate its own direction. b. Incorporate group recommendations, but see that objectives are met. c. Redefine goals and supervise carefully. d. Allow group involvement in setting goals, but don't push.
6. You stepped into an efficiently run situation. The previous administrator ran a tight ship. You want to maintain a productive situation, but would like to begin humanizing the environment.	a. Do what you can to make the group feel important and involved. b. Emphasize the importance of deadlines and tasks. c. Intentionally do not intervene. d. Get the group involved in decision making, but see that objectives are met.

*Instrument developed by Paul Hersey and Kenneth Blanchard. Reproduced by special permission from the February 1974 *Training and Development Journal.* Copyright © 1974 by the American Society for Training and Development.

7. You are considering major changes in your organizational structure. Members of the group have made suggestions about needed change. The group has demonstrated flexibility in its day-to-day operations.

   a. Define the change and supervise carefully.
   b. Get the group's approval on the change and allow members to organize the implementation.
   c. Be willing to make changes as recommended, but maintain control of implementation.
   d. Avoid confrontation; leave things alone.

8. Group performance and interpersonal relations are good. You feel somewhat unsure about your lack of direction of the group.

   a. Leave the group alone.
   b. Discuss the situation with the group and then initiate necessary changes.
   c. Take steps to direct subordinates toward working in a well-defined manner.
   d. Be careful of hurting boss-subordinate relations by being too directive.

9. Your superior has appointed you to head a task force that is far overdue in making requested recommendations for change. The group is not clear on its goals. Attendance at sessions has been poor. Meetings have turned into social gatherings. Potentially they have the talent necessary to help.

   a. Let the group work it out.
   b. Incorporate group recommendations, but see that objectives are met.
   c. Redefine goals and supervise carefully.
   d. Allow group involvement in setting goals, but don't push.

10. Your subordinates, usually able to take responsibility, are not responding to your recent redefinition of standards.

    a. Allow group involvement in redefining standards, but don't push.
    b. Redefine standards and supervise carefully.
    c. Avoid confrontation by not applying pressure.
    d. Incorporate group recommendations, but see that new standards are met.

11. You have been promoted to a new position. The previous supervisor was uninvolved in the affairs of the group. The group has adequately handled its tasks and direction. Group inter-relations are good.

    a. Take steps to direct subordinates toward working in a well-defined manner.
    b. Involve subordinates in decision making and reinforce good contributions.
    c. After discussing past performance with the group, work alone in examining the need for new practices.
    d. Continue to leave the group alone.

12. Recent information indicates some internal difficulties among subordinates. The group has a remarkable record of accomplishment. Members have effectively maintained long-range goals. They have worked in harmony for the past year. All are well qualified for the task.

    a. Try out your solution with subordinates and examine the need for new practices.
    b. Allow group members to work it out themselves.
    c. Act quickly and firmly to correct and redirect.
    d. Make yourself available for discussion, but be careful of hurting boss-subordinate relations.

FIGURE 7-1

Basic leadership behavior styles

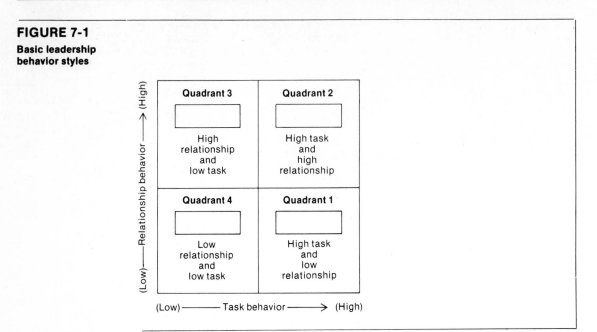

FIGURE 7-2

Determining leadership style and style range

		Alternative actions			
	1	A	C	B	D
	2	D	A	C	B
	3	C	A	D	B
	4	B	D	A	C
	5	C	B	D	A
Situations	6	B	D	A	C
	7	A	C	B	D
	8	C	B	D	A
	9	C	B	D	A
	10	B	D	A	C
	11	A	C	B	D
	12	C	A	D	B
Quadrant		(1)	(2)	(3)	(4)
Quadrant scores					

FIGURE 7-3

Tri-dimensional leadership effectiveness model

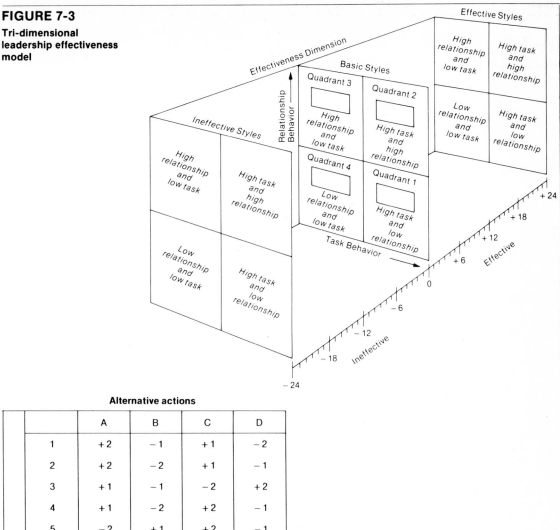

Alternative actions

		A	B	C	D
	1	+ 2	− 1	+ 1	− 2
	2	+ 2	− 2	+ 1	− 1
	3	+ 1	− 1	− 2	+ 2
	4	+ 1	− 2	+ 2	− 1
	5	− 2	+ 1	+ 2	− 1
	6	− 1	+ 1	− 2	+ 2
	7	− 2	+ 2	− 1	+ 1
	8	+ 2	− 1	− 2	+ 1
	9	− 2	+ 1	+ 2	− 1
	10	+ 1	− 2	− 1	+ 2
	11	− 2	+ 2	− 1	+ 1
	12	− 1	+ 2	− 2	+ 1
Subtotal			+		+		+	

= Total

FIGURE 7-4

Determining style adaptability

CASE
OUTPATIENT SCHEDULING DEPARTMENT*

Community Medical Center is a 350-bed voluntary, not-for-profit hospital in a large metropolitan city. The hospital has operated an emergency department for twenty-five years and the hospital has all the ancillary services common for such a medical center. In the early 1970s, because of the sophistication of the medical technology in the hospital, the physicians began referring many patients to the hospital for outpatient tests and procedures. All outpatients, both for the emergency room and those scheduled for ancillary tests, were processed by the secretary assigned to the emergency department. Processing involved interviewing each patient and preparing the medical record, which includes both personal and financial information. In 1973 the hospital began to remodel the emergency department because of the increase in demand for its services.

Since the demands for outpatient tests and procedures were also increasing, it was the consensus of the administration to develop an outpatient scheduling department. This new department's responsibility would be to process all the outpatients and to coordinate the scheduling of all outpatients to the different ancillary services.

The hospital hired Mr. Joe Campbell to coordinate this new department. Mr. Campbell had been trained in the army medical corps and was knowledgeable about many of the tests and procedures performed in the ancillary departments. Mr. Campbell spent three months working with all the ancillary department heads, coordinating an information system that would be necessary for the smooth flow of patients into the hospital, through the system, and then out of the hospital if the attending physician so desired. Much of the initial organizing of the outpatient system was accomplished by Mr. Campbell working one to one with these different department managers. It was the plan of Mr. Campbell and the administration to initiate this program in July 1974 at the same time the new emergency department was dedicated.

All went on schedule, and the outpatient department began to function in July 1974. Under Mr. Campbell's program, physicians called the outpatient scheduling department when they had patients who needed tests or procedures to be performed in the hospital. Mr. Campbell had obtained from each ancillary department a preferred

*This case was contributed by Tom J. McClain. Reprinted by permission of the author.

list of possible appointment times. When a physician called, the patient was given a specific time and date for the appointment as well as instructions on how to prepare for the test. At the end of each business day, the outpatient department would inform the other ancillary departments of the next day's outpatient schedule. If Mr. Campbell or his staff had any particular scheduling problems, they would communicate directly with the department involved to co-ordinate an appropriate schedule for the patient.

Since the program was new and had many shortcomings in the beginning, the hospital administration developed an outpatient committee. Mr. Campbell was appointed chairperson and each ancillary department had representation on the committee. Monthly meetings were held for the first year. Many of the agendas addressed specific problems of the system. Communication between the participants was good, but Mr. Campbell seemed to dominate all meetings and at times even forced cooperation among the different department heads. The committee was accomplishing its goal to make the system work. As specific problems became fewer, there seemed to be no need to come together to discuss the system, and in August 1974 the committee was dissolved.

After this time, Mr. Campbell made the system work. He dealt directly with the physicians and the particular department heads when any problem or conflict arose. It was Mr. Campbell's style to speak with the conflicting parties individually and find a solution that each would accept, communicating this solution back to the parties involved. The department heads resented Mr. Campbell's dogmatic style, but accepted his solutions of conflicts since it was "his" system. The system progressed through the year with only minor problems that "Mediator" Campbell seemed to solve easily.

In June 1976, feeling complacent about his system, Mr Campbell took a week's vacation. The following situations developed:

Ms. Betty Lyons, the head technician in the nuclear medicine department, has been in her position for six months. She has had little contact with the laboratory personnel since very few nuclear medicine outpatients have lab tests. On Monday, Dr. Bills scheduled a patient for a very uncommon lab test (thyroid profile) and a very common nuclear medicine test (thyroid scan). Dr. Bills' patient, Helen Smith, arrived late and was sent to the lab and instructed to go to nuclear medicine after the lab test was completed. When the patient had not arrived as scheduled in nuclear medicine, Betty Lyons went looking for the patient. Finding her in the laboratory waiting area, Ms. Lyons took Mrs. Smith to her department for the scan without clearing it with any lab technician. Ms. Lyons assumed that the patient was lost. Upon completing the test, Ms. Lyons discharged the patient. When Dr. Bills did not receive the lab test result, he called Mr. Campbell. Finding Mr. Campbell was on vacation, he complained to Mr. Robert White, the associate administrator.

Mrs. Berman, an outpatient clerk, has been working in the department for two years. She has always been pleasant with the patients but many times has imposed her personal feelings on them about overusage of the emergency department. Mr. Campbell recognized this fact and counseled her about it. During the week that Mr. Campbell was out of the department, the emergency room staff received many complaints about Mrs. Berman hassling them at the reception desk. Mrs. Berman has still not realized her importance to the team concept or recognized that her only duty is to process the patients without imposing her views on them.

Charles Black is a patient of Dr. Sommers. He was scheduled for a chest x-ray and an EKG. Upon completion of his chest x-ray, the technician remarked, "You're finished, you can go now." The x-ray technician had no idea that Mr. Black also was to have an EKG. Mr. Black, assuming that he *was* finished, left the hospital. Dr. Sommers also complained to Mr. White when he could not contact Mr. Campbell.

Since Mr. Campbell had always solved these problems, Mr. White had no idea that the system was so vulnerable to mistakes. He had to analyze the system.

ASSIGNMENT 1
POWER

In what situations do you feel particularly powerless or unable to influence anything that happens? How does this lack of power affect the way you feel about these situations?

ASSIGNMENT 2
INFLUENCE

Think of a "typical" week in recent months. What five people have had the most influence over you during that week? After identifying them, state why you think they were influential. Using the Raven and French classification (see Chapter 7 in text), analyze the type of power you feel they exerted on you.

ASSIGNMENT 3
LEADERSHIP STYLE

Using the leadership concepts studied in Chapter 7 of the text, present an analysis of your leadership philosophy and style.

DISCUSSION QUESTIONS

1. Discuss the possible origins of the "trait theory" of leadership and how some of its principles may still persist today in our society.
2. If you use the word "leader" rather than the term "leadership," does it make you think of a person rather than the functions which might be carried out? Does one person (i.e., the so-called leader) perform all the functions for a group? Can this person do it? Or should he or she do it?
3. Compare the main points of the contingency theory with the development of "life-cycle theory" to explain how some styles of managing may be more effective than others.
4. If power depends on resources, dependencies, and alternatives, do all these have to be together to establish a power relationship? In other words, how are those factors related in actual situations to produce power?
5. We sometimes speak of power as a dangerous or even an evil thing. Do you feel that way about power? In what ways is power healthy and effective for organizations?

CHAPTER 8

GROUP COMMUNICATION PROCESSES AND DECISION MAKING

ACTIVITY 1
WHO GETS THE SPACE: MULTIPLE ROLE PLAY

Purposes: 1. To experience the dynamics of decision making in small groups.
          2. To explore the effects of hidden agendas on decision making.
          3. To assess the role of bargaining power in small groups.
          4. To discuss the meaning of fairness in deliberations involving the allocations of scarce resources.

Class size: Any size. Class is to be divided into groups of seven members each. Any students not in a group will function as observers.

Time required: Between 1 and 1½ hours.

Materials needed: General information sheets for all participants. Specific role sheets for each of the seven members in each team. Seven place cards for each group with the role names printed in broad letters to facilitate group discussion. A copy of Instructions for Observers for each observer.

Physical setting: A classroom large enough to accommodate all groups without two much interference.

PROCEDURE

1. Groups of seven members each are formed. The instructor assigns roles in each group by handing a place card and the corresponding specific role sheet to each group member, together with a copy of the general information sheet.

2. The instructor asks the group members to read all instructions and tells the hospital directors they can lead the discussion any way they wish. If, however, the group is unable to reach a decision by the end of 30 minutes, the hospital directors will have to decide what to do with the space. The instructor tells all students to "get into the roles" as much as they can.

3. The groups discuss the problem of space allocation for about 30 minutes.

4. On the board record the following information for each group:

    Who got the space?
    Were there any trade-offs, arrangements, sharings, etc.?
    Who made the decision (the director, the group as a whole by consensus, one vocal group member, the groups as a whole by vote)?
    How many members of the group are satisfied with the decision?
    Is the hospital director satisfied with the decision?
    Is the decision in the best interest of the hospital?

5. Class discussion can center around the following issues:
    a. What is a fair decision?

    b. How can you determine what is in the best interest of the hospital?

    c. What role should the hospital director play in deciding issues?

    d. What are the advantages of group consensus in decisions about allocation of scarce resources?

    e. What are the disadvantages of group consensus in such decisions?

WHO GETS THE SPACE*

General Information

You all work for a veterans hospital in a south Texas city. One of the group will take the role of the hospital director (HD), and the rest will be chiefs of various service areas which are interested in occupying newly released space in the central wing of the hospital. The space will have to be remodeled, and there is a budget of $150,000 for the job, but according to the budget grant, if the work can be done less expensively the funds can be reallocated to any other physical plant or furnishing activity of the hospital. Five service areas have been selected to present their arguments for use of the space because they seem to be most closely related to the section of the hospital in which the renovation will take place, and also because the space has been very vehemently requested by their chiefs. The HD has been advised to attempt to reach a solution to allocation of the space by a *participatory method*: All the concerned chiefs should reach a consensus on space allocation within the budget figure for renovation and furnishing.

Here are some facts about the service chiefs, and in Figure 11-1 you will find a rough map of the areas now occupied by each service and of the new area, approximately 40 by 40 feet, which is to be assigned by your group's action.

Pharmacy. The chief has been at this hospital in this job only two years. Needs a central location for controlling, compounding, allocating, and dispensing, and must be secure; serves both medical and psychiatric wings. Very recently pharmacy had some of its storage and accounting work space taken away for use by admitting and by fiscal, and it also lost a few square feet of space to a flower shop operation run by a veterans' group.

Social work. The chief has been in this position, his or her first supervisory job, for five years; the position is a new one, created when the present chief took over. Needs to be closer to the mainstream of patient and visitor traffic; does considerable family counseling and

---

*This simulation was written by Gail E. Myers and Michele T. Myers.

FIGURE 8-1

Physical plant

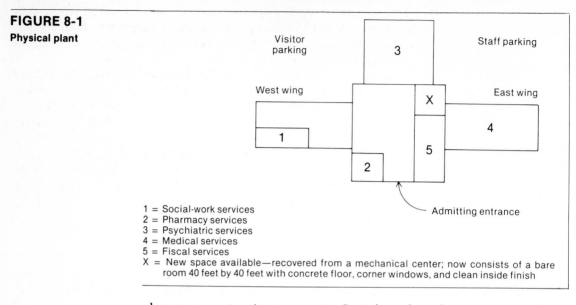

1 = Social-work services
2 = Pharmacy services
3 = Psychiatric services
4 = Medical services
5 = Fiscal services
X = New space available—recovered from a mechanical center; now consists of a bare room 40 feet by 40 feet with concrete floor, corner windows, and clean inside finish

has many outpatient contacts. Social work took over a very dilapidated and poorly furnished area from canteen services when that function was moved into another building. The department has been difficult to find, and for that reason many appointments are not being kept. This is the fastest-growing service in the hospital despite its distance from the central area.

Psychiatric service. The chief has seniority in this group, having been here seventeen years. Needs additional room for group activities and for a seminar room for staff casework; rapidly expanding. Visiting doctors do not have a decent facility of their own, and the number of consulting psychiatrists is increasing very rapidly. The present system, by which visiting doctors share facilities with staff psychiatrists, has not been entirely satisfactory. Grand rounds are not held regularly because the service's space is shared with an in-service training program scheduled for the same conference rooms in the west wing.

Fiscal services. The chief has been at this hospital eight years, after holding other positions for twelve years. Gave up 6 by 10 feet of extra space for admissions and records last year, and held back on expansion of the computer terminal array which had been proposed (and funded) but could not be installed because of lack of suitable space. Inventory control, accounts payable and receivable, budget control, and fiscal planning are all being conducted in less than ideal fashion without a central location adjacent to the present opeations.

Medical services. The chief has been at this hospital ten years.

Has needs very much like those of psychiatric services. Visiting doctors do not have adequate consulting space and must share with staff; grand rounds are not held regularly because of difficulty scheduling the only conference room; intern meeting rooms are needed for staff casework.

It should be emphasized that these data are not complete, as they give only a brief sketch of each service and its space needs. Accept the facts as given (even if they seem unusual in your experience). If facts or events arise in the role play which are not covered by the general information or your hidden agenda, make up things which are consistent with the way they might be in a real-life situation.

In addition to the stated positions, participants have a set of Hidden Agendas given to each one individually. Try to assume the role described in your hidden agendas and let your feelings develop in accordance with events.

INSTRUCTIONS FOR OBSERVERS

The following items are furnished as a guide to observing communication patterns and interactions in the group: what the leader did and how the members reacted and interacted.

1. How did the leader present the problem?
   a. Did he or she appear to be genuinely asking for consensus and help?
   b. Did the leader present the problem objectively? Was the presentation brief and to the point?
   c. Did the leader avoid suggesting a solution?
   d. Did he or she exhibit any stereotyped reactions about his chiefs or their services?
2. What kinds of things went on during the discussion?
   a. Did all members participate?
   b. Was there a free exchange of feelings among group members?
   c. Were there evidences of "social pressure" on any members?
   d. Was the leader permissive? Did he or she take sides or favor anyone?
   e. Did each member's hidden agenda show up?
   f. How much time did the group spend talking about the room allocation in relation to other items not concerned with their decision?
   g. If there were points of disagreement among members, did they seem to be disagreements on (1) facts, (2) logics, or (3) emotions?
3. What did the leader do to help solve the problem?
   a. Did the leader ask questions and avoid hurrying the group to develop a solution?

b. Did the leader accept all ideas equally and avoid favoring one solution?

c. Who supplied the final solution?

d. What, if anything, did the leader do to get agreement on the solution?

e. Did the leader try to have members talk to each other and not just talk to him or her?

ACTIVITY 2
Glazier Electronics Company*

Purposes: 1. To explore problems of coordination, conflict, and integration arising from division of work.
2. To experience conflict among departmental goals and organizational objectives.

Class size: Five groups, up to eight members each, plus two students to play the roles of president and vice-president of the company.
Time required: About 1½ hours.
Materials needed: A role sheet for each participant.
Physical setting: A regular classroom with a central table, seating seven persons, to conduct the executive committee meeting.

PROCEDURE

1. The class selects one president and one executive vice-president. The rest of the class are divided into five groups: production, marketing, finance, personnel, and research. Read background information on the Glazier Company and then the appropriate part for your department. There is a separate part for the president and the executive vice-president.

2. In a twenty-minute meeting, each group selects its own VP and then holds a departmental meeting to determine its position on the proposal by the marketing department to work up an improved model of the integrated analyzer. You may use and extend in any way you choose the information in the background material and in the material describing the situation for your department. The only

*Frederick E. Finch, Halsey R. Jones, and Joseph A. Litterer, *Managing for Organizational Effectiveness: An Experiential Approach,* McGraw-Hill Book Company, New York, 1976. Reprinted by permission of the author.

provision is that the extensions you make must be consistent with the facts of the case and the realities of business life. Also remember you will have to live with any position you decide to adopt in the forthcoming meeting with the president.

3. While the departments are holding their meetings, the president and executive vice-president prepare their agenda for the meeting of the executive committee.

4. At the end of the 20-minute meetings, the president calls the meeting of the executive committee and conducts it according to the instructions given the president (below).

5. After the meeting is completed, students are asked to discuss what they observed while the meeting was in progress. The instructor calls on class members who were not on the executive committee to share their observations with the whole class.

6. General class discussion can center around the following points:
   a. What things helped or hindered the executive committee in making its decision?
   b. What sorts of things happened during the ten-minute break when the vice-presidents went back to their respective departments?
   c. In what way was the meeting different after the break?
   d. On what basis were the president and executive vice-president selected by the class at the beginning of the simulation? How was each vice-president selected in the departments?
   e. Did the vice-presidents seem to support their departmental interests or the overall company objectives?
   f. Was the behavior of the vice-presidents toward each other different from their behavior toward the president?

BACKGROUND OF GLAZIER ELECTRONICS COMPANY

Glazier Company is a medium-sized manufacturer of instruments and testing equipment for monitoring and correcting various industrial processes. It has been known over the years for producing very reliable equipment. Although it did not typically lead the field in developing products, when it has introduced new products or modifications of existing ones they have usually been equal or superior to any others in the field. Since these instruments and test equipment are used to control automatic or semiautomatic manufacturing and chemical processes, the need for reliability and easy maintenance is of great importance.

For the first thirty years of the company's existence, its prime competitors were a few well-established American firms. In the last decade, however, rapidly increasing and very intense pressure has been felt not only from new American firms but also from foreign

competitors, notably in Germany and Japan. Two years ago, changing
its long-standing policy, the company launched a major research and
engineering effort to come up with new instruments that would lead,
rather than just keep abreast with, the field. The scientists and
engineers involved have been extremely pleased with the work done
thus far and are very optimistic about the outcome. Nontheless, it
looks as if at least another two years will be necessary before
prototype instruments will be available for starting production.

Just recently, some of the foreign competitors introduced new
models of existing test equipment with new, flexible features which
have made them very attractive. In particular, one of the Glazier
Company's most successful products, the integrated analyzer, has
been severely challenged by products with new and very desirable
features. Sales of the integrated analyzer have fallen off sharply, and
the company is facing severe financial problems as a consequence.

The company president has recently summarized the firm's
position as follows: "New developments currently under way in
research and engineering, when completed, will completely supplant
the integrated analyzer or any of the later variations of that type of
instrument currently on the market. Unfortunately, it will be a
minimum of two and very possibly three years before production is
even possible on these new developments." In the meantime, the sales
department has been making progressively more desperate demands
for modifications to be made in the integrated analyzer to make it
competitive with the new models on the market. Further, the vice-
president of finance has reminded the president that the expensive
research and engineering effort was undertaken on the assumption of
maintaining existing market revenues and profits. Now that revenues
are beginning to fall off, these heavier expenses have brought the firm
to a point where it is beginning to incur operating losses. The
president has called a meeting of the executive committee to discuss
the proposal from the marketing department.

**MARKETING
DEPARTMENT
SITUATION**

For the last year, there has been a boom in the industries in which the
integrated analyzer is most typically used. Many of the companies
building new plants in new locations are consequently looking for
new and varied approaches to their manufacturing problems. They
have been particularly receptive to the new flexible features on
analyzers developed by the Japanese and German competitors. Sales
of the Glazier Company's integrated analyzer have fallen off and will
probably continue to do so. There seems little that improved selling
efforts can do to increase the demand for the product, which cannot
match the more attractive competing instruments. Salesmen in the

field are becoming increasingly discouraged. It is harder to keep up their morale, and this is apparently influencing their sales of other company products. Further, it is very difficult to hire new salesmen in this declining situation. Innovative modification of the existing integrated analyzer to meet competition is essential.

Personnel Department Situation

The personnel department has felt very proud of its ability to maintain training and morale programs which have kept turnover and absenteeism low. Manufacturing employees in particular are stable, highly motivated, and competent. The last major effort by the personnel department, successfully completed about two years ago, was to attract and integrate the new engineers and scientists for the expanded research and engineering program. Recently, the personnel department has been getting requests for help from the marketing department on two issues—one, the increasingly difficult task of recruiting new salesmen, and two, problems of morale among existing salesmen.

Research Department Situation

Morale has never been higher in the expanded research and engineering department. Once development began on the new line of instruments, work has gone extremely well. The men are very pleased and are quite confident that within two years they will have successful operating prototypes. It is anticipated that these new instruments will be so far superior to anything currently available that they will give the company a commanding marketing position. In addition, the men are extremely proud of working on such sophisticated and professionally challenging work. The rumors that the marketing department wants a revision of the old integrated analyzer were at first ignored but more recently have been viewed with considerable alarm. First, reworking a thirty-year-old product is viewed as hackwork—an extremely unpleasant assignment for any engineer or scientist. Second, the revisions would require considerable manpower; substantial numbers of research and engineering personnel would have to be removed from their assignments on the new instruments to work on the old product. Morale would doubtless suffer, and the work on the new products would be delayed not only because of the time displaced but also because of the morale problems. It is estimated that half of the research and engineering personnel would have to work full-time for six months to make substantial revisions in the integrated analyzer. However, the delay in completing work on the new instruments would probably be twice that.

Finance Department Situation

The company has always had a record of being a solid, conservative firm. It has never made particularly large profit margins on either sales or investments, but profits have always been steady and reliable. However, it has become obvious that the old product and marketing policies will have to change to meet the new situation. When research on the new products was undertaken, it was with the knowledge that the expanded research effort would cut substantially into the rather modest profit margins but that this could be tolerated, given the long-run favorable outlook. However, the firm was left particularly vulnerable to any substantial market decline—which, unfortunately, has occurred with the drop in sales of the integrated analyzer. Sales of some other product lines have also fallen slightly. Increasing revenues seems imperative. To wait two years without profits while the new line of products is developed would put the firm in a particularly bad position. The money market is very tight at this time. While additional funds probably could be found, the firm's profit picture for the next several years would make it necessary to pay prohibitively high interest rates.

Production Department Situation

The production department has always felt that a considerable proportion of the company's success rested on its capacity to manufacture reliable and competitively priced products. This has resulted from carefully training technicians to make these instruments and from not trying to move quickly with the market; instead, the firm has brought out product changes only when long production runs were ensured and the most efficient methods could be employed. The production department, on hearing of the prospect of a revision in the integrated analyzer, foresees several problems. First, there will doubtless be pressure to manufacture the new product almost immediately after the design revisions have been completed, allowing little time to train workers to make the modified product. Second, the revised product will soon be supplemented by the radically new product research and engineering are working on. Further, it will be very hard to liquidate the training and other setup costs for the revisions. Consequently, it will be very difficult to keep either quality or cost at the levels the department has traditionally maintained.

INSTRUCTIONS TO THE PRESIDENT AND EXECUTIVE VICE-PRESIDENT

It is your job to prepare an agenda for the forthcoming meeting of the executive committee. After the meeting has been under way twenty minutes, you will call a break and allow a ten-minute period in which the vice-presidents will check with their respective departments to gather any information they think necessary. After that point, you will reconvene the meeting and conduct the second portion of the meeting for a remaining thirty minutes.

INSTRUCTIONS FOR THE REST OF THE CLASS DURING THE MEETING

While both phases of the executive committee meeting are going on, the rest of the group act as observers. They should look at the following things:

1. Do people listen to each other's comments? How can you tell?
2. Were the various vice-presidents committed to the overall company problem or to their particular department problems?
3. Where there were conflicts in the meeting, identify those involved.
4. How were conflicts handled? Were they solved, ignored, continued, etc.?
5. Did the group, or members of it, pay any attention to maintenance problems during the meeting, or was attention given exclusively to content?
6. In what way did the president and executive vice-president handle the meeting to influence the outcome of the meeting?
7. Did the group spend any time discussing the objective of the meeting? How the meeting was to be conducted?

ACTIVITY 3
NASA EXERCISE

Purpose: To compare the results of individual decision making with the results of group decision making.

Class size: Any number of groups of six to eight members.
Time required: 45 minutes to an hour.
Materials needed: A copy of the Individual Worksheet and the Direction Sheet for Scoring for each student; a copy of the Group Worksheet for each group; pencils.
Physical setting: Regular classroom.

PROCEDURE

1. The class is divided into groups, and each group is seated in a circle. Each student is given the Individual Worksheet and is instructed to complete it within 8 to 10 minutes.
2. Groups are instructed to discuss and arrive at a group consensus for the rankings. A group recorder is selected to record the group rankings onto the Group Worksheet.

     a. Students are not to change answers on their Individual Work-sheets as a result of group discussion.

     b. Groups have about 20 minutes to complete the task.

3. Each student is given a Direction Sheet for Scoring and scores his or her individual worksheet. The group recorder then computes the average of individual scores as well as the score for the group resulting from group discussion.

4. The instructor records all data on the board in the following manner:

	Group 1	Group 2	Group 3	Group 4
Group Worksheet Score (Consensus Score)	_____	_____	_____	_____
Average of Individual Scores	_____	_____	_____	_____
Range of Individual Scores	_____	_____	_____	_____

NASA EXERCISE INDIVIDUAL WORKSHEET

Instructions

You are a member of a space crew originally scheduled to rendezvous with a mother ship on the lighted surface of the moon. Due to mechanical difficulties, however, your ship was forced to land at a spot some 200 miles from the rendezvous point. During landing, much of the equipment aboard was damaged, and since survival depends on reaching the mother ship, the most critical items available must be chosen for the 200-mile trip. Below are listed the fifteen items left intact and undamaged after landing. Your task is to rank-order them in terms of their importance to your crew in reaching the rendezvous point. Place the number 1 by the most important item, the number 2 by the second most important, and so on, through number 15, the least important. You have ten minutes to complete this phase of the exercise.

_____ Box of matches

_____ Food concentrate

_____ 50 feet of nylon rope

_____ Parachute silk

_____ Portable heating unit

_____ Two .45 caliber pistols

_____ One case dehydrated Pet milk

_____ Two 100-pound tanks of oxygen

_____   Stellar map (of the moon's constellation)

_____   Life raft

_____   Magnetic compass

_____   5 gallons of water

_____   Signal flares

_____   First-aid kit containing injection needles

_____   Solar-powered FM receiver-transmitter

NASA EXERCISE GROUP WORKSHEET

Instructions

This is an exercise in group decision making. Your group is to employ the method of *group consensus* in reaching its decision. This means that the prediction for each of the fifteen survival items *must* be agreed upon by each group member before it becomes a part of the group decision. Consensus is difficult to reach. Therefore not every ranking will meet with everyone's complete approval. Try as a group to make each ranking one with which all group members can at least *partially* agree. Here are some guides to use in reaching consensus:

1. Avoid *arguing* for your own individual judgments. Approach the task on the basis of logic.
2. Avoid changing your mind *only* in order to reach agreement and avoid conflict. Support only solutions with which you are able to agree at least somewhat.
3. Avoid "conflict-reducing" techniques such as majority vote and trading.
4. View differences of opinion as helpful rather than as a hindrance in decision making.

_____   Box of matches

_____   Food concentrate

_____   50 feet of nylon rope

_____   Parachute silk

_____   Portable heating unit

_____   Two .45 caliber pistols

_____   One case dehydrated Pet milk

_____   Two 100-pound tanks of oxygen

_____ Stellar map (of moon's constellation)

_____ Life raft

_____ Magnetic compass

_____ 5 gallons of water

_____ Signal flares

_____ First-aid kit containing injection needles

_____ Solar-powered FM receiver-transmitter

NASA EXERCISE DIRECTION SHEET FOR SCORING

A group member will assume the responsibility for directing the scoring.

1. Individuals score the net difference between their answers and the correct answers given by the instructor. For example, if your answer was 9 and the correct answer was 12, the net difference is 3, which becomes the score for that particular item. If your answer is 12 and the correct answer is 9, your score for that item will be 3.
2. Individuals total all item scores to obtain their individual scores.
3. The member responsible for directing the scoring then totals all individual scores and divides by the number of participants to obtain the average of individual scores.
4. The member in charge of the group worksheet scores the group worksheet in the same fashion individual scores were obtained.
5. The group consensus score and the average of individual scores are then given to the instructor, who records them on the board. The range of individual scores (the lowest and the highest) in each group is also given to the instructor.

Ratings

0–20	Excellent
20–30	Good
30–40	Average
40–50	Fair
Over 50	Poor

CASES

In each of the following cases, explain how you would make your decision. Explain as thoroughly as possible the reasons for your approach to the decision and the specific process you would go through in making the decision. (You should be specific about the outcomes you intend and aware of some possibilities of other outcomes as well.)

CASE 1
THE PRINTING SHOP MANAGER

As the manager of the printing and reproduction facility for the company, you have four section chiefs reporting to you and a total staff of sixty people. Recently you have installed new machines and put in a new and simplified work system after comparing your previous system with more modern ways of handling the copying and reproduction functions for a firm your size. You expected an increase in both quality and quantity of production. Neither has happened. In fact, the output is down and the rejection rate of finished work has gone up steadily, indicating a decrease in quality as well as quantity of production.

You invite representatives of the new equipment manufacturers to look at your installation, and they assure you the machines are all working well and should be doing more for you. They show you figures from other similar installations to prove the machinery is OK.

Your four section chiefs have no simple explanation for the change in production. They suggest that operators have not been given good training, that morale dropped when the new machines were installed, that the operators think they should be getting higher pay for taking on the more sophisticated machinery, and that the new work system did not take into account the correct factors for compensation and for promotion and work assignments, and was not clearly understood by operators. Each section chief is willing to blame slower production on different factors, and each feels very defensive about the bad work being produced. Their own compensation is linked to the section production, so they are bickering among themselves trying to assess the blame.

Your boss has now called you about complaints from all parts of the company. Work is arriving late and being done badly. Your boss asks what you intend to do about the situation and gives you three days to report back with your plan for correcting the problems.

CASE 2
ELECTRONIC WIZARD

A few years ago you started a small electronic assembly firm which, by virtue of changes in technology, your own sales aggressiveness, and the good fortune of a booming economy, suddenly became a very successful and expanding company. You are hailed by the local newspapers and the chamber of commerce as the "electronic wizard" for the way you guided the company's growth. Although none of the engineering or electronic technology was the result of your own invention, you did put the company together and are seen as the reason for its success. Your staff has grown substantially in three years, and you find yourself in charge of vice-presidents and division heads who believe your press clippings: They openly refer to you as a genius. They will not make decisions without you. They ask your advice on all items, whether it is sales, technical, accounting, marketing, production, or purchasing.

You want to develop another similar major company in another city and are interested in getting advice from your subordinates. You want some of them to take on leadership in that new venture, and you know the situation will have some risks in spite of a great chance to succeed. How do you proceed to organize your staff to take on the responsibility of expansion?

CASE 3
TRANSFER TRAUMA

You are the supervisor of a section of ten reproduction operators whose specialties include setting type on a composing typewriter, making multiple copies, and then collating and binding the finished product. The section's major responsibility is to prepare (1) specification proposals for suppliers and (2) highly technical government bids which must be very accurate and must also be typeset and reproduced in a very attractive and professional manner. All ten of your people can do the same work, and they work well together as a team.

The engineering drafting department has just been given a large job to complete in a short time and needs composing and reproduction services. Because they are located several miles from the main plant, they have a few pieces of reproduction equipment but no permanent operators. Your section has the only trained operators in the company. Engineering has asked that three of your operators be assigned to them for six weeks to help complete the presentation proposals they have already begun.

As supervisor you have been instructed to select three of your people to be reassigned to the engineering drafting department for that period of time. Your section has its own work to do, and the equipment and working conditions at engineering are well known to be not as good as in your main shop. How do you go about finding the right people to send to engineering for this temporary assignment?

ASSIGNMENT 1
THE COMMITTEE MEETING

Choose an organization such as a campus club or association, a business, or a religious group, and ask for permission to observe a regularly scheduled meeting of a committee or group with no more than twelve members.

Analyze group behavior at the meeting, as well as individual members' behaviors, using one of the classification systems discussed in Chapter 8 in your text.

ASSIGNMENT 2
GROUPTHINK

Discuss a recent example of groupthink you have observed.

DISCUSSION QUESTIONS

1. What has been your experience with groups? Do you agree with some of the negative quips and comments about groups? What makes some groups more effective than others?
2. Of the types of groups listed in Chapter 8 (casual, cathartic, learning, policy-making, and action) which are ones you prefer to work in? Why? Do they act differently from the others? Do they produce different outcomes which interest you? Do some satisfy you more than others?
3. Describe a group you know which tends to produce only (or nearly) programmed decisions rather than nonprogrammed ones. What makes the group operate that way? External forces? Internal forces?
4. Do you have another decision-making sequence which works for you and an organization which you've seen use it? Has anyone suggested that you can use "brainstorming" as a decision-inducing process?
5. Of the many factors to take into account when planning a meeting, which seem to be the most easily overlooked? Are they less important? Are they most difficult to control?

CHAPTER 9

MANAGING CONFLICT

ACTIVITY 1
CONFLICT STYLES: ORGANIZATIONAL DECISION MAKING*

Purposes: 1. To identify ways of dealing with organizational or group conflict.
2. To discuss when and why different methods of resolving conflict are appropriate to different situations.
3. To provide an experience in group decision making.

Group size: Any number of groups of five to seven participants each.
Time required: Approximately 1½ hours.
Materials needed: A Conflict Styles Worksheet for each participant and an extra copy for each team; a pencil for each participant; newsprint and a felt-tipped marker.
Physical setting: A room large enough to accommodate all participants, with adequate tables and chairs available for each team.

PROCEDURE

1. The instructor introduces the experience by commenting on the inevitability of conflict in groups and how conflict can be used as a constructive force.
2. The instructor then gives the participants copies of the Conflict Styles Worksheet and instructs them to complete the worksheet in 15 minutes.
3. At the end of this time, the instructor divides the participants into groups of five to seven members each and appoints one observer for each group. Observers are briefed on what to look for.
4. A copy of the Conflict Styles Worksheet is given to each group, and the groups are instructed to complete the work sheet *as groups.* They are advised to avoid conflict-reducing techniques such as the use of majority power (voting), minority power (persuasion based on pressure), or compromise (giving in to keep the peace). The instructor also urges the group to view differences of opinion as constructive and to make their ranking decisions as a group, based on logic as well as mutual understanding. The groups are told they will have forty-five minutes in which to complete the worksheet.
5. After the work period is over, each group observer reports to his or her group on how it handled the ranking task and any conflict that arose. Specific incidents are described to provide the group members with pertinent feedback.
6. When the observers have finished their reports to the subgroups, the total group is reassembled, and each group's decision is posted on newsprint. If any groups' decisions differ widely (a "1" and a "5" choice for the same problem), the instructor may focus on *intergroup*

*Reprinted from J. E. Jones and J. W. Pfeiffer (eds.), *The 1977 Annual Handbook for Group Facilitators,* University Associates, San Diego, Calif., 1977. Used with permission.

conflict by having each of the small groups explain the rationale for each of its responses.

7. The instructor discusses the five styles of handling organizational conflict. He gives an example of each style, when it might be appropriate, and so on. Participants may be urged to discuss the styles in terms of what they have just experienced. The participants then identify by style the ways of dealing with conflict listed for each case on the Conflict Styles Worksheet. (Usually they are able to identify the responses correctly.)

8. The instructor sums up the activity for the group by pointing out what things the group have gained from the experience and by applying these lessons to real-life situations. Major points are listed on newsprint.

VARIATIONS

1. The instructor can increase the pressure on the small groups by reducing the time allotted for the ranking task to thirty minutes.

2. The situations described on the Conflict Styles Worksheet can be rewritten to reflect the interests or needs of the participants or groups involved (supervisors, sales personnel, governmental or clerical staffs, educators, etc.)

CONFLICT STYLES WORKSHEET

Instructions

Your task is to rank the five alternative courses of action under each of the four cases below, from the most desirable or appropriate way of dealing with the conflict situation to the least desirable. Rank the *most* desirable course of action "1," the next most desirable "2," and so on, ranking the *least* desirable or least appropriate action "5." Enter your rank for each item in the space beside it.

Case 1

Pete is lead operator of a production molding machine. Recently he has noticed that a man from another machine has been coming over to his machine and talking to one of his men (*not* on break time). The efficiency of Pete's operator seems to be falling off, and there have been some rejects due to his inattention. Pete thinks he detects some resentment among the rest of the crew. *If you were Pete, you would:*

    _____   a. Talk to your man and tell him to limit his conversations during on-the-job time.

    _____   b. Ask the foreman to tell the lead operator of the other machine to keep his operators in line.

_____ c. Confront both men the next time you see them together (as well as the other lead operator, if necessary), find out what they are up to, and tell them what you expect of your operators.

_____ d. Say nothing now; it would be silly to make something big out of something so insignificant.

_____ e. Try to put the rest of the crew at ease; it is important that they all work well together.

Case 2

Sally is the senior quality-control (QC) inspector and has been appointed group leader of the QC people on her crew. On separate occasions, two of her people have come to her with different suggestions for reporting test results to the machine operators. Paul wants to send the test results to the foreman and then to the operator, since the foreman is the person ultimately responsible for production output. Jim thinks the results should go directly to the lead operator on the machine in question, since he is the one who must take corrective action as soon as possible. Both ideas seem good, and Sally can find no ironclad procedures in the department on how to route the reports. _If you were Sally, you would:_

_____ a. Decide who is right and ask the other person to go along with the decision (perhaps establish it as a written procedure).

_____ b. Wait and see; the best solution will become apparent.

_____ c. Tell both Paul and Jim not to get uptight about their disagreement; it is not that important.

_____ d. Get Paul and Jim together, and examine both of their ideas closely.

_____ e. Send the report to the foreman, with a copy to the lead operator (even though it might mean a little more copy work for QC).

Case 3

Ralph is a module leader; his module consists of four very complex and expensive machines and five crewmen. The work is exacting, and inattention or improper procedures could cause a costly mistake or serious injury. Ralph suspects that one of his men is taking drugs on the job or at least is showing up for work under the influence of drugs.

Ralph feels that he has some strong indications, but he knows he does not have a "case." *If you were Ralph, you would:*

_____ a. Confront the man outright, tell him what you suspect and why and that you are concerned for him and for the safety of the rest of the crew.

_____ b. Ask that the suspected offender keep his habit off the job; what he does *on* the job *is* part of your business.

_____ c. Not confront the individual right now; it might either "turn him off" or drive him underground.

_____ d. Give the man the facts of life; tell him taking drugs is illegal and unsafe and that if he gets caught, you will do everything you can to see that he is fired.

_____ e. Keep a close eye on the man to see that he is not endangering others.

Case 4

Gene is a foreman of a production crew. From time to time in the past, the product development section has "tapped" the production crews for operators to augment their own operator personnel to run test products on special machines. This has put very little strain on the production crews, since the demands have been small, temporary, and infrequent. Lately, however, there seems to have been an almost constant demand for four production operators. The rest of the production crew must fill in for these missing people, usually by working harder and taking shorter breaks. *If you were Gene, you would:*

_____ a. Let it go for now; the "crisis" will probably be over soon.

_____ b. Try to smooth things over with your own crew and with the development foreman; you all have jobs to do and cannot afford a conflict.

_____ c. Let development have two of the four operators they requested.

_____ d. Go to the development supervisor or foreman and talk about how these demands for additional operators could best be met without placing production in a bind.

_____ e. Ask the supervisor of production (Gene's boss) to "call off" the development people.

INSTRUMENT
FINAL COURSE EVALUATION

This form is designed to provide you with an opportunity to evaluate the course and your instructor. Please fill out the form anonymously.

1. Please rate the course as a whole according to the following scale:

   5 Agree strongly
   4 Agree somewhat
   3 Neither agree or disagree
   2 Disagree somewhat
   1 Disagree strongly

	5	4	3	2	1
a. I am very satisfied with the course	____	____	____	____	____
b. I have learned a great deal.	____	____	____	____	____
c. The material was very useful.	____	____	____	____	____
d. The material was very challenging and interesting.	____	____	____	____	____
e. The material was applicable to practical situations.	____	____	____	____	____
f. I would recommend the course to other students.	____	____	____	____	____

2. What did you like *most* about the course? What aspects of the class seemed of *most* value to you?

3. What did you like *least* about the course? What aspects of the class seemed of *least* value to you?

4. Comment about the assignments: their usefulness in helping you learn the material, their difficulty, how much you enjoyed or did not enjoy doing them, etc.

5. Did you feel free to participate in class? Why or why not?

6. What are your reactions to the textbook used in the course and to the other reading assignments (if any)?

7. Please rate your instructor on the following items:

	5	**4**	**3**	**2**	**1**
a. The instructor was knowledgeable and up to date.	_____	_____	_____	_____	_____
b. The instructor came to class prepared.	_____	_____	_____	_____	_____
c. The instructor is concerned about the effectiveness of his or her teaching.	_____	_____	_____	_____	_____
d. The instructor communicated the material in a clear, organized, and meaningful manner.	_____	_____	_____	_____	_____

	5	4	3	2	1
e. The instructor made good use of examples and illustrations.	——	——	——	——	——
f. The instructor encouraged student/teacher and student/student discussion.	——	——	——	——	——
g. The instructor used varied methodologies (lectures, simulations, experiential activities, discussions, group projects, role playing, etc.) appropriate for the learning objectives of the course.	——	——	——	——	——
h. The instructor was available for individual help.	——	——	——	——	——
i. The instructor clearly defined student responsibilities in the course.	——	——	——	——	——
j. The instructor gave adequate information during the course regarding student progress through tests, assignments, and other feedback methods.	——	——	——	——	——
k. The instructor gave exams based on the material covered.	——	——	——	——	——
l. The instructor gave exams that were good measures of my knowledge and understanding of the material.	——	——	——	——	——
m. The instructor graded fairly.	——	——	——	——	——

8. Circle an overall grade for the course: A B C D F

9. Circle an overall grade for your instructor: A B C D F

10. Any other comments, criticisms, questions, suggestions, etc.?

CASE 1
BOB LEE

Bob Lee was taking a difficult, required course during his junior year at Strivemore University. Bob needed a B average to keep his scholarship, but no matter how hard he studied, he could only get F's and D's on the weekly tests that would form the major part of his grade in the course. The professor curved the grades of the thirty students in the class, and Bob just could not seem to come out on the top of the curve.

After the fourth test, Bob was complaining about the situation to a fraternity brother who also was in the class. The brother sized him up and decided that since Bob was a good guy and part of the group, he'd give him the inside dope on the course. He swore Bob to secrecy and then told him the whole story. It seemed that the professor didn't correct his own papers, but used a graduate student grader. The grader had found a new way to work his way through college. He had arranged, through a star football player in the class, to provide cram sessions before each test based on the key the professor gave him. For $5 per test he "tutored" nine of Bob's classmates, or for $10 he would give a student the answers to memorize. For just "five or ten bucks" a week, Bob could join the group and his problem would be solved.

Bob had a little money saved from his summer job, but he wasn't immediately ready to invest it in an A. Wasn't the whole thing unethical? Shouldn't the professor be told? But then again, what if his fraternity brother or the football player were expelled? Still, what about the students at the bottom of the curve?

All these questions and more went through Bob's mind. He had to decide soon or it would be too late to save his grade.

If you were Bob, what would you do? Why?

CASE 2
MARY JONES

Mary Jones is working for Dr. Calley and Dr. Casey. Among other duties, she has charge of instruments and preparations of injections. The doctors operate in a small county hospital with limited surgery facilities.

Shortly after coming on the job, Mary Jones discovers that sterile techniques are not being observed. The very busy doctors reuse instruments and syringes and don't pay attention to scrub techniques. After a week, Mary is completely frustrated in her attempts to maintain the kind of regime she has learned and practiced for three years before coming to work with the doctors. She is also concerned that her failure to maintain the techniques will someday have serious consequences, although she is not aware that there has been any difficulty in the past.

New residents of the small community where they plan to make their home, Mary Jones and her husband both need to work to support their three young children. The county hospital is about the only medical facility for miles around.

What are the real problems here? How might they be solved?

ASSIGNMENT 1
NEGOTIATIONS

Select a real situation in which you experience a conflict or disagreement with someone (roommate, parent, spouse, friend, teacher, co-worker, etc.) which you would like to settle.

1. Determine what you would like to see happen or change.
2. Determine what you would settle for.
3. Figure out a strategy you will use with the other person.
4. Ask to meet with that person for the purpose of settling the conflict or disagreement, and actually negotiate toward a settlement.
5. Write a short report in which you analyze the process and outcomes of your negotiations.

ASSIGNMENT 2
STYLES OF CONFLICT MANAGEMENT

In a short paper describe your parents' style for dealing with conflict in the family. Include the specific examples that you can recall. In what ways have their styles influenced yours?

ASSIGNMENT 3
CONFLICT LOG

For two weeks, keep a log of your interactions with others in which disagreements/conflicts occurred. For each incident, state briefly:

1. The content of the disagreement
2. The other people who were involved
3. What you did
4. What the other persons did
5. Your feelings and reactions
6. The outcomes of the incident—even if no resolution occurred

After two weeks, read your log again and determine whether you see a pattern in the types of conflicts you engaged in, the types of people you had disagreements with, and your style of coping with these incidents.

Write a short paper analyzing your findings.

DISCUSSION QUESTIONS

1. What was the attitude about conflict in the family you grew up in? In the school you attended? In any business you first began to work with? In your church group or club?
2. Describe how conflict can absorb the time and energies of people working in an organization. (Use examples of what these people might actually do.)
3. Is raising the competitive spirits of the members of an organization by conflict a potentially useful activity? Should a manager induce conflict to develop competition and team spirit? In what situations might it be useful?
4. Discuss some situation in which a win-lose (or a lose-lose) strategy could have been turned into a win-win strategy. Is win-win an unfamiliar way to manage conflict?
5. In managing conflict or negotiating settlements of conflicts, what are the most important communication skills you would need to develop? How does such negotiation relate to earlier chapter discussions of (a) power, (b) leadership, (c) meanings, or (d) listening?

INDEX